FROM THE HISTORY AND CONTENTS OF THE FIRST SECTION OF THE ESOTERIC SCHOOL

1904–1914

RUDOLF STEINER (1905)

FROM THE HISTORY AND CONTENTS OF THE FIRST SECTION OF THE ESOTERIC SCHOOL

1904-1914

Letters, Documents, and Lectures

TRANSLATED BY JOHN WOOD
EDITED BY HELLA WIESBERGER
INTRODUCTION BY CHRISTOPHER BAMFORD

RUDOLF STEINER

SteinerBooks

CW 264

SteinerBooks
Anthroposophic Press

610 Main Street
Great Barrington, Massachusetts 01230
www.steinerbooks.org

Translated from the German by John Wood

This book is volume 264 in the Collected Works (CW) of Rudolf Steiner, published by SteinerBooks, 2010. It is a translation of the German *Zur Geschichte und aus den Inhalten der ersten Abteilung der Esoterischen Schule 1904-1914,* published by Rudolf Steiner Verlag, Dornach, Switzerland, 1984.

Library of Congress Cataloging-in-Publication Data is available.

ISBN 978-0-88010-640-5

Printed in the United States

CONTENTS

PART III

The Relationship between the Movement, the Esoteric School, and the Society

APPENDICES

INTRODUCTION

CHRISTOPHER BAMFORD

THE GERMAN SECTION of the Theosophical Society was founded on October 20, 1902, with Rudolf Steiner as General Secretary and Marie von Sivers as Secretary. During the proceedings, Steiner asked Annie Besant, who had traveled to Berlin to bestow the Charter, to enroll him as a member of the "Esoteric School." From this deed, two inferences follow. The first is that esoteric, inner development was personally important, even central, to Rudolf Steiner's own path and that he was eager to experience the inner teachings, exercises, and practices developed by Theosophy. And the second is that he understood that without inner development, practiced seriously and assiduously by at least a dedicated core group of committed students, any esoteric or spiritual movement was bound to be ineffective. In other words, Rudolf Steiner understood that the success of what he was about to undertake—which was to renew the "Mysteries" by planting the cultural and transformative impulse of Anthroposophy into the world—would depend to a very great extent on the quality of the inner work that he could inspire in his students. The Esoteric School, then, would give him both a place to start and an insight into the historical source from which his own work—his own "Esoteric School"—would have to grow.

The origins of the School dated back at least to 1884, when certain members of the London Lodge "petitioned the Masters for the formation of an inner group" for deeper esoteric training. Following that initial call for experience rather than theory, the number of Theosophists seeking to become practicing "disciples" rather than simply "students" of the doctrines grew, until, in 1888, in response to demand, the Esoteric School was founded "to promote the esoteric interests of the Theosophical Society by the deeper study of esoteric philosophy…"

The constitution and sole direction of the School was vested initially in Madame Blavatsky herself, who was responsible to its Members. The School had no official or corporate connection with the Exoteric Society, "save in the person of the Founder-President." In other words, the Esoteric Section derived directly and solely from Madame Blavatsky—that is to say, from the Masters, "the *real* founders of the Theosophical Society." The lineage through Blavatsky to the Masters was important to Steiner. It authenticated on the historical plane Steiner's own direct connection to them. Preservation of continuity was for Rudolf Steiner always a cardinal rule, which he followed, as Hella Wiesberger puts it, by outwardly "linking in every case to an already existing situation and seeking to transform it into something more perfect."

Spiritually, of course, his own experience was all the legitimization he needed.

The School's leadership continued under Blavatsky until her death in 1891, when Besant assumed the leadership with William Q. Judge, and then, after his death in 1895, alone.

*

From the beginning of his association with the Theosophical Society, Steiner was asked for esoteric instruction. He invited it, because he himself practiced what he taught, knew what he was speaking of, and spoke only from experience. At the same time, he taught that this experience was available to anyone who with reverence, devotion, and humility dedicated themselves to it.

Steiner's path had in fact always been one of experience. He was not an "armchair" thinker or one who reveled in building logical systems: he wanted to experience the truth and act on it. He was a true philosopher. It was no secret, then, that, for him, "theosophy" was living knowledge, actual spiritual experience, not theory—that he was a practical person, a person of real action, who always sought to get to the heart of a matter: to learn it, master it, and make it fruitful.

Entering the "armchair" atmosphere of the Theosophical Society, he realized immediately (as he wrote in a letter to Marie von Sivers in April 1903) that "without a body of true Theosophists to improve the karma of the present by hard-working meditation, theosophical teachings would be expounded merely to half-deaf ears."

For this reason, on becoming General Secretary of the Theosophical Society's German Section, he joined the Esoteric School as soon as he could; and, even though it was not until, visiting Anne Besant in London in May 1904, that he was officially named "Arch Warden" of the Esoteric School (i.e. "authorized" to teach), he gave spiritual instruction as soon as he was asked for it.

For this reason, too, *Theosophy* (1904) contained a significant last chapter on "The Path to Knowledge" and *How to Know Higher Worlds* (1904/5) was entirely dedicated to the path. Each of these contains precious background material for understanding the inner work of the Esoteric Section.

"Path to Knowledge" makes several important points. It begins by stating "we can find our own path to knowledge only by taking thinking itself as our starting point." However, he then goes on to say that to present "an image of the higher worlds," as he has done in Theosophy and as he often does in the meditations he gives, whose reality we may not be able to perceive for ourselves and thus not fully understand, is not without its purpose because:

> Thoughts that have been supplied for us constitute a force that keeps on working in our world of our thoughts. This force becomes active within us, arousing potentials that lie dormant within us. It is a mistake to believe that we waste our time by dwelling on an image in thought form. This opinion assumes that thoughts are unreal and abstract, while in actuality they are founded on a living force. To someone who has acquired knowledge, thoughts are present as a direct expression of what is perceived in the spirit, it lives on in that person as a seed that will grow and bear knowledge as its fruit.

Implicit here is the understanding that spiritualized thinking involves the practice of a kind of active receptivity or devotion: "We should allow things and events to speak us to more than we speak about them, and we should extend this principle to our thoughts as well..." But receptivity, devotion, is only the beginning. It must be framed by a true spiritual objectivity that allows what is received—the other—to exist for itself, in its uniqueness. This requires equanimity. We must allow our thinking to become a transparent eye-like organ for the transmission of spiritual impressions. For this, our thinking, feeling, and willing—our soul-life—must become orderly, controlled, and disciplined. In other words, as a prerequisite for "true receptivity," we must practice the so-called "six subsidiary (or complementary) exercises": control of thoughts, control of actions, equanimity (inner composure, detachment, imperturbability), freedom from prejudice (positivity), openness, inner harmony, and freedom.

Similarly, and in much greater detail, *How to Know Higher Worlds* starts with the path of reverence (receptivity and devotion to truth and knowledge. "Only those who have acquired this fundamental mood or attitude can become members in an esoteric school." Reverence, as inner attitude, leads quite organically, on the one hand, to humility, and on the other, to respect. Humility, in turn, will lead to sense of gratitude; respect, in the sense of always see (k)ing the good in all will lead to an enlarged vision. We will see things we did not see before. At the same time, the practice of these virtues must be accompanied by the development of an inner life. We must become familiar with inner experience. Inner peace is necessary for this; as well as a sense of objectivity with regard to the world and ourselves. But inner experience by itself without a corresponding perfection of outward, ethical life is fruitless. Hence: every idea must become an ideal; and three steps in moral growth must accompany every step in increased knowing. Against this background, *How to Know Higher Worlds* then gives a series of inner exercises and practices for the healthy development of a selfless willing, feeling, and knowing human being. Finally, the critical inner experiences of encountering the two Guardians of the Threshold are described.

How to Know Higher Worlds appeared in installments in the journal *Luzifer-Gnosis* as the Esoteric Section was developing and must have been read (and practiced) by the members of the School.

*

Esoteric work depends above all upon a discipline, whose purpose is both to introduce rhythm into a student's life and orient that student toward the spiritual world. The rules of the Esoteric School, in the form that Rudolf Steiner gave them, were more or less as follows:

1. Every morning, rise at a fixed time and, preferably before eating, sit for a half-hour period of meditation.

For instance: first, inner control, silence, peace; then, a sense of devotion to the divine in the universe, coupled with the inner understanding that one is united with it, to which end the following is held in the heart and allowed to penetrate one:

> More radiant than the Sun,
> Purer than the snow,
> Finer than the ether,
> Is the Self,
> The Spirit in my heart.
> This Self am I.
> I am this Self.

Concluding, one concentrates on a sentence: such as, "Before the eyes can see they must be incapable of tears. Finally: a mood of reverence toward what one holds as divine.

2. In the evening, before retiring the member should first meditate (inwardly repeat) for at least a quarter of an hour a sentence given by Rudolf Steiner and then conduct a "backward review" of the day.

3. At least half an hour daily should be devoted to study of a suggested book.

4. Every two weeks, the member should report what exercises have been practiced and, if they have not been practiced, state why not.

5. The member should keep a daily record in a notebook of exercises practiced.

6. Alcohol was prohibited.

7. Abstention of animal food was not compulsory, but a vegetarian diet was recommended.

Within the School, there were different grades or classes: the Probationary Order of Hearers; the First Class; and after that the Second Class, and so on. Members of all Classes would probably have attended the Esoteric Lessons contained here. Details of the "Second" (and "Third") Classes are to be found in the volume entitled "*Freemasonry" and Ritual Work: The Misraim Service* (CW 265).

Instruction was of three kinds. 1. There were rules and exercises practiced universally by all students. 2. There were individual exercises and practices given by Rudolf Steiner personally. 3. There were the esoteric lessons. The function of the lessons was to address intimate aspects of the path, while at the same time to direct students to the Masters who were the true leaders of the School.

✳

Rudolf Steiner's path to Theosophy and its Esoteric Section was essentially, as one might have inferred, a cognitive path of thinking—but clearly not the kind of thinking we usually and automatically assume. The kind of thinking that Steiner practiced was living, present, wordless, meditative thinking. Such thinking is an experience and activity of the whole person. To engage in it is to change: to be changed utterly. In what must be about the first piece of writing from him that we have, a letter to a friend when he was nineteen, he writes:

On January 13, 1881
Twelve o'clock midnight

Dear, trusted friend,

It was the night from the 10th to the 11th of January, in which I had not a moment's sleep. I had busied myself until half past twelve in the morning with certain philosophical problems and finally threw myself onto my couch. The previous year my striving had been to research whether what Schelling said was true: "There dwells in all of us a secret, wondrous capacity to draw back from the stream of time, out of the self clothed in all that comes to us from outside, into our innermost being, and there in the immutable form of the eternal, to look into ourselves." I believed, and still believe, that I discovered this capacity quite clearly in myself. I had long had an inkling of it. Now the whole of idealist philosophy stands before me in an essentially modified form. What's a sleepless night compared to that.

In his next letter to the same friend, he writes: "I follow a quite specific goal, an ideal goal: cognition of the truth."

To cognize—or know—the truth is a different kind of thinking.

Steiner's first experience of the path to cognition of the "truth" came with his introduction to geometry. It was also his first experience of happiness. He was about eight or nine, when the assistant teacher in the village school of Nuedörfl lent him a geometry textbook for private study. He plunged into the world of "triangles, quadrilaterals, and polygons" and "wracked his brains" over the theorem of Pythagoras and "the question of where parallel lines actually intersect." He writes: "I derived a deep sense of contentment from the fact that one could live with the soul in building forms that are seen wholly inwardly, independent of the outer senses... The ability to grasp something purely through the spirit brought me an inner joy."

Very early, then, Steiner was on the way to understanding two fundamental principles: first, that to arrive at true thinking requires that one experience the difference—and be able to distinguish—between the living act and process of thinking and finished thoughts, the traces or arrested products of that process; and second, that the path to this experience lies in overcoming what Coleridge called "the despotism of the eye"—or senses generally—under the influence of which, as Coleridge again says, "the Reasoner must have a picture, and mistakes surface for substance." True thinking, then, is not representational: it is not the manipulation of representations or ciphers of outwardly or otherwise independently existing "objects." In his *Autobiography*, Steiner puts it thus:

...My relationship to geometry was the beginning of a view that took shape gradually within me. During childhood, it lived in me more or less unconsciously; by my twentieth year it had assumed a definite, fully conscious form. I would have said that the objects and events seen by the senses exist in space, the space outside the human being; but a kind of soul space exists within as the setting for spiritual beings and events. *I could not see anything in thoughts that were like pictures we form of things; rather they were revelations of a spiritual world on the stage of the soul.* To me geometry seemed to be a knowledge that we ourselves produce; but its significance is completely independent of us. *(Italics added)*

In other words: meditative thinking depends upon our activity but, paradoxically, the goal of this activity is not any "thing," but to disclose a kind of cognitive *receptivity*—or inner soul space—in which cosmic meanings (spiritual beings and events) may be cognized as intuitions.

But still the problem of inner and outer, visible and invisible, remained.

At this point in the development of his path, Steiner was aided, in the first place, by thinking through the contributions of German idealist philosophers: Kant, Fichte, Hegel, and Schelling. *Kant* resolved the riddle of the relationship between inner and outer in the starkest terms: for him, there wasn't one. Steiner however felt instinctively that living thinking (in contrast to mere cogitation) provided a way out of Kant's dualistic conviction that placed "things in themselves" irrevocably beyond thinking's capacity to apprehend them. It was untenable to him that something should remain beyond thinking and unknowable in this sense. *Fichte* offered an initial resolution to this problem by focusing attention on the primacy of the "I" as the source of all. Here Steiner found an explanation of the activity of thinking in its relation to the world. He writes: "Previously I had agonized over finding concepts that apply to natural phenomena, from which one could them derive a concept for the I. Now my goal was just the opposite: beginning with the I-being, I wanted to penetrate the creative processes in nature." *Hegel,* for his part, "the greatest thinker," provided the necessary clue that "thinking" and "spirit" were related—sometimes identical, often interchangeable—realities. For Hegel, the spiritual world was within thinking—but he lacked, as Steiner puts it, "a feeling for the world of the spirit." Something of this feeling, however, came through in *Schelling*, for whom "nature is visible spirit, spirit invisible nature": one and the same being in two different forms. It was the conscious realization of this reality that Steiner sought through his path of meditative thinking.

None in the modern era, before Steiner himself, had as gone as far in the realization of this project than Goethe—in whose company Steiner lived, worked, and meditated for more than ten years. Asked to edit Goethe' scientific writings, over a ten year period of intense study, he wrote introductions to these, as well as two separate books. Living in this way with Goethe was a transforming moment. It was thus Goethe above all who honed and grounded the path of meditative thinking that Steiner had begun in geometry and continued through philosophy. Goethe, who claimed never to have thought about thinking, added something radically new to the equation: he drew directly (rather than indirectly) on the Hermetic, alchemical, and Rosicrucian traditions of ancient sacred science.

The encounter with Goethe was therefore a matter of intense, personal karma for Steiner. It put him into intimate conversation with his destiny in a different way than his encounters with the philosophers had. That this was so is confirmed by the events in his life that coincided with his entering into the life-changing commission to become the editor of Goethe's scientific writings: he met the herb gatherer Felix Kogutski. Kogutski was a living repository of folk traditions of nature wisdom and Steiner learned much from him. But his most important function was to lead Steiner to an initiatory meeting with, as he puts it, the "M (aster)," reputedly Christian Rosenkreutz. As a result of his meeting, Steiner understood his task: to build a bridge between Rosicrucian wisdom and contemporary, modern scientific consciousness.

Goethe was the medium at hand for the accomplishment of this task, for Goethe still understood the power and capacity of thinking "to approach the truth, to penetrate to the depths of the world through its own power." In this regard, for Goethe, thinking, intimately united with sense perceiving, was able to raise it to the perception of higher phenomena. In this sense, it was in itself an organ of perception not for sensory realities but for the universal world of living ideas, which we all share, displayed through them. Goethe always began not with concepts but with "actual facts," that is, experiences. Holding, arranging, comparing experiences led him to the experience of the reality that united them. "Truth is Godlike," he wrote, "and does not appear directly; rather it must be apprehended through its manifestations." In this way, Steiner was led to the fundamental realization: *Beholding the idea in reality is the true communion of humanity.*

The following years (and by that token those preceding the turn of the century, the entry in Theosophy, and the assumption of the mantle of spiritual teacher) were continually transformative for Steiner. After all, blessed by the spiritual world and karma, he was on the path to the realization of his destiny. Study and meditation through Goethe, the philosophers, the mystics, and the alchemists were but way stations. The goal was transformation of being—ontological change in the structure of consciousness itself. Such change is not accomplished by changing the content of consciousness: it is not a matter of what we think about, but how we think and *are*. It is in this sense that Rudolf Steiner's Christ experience, when he "stood spiritually before the Mystery of Golgotha in a deep and solemn festival of knowledge"—happened around 1897—must be understood. He did not simply "add" Christianity—or the meaning of the Incarnation—to his wardrobe of concepts: he experienced in a profound and shattering way Christ's transformative presence in human, cosmic, and divine being. The fruits of this period, coming eight to ten years after Steiner began his Goethe studies in 1884 are contained in *Truth and Knowledge* (1892)—his doctoral dissertation—and *The Philosophy of Freedom* (1894). These works provide the philosophical basis for the meditative work that will become Anthroposophy: "In thinking we hold a corner of the world process where we have to be present if anything is to occur." Essentially, they lay the groundwork for the reality of sense-free thinking—that fundamental capacity of human nature to live "consciously within the spiritual foundations of existence," which is, of course, also the goal of meditation. At this stage in Steiner's practice, his meditative path was not the *via negativa* of the stripping off of all concepts to plunge in nakedness into the soul's depths, but rather the *via positiva* of uniting with the soul's depths "accompanied by the full, clear content of ideas." To enter into the depths of the soul without ideas seemed to be to enter into feeling alone. As he wrote in his *Autobiography*: "I wanted to carry the light of the idea realm into the warmth of the inner experience."

*

Steiner was forty when entered the Theosophical world as a spiritual teacher. He had half a lifetime of spiritual experience and practice behind him. Thus, in some sense, he was ready—and needed only—to come out to assume his task. Yet the Theosophical world in which he as to begin his mission provided a certain context. He had to allow his mission to grow forth organically from what Madame Blavatsky and her successors had created. This meant first mastering Theosophical literature, which he did thoroughly and meditatively, and then building a bridge between it and what he himself was charged to bring. Chief among these texts, besides *The Secret Doctrine*, were the two short meditation texts: Blavatsky's *The Voice of the Silence* and Mabel Collins' *The Light on the Path*. These two, especially the latter, lie behind the early work in the Esoteric Section. The beginning of *The Light on the Path* makes it clear how deep and hard the path will be:

> Before the eyes can see, they must be incapable of tears. Before the ear can hear, it must have lost its sensitiveness. Before the voice can speak in the presence of the Masters it must have lost the power to wound. Before the soul can stand in the presence of the Masters its feet must be washed in the blood of the heart.

1. Kill out ambition.
2. Kill out desire of life.
3. Kill out desire of comfort

4. Work as those who are ambitious. Respect life as those who desire it. Be happy as those who live for happiness. Seek in the heart the source of evil and expunge it...
5. Kill out all sense of separateness.
6. Kill out all desire for sensation.
7. Kill out the hunger for growth....

Such injunctions must be understood and processed in and by the heart. They cannot be accomplished by the "hard will" of the ordinary ego. To attempt to do so would be a kind of black magic and would accomplish the opposite of what was intended. Meditation, spiritual practice, is a long-term process of the gradual and profound transformation of the whole person. As Rudolf Steiner teaches it (and as any kind of immersion in the volumes dedicated to the Esoteric School, as well as those written works that deal with different aspects of the inner life, will make clear), the long-term process has two components: the gradual development in all our capacities of the universal capacity of concentration and attention accompanied by the rhythmic, repeated, and continued placing into the depths of our being of mighty seed ideas. These, over the long haul, will transform us silently and secretly from the inside out. As he writes to Clara Smits in 1903 on page 33:

Much remains *unconscious* in us to begin with. And therefore I beg of you to continue the mediation steadfastly. We make progress only when we do that, and are aware of the fact that no day is wasted when we devote ourselves to this end. Every day lays up knowledge within us, and that day will surely come when it will reveal itself to us in full consciousness. The sentences that we meditate upon are not just sentences for our understanding, which have to be merely comprehended; I can only say again and again: they are sentences that are alive and that we ourselves must live with as we live with children. We are quite familiar with children too, but nevertheless we busy ourselves with them every day. Thus it should be with our meditation sentences.

Translator's Foreword

The English translation of this volume was begun by John M. Wood in 1985, soon after it had appeared for the first time in German. From the start it caused controversy among members of the Anthroposophical Society, some of whom thought that it might present a danger to those not sufficiently acquainted with the teachings of Rudolf Steiner.

This danger can be avoided if people pay sufficient heed to what the title states. It is a *history* of the early phase of the society when it was still joined to the Theosophical Society of Mrs. Besant. The correspondence and documents included herein are in part directed toward individual esoteric pupils already familiar with exercises practiced in the Theosophical Society. When Dr. Steiner broke away from the Theosophical Society and formed his own Anthroposophical Society, many of the former ways of working were changed. It would not be right to carry out the exercises as given here without considering the instructions given by Rudolf Steiner in later times.

As a close friend of Rudolf Steiner explained, "The Western way of esoteric development is not to seek enlightenment by regulating the breathing (yoga), but just the reverse: to bring about a change in the rhythm of breathing by engendering the right thoughts. The breathing is slowed down or halted when the mind is engrossed in contemplation of something that inspires it with admiration!"

Or, as Rudolf Steiner himself expressed it in *An Outline of Esoteric Science*,[1] "The ultimate ideal is that no exercises of any kind should be done with the physical body as such, not even breathing exercises, so that whatever happens in the physical will occur simply and solely as an *outcome* of the exercises for Intuition."

---

1. Anthroposophic Press, NY, 1997. Also published as *An Outline of Occult Science*.

The present volume forms part of the complete edition of the works of Rudolf Steiner, which is divided into three large sections: writings, lectures, and artistic work.

Rudolf Steiner (1861–1925) supported anthroposophically-orientated spiritual science from 1900 until his death by means of publications, and many lectures and lecture courses. At the request of German theosophists, Steiner began his spiritual scientific activity in connection with the Theosophical Society, founded in 1875 by the Russian Helena Petrovna Blavatsky and others. The German Section of this was founded and established, with Rudolf Steiner as its General Secretary, in 1902. When, ten years later (1912–1913), the exclusion of the German Section from the main Theosophical Society occurred, due to their serious differences of opinion with the headquarters in India, the German Section formed an independent society under the name of the Anthroposophical Society.

Alongside his publishing and lecturing activities, Rudolf Steiner also taught in his Esoteric School. This existed in three sections from 1904 until it closed in 1914 due to the outbreak of World War I. It was not until ten years later that it was revived in connection with the necessary reorganization of the whole anthroposophical way of life. In accordance with the needs of the age for complete frankness, the Esoteric School now had to be established as the "Free High School for Spiritual Science at the Goetheanum," with three esoteric Classes as well as Sections of the Sciences and the Arts. [2]

From the beginning, he appointed Marie Steiner (1867–1948) to administer the stenographic and other written reports of his many lectures, and for the necessary revision of the texts for publication, and he made her the legal heir to his literary legacy. Some years before her death, she instituted the administrative body for Rudolf Steiner's Estate (*Nachlassverwaltung*) for the further accomplishment of her task, which, in the first place, was to bring out the needed complete edition of Rudolf Steiner's works (*Gesamtausgabe*, or "GA"). According to her general instructions, it was to have

---

2. See *The Constitution of the General Anthroposophical Society and the Free High School for Spiritual Science* (CW 260a).

included the esoteric teaching material, which she had already begun to publish.

The present documentation forms the beginning of a series. It comprises numerous documents, to be sure, but they cannot give a comprehensive picture on their own. Consequently, contrary to the usual practice of publishing works in a complete edition without commentary, notes with historical and practical bearing have been added. Even so, it is necessary to recognize that what has been preserved can illuminate only a part of these connections, mainly the historical part, because the chief part of the activity of the Esoteric School rested on a personal relationship between teacher and pupil.

The conditions laid down by Rudolf Steiner concerning judgements made about his statements that were not originally intended for publication are particularly applicable to the present volume: "... *at least* a knowledge of the human being and of the cosmos in so far as these have been presented in the light of Anthroposophy, and also knowledge of what exists as 'Anthroposophical History' in what has been imparted from the spiritual world" (Rudolf Steiner: *Autobiography*, SteinerBooks, 1980, p. 388).

The insertions in Rudolf Steiner's text in parentheses ( ) exist thus in the original; the insertions made by the editor or translator are in brackets, [].

GA (Gesamtausgabe, German edition) or CW (Collected Works, English edition) is the same as Bibl. (Bibliography).

Rudolf Steiner's Position in the History of the Esoteric Movement

FREE ESOTERICISM: A QUESTION OF METHODOLOGY

> *Rudolf Steiner has become the pioneer in the very domain where, through his indications, human beings for the first time have been allowed freedom.*[3]

As the first modern scientist of the supersensible, Rudolf Steiner was completely thrown back upon his own resources. He taught only what he could vouch for out of personal experience. Looking far ahead of his time he had discerned that the turning point of the end of the nineteenth century was not merely the beginning of a new century, but the beginning of a totally new epoch, when humanity would be faced with social upheavals of unimagined magnitude. He saw that with the increasing awareness of the individual, a tremendous struggle for freedom would ensue; through the ever more prevalent influence of the agnostic and pragmatic ways of thinking of the mechanical-materialistic sciences, great advances would certainly be made but, at the same time, the last vestiges of ancient inherited wisdom, which sees the creative-spiritual world as the origin and goal of all existence, would be lost. The inevitable result of this would be a universal devastation of the spiritual and a feeling of meaninglessness in life.

Through this insight Rudolf Steiner was convinced that this historic process, necessary for general progress, can be met by only one thing:

---

3. From Marie Steiner's preface to Rudolf Steiner's *The Stages of Higher Knowledge*, SteinerBooks, Great Barrington, MA, 2009. She goes on to say, "... he had to build a basis and create a spiritual attitude through which—by finding the solid moral support within—one might in this freedom avoid falling prey to temptation and aberration."

a view of the world and of life founded on individual awareness, orientated toward what is spiritually creative. And so he developed modern spiritual science—*Anthroposophy*—out of his own firsthand knowledge of the supersensible guidance of the world and of human destiny, and lived and taught in accordance with the spirit of modern times, according to the precept: Freedom in the spirit of modern science as well as in the realm of the supersensible, the esoteric.

With this basic aim he at the same time effected a historic turn in the esoteric movement, for this movement had acquired its store of wisdom from a consciousness springing from other sources. It was derived from the so-called archetypal wisdom that had been revealed to humanity during primeval times, and had endowed it with an extensive control over the material powers of existence. As long as human beings still acted without individual responsibility, in full accord with the intentions of the spiritual worlds, this wisdom was a part of the heritage of knowledge belonging to the whole of humankind. But when, on the road to the development of personality, egoism arose, and the unquestioned connection with the supersensible worlds faded, the supersensible knowledge, which was a source of power, had to be protected from misuse. It was withdrawn into the Mysteries. But from there it directed the public life of culture for a long time, even into the beginning of the Christian era. Through Christianity and growing intellectualism, when the progressive cultural consciousness directed its attention more and more strongly toward the cognition of the laws of the material universe, the Mysteries gradually lost their dominant position and were finally extirpated as *public* institutions. Since then, the ancient wisdom of the Mysteries could only be cultivated within restricted, secret circles. There it was strictly guarded until, in the nineteenth century, the signs of the times demanded that a spiritual counterpart be set against the purely materialistic-agnostic way of thinking of civilized society.

This task had given rise to a question, which had become a weighty problem for the esoteric movement of the nineteenth century. Should this body of knowledge still be kept secret, or would it be better to make it generally known? This question so deeply touched the pulse of existing practice—for since early times, to ensure against their misuse, higher truths had been handed on only to those who had been specially prepared to receive them—that a decision could not immediately be made to popularize them. A compromise solution was tried, first testing, as it were, public reaction to the announcement proclaiming the existence of spiritual worlds and beings. Thus came about the spiritualistic-mediumistic movement of the 1840s to the 1870s. The result was certainly different from what had been expected but, nevertheless, the dam of strict secrecy had been broken and it now became inevitable that at least the main truths should be openly revealed. This came about through the Theosophical Society founded in 1875 by a Russian, Helena Petrovna Blavatsky, and an American, Henry Steel Olcott.

These two experiments certainly gave rise to sensational movements (Spiritualism and Theosophy), but in a deeper sense, they must be considered to have failed in their intention, mostly because the cultural norm of natural-scientific thinking rejected the mediumistic way as unscientific. This was justified inasmuch as this way signified not only a going back to former stages of consciousness, but also a curtailing of the free choice of the individual. On the other hand, mediumism had up till then been the only surviving method of spiritual investigation.[4]

While this dilemma was still being faced by the occult movement at the end of the nineteenth century, the problem had been solved by Rudolf Steiner along his own individual path to the spirit. He had gained the crucial understanding that supersensible knowledge and reality can unite in a healthy way with modern civilized life, only when the method employed ensures that exactness and independence are equally achieved, as with modern natural science. He had not acquired this knowledge from the traditional teaching guarded by the occult societies, but from what he had acquired quite naturally through his childhood experiences, and by mastery over the

---

4. For more detail see *The Occult Movement in the Nineteenth Century,* Rudolf Steiner Press, London, 1973 (CW 254). Compare also the two lectures translated from CW 52, "The History of Spiritism" and "The History of Hypnotism and Somnambulism," Berlin, May 30, 1904 and June 6, 1904. Further lectures in this series have not yet been translated.

mechanical-materialistic manner of thought he had encountered in his natural-scientific upbringing.

Based on this knowledge he made his first task the development of a method of supersensible investigation founded entirely on natural-scientific principles. By strict self-discipline, leading from sense-imbued thinking to thinking free of the senses, he found the necessary certitude regarding the spirit as such. At the same time he recognized freedom as an actual experience and as the bearer of true morality. Thinking that is free of the senses thus became for him the starting-point for a scientifically clear connection to the supersensible world and for a science of freedom as the basis of "ethical individualism."

The logical extension of the inner experience of the I led, furthermore, to the perception of the macrocosmic representative of I-being, the Christ Spirit, whose nature is expressed in true freedom and love. Thereby, Rudolf Steiner had also paved the way to the understanding of the two Christian ideals appropriate to our time: freedom and love, which he constantly referred to as the basic impulses behind the central event of humanity's development, the Mystery of Golgotha. And connected with it is humanity's greatest task: "to transform the Earth into a cosmos of freedom and love."[5]

This relationship of the human I to the World-I is later touched on by Rudolf Steiner in a lecture given in Dornach on May 24, 1920:[6] "The 'ethical individualism' of my *Philosophy of Spiritual Activity*[7] is, in reality, founded upon the Christ-impulse in humanity, although this is not expressed in the book." He also said later that, at the present time, the only way to directly convey the original wisdom springing from initiation is to preserve one's association with Christ.[8]

This association, acquired through sense-free thinking in what Rudolf Steiner calls "the emancipation of the human being's higher

---

5. *The Spiritual Hierarchies and the Physical World: Zodiac, Planets, and Cosmos*, SteinerBooks, Great Barrington MA, 2008, lecture 10, April 18, 1909.
6. *The Redemption of Thinking*, Anthroposophic Press, NY, 1983, pp.109–110.
7. Published as *Intuitive Thinking as a Spiritual Path*, Anthroposophic Press, NY, 1995.
8. *Polarities in the Evolution of Mankind*, Anthroposophic Press, NY, 1987, lecture of March 7, 1920 (CW 197).

consciousness from the fetters of every authority,"[9] provides the necessary condition whereby esotericism could be set free in a wholesome way from attachment to certain brotherhoods. If, in the past, one had been able to penetrate to the world of spiritual realities only through a dimming-down of one's consciousness, and under the guidance of a spiritual leader whose authority had to be unconditionally acknowledged, now, through Rudolf Steiner's pioneering deed, every serious aspirant can achieve this in a clear state of consciousness and with free responsibility for his or her own actions.

The only condition attached to this, to which everyone is obliged individually, is activity of soul and spirit. This is essential not only for the individual, but for the general progress of humanity. Indeed, this is so to such an extent that civilization must cease altogether unless every single person is prepared to bring to it a new impulse through a renewed knowledge of the spirit. This was expressed by Rudolf Steiner more than six decades ago.[10]

It is just in this matter of activating the will of the individual to social responsibility that anthroposophical spiritual science differs so fundamentally from the ancient wisdom guarded in the esoteric brotherhoods. For concepts springing from the latter source, proceeding as they do from revelations out of a period in human history still rooted in a group-soul consciousness, can provide no new, valid social impulses. On the other hand, no new impulses can be developed where no knowledge arises through initiation. For this reason Anthroposophy can be explained out of social necessity as an instrument to produce new spiritual revelations, which take into account the consciousness of the individual. It had become a task of culturally historic importance to make the new revelations of the spirit understandable to human beings, especially those that had appeared after the end of the Kali Yuga period in 1899. Through this, the greatest event of humanity's history—the Mystery of Golgotha—was rendered accessible again, and to this end Rudolf Steiner dedicated his efforts.

---

9. *Letters* II, Rudolf Steiner to Rosa Mayreder, December 14, 1893 (GA 39).
10. *Psychoanalysis & Spiritual Psychology*, Anthroposophic Press, NY, 1990, end of last lecture, Dornach, July 2, 1921 (CW 143).

He remarked on one occasion, "Anyone who cannot understand Anthroposophy in this sense is unable to understand it at all."[11] Therefore, when he began lecturing about the social question, he appealed to his hearers' power of discernment:

> Who can speak about the burning questions of the moment in a really modern and pertinent way, so that it goes to the heart of the matter? You cannot discover this in the rituals and statutes of this or that Masonic or Confessional Body. One would like to see a capacity for discernment taking hold of people.[12]

In this same connection he asserted that the spiritual current he represented had never been dependent on any other, and that he was therefore not obliged to anyone to be silent about anything that he thought should be spoken about at the present time:

> A pledge of silence cannot be imposed on him who is not indebted to anyone else for his store of spiritual insight. That forms the basis for discriminating between this movement and other movements. For whoever would assert, at any time, that what is proclaimed by anthroposophically-orientated Spiritual Science differs from the sense of what is expressed in my book *Theosophy*—the words of which I can personally certify—that person is saying something untrue, whether it be out of ill will or not; and, as far as I am concerned, the judgement may be made in ignorance of the circumstances, or often the person may not have been present and may have been judging from outward appearances only. He, however, who has been with us much and states something different, using another spiritual movement to substantiate what he says about, say, a past event or connection of this movement, when he knows the circumstances here—that person is telling a lie. Those are the facts of

---

11. *Die soziale Grundforderung unserer Zeit—In geänderter Zeitlage*, Dornach, December 20, 1918, untranslated (GA 186).
12. Dornach, December 15, 1918.

the case. Either a person is stating an untruth out of ignorance of the circumstances, or he is telling a lie in knowledge of those circumstances. That is how all opposition toward our movement is to be understood.

Therefore I must emphasize repeatedly: I need remain silent only about those things that I know may not be divulged because the people of today are unripe to receive them. But there is nothing that I have to remain silent about because of a pledge or anything of that sort that I have made to anyone. Never has anything entered into this movement that has come from elsewhere. This movement has never been spiritually dependent on any other; the connections were only external.[13]

This statement leads to the question: Why did Rudolf Steiner then link to other movements at all, when he felt obliged to reject both the old method of keeping everything secret, as well as the old practices used in their investigation?

This contradiction is only solved when one takes into account the two main rules of esoteric life, that Rudolf Steiner always worked to comply with when at all possible. They are the rules of absolute truthfulness and to preserving continuity. These two rules were placed ever and again before the souls of his esoteric pupils.[14] He adhered to the rule of absolute truthfulness in that he only taught the things he knew to be true through his own investigation. He followed the rule of preserving continuity by not simply putting something quite new and more perfect in the place of the less perfect, but by linking in every case to an already existing situation and seeking to transform it into something more perfect. This signified an awakening to life within him of the deepest Christian concept, the concept of resurrection. If we are able to experience within ourselves how the present can be carried over into the future in a living way, thus fulfilling the Gospel words that we

---

13. Dornach, December 15, 1918.
14. Disclosed by a member of the Working Committee of the Esoteric School, in a letter from Adolf Arenson to Albert Steffen, December 24, 1926.

should remain related to one another not only in the body through the blood, but should relate to one another in the soul life through the spirit, then the way to an understanding of the Mystery of Golgotha has been discovered.[15]

Much could be gained, according to Rudolf Steiner's conviction, if people of a later generation would take their guidance from the dead, whereby a continuity of development would be consciously preserved. When he wrote about Goethe, he completely ignored his own opinion and attempted to express only the thoughts originating from Goethe; he wrote a theory of knowledge of Goethe and did not give his own philosophy of life. Just as in the case of Goethe's world conception, he also immersed himself in the thought-worlds of Nietzsche and Haeckel, for we are able to attain to true knowledge only if we do not absolutely insist on our own point of view, but submerge ourselves in the spiritual views of others. And only after he had struggled to work in this way for twenty years to gain the right, so to speak, to work on the living, did he begin to disseminate spiritual science in public. For then no one could any longer rightly maintain: This occultist speaks about the spiritual world because he is ignorant of the philosophical and natural-scientific achievements of the age.[16]

This path, so unusual to ordinary understanding and perception, was incomprehensible to Rudolf Steiner's opponents, and was understood only with difficulty by friends sympathetic to spiritual-scientific outlook. Because he was aware of this difficulty, he took pains again and again to make clear, at least to his anthroposophical friends, that the spiritual current to which he adhered had never depended upon other currents, and that certain connections had only been outward ones. He admitted, however, that the distinction had been made more difficult through historical happenings. But

---

15. A reference to Matthew 12:47–50 [Trans.]; see Rudolf Steiner, *Building Stones for an Understanding of the Mystery of Golgotha*, Rudolf Steiner Press, London, 1972, Lecture 8, Berlin, April 24, 1917 (CW 175).

16. See "On the Connection of the Living and the Dead," Berne, Nov. 9, 1916, in *Life Beyond Death: Selected Lectures by Rudolf Steiner*, Rudolf Steiner Press, London, 1995 (CW 168); see also the autobiographical sketch of 1907 in *Correspondence and Documents 1901–1925*, Anthroposophic Press, NY, 1988 (CW 262).

though it might appear to outward view that it would have been more advisable to have founded the Anthroposophical Society independently of other societies, the connections were nevertheless justified in terms of karma.[17]

This remark makes it evident that the linking up with other societies, which took place at that time, was necessitated by the interplay of forces arising between the polarities of *freedom* and *love*, as they are justifiably expressed in esoteric life as *truthfulness* and *continuity*. Working toward truth and knowledge requires freedom, but at the same time, what has been recognized as true must link in fellowship to what already exists in the world. It is significant that even Rudolf Steiner's great strength was not always sufficient to reconcile the polarities of a life devoted in freedom and truth to the search for knowledge while trying to preserve continuity in the cause of fellowship. This was objectively unattainable because, where continuity is concerned, the world is involved, and though Rudolf Steiner respected continuity in a far greater measure than is normally the case, nevertheless, he could not sacrifice truthfulness to the cause of fellowship. When this became an acute problem in the Theosophical Society it led to separation.

Only by failing to consider Rudolf Steiner's discernment toward these polarities of esoteric life can misunderstandings and wrong judgements occur with regard to his spiritual independence. But, beyond all such fleeting opinions, the historical importance of Rudolf Steiner's cultural act—that of creating, through his method of spiritual investigation, a science that allows freedom to be found in the realm of the esoteric—will become more and more acknowledged.

Here it might be interposed that, through the creation of his Esoteric School, Rudolf Steiner did impose a rule of *secrecy* after all. This argument is not justified, however, for, in Steiner's view, it was never a case of keeping anything secret in the accepted sense of the term, not even in the Esoteric School. For him it was a matter of upholding a truly scientific attitude that, in the cultural life of our

---

17. Dornach, December 15, 1918.

time, demands as a matter of course that serious knowledge can only be acquired step by step. For example, no one who has not received the requisite grounding can be instructed in the higher stages of geometry. Whereas this is clear to everyone in the case of geometry, the most widespread belief is that in the realm of supersensible knowledge everything can be comprehended and judged without any kind of preliminary requirements.

Solely in accordance with this impartial and methodical approach, Rudolf Steiner's way of teaching ranged from what was completely free and public to what was conditional. The common basis of all these stages of instruction subsisted in what he proclaimed as his "act of inauguration," which occurred at the commencement of his public activity on behalf of a science of the supersensible.

> I will build on the strength that enables me to lead the pupils of the spirit along the pathway of development. This will be the sole meaning of my act of inauguration.[18]

The Esoteric School served this purpose in its particular way insofar as its pupils received their instruction entirely in accordance with their individual needs and capabilities. Yet, when the Esoteric School was refounded in 1924 under the title "The Free High School of Spiritual Science," the esoteric instruction was thereafter built up according to strict rules, which applied throughout. It is true that this could be carried out only for the First Class. The decline of Rudolf Steiner's physical powers in the autumn of 1924 made it impossible for him to carry the great plans of his final project to a conclusion.

Hella Wiesberger

---

18. Letter of August 16, 1902 to the representative of the German theosophists, Wilhelm Hübbe-Schleiden, from *Letters* II (untranslated).

FROM THE HISTORY AND CONTENTS OF THE FIRST SECTION OF THE ESOTERIC SCHOOL

1904–1914

Rudolf Steiner

PART I

THE FOUNDING OF THE FIRST SECTION
OF THE ESOTERIC SCHOOL
AND SOME OF THE MATERIAL USED
1904–1914

FURTHER INTRODUCTORY REMARKS

BY HELLA WIESBERGER

On the occasion of the refounding of the Anthroposophical Society at Christmas 1923–1924, Rudolf Steiner spoke about his plan to establish three classes in the new Esoteric School to be known as "The Free High School of Spiritual Science," and he pointed out that three such classes had existed previously, though in a slightly different form. He was referring to the three *study circles*, or sections, of the Esoteric School as they had existed from 1904 until the First World War in the summer of 1914. True to the rule of preserving continuity as far as possible, he had already linked in these circles to whatever was reconcilable with his aims: he linked the First Circle to the Esoteric School of Theosophy in the Theosophical Society; the Second and Third Circles, out of which the Cognitive-Ritual Section was formed, were linked to a society with Masonic-ritual affinities.[19]

Concerning the Structure of the Esoteric School

The Esoteric School of Theosophy, abbreviated as *EST* or *ES*, was founded in 1888 by H. P. Blavatsky, and remained under her sole leadership until her death in 1891. Her pupil Annie Besant then took over the leadership, at first with William Q. Judge and, from 1895 on, alone.[20] The few German theosophists who sought esoteric instruction were affiliated to this London ES. A German Esoteric School was founded for the first time by Rudolf Steiner along with the German Society.

---

19. See *Rosicrucianism Renewed* (CW 265).
20. For the history of the founding of the ES see the second part of this volume.

It has been possible to reconstruct the following details about the successive stages in the building up of the First Circle, which was originally attached to the EST.

The German Section of the Theosophical Society, centered in Berlin, was officially founded October 20, 1902, with Rudolf Steiner as General Secretary and Marie von Sivers as Secretary. Annie Besant, who was then one of the most active representatives of the Theosophical Society and leader of the Esoteric School, came to Berlin with the foundation charter. At this occasion Rudolf Steiner allowed her to enroll him as a member of the ES.[21] The following account is given by Steiner:

> In this connection I must mention something constantly brought forward by our opponents, wrapped in a fog of misunderstandings. I need not have mentioned this on any inner ground, for it has had no influence whatever on the course of my life or my public activities. As regards all that I have to describe here the matter has remained a purely "private" affair. I refer to my joining the *Esoteric School,* which existed within the Theosophical Society.
>
> The Esoteric School dates back to H. P. Blavatsky. She had created, for a small inner circle of the Society, a place in which she gave out what she did not wish to say to the Society in general. Like others who are cognizant with the spiritual world, she did not consider it possible to impart to the generality of persons such profound teachings.
>
> All this is connected with the way H.P. Blavatsky arrived at her teachings. There has always been a tradition in regard to such teachings, which goes back to the ancient Mysteries. This tradition was cherished in many different societies, which took strict care to prevent any of the teachings from spreading beyond the limits of such societies.

---

21. October 23, 1902. Marie von Sivers had already become a member of the ES at an earlier date.

But, for some reason or other, it was considered proper to impart such teaching to H. P. Blavatsky. She then united what she had thus received with revelations that came to her personally from within; because of a remarkable atavism, she was a human personality in whom the spiritual world worked as it had once worked in the leaders of the Mysteries—in a state of consciousness that was dreamlike—in contrast with the modern state illuminated by the consciousness-soul. Thus, in the human being "Blavatsky," what in primitive times was kept secret in the Mysteries was renewed.

For modern human beings there is an infallible method for deciding what portion of the content of spiritual perception can be imparted to wider circles. This can be done with everything that the investigator can clothe in ideas that are current both in the consciousness-soul itself, and in appropriate form in acknowledged science.

This is not the case when spiritual knowledge does not live in the consciousness-soul, but rather in the forces in the subconscious soul powers. *These* are not sufficiently independent of the forces active in the body. Therefore the imparting of such teachings drawn from the subconscious may be dangerous; for such teachings can in like manner be taken in only by the subconscious. Thus both teacher and learner are then moving in a region where what is wholesome for humanity and what is harmful must be handled with the utmost care.

All this, therefore, does not concern Anthroposophy, because this lifts all its teachings entirely above the subconscious.

The inner circle of Blavatsky continued to live in the Esoteric School. I had placed my anthroposophical activity into the Theosophical Society. I therefore had to be informed about all that had occurred in the latter. For the sake of this information, and also because I considered a smaller circle necessary for those advanced in anthroposophical spiritual knowledge, I caused myself to be admitted as a member into the Esoteric School. Of course, my smaller circle was to have a different meaning from this school. It was to represent a higher class, a higher participation, for those who had absorbed enough elementary knowledge of Anthroposophy. I now intended to link up everywhere with what was already in existence, with what history had already provided. Just as I did this in regard to the Theosophical Society, I wished to do likewise in reference to the Esoteric School. For this reason my "more restricted circle" arose at first in connection with this school. But the connection consisted solely in the *plan*, and not in what I imparted from the spiritual world. So in the first years my more restricted circle appeared to be like a section of the Esoteric School of Mrs. Besant. Inwardly it was not in any way the same as this. And in 1907, when Mrs. Besant was with us at the Theosophical Congress in Munich, even the external connection came to an end according to an agreement between Mrs. Besant and myself.

That I could have learned anything special in Mrs. Besant's Esoteric School is beyond the bounds of possibility, and from the beginning I never participated in the exercises of this school except in a few instances where my participation was for the sole purpose of informing myself as to what went on there.

At that time there was no other real content in the school, except what was derived from H. P. Blavatsky, and that was already in print.[22] In addition to these printed exercises, Mrs. Besant gave all sorts of Indian exercises for progress in knowledge, to which I was opposed.

Until 1907, then, my more restricted circle was connected, as to its plan, with what Mrs. Besant fostered as such a circle. But to make of these facts what has been made of them by opponents is wholly unjustifiable. Even the absurd idea that I was introduced to spiritual knowledge entirely by the Esoteric School of Mrs. Besant has been asserted.[23]

---

22. *Esoteric* (third volume of Blavatsky's *The Secret Doctrine*) from the posthumous works published by Annie Besant in 1897.
23. Rudolf Steiner, *Autobiography*, SteinerBooks, Great Barrington, MA, 2006, pp. 221-222.

The collected letters of the first part of this volume record that Rudolf Steiner was asked for esoteric instruction immediately after the founding of the German Section, that is, even before he was officially nominated as the first Arch-Warden (*Landesleiter*) of the Esoteric School in 1904. The institution of the restricted Circle, which he regarded as so essential, and so much desired by his first pupils, is touched upon in the letter to Marie von Sivers of April 16, 1903:

> Without a body of true theosophists to improve the karma of the present by hard-working meditation, theosophical teachings would be expounded merely to half-deaf ears.
>
> (*Correspondence and Documents*, p.28)

This is exemplified also by the answer given to a corresponding question by Mathilde Scholl:

> It would be really wonderful if the *newer* members of the German ES could somehow come closer together. This is just what is needed in Germany, for the ES must become the heart of the Theosophical Society. (May 1, 1903)

A year after this statement, in May 1904, Rudolf Steiner stayed for a week in London with Marie von Sivers, to discuss his functions in the ES with Annie Besant. Marie von Sivers was always present during his personal discussions with Annie Besant to act as interpreter. In an open letter of May 10, 1904, to all members of the ES in Germany and Austria, Annie Besant proclaimed that Rudolf Steiner was authorized as her representative in Switzerland and Hungary.[24]

---

24. The letter, reproduced on p. 8, appointed Rudolf Steiner to the office of "Arch-Warden" of the ES in Germany and the Austrian Empire—ED.

31, St. James' Place,
London, S.W.
May. 10. 1904.

To all members of the E.S.
in Germany & Austria.

I hereby appoint Dr Rudolf
Steiner as Arch-Warden of the
E.S. in Germany & the Austrian
Empire, with full authority, as
my representative, to call meetings
of the School, to organise groups
& appoint Wardens, & to do all
else necessary for the welfare of the
School, remaining in direct communication with myself.

Annie Besant

Facsimile of Mrs. Besant's letter to the members.

From London, Rudolf Steiner returned to Berlin and began working to build up his Esoteric School, alongside his other activities of spreading spiritual science and developing the Society. Since from the very beginning the main emphasis of his work was on his public work, he started to propagate the ideas of the Christian-Rosicrucian means of development—of great importance for the West—in a series of articles that appeared in the publicly available theosophical periodical *Lucifer-Gnosis*, which he founded and published. These articles appeared between June 1904 and 1908 as "How to Attain Knowledge of the Higher Worlds," and they were first published as a book in 1909.[25] June 1904 is also notable as the first recorded date that he functioned as Arch-Warden in the ceremonies of the ES, during the Theosophical Congress in Amsterdam, which took place from June 18–21. Apart from Rudolf Steiner and Marie von Sivers, other German Theosophists also took part, among them Mathilde Scholl from Cologne, Sophie Stinde and Pauline von Kalkreuth from Munich, Günther Wagner from Lugano and his sister, Amalie Wagner, from Hamburg. Mathilde Scholl recounts that Amalie Wagner was admitted into the ES on that occasion and that Rudolf Steiner performed this act in her hotel room. But that can only refer to a kind of preliminary event, as the official ES work was only begun in Berlin after the Amsterdam Congress. There the first esoteric lessons took place on July 9 and 14 of 1904—at least those are the first recorded dates of esoteric lessons in Berlin, and from the available records it is to be assumed that the work of the ES first took place in Berlin at that time. But these ceremonies must also be reckoned as merely a preliminary proceeding, which basically continued into the autumn of 1905. For only when the Second and Third Sections were added was the School fully complete.

During the holiday month of August 1904, Rudolf Steiner sent personal letters to several members living at a distance, whom he thereby either admitted to membership of the School or invited to join. A further ES gathering was planned for the beginning of September

---

25. *How to Know Higher Worlds: A Modern Path of Initiation*, Anthroposophic Press, Hudson, NY, 1994.

(according to a letter of August 29, 1904 to Günther Wagner), however, it is not known if this actually took place.

In the second half of September 1904, Steiner accompanied Annie Besant on her lecture tour of several German cities, and gave a resume in German of her public lectures given in English. At the last place they called, in Cologne, both stayed at the home of Mathilde Scholl, who reported that a gathering of ES members occurred:

> Mrs. Besant, Dr. Steiner, Fräulein von Sivers, Miss Bright, Mr. Keightley, Mathilde Scholl, in Mrs. Besant's room. Before we left the room Mrs. Besant spoke to Dr. Steiner about the study material for pupils of the ES. Mrs. Besant recommended Leadbeater's *The Christian Creed.* Politely but firmly Dr. Steiner answered that he could not make use of this book for his pupils.

A few esoteric lessons then took place until May 1905 in Berlin. But the first official communication through the "long-prepared circular to the German ES members" containing rules appeared only at the beginning of June 1905.

At the General Meeting in October 1905, the School was extended to include the *Cognitive-Ritual* (that is, the second and third sections), and members, at the specific request of Rudolf Steiner, flocked in greater numbers to Berlin, where several ES lessons occurred. The contents of the lesson of October 24, 1905 were written personally by Rudolf Steiner for Anna Wagner, the wife of Günther Wagner, who was unable to take part for health reasons.[26] Apart from the short summing-up of the lesson of October 4, 1904, for Adolf Kolbe in Hamburg, this is the only version of an esoteric lesson given in Rudolf Steiner's own handwriting. All that has otherwise been preserved of the contents of such lessons were written afterward from memory by those present, and who were not allowed to make notes during the lessons.

---

26. The lesson content is contained in *Guidance in Esoteric Training: From the Esoteric School*, Rudolf Steiner Press, London, 1994, pp. 83–86 (CW 42/245).

More and more esoteric lessons took place from that autumn of 1905 on, not only in Berlin, but also in other German cities, and later in other countries also where pupils of Rudolf Steiner were working in this way. After the start of the First World War in the summer of 1914, the esoteric activity came to an end, because work in strictly closed circles could have aroused suspicion, but also because it would have been impossible to undertake any esoteric activity at a time charged with such strong emotions. It was ten years before an Esoteric School could again be inaugurated, this time in connection with the refounding of the Anthroposopical Society.

The General Rules of the School

The relevant documents reveal that during the initial stages of the first Esoteric Study Circles, "Rules" were given, modeled on those of the EST. The latter are said to have been originally very strict, but were in many respects modified over time. At the time Rudolf Steiner joined, one could apply for membership after two years in the Theosophical Society. The School was divided into degrees, acquired according to four different paths, or methods of discipline: a general discipline, a discipline related to yoga, a Christian-Gnostic discipline, and a Pythagorean one. But before admittance to the training proper one had to have belonged to the Probationary- or Hearer-Degree (the *Shrâvaka*-Degree of India) for at least one year, and later two. At the time of admittance a written "promise" had to be submitted, affirming that the papers received would be handled in confidence and returned on demand. After the predetermined trial period one could be accepted into the actual first degree, upon giving a written statement that Theosophy would be made the all-determining factor of one's life.

Because Rudolf Steiner's first Esoteric Study Circle was outwardly joined to the Probationary-Degree of the EST, and actually came within the general discipline, his pupils were obliged to make the compulsory "promise," which is evidenced by various letters. Meanwhile, he led his Study Circle quite independently. For example, there was no choice of discipline, even though in a letter to Anna and Günther Wagner on January 2, 1905 the four disciplines were mentioned.[27] But at this time everything was in a transitional state, and before long it was taken as a matter of course that everything should be determined according to Rudolf Steiner's intentions. Thus on January 23, 1905 he received a letter from Mathilde Scholl who, through his intercession, had been admitted by Annie Besant into the first degree of the EST in London, in May 1904, but had not yet received its instructions:

> For me personally, it is not a matter of importance whether Mrs. Mead sends the writings or not, for all that I need is given me by you, and will continue to be given me; and that is in such profusion that I can only look forward with respectful astonishment to all that is to come.

Something similar is expressed in a letter from Günther Wagner, April 3, 1905:

> Some months ago I already received a printed article in English from Mrs. Oakley that gave information about the four ways that were practiced in the ES, and which you mention in your valued and kind letter to my wife. My wife and I have decided on the "Christian" path, and we would now ask if we may also begin on the first of April in Germany, as described in the article printed in English. Is a German set of instructions going to be made available? This will most probably be the case, because you will be unable to provide written instructions to all ES members who live at a distance. I would also like to know if pupils of the first degree (old order) should receive other instructions than those from the article printed in English, or whether these now apply to all pupils. You prescribed for my wife on January 2, that she should carry out the exercises from January 6 for about four weeks. She has done so and is continuing with them, but she requests new instructions from you.

---

27. Letter on p. 66.

These questions were answered in the first ES circular letter of June 5, 1905, and were further elaborated in later instructions.

No more can be reconstructed of the gradual development of the First Circle. The question of how the "promise" of the EST was dealt with remains open, for Rudolf Steiner's pupils did not enter the degrees of the EST and yet some of these "promises" are still extant which, as far as they are dated, originated in 1906. It is not known if they were given on admission to the first degree of the Cognitive-Ritual Section, or in some other connection. At any rate, Rudolf Steiner wrote to an esoteric pupil in the same year, 1906:

> Please do not regard the keeping secret as a strict injunction, but as a temporary one, due to the present confused circumstances in the ES and TS.... I would also be pleased if this were not necessary.

This statement agrees with the fact that nothing has come down to us—even though the circle of pupils had already grown—to say that after the separation from the EST in May 1907 written "promises" were still asked for by Rudolf Steiner. In fact, at the refounding of the Esoteric School in 1924, the obligation to treat the lesson material confidentially was left to the individual's consciousness of responsibility. In this sense Marie Steiner wrote after Rudolf Steiner's death:

> It was not his opinion that esotericism could still be practiced in the greatest seclusion and with strictly binding vows as in former times. That could not have been reconciled with the feeling of individual freedom. The soul must stand before its own higher self and recognize what it owes to this higher self and the spiritual world in the way of respectful silence.[28]

---

28. Foreword to the first edition of *Karmic Relationships of the Anthroposophical Movement* (not included in current edition, *Karmic Relationships: Esoteric Studies*, vols. 1–8, Rudolf Steiner Press, London, 1975).

The Lesson Material

The instruction was, as it were, divided into three parts: the rules and exercises that applied to all equally; the personal exercises; and the esoteric lessons, which mainly dealt with intimate aspects of the path of development and directed the consciousness toward the Masters of Wisdom and of the Harmony of Sensations and Feelings, as the true leaders of the School. The ideal aim of the instructions lay, after all, in the gradual attainment of personal access to the Masters through the higher consciousness developed through the exercises.

The descriptions of the nature and activity of the Masters given in the esoteric lessons were meant as a guide along this path. The little thereof that has been handed down to us is summarized in the section dealing with the Masters. However, as Rudolf Steiner has spoken about them not only in esoteric lessons, but also in lectures to Society members, and even in public, they can be adequately grasped from the picture presented there.[29]

Knowledge of the Masters had been of basic importance in the Theosophical Society and its Esoteric School since their founding.[30] For Rudolf Steiner the existence of the Masters had been a personally experienced reality decades before his connection with the Theosophical Society, as he testified many times.[31] Also, that it was his own Master who convinced him of the necessity of spreading the truth of esotericism in the world is vouched for by his own testimony:

> I can only say that had the Master not convinced me that, in spite of all this, Theosophy is necessary for our age, I would only have written philosophical books and lectured on literature and philosophy even *after* 1901 (*Correspondence and Documents*, p. 47).

---

29. Cf. the survey in the Supplement beginning on p 207.
30. Further details are given in the introductory remarks at the beginning of Part II.
31. See the notes for Edouard Schuré and letters to Marie Steiner-von Sivers, both in *Correspondence and Documents: Rudolf Steiner/Marie Steiner-von Sivers* (hereafter referred to as "*Correspondence and Documents*"), Anthroposophic Press, Hudson, NY, and Rudolf Steiner Press, London, 1988 (CW 262); see also *Self-Education: Autobiographical Reflections 1861–1893*, Mercury Press, Spring Valley, NY, 1985.

And he only joined the Society after having recognized "at the culmination of many years of inner development" that "the spiritual powers which I serve are to be found within the TS."[32]

However, whereas in the TS the Masters were only referred to as the "Masters of Wisdom," Rudolf Steiner spoke of them as "The Masters of Wisdom and of the Harmony of Sensations and Feelings," or sometimes "of the Feeling-Life of Humanity," because they possessed not only a high degree of wisdom, but also a "limitless source of human love" (From the letter to Amalie Wagner on August 2, 1904).[33] This aspect points, as everything of his does, to the central theme of his spiritual knowledge—the unique significance of the Christ-Principle for the whole of the development of humanity and Earth. For him Christ was the Master of all Masters, and the "Masters of Wisdom and of the Harmony of Sensations and Feelings" were those who "stand in direct relationship to the forces of the higher hierarchies" (lecture given in Düsseldorf, June 15, 1915),[34] and who have comprehended the fact that "the progress of humanity depends upon the understanding of the great significance of the event of Golgotha" (Berlin, March 22, 1909).[35]

What Dr. Steiner said in one of his earliest public lecture cycles, given in Berlin, may be considered the most revealing statement of his personal relationship to the Masters. Referring to those highly developed individualities as described in Sinnett's *Esoteric Buddhism*, he attempted to show that for the European way of thinking the concept of the Masters did not necessarily bear any great significance, when we consider that on the ladder of development—from the less advanced to, for instance, a Goethe, or beyond—there are an infinite number of possible stages. And then follow the words of such significance for himself:

---

32. From the rough draft of a circular to the German Theosophical Lodges in the summer of 1902, before the founding of the German Section. (In *Correspondence and Documents, 1901–1925*, Anthroposophic Press, Hudson, NY., 1988 (CW 262).
33. Letter on p. 44.
34. "Preparing for the Sixth Epoch" (booklet of one lecture), Anthroposophic Press, Hudson, NY, 1979.
35. *The Deed of Christ and the Opposing Spiritual Powers: Lucifer, Ahriman, Mephistopheles, Asuras*, Steiner Book Centre, North Vancouver, B.C., 1976.

... the so-called Masters are great inspirers—nothing more than that—great inspirers on the spiritual level. To be sure, their development extends far beyond the measure offered by our present day culture. They are our great inspirers. They do not, however, demand belief in any kind of authority, or in any dogma. They only make a demand on the individual's human understanding and give instruction, through certain methods for developing the powers and abilities dormant in every human being, which lead upward to the higher domains of existence. (Berlin, October 13, 1904)[36]

In his next lecture he characterized the Masters in a way that makes clear that they respected human freedom to the highest degree, so that no kind of dependence could arise. No one, for instance, can suffer any harm from the rules given in *How to Know Higher Worlds*, as opposed to many other books of a similar nature that certain people recommend. But because so much is recommended that is not only valueless, but can also be harmful, "the Masters have given permission for the publication of such rules" (Berlin, December 15, 1904).[37]

If one looks at the various statements about the Masters they appear at first glance to be contradictory. In particular, what is quoted above from the lecture of October 13, 1904 in Berlin appears to contradict what can be read in letters to esoteric pupils:

I am able and allowed to be your leader only insofar as the exalted Master by whom I myself am guided gives me instruction.

(Letter, August 11, 1904)[38]

or also where it states that the theosophical doctrines refer back to the Masters:

---

36. *Ursprung und Ziel des Menschen. Grundbegriffe der Geisteswissenshaft*, untranslated (CW 53).
37. Ibid.
38. Letter on p .48.

We affirm quite rightly that Theosophy did not come into the world through this or that book, through this or that set of dogmas. Theosophy springs from those high individuals, whom we call the Masters of Wisdom and of the Harmony of Sensations and Feelings, for they have uncovered the sources of the spiritual life that can henceforth flow into humanity.

(Berlin, June 21, 1909)

Spiritual life can be traced back to those sources, which are to be sought in the individualities we call the *Masters of Wisdom and of the Harmony of Sensations and Feelings*. It is by them that we can find the impulses, if we truly search for them, that help us to work from epoch to epoch, from age to age.

(Berlin, December 26, 1909)

If, however, one looks more closely at these statements, then the apparent discrepancy between them is resolved. It becomes clear that Rudolf Steiner himself belongs to those initiates who receive the impulses of the Masters through their free powers of reasoning and whose task is to elaborate those impulses for the progress of humanity. The world of the supersensible, and also of the Masters, has its own language. It is revealed through signs and symbols that can be studied and deciphered only by means of a special training. How the esoteric language of revelation is interpreted and used depends entirely on the extent to which the capacity of understanding penetrates, and also on the moral awareness of responsibility of the one who uses it. Rudolf Steiner's achievement on behalf of cultural progress quite obviously rests on his ability to convert the symbolic language of the creative-spiritual basis underlying all existence into a conceptual language appropriate to the modern consciousness, which is expressed in Anthroposophy. He had to stand by this personal deed in the eyes of the world without relying on the authority of the Masters. His manner of teaching was quite personal. Perhaps this helps to explain why he ceased to speak in the same intimate fashion about the Masters as he did in earlier times, the more he developed the scientific character of Anthroposophy. This is especially the case in the years after the First World War.

Concerning the Method of Instruction in the Esoteric School

Whereas, in the above sense, Rudolf Steiner took personal responsibility for the supersensible knowledge he gave in public, this did not apply in the same way to the Esoteric School. He stated that the School stood under the direct guidance of the Masters and that therefore all that flowed through it must emanate only from the Masters of Wisdom and of the Harmony of Sensations and Feelings, and from no other source. The chief obligation of the pupils of the School was to apply all the common sense they had to what was taught them and to ask themselves if it was a reasonable path to follow (from an esoteric class, Düsseldorf, April 19, 1909).

It was apparently not always the case, but in certain of his esoteric lessons, or at certain moments during his esoteric lessons, Rudolf Steiner spoke as the direct mouthpiece of the Masters. A participant in the Düsseldorf lesson of April 19, 1909 reported that this particular lesson commenced with the following words: "My dear Sisters and Brothers, this esoteric lesson is one where the responsibility does not rest with the one who is speaking!" Those words were uttered because, in the following description of how Zarathustra had once received initiation from the Sun Spirit, Rudolf Steiner himself *was* Zarathustra at that moment. It must have come as a grand experience that "our great teacher, who had shared the results of his investigations with us, could now demonstrate through his own person how an ancient leader of humanity revealed himself by means of inspiration"[39]—that is, how Rudolf Steiner, as the first of the modern age, could transform himself through his own strict inner discipline into a serviceable tool for spiritual beings to work through, not as a medium, but as a fully conscious spiritual investigator.

There are very few accounts of this particular feature of Rudolf Steiner's activity in the esoteric lessons where he could be experienced as the Messenger of the Masters. The following account is from memory:

---

39. Lecture by Elizabeth Vreede in Stuttgart on July 9, 1930. See Elizabeth Vreede and Thomas Meyer, *The Bodhisattva Question*, Temple Lodge Press, London, 1993.

I remember exactly how Rudolf Steiner entered the room. It was he and it was not he. When he came to the esoteric lesson he did not look like Rudolf Steiner, but only like his outer sheath. "Through me are speaking the Masters of Wisdom and of the Harmony of Sensations and Feelings," he began. It was always a solemn occasion. One is quite unable to forget it—the expression of his countenance.[40]

Another person wrote of the deep impression he had when first attending an esoteric lesson:

Everyone sat in silence. When Rudolf Steiner entered the room it seemed to me that a super-earthly radiance still shone upon his features out of that realm from which he had come to us—it not only appeared this way; it was so. As though with direct knowledge and understanding, he spoke of the great Masters who guide our life and our endeavors from above: Kut Hoomi, Morya, Jesus, and Christian Rosenkreutz—the "Masters of Wisdom and of the Harmony of Sensations and Feelings."

This much can be said: that the sanctity of this hour was indescribably beautiful. Rudolf Steiner appeared at this moment entirely as the Messenger of a higher realm. The impression is unforgettable.[41]

In greatest detail and in the most delicate phrasing, the Russian poet Andrei Belyi described in his memoirs *Verwandeln des Lebens* (Basel, 1975), how he experienced it as his task in the "Probationary-Degree" to train his attention more on the "how" than on the "what." There was no outer distinction between the esoteric lectures and the other lectures, for all of them had an esoteric nuance. The more they were given in popular form, the more subtle was the wording. What, however, could be experienced in concentrated form in the esoteric lessons was precisely that the *how* had become the *what,* and outshined everything else.

---

40. Jenny Schirmer-Bey in "*Was in der anthroposophischen Gesellschaft vorgeht.*" *Members' News Sheet,* September 1, 1974.
41. Ludwig Kleeberg, *Wege und Worte,* Stuttgart, 1961.

LETTERS TO ESOTERIC PUPILS

WITH EXERCISES

The letter of September 20, 1907, is placed at the beginning because it contains basic information about esoteric training. Then follow in chronological order the letters that Rudolf Steiner wrote in his capacity as esoteric teacher, insofar as they are known and have been preserved. The letters to Mathilde Scholl were made available by those responsible at the Goetheanum.

The times indicated in the letters for starting the meditation are connected with the phases of the Moon. They should be begun only during the time of the waxing Moon.

In connection with individual exercises and the explanations mentioned concerning *Light on the Path* by Mabel Collins and *The Voice of the Silence* by H. P. Blavatsky; cf. *Guidance in Esoteric Training*, CW 245.

Letter to Martha Langen in Eisenach concerning basic information relating to esoteric training:

Berlin, September 20, 1907

Esteemed Frau Langen:

Only today am I able to answer your letter.[42] To be sure it would only be possible to give a complete answer orally; nevertheless, I would like to send you a few observations to begin with, so that you can judge whether the journey to Hanover would prove practical and desirable.

---

42. This letter of inquiry is unavailable.

Because of the way that Theosophy needs to be propagated today, misunderstandings can all too easily arise about its basic principles; for example, in respect to esotericism and its study. Such a misunderstanding, for instance, is the belief that Theosophy requires anyone engaging in it in any way to accept esoteric instruction. That, however, is certainly not the case. Esoteric truths can be *discovered* only by those trained in esotericism; they can be *grasped* by ordinary human reasoning, and also *applied* in practical life on the basis of an understanding attained by the ordinary soul faculties. I will never impart any information discovered by esoteric means that cannot be grasped by the ordinary soul-powers when *voluntarily* applied. Theosophy is necessary in our age, and humanity must necessarily fall into desolation and universal sterility if it cannot receive this as a mighty stream of power. It would, however, be fatal if every theosophist also wished to become an esoteric pupil. That would be (excuse the trivial comparison) as though everyone needed to become a tailor just *because* all people need to have clothes. All people are in need of Theosophy under certain circumstances; few are in need of esoteric training.

On the other hand, no one who is a suitable candidate may be denied this training; for, however many apply, at present there will not be *over* many. Therefore, in a certain sense, there is no hindrance in the path of anyone wishing to apply for esoteric training. However, because many today wish to take up such a training, misunderstandings are bound to occur under such circumstances, even among the trainees themselves. Today everyone thinks that what is good for them must also be good for other people.

Thus *generalized* views about the training are propagated that are fundamentally erroneous. The esoteric teacher is naturally obliged to admit that the course followed by someone who is ascetic in sexual life is different from the course of one who does not avoid being of service to humanity in this way. This is soon changed into the statement: Asceticism is a requisite of esoteric development. The truth is something completely different. Asceticism with regard to sexual matters makes it *easier* for the esoteric pupil, makes the task more comfortable, as it were. Whoever, therefore, wishes primarily to gain "insight" through the pure egoism of acquiring knowledge can be assured that a certain ambition will be achieved in this direction by practicing a kind of asceticism. There can, however, be no *obligation* regarding asceticism, but only a *right* to it, which must first be earned. One must acquire the possibility of rendering a *valid* recompense to humanity for the avoidance of a *duty*, which would otherwise provide souls with an opportunity to incarnate. You see, therefore, that asceticism cannot be a rule in this respect, but may be permitted to some esotericists only under certain circumstances.

According to the opinions you bring to esotericism, you will easily understand, moreover, that *every* kind of egoism, however hidden or masked it may be, will prevent a person from getting very far along the path of esoteric training. A woman who does not avoid her womanly duties, but fulfills them according to their proper requirements, will naturally soon progress further than one who strives to gain "insight" through basically egoistic renunciation, unheeding of the destiny of the rest of humanity.

Therewith a large part of the questions from your letter has been answered. Esoteric training can never divert people from their life's task, unless they are on the wrong road. Certainly, you may find many so-called "pupils" whom you may regard as unsuited to fulfill a useful purpose. But one comes to a wrong conclusion if one compares *these* "pupils" with those who fulfill their life's tasks without wishing to know anything about Theosophy. One should not compare the former with the latter, but should ask oneself: How futile would be the former if they did not have Theosophy? And, as for the latter, the proper question would be: How much greater would be the content of their activities in life if they could include Theosophy, or even esoteric training itself?

To practice without guidance is not to be recommended. To persuade anyone to embark upon "training" is not my wish. It must be one's *own* free decision.

The occurrences of your inner and outer life compel you toward this inner training. You will certainly be able to fulfill your life's tasks more easily and surely with the help of this instruction. Your husband has far more difficulty with Theosophy than you do. That can be judged only by someone who knows that a learned education presents an almost insurmountable *inner* obstacle to theosophical truths at the present day. And perhaps, on the other hand, nothing is so suited to overcoming these obstacles as practical employment, such as is being offered to your husband at the moment.

Your inner training will be the right one only if it does not take anything away from you, but adds to what you already have: good health, strength in your life, security in your way of working, and inner peace, that human beings need, not for their own sake, but for the sake of others. No activity serves humanity that does not spring from inner peace. *Every* activity that stems from an inwardly dissatisfied soul disturbs the healthy human development wherever it makes its appearance.

Should you wish to undertake this after what I have here imparted to you, I will offer you every possible support. I shall be in Hanover from the evening of September 21 until October 4. If you care to announce your arrival by postcard I will arrange everything for a thorough exchange of views. Address: Dr. Rudolf Steiner, at present in Hanover, c/o Fleissner, Ferdinandstrasse 11.

With hearty greeting to your dear husband and be heartily greeted yourself, also, from

Dr. Rudolf Steiner

To Mathilde Scholl in Cologne

Mathilde Scholl wrote to Rudolf Steiner on February 11, 1903:

… With reference to our conversation I wish to ask the following. On plate XXVI of Leadbeater's book (*Man, Visible and Invisible*) the aura of a pupil of Buddha is depicted, a pupil who has attained the fourth degree, the level of an Arhat. The aura is arranged concentrically, the color sequence, starting from the center, is as follows:

1. Yellow = Intelligence
2. Rose pink = Love
3. Light blue = Devotion
4. Green = Sympathy
5. Violet = Spirituality

All this is surrounded by a rainbow-colored or rather, mother-of-pearl, circlet of rays and irradiated by living rays of light, which issue from the body of the Arhat. Leadbeater maintains that the *nature* of the *Arhat*, respectively also of his teacher, can be recognized by the sequence of colors.

Of what nature, or to which hierarchy, would a being belong whose aura, starting from the center, consists of:

1. Light blue = Devotion
2. Rose pink = Love

The sequence is similarly concentric, exactly like the one depicted, and yet no other colors were visible apart from light blue and pink (from a dream experience). However, the physical body appeared only in outline and was transparent, *not* plastic—and within it there were centers (like the swastika, or like wheels), which turned upon their own axes with the greatest rapidity and radiated light. The face had the features and expression of the Master M.

If you are able and permitted to tell me who this being is, or in what way I can find an explanation for it myself, I would be very happy....

I would be very pleased if a union with the ES in Germany could take place later. Some external considerations are still of help to me. For instance, I would like to have regular sets of instructions to study—in the beginning, that is two and a half years ago, one of the instruction sheets indicated which verse I should commit to memory in the evenings. But as no further instructions arrived thereafter, I started to study *The Bhagavad Gita* in this way, and after that *The Voice of the Silence*, where I have now arrived at the end of the second book. It would be of help to me not to be without guidance in my studies and to be assured, for instance, that when I make my meditation in the mornings many others are turning their thoughts in the same direction as I am—to know that many other people are studying the same book, and several other things that lie in this direction....

Rudolf Steiner answered:

Schlachtensee, nr. Berlin, May 1, 1903

Most esteemed Fräulein Scholl:

I should have written to you long ago. But even those duties only connected with *Luzifer*[43] have been somewhat pressing of late—on top of everything else. Now, at last, it will appear in print within a few days, and I hope that I will then be able to get back into a settled routine. At any rate, I shall not wait so long with my answering in future as, unfortunately, has been the case until now.

First of all allow me to deal with your main question. The aura that you describe is not distinct enough for me to be able to say anything of any note about it. You do not mention anything about rays emanating from the being you describe. Now there are always rays present in the *causal body* of *more advanced* persons.[44] These rays are the expression of active forces that human beings build into their constantly progressing karma. It appears, therefore, that what you are describing is not the picture of a causal body. I will, however, not say that we are not dealing with a highly developed being in what you mention, but in this particular case it could merely refer to the *projection* of the causal body in the substance of

---

43. The periodical founded and edited by Rudolf Steiner, collected in *Lucifer-Gnosis* (CW 34); some individual articles have been translated.

44. *Causal body* = the I-being; "The Spiritual thinking Ego," or permanent element of the human being that reincarnates; "For it is the Buddhi-Manas which is called the *Causal body*, (the United 5th and 6th Principles), and which is *Consciousness*, that connects it with every personality that inhabits on earth. Therefore, Soul being a generic term, there are in men three *aspects* of Soul—the terrestrial, or animal; the Human Soul; and the Spiritual Soul; these, strictly speaking, are one soul in its three aspects. Now of the first aspect, nothing remains after death; of the second (*nous* or Manas) only its divine essence *if left unsoiled* survives, while the third in addition to being immortal becomes *consciously* divine, by the assimilation of the higher Manas." (H. P. Blavatsky, *The Key to Theosophy*, Theosophical University Press, Pasadena, 1972, pp. 121–122).

See also Allan Combs, *The Radiance of Being: Complexity, Chaos and the Evolution of Consciousness* (Paragon House, New York, and Floris Books, Edinburgh, 1995), where the *causal body* is described as the "sheath of bliss," or the *Anandamaya kosha*, in which one experiences rapture, the body that provides the initial "religious" experience, and which is not the goal but must be developed (p. 123).

the mind. And in that case I am unable to explain the swastikas, which point again to an astral element. I therefore ask you to write to me in greater detail on this point. I would very much like us to get clear on this matter.[45]

It would be really wonderful if the *newer* members of the German ES could somehow come closer together. That is just what is needed in Germany, for the ES must become the heart of the Theosophical Society. In Germany this is especially important, for we have long hoped for an inner cooperation only in the case of *individuals,* and accept the fact that larger circles can only come together in an external way. But the individuals will then form a nucleus of people that will be all the more true, secure and vigorous. And that is what we need, because so much has got into a muddle with us.

Everything went very well in Weimar. We now have a Lodge there too. The lectures were exceptionally well attended. I would like to visit Cologne for the most diverse reasons, also to lecture there. Perhaps you might be able to prepare the ground for it a little, if you would be so kind. Much, very much, depends on our creating *new* centers. Until now almost all the German theosophists have wanted to maintain a much too loosely knit connection with the English Society, from which their movement sprang. And only *from this source*, in the closest connection with the mother movement, is it possible for *us* to work at present. In Germany there has been too much inclination toward dogmatization, toward *merely* intellectual

---

45. Mathilde Scholl replied on May 7, 1903, "My most sincere thanks for the reply to my question. The dream picture I described certainly radiated light, and this light seemed to emanate from the swastikas situated in the head and upper part of the body. Only the head and upper part of the body were visible, and that only in outline. The being did not appear to be physical, but only a phenomenon of light. The impression it made was so strong, however, that in my dream I believed I threw myself at its feet and became unconscious. On awakening everything appeared vivid to my eyes, and I felt deeply stirred for a long while afterward. I did not try to find an explanation at all at first. Through Leadbeater's book I learned how such a color sequence could be seen by someone. But I would love to know who this being was, because, although it seemed to have the features of the Master M, that may just as easily depend on my personal frame of mind as on reality." Rudolf Steiner's answer to this question is unknown.

comprehension of the doctrines, while no real understanding exists for living spirituality. We can make progress only when this latter is aroused and when our eyes are opened to the need not only for the learning of dogmas (Hartmann), but for spiritual union with the central individuals, the source of this wisdom and from whom this wisdom continues to flow—only then can progress be made. We have to make clear (not in words, but more subtly) that we are here dealing with the continuous fructification, by leading individuals, of those who carry the work of the TS. Only those who work esoteri-cally will fully comprehend these matters, and for that reason they must stick together in a conscious and self-assured manner and be able to rouse the others to activity.

It was very satisfying to me to be able to spend a few hours with you in Düsseldorf. That is the sort of satisfaction we have when we see other people travelling along the path where the milestones always register an advance. For a theosophist there is only the door one passes through just once—on the *outward* journey—and never a second time—on the return.

In Germany there are only four or five really reliable personalities; therefore we have to work intensively. If we do so, we shall find ways and means of advancing. If not, we shall miss something *now* that cannot so easily be put right again in Germany.

My forthcoming exoteric task is to spread the teaching to the best of my ability.

I hope that you will settle down well in Cologne, dear, most esteemed Fräulein Scholl, and will be able to work there in our affairs and find satisfaction therein. How is the person committed to your care?

In hope of hearing from you again soon, with hearty greetings, I remain

Yours sincerely,

Rudolf Steiner

Fräulein von Sivers sends you hearty greetings.

To Günther Wagner in Lugano

*Günther Wagner had written the following to Rudolf Steiner
on November 14, 1903:*

Esteemed Herr Doctor:

Enclosed—that is, posted at the same time—I am sending you the manuscript of Leadbeater's article "Our attitude toward children," which you asked me for on my visit to Berlin, in order to have it printed in *Luzifer.*[46]

It was a great pleasure to me to have made your acquaintance at the Annual Meeting, and I hope that we shall long continue in our joint work and will continue to support one another.

It would give me great pleasure if you would care to supply me with a particular piece of information. The allusion to a riddle that each Race [Epoch] has to solve was quite new to me; I could not find anything about it in the *Secret Doctrine.* Can you name the four riddles, which the first four epochs have (apparently) solved? I would also like to read H. P. Blavatsky's indications about it. Perhaps you could give me the exact reference.[47]

In the meantime I remain yours most respectfully,

Günther Wagner

Rudolf Steiner replied:

Berlin, December 24, 1903

Very confidential.

Dear esteemed Herr Wagner:

On page 42, Vol. I of the facsimile edition of *The Secret Doctrine*, in an explanation of the sixth stanza of the *Book of Dzyan*, stand the

---

46. It appeared in Issue 7 of the journal *Luzifer.*

47. The question refers to what Rudolf Steiner said at the first general meeting of the German Section in Berlin on October 18, 1903, in which Günther Wagner took part. Compare this with what is given at the end of the supplementary remarks to this section by Hella Wiesberger relating to "the fifth of the seven great life-secrets," beginning on p. 215.

words: "Of the Seven Truths or Revelations only four are manifested, because we are still in the Fourth Round."[48] I have indicated—while you were in Berlin—that, in the sense of a particular
esoteric tradition, the fourth of the above-mentioned Seven Truths
is derived from seven *esoteric Root-Truths*, and that of these seven partial truths (the fourth being considered as complete), one is
divulged (as a rule) to each Race [Epoch]. The fifth will be fully
manifested when the Fifth Race will have reached the goal of its
development. Now, I would like to answer your question as best I
can. At the moment the matter stands thus, that the four partial
truths are the subject of meditation-sentences for the aspirants in
the Mysteries, and that *nothing* else can be given apart from these
(symbolical) meditation-sentences. Something of a higher nature
emanates from them, by esoteric paths, to the one who meditates. I
therefore set down these four meditation-sentences, transmitted
from the symbolic sign language, as follows:

1. *Consider*: how the point becomes the sphere and still remains
   itself. If you have understood how the infinite sphere is, after all,
   merely a point, then return, for then the infinite will appear as
   finite within you.
2. *Consider*: how the grain becomes an ear [of rye] and then return,
   for then you will have understood how what is living exists in
   number.
3. *Consider*: how light desires the dark, heat the cold, how the male
   desires the female, then return, for then you will have understood which aspect the great Dragon of the Threshold will turn
   toward you.
4. *Consider*: how one enjoys hospitality in someone else's house,
   then return, for then you will have understood what awaits one
   who sees the Sun at midnight.

---

48. On p. 140 of the English facsimile edition it is rendered as: "Of these (the
Seven Elements) four of the elements are now fully manifested, while the fifth,
ether, is only partially so, as we are hardly in the second half of the Fourth Round,
and consequently the fifth Element will not manifest fully until the Fifth Round."

The fifth secret then arises, if the meditation was successful, out of the other four. Let me state, provisionally, only this much, that Theosophy—the fragment of Theosophy that could be found in *The Secret Doctrine* and its esotericism—is made up of partial truths contained in the fifth secret. An indication of how one can get beyond this point is to be found in the letter from the Master KH [Kut Hoomi] published by Sinnett, beginning with the following words: "I have to read each word..." (A.P. Sinnett, *The Occult World,* pp. 126–127).[49]

I can only give you the assurance that in the sentence by Kut Hoomi: "When science will have learned how it is that impressions of leaves can appear on stones...," practically the whole of the fifth secret lies hidden.

That is all that I am able to tell you *at present* with regard to your question. Perhaps I will be able to enlarge on it when more questions are forthcoming.

The above four sentences are what one calls *living* sentences, that is to say, they begin to sprout during meditation and send forth shoots of knowledge.

With joyful Christmas greetings.

Yours faithfully, Rudolf Steiner

Berlin W., Motzstrasse 17

---

49. The exact rendering of Kut Hoomi's words as given by A. P. Sinnett as follows: "Of course I have to read every word you write, otherwise I would make a fine mess of it. And whether it be through my physical or spiritual eyes, the time required for it is practically the same. As much may be said of my replies; for whether I precipitate or dictate them or write my answers myself, the difference in time saved is very minute. I have to think it over, to photograph every word and sentence carefully in my brain, before it can be repeated by precipitation. As fixing on chemically prepared surfaces of the images formed by the camera requires a previous arrangement within the focus of the object to be represented, for otherwise—as often found in bad photographs—the legs of the sitter might appear out of all proportion with the head, and so on—so we have to first arrange our sentences and impress every letter to appear on paper in our minds before it becomes fit to be read. For the present it is all I can tell you. When science will have learned more about the mystery of the lithophyl (or lithobiblion), and how the impress of leaves comes originally to take place on stones, then I will be able to make you better understand the process. But you must know and remember one thing—we but follow and servilely copy Nature in her works." With reference to these so-called precipitated letters from the Masters, see Hella Wiesberger's foreword to the section on the separation from the Esoteric School of Theosophy, p. 228.

To Mathilde Scholl in Cologne (postcard):

Berlin, December 24, 1903

Most esteemed Fräulein Scholl,
  Hearty good wishes for Christmas to the three of you,[50] with the news that you are about to receive the diploma and explanations to L.o.t.P., [*Light on the Path*] on Saturday. Please have patience until then.
  With best wishes,
                          Yours, Dr. Rudolf Steiner
Berlin W., Motzstrasse 17

To Mathilde Scholl in Cologne:

Berlin, December 28, 1903

Esteemed dear Fräulein Scholl,
  Herewith begins the interpretation of *Light on the Path*, which will indicate the way the book should be meditated. I shall continue the interpretation for you in a very short time.[51]
  I shall send the diploma to you by tomorrow at the latest. I want this letter to be sent off to you *immediately.*
  With hearty greetings to your dear house-residents, and for yourself the heartiest greetings.
                          Dr. Rudolf Steiner
Berlin W., Motzstrasse 17

---

50. This refers to Mathilde Scholl's friends and house-residents, Maud and Eugen Künstler.
51. See Appendix D, p. 424.

To Clara Smits in Düsseldorf:

Berlin, December 28, 1903

Most esteemed Madame!

You will no doubt have continued the exercises in the manner they were begun. I would ask you now, during January too, to proceed further in exactly the same way as I described to you in my letter.[52] I would only ask that you replace the sentence I then gave you with the following one:

> Every living being that you bestow your love upon reveals itself to you; lack of love is a veil overlying the things of the world and shrouding them from view. Inasmuch as you send out love you will receive knowledge in like measure.

. . . . . .

I would like to add something to this meditation-sentence that will make it more understandable. It is certainly so that as much knowledge flows into us from the world as we give of our love. Nevertheless, we must not imagine that in every phase of development all knowledge is immediately *conscious* to us. Much remains *unconscious* in us to begin with. And therefore I beg of you to continue the meditation steadfastly. We make progress only when we do that, and are aware of the fact that no day is wasted when we devote ourselves to this end. Every day lays up knowledge within us, and that day will surely come when it will reveal itself to us in full consciousness. The sentences that we meditate upon are not just sentences for our understanding, which have to be merely comprehended; I can only say again and again: they are sentences that are alive and that we ourselves must live with as we live with children. We are quite familiar with children too, but nevertheless we busy ourselves with them every day afresh. Thus it should be with our meditation-sentences.

Therefore everything else in your meditation remains throughout January as it was before; only the sentence for December must give place to the one mentioned above. I would beg of you, most

---

52. Unavailable.

esteemed lady, to continue everything as it was given you until I write to you again. You may rest assured that from time to time you will receive the relevant letter. If this should happen a few days after the expected time, it will not matter.

It also pleased me very much to see you in Cologne on my last visit. I would have liked to have looked you up once again during that visit, but time was pressing. Lohf now has the possibility of finding at least six people in Düsseldorf with whom he can reconstitute the group. That would be *very welcome*. As to you, most esteemed lady, I know that you will do all you can. I also know how difficult it is. But, through our united efforts, the requirements of the theosophical movement must occur through those who recognize its importance. No one who has recognized its importance can then withdraw from this movement.

I hope we shall see each other again very soon.

Yours cordially,
Dr. Rudolf Steiner

Berlin W., Motzstrasse 17

To Clara Smits in Düsseldorf:

Berlin, February 24, 1904

Esteemed Frau Smits:

I hope to see you then during the next few days. Fräulein Scholl told me that you want to get some people together in Düsseldorf on Monday. That will be fine, even if it is only very few. Please just choose a suitable time. I will fit in with whatever you find best.

I shall be very pleased to be able to talk to you again about your meditation. I hope that all has gone well until now. I will give you exact notifications about the way to proceed with it when I am with you.

Good-bye for now, then,

Yours truly, Dr. Rudolf Steiner

Berlin W., Motzstrasse, 17

To Doris and Franz Paulus in Stuttgart:

Zurich, April 14, 1904

Most esteemed Frau and Herr Doctor:

Before the 16th comes along I would like to write you a few lines about the next days of the meditation. I beg you therefore to proceed with the part of my explanations, which I have marked with the *Voice of the Silence,* in such a way that the first two sentences remain in our field of consciousness during the first fortnight. I mean (with the exception of the very first sentence) the following:

He who would comprehend the voice of the spirit without, he has first to experience his own spiritual self.[53]

When the seeker no longer desires to listen to the world of the senses alone, so must he search for Him who created this world. He must live in thoughts that turn the sense world into the world of illusion.[54]

We do not depend on speculation about these sentences, but on living with them for a few minutes. One must also have become so familiar with their content that one is able to survey it with spiritual insight, place it before the mind's eye and, without speculating about it, allow it to work upon one in self-surrender. For the meditation can prove fruitful only if one allows the thought that one meditates to stream into oneself in complete calm.

If anything is incorrect or unclear, I would beg you to ask me about it and I will reply right away. I will write the promised interpretation of the seven voices for you from Lugano. They are due within the second fortnight.[55]

---

53. According to Blavatsky, *The Voice of the Silence,* fragment: "He who would hear the *Voice of Nada,* [the Soundless Voice], and comprehend it, he has to learn the nature of *Dharana* [intense and perfect concentration on an inner object]...."
54. According to Blavatsky: "... having become indifferent to objects of perception, the pupil must seek out the rajah of the senses, the thought-producer, he who awakens illusion."
55. This was given in the letter of August 11, 1904, p. 48.

Similarly I will write about the Bresch performances immediately I arrive.[56]

Today I only want to say to you both that I am filled with the greatest satisfaction with respect to your inclinations toward Theosophy. When one knows about the world mission of Theosophy, then one is able to appreciate the participation of people of deeper understanding. I will still have several things to write to you, about the statements of Frau Doctor, in the next days. In Munich every hour of the day was filled up, and also here in Zürich the theosophists from here and the surroundings are gathered together. In a short time, however, the train will depart.

Therefore, for the time being, all the best to both of you and the Arensons.

Yours, Rudolf Steiner

Present address:

Dr. Rudolf Steiner

c/o Herrn Günther Wagner

Lugano, Castagnola

(Switzerland)

To Doris and Franz Paulus in Stuttgart:

London, May 14, 1904

Very confidential.

Most esteemed Frau and Herr Doctor:

Until today I have been prevented by all kinds of work and traveling from giving you a detailed reply to your kind letters. Your most recent letter was particularly welcome, as I see from it that you have continued the work of meditation, and I would beg you to hold to that. You may rest assured that you will always receive what you need from me at the proper time. On account of the esoteric work in Germany I was obliged to spend the last days here in London

---

56. It is not known if this was carried out.

with our spiritual head, Mrs. Besant, in order to receive from her the full esoteric authorization for all that I am doing in this connection. For you may be certain that in esoteric matters every instruction, every piece of advice, is given in the most careful manner and under the true guidance of the great spiritual leaders of humanity. Do not doubt that, sooner or later, you yourselves will find the way to these leaders through the work of meditation. Whoever has experienced what I have experienced is entitled to speak in this manner. I would beg you now, and during the next weeks too, to meditate that part of the *Voice* [*of the Silence*] that precedes "The Seven Voices." In the next days I shall interpret these "Seven Voices," under authorization, and you will receive one of the first copies. It will then be of much more value to you than if I were to have given it to you a fortnight ago without this full authorization. For my *esoteric* work has only just received its final blessing during the last few days.

Now I turn to your questions, dear Frau Doctor. If I were not an esotericist and if I did not have a connection to spiritual life, I would perhaps say: Your questions in Stuttgart and, later, those asked in your letter have caused me surprise. But, as a result of the aforementioned circumstances, I was fully prepared to recognize your deep psychological insight. I can only say to you: You have *good* psychic gifts and fine prerequisites both for spiritual insight, as well as for being able to *work* in the physical world from a spiritual level. What you experience simply shows that you have a connection to the spiritual world-powers, and also your whole nature shows that you are called upon to use these spiritual gifts in a noble fashion for the benefit of all humanity. Among other things, you have repeatedly asked me who I am. The time will also surely come when we can talk about it. But today I shall only say that I am entitled to the belief that, in a former life, you once rendered me a very great service. Do not misunderstand me. Errors should not, of course, be excluded from spiritual observations. But I am not someone who lives in illusions. I am one of those whom one would call cautious, and even "matter of fact" in spiritual matters. That is why I can talk of justified belief.

There was a person in my former life, centuries ago; she played the part of someone who tore me away from family connections and paved the way that led me to my calling that, at that time, was as a Catholic priest. In those times the Church was not yet so entirely degenerate as it is today. At that time *you* showed the freedom from prejudice that impresses me about you so much today. You indeed created the conditions for your present life at that time. Those are indications that I beg you to accept as critically as possible; but I can only say that I have a reason for finding them fully justified. If what I have said appears plausible to you, it will be clear to you that you are called to a psychic way of life. Do not be frightened by these talents. We must look upon such gifts as something holy; we must live with them as intimately as we live with tables and persons in our physical surroundings. We must accept them quite objectively and always keep our self-esteem, the *I*, intact as the firm center of our being.

We must never allow ourselves to become *unfree* owing to such influences. They have been bestowed upon us, but never with the intention of overpowering us. Whatever happens hold fast to the principle: All the powers in the world, physical as well as spiritual, are present at this stage of evolution for the purpose of enabling humankind, as free, self-conscious, *thinking*, independent beings, to fulfill their task *here* on Earth. The spiritual powers and influences are there only as guides to show them the proper path *here* on the Earth. And today women especially are called upon to discover their selfhood and make it valid. Everything that happens in this way will contribute to the welfare of humankind.

I shall probably be in Berlin again on the 17th of May and will then continue this letter.[57]

For today I send you both my most hearty greetings from here.

Yours truly,
Rudolf Steiner

---

57. Letter of August 11, 1904, p. 48.

The letter to Adolf Arenson in Bad Cannstatt, from London, May 14, 1904 has not been preserved, but the reply to Rudolf Steiner from Adolf Arenson on May 27 was as follows:

Dear Herr Doctor:

Your friendly message from London gave me great pleasure and happiness. Thank you for your trust in me—I shall certainly live up to your expectations, even if my attempts at meditation may perhaps not be all that could be desired. Not only is this conditioned by my will, but I already feel that this daily concentration is having an influence on my character and making me more strict with myself. On the one hand I experience my shortcomings more intensely than ever, on the other hand there is nevertheless a greater sense of inner peace, because I know that I am on the right path.[58]

That is all that I have to tell you.

Most respectfully,
Yours, Adolf Arenson

To Mathilde Scholl in Cologne, Berlin, May 18, 1904:

Dear esteemed Fräulein Scholl:

I have just returned from London. On the way here I also delivered a lecture in Hanover.[59]

58. Rudolf Steiner's letter obviously included the announcement that Adolf Arenson was to be admitted into the Esoteric School. He had, however, already received instructions from Rudolf Steiner (see the section: "Exercises given to individuals"), for he wrote to him on May 9, 1904: "According to our agreement I shall give you a report today on the progress of my attempts at meditation.[And his letter concludes:] Then I would ask you to put my name forward for the Esoteric School. On your last visit I expressed to you my wish to join. It is true that I do not know what conditions are laid down, or what obligations are entailed; but whatever is demanded, I feel within me the honest intention, if not the strength, to strive continually toward this end. Must I make a direct request for acceptance? I should be very grateful to you if you would grant me a sentence of reply to these questions."
59. A public lecture on May 15, "Birth and Death in the Life of the Soul. A Look into the Theosophical Worldview." (copy unavailable).

It is incumbent upon me, first of all, to consider your meditation work. Your letter of the 15th[60] expresses a feeling that you have about your inner experience. You say: "I am not in despair any more when, at times, I feel the spiritual life less strongly." That is the proper mood of *inner composure* that those people working on themselves must acquire to a greater and greater degree. The right progress will come about more as one acquires the mood: "take everything that comes with *calmness and resignation.*" One should not force anything but *wait* in patience for what comes. However it may appear to you that you have progressed and will continue to make further progress. I have spoken to Mrs. Besant about you in this connection, for my mission to London at the present time was mainly to discuss the ES and its task in Germany with Mrs. Besant. Mrs. Besant could already appoint me as "Arch-Warden of the ES" with the agreement that what I do is done in her name. One of the next things that I had to discuss with her was that *you* should really become a member of the "first degree" of the School. I will now send you the "Rules" of the "first degree" in a few days and you will then tell me what your attitude is toward them. But, first of all I have to tell you that members of the ES, through their acceptance into the "first degree," enter into real esoteric communication with the spiritual current that emanates from the Masters, and that in the course of time this will become more and more conscious to you—if perhaps only slowly. I can fully vouch to the "Blessed Masters" for your having reached the stage of being accepted. What I have to say to you orally I will tell you when we next meet—in Amsterdam, I suppose.[61] The success of the German theosophical movement depends on our having a nucleus of the kind of theosophists able to work esoterically. You are destined to help mainly in this direction as well. These are serious words that I now address to you, but you are one who is always prepared to take serious things seriously.

---

60. This letter is unavailable.
61. At the Congress of the Federation of the European Sections of the Theosophical Society, June, 1904.

I will write to you about everything else of this kind in more detail presently.

Above all else, do not allow yourself to be scared by such things as, according to your letter, you have experienced. Such things are the reactions on the etheric, and through that on the physical body, caused by the astral body being occupied in meditation. *What* you see are primarily physical-etheric processes, partly caused by your own physical organs. The *causes* lie in your astral body, which has become aroused by the meditation. That will all be overcome, and in its place true spiritual experiences will be born in you. Everything must simply be endured. In calmness.

I enclose the diploma for Fräulein von Dessauer;[62] please settle all further matters with Fräulein von Sivers.

Everything is going well in Cologne. It would be most necessary for the formal union to take place in Düsseldorf quite soon.

Give greetings to your house-residents, and hearty greetings for yourself,

Yours, Dr. Rudolf Steiner

Berlin W., Motzstrasse, 17

To Mathilde Scholl in Cologne

Mathilde Scholl wrote to Rudolf Steiner on July 13, 1904:

Frau Lübke has just written to me that she has signed the "pledge" in England, and urgently draws my attention to the necessity of asking you to let me also sign the "pledge" very soon, in case you are unable to send the other papers yet. Some changes have been made in the School, however, about which she cannot give me any details *until* I have signed the "pledge."

---

62. Refers to her membership in the Theosophical Society.

I have not said anything about the fact that I have not yet given my signature, nor received any papers, because I did not consider it very important. I am telling you about this because Frau Lübke appears to be troubled about it. What I consider to be of sole importance is that you and Mrs. Besant have accepted me. You know completely my thinking on this, whether or not I have given a special promise verbally or in writing. You know that I am basically prepared for anything that you may ask of me. I do not understand how it is that outer changes in the School can have an influence on the degree of a person's development. However, there must be something of a serious and important nature involved, as Frau Lübke, whose right hand is out of action and receiving medical attention, wrote to me with great difficulty with her left hand. I am certainly grateful to her for it, but I believe that she is upsetting herself about it for no reason. You will see what you intend to do.

Rudolf Steiner replied:

Berlin, July 14, 1904

Dear Fräulein Scholl:

Enclosed is the pledge. I would ask you to make a copy of it and to send this to me along with your signature for forwarding to Mrs. Besant.[63] What unites the members of the ES is contained in the

---

63. This occurred July 15, accompanied by the following letter: "Enclosed is the 'pledge.' I make it gladly, and in all points with my whole heart. May I be able to fulfill it as faithfully as possible.

"Thank you very much for your friendly words. I can draw constantly much peace, courage, and strength from what you tell me, and similarly from what you give through your writings, as now through the last issue of *Luzifer*. As much as I rejoice over every line you write, and as much as I would like to receive the further installments of the explanations to *Light on the Path*, I would beg of you, that you only write this to me when you find the time, without infringing on your very necessary leisure hours. The preservation of your strength is of primary concern. For that reason you should on no account overwork yourself physically. We are all concerned about this. But I trust that you see for yourself the necessity of keeping yourself fit for our sakes and for the world. There is so much that we all have to hear and learn from you."

pledge. All the obligations that the Shrâvaka has undertaken already, naturally remain valid. When you have sent me the pledge with your signature I will also send you some papers *provisionally.* Nothing further can be given at the moment, but soon.

Regardless of any changes that may occur in the School, you have not the slightest need for worry. Such things never concern the inner development of the individual member, but only the way that the School works down from above onto the physical plane *in the eyes of the world* and *in* the world. One must, of course, always consider how the world is going to benefit. The fact that you who are a faithful devoted pupil of the ES and are absolutely on the right path will not be seriously affected in any way by the change.[64]

It is necessary to stick to each of the points in the pledge if we are to get anywhere along the esoteric path. Nothing need be taken pedantically however—but *strictly.* It all depends upon one's *attitude. How* one supports the theosophical movement is left entirely to one's own decision. Because of one's office or position in life it may even be necessary not to *speak* about the fact that one is a theosophist. If one works *ardently—however quietly*—one has kept one's word.

Much depends on how one speaks, so that others are less and less injured by what is said. By that means the doors can be opened that otherwise shut us off from the Masters. The weaknesses of others must *never* receive censure from us—at least not as coming from the heart—but we should always try to *understand* in every way possible.

Such is a duty to be undertaken by every ES pupil.

You will certainly receive the interpretation of *Light on the Path* very soon.[65] I shall also surely reply to all the other things during this week.

With hearty good wishes,

       Yours, Dr. Rudolf Steiner

Berlin W., Motzstrasse, 17

---

64. Details unknown.
65. See letter of August 9, 1904, p. 47.

To Amalie Wagner in Hamburg:

Berlin, August 2, 1904

Dear esteemed Fräulein Wagner:

I can send you the first news of the ES today. The first thing must be to speak about the significance of the School. The Esoteric School is an esoteric affair, that is to say, it is guided by highly developed individualities—those who have already come to the end of the pathway that still lies ahead for the majority of humankind. Such highly developed individualities possess a high degree of wisdom; they are endowed with an inexhaustible source of human love and with the capacity to help those who wish to tread the path to perfection.

Those who enter the Shrâvaka Order do not commit themselves to anything apart from working consciously toward perfecting themselves, so far as it is in their power to do so. They can therefore also serve more and more in the perfecting of the whole of humanity. No one can, of course, do more than lies within one's power. The School demands nothing. It only provides the means whereby anyone can perfect themselves as necessary, for the individual and humankind. And to attain that, such perfected individualities are of help in an esoteric way. For those who sign the pledge, the influence of the perfected individualities begins to take effect, though at first, perhaps, one is quite unaware of it. Thus one works for the good of all humanity through simply being a member of the School. All the obligations to which the S. [Shrâvaka] is committed are taken up only through one's own responsibility. For, if one does not hold fast to these commitments it is impossible to attain to the desired goal; and then the membership of the School would be without purpose.

Esteemed Fräulein Wagner: I will now detail to you in all brevity what you need to do. You can only begin everything on August 18, and I must ask you to make a beginning on this date. For reasons known only to esotericists, the commencement must be made at quite definite times. Later on everything will become clear to you.

Then the following must be done:

1. In the evening, before going to bed—best of all just before going to sleep—I would ask you to repeat to yourself in your thoughts—every evening—the following sentence:

> More radiant than the Sun,
> Purer than the Snow,
> Subtler than the Ether,
> Is the Self,
> The Spirit within my heart.
> I am that Self,
> That Self am I.[66]

When you have pondered this, but pondered in such a way that no extraneous thought enters your consciousness while keeping this thought in your mind:

2. Then spend 4–5 minutes looking backward over the events of the day. So I would ask you to let these events of the day pass quickly before your mind's eye, and make yourself aware of what your attitude is toward them. In this way one observes oneself and asks if and to what extent one is satisfied with what one has done, what experiences should have been made and what could have been done better. Thus one becomes a self-observer. The meaning of this is that one looks at oneself from a higher level, and gradually, by this means the "higher self" becomes the master over the ordinary human being. In this way, however, everything that approximates to grief and sorrow about one's experiences should fall away. We should merely learn from our own life and take it as a lesson. We should not regard the past with regret—there is plenty of time during the rest of the day for that—but we should courageously make use of the past for the future. Then we learn something for our own present life and we learn, above all, for that time lying beyond death.

3. After completing the retrospect of the day in this way, one then goes to sleep with thoughts about the people one loves or would like to help.

---

66. Original English version by Annie Besant.

4. And following that, one can visualize an aim in life with which one feels particularly connected.

Now for morning. As soon as possible after awaking a short meditation should be undertaken, consisting of the following:

1. The thoughts from the previous evening should be reviewed: More radiant than the Sun..."
2. The meditation itself (6–8 minutes)
   In addition, I would ask you to take up a sentence from Thomas à Kempis's *The Imitation of Christ* every day, and to do it as follows: During the first week you take the sentence: "Happy is the person who is instructed by truth..." [beginning of chapter 3]. Impress this sentence well into your mind so that you know it by heart. Then fill your entire consciousness with this sentence for the stated 6–8 minutes. Every other thought must be excluded from your mind. Through this we can absorb such a spiritually alive thought into our whole being. We let it penetrate us, and it then radiates its strength over all that we do and are. You keep the same sentence every day for a whole week. Then comes the next sentence, and so on.
3. The third part of the morning meditation is devotion toward what for us is of divine holiness; for example, Christ. That ought to last at least 4–6 minutes and consist of devoted worship of this Holy Being.

These are all the exercises for the moment. By means of these exercises the perfected beings (the Masters) will be able to approach us and receive us into the paths leading to perfection. And now, with reference to the sixth rule.[67] I would simply mention that during Holy Communion is the only exception where a sip of wine may be taken; in that case the harmful influence is no longer present because it involves a ceremony. Otherwise this abstention should indeed be quite rigorously adhered to. It is not a matter of carrying out a duty toward the School, but of promoting perfection.

---

67. The rules and text of the pledge were included with the letter.

It will be sufficient especially in the case of the Shrâvaka if, *for the most part*, the drinking of alcohol is avoided. But even here "better is better."

I will be writing the third book soon.[68] "Engel" is the [Julius] Engel from Berlin. He translated *Letters That Have Helped Me.*[69] I would ask you, however, not to practice what is given in that ... [End of letter missing].

To Mathilde Scholl in Cologne:

Berlin, August 9, 1904

Esteemed dear Fräulein Scholl:

With this I am sending what you require.[70] The sequel will follow *very soon.* Regarding Herr Künstler's question, a letter will follow immediately.[71]

Most heartily,

Dr. Rudolf Steiner

Berlin W., Motzstrasse, 17

---

68. This presumably refers to *An Outline of Esoteric Science* as the third theosophical book after *Christianity as Mystical Fact* (1902), and *Theosophy* (May, 1904). *An Outline of Esoteric Science* was originally planned as the second part of *Theosophy* and was announced for publication beginning in 1905; because of too many commitments, however, it did not appear until the end of 1909.

69. *Letters that have Helped Me* by William Q. Judge. Theosophical University Press, Pasadena, California. First published in 1891 as a book. Julius Engel translated this into German.

70. From Mathilde Scholl's reply (August 10, 1904) it appears that enclosed was instructions for a meditation and the sequel to the explanations for *Light on the Path*, which he had promised her in a letter (December 28, 1903, p. 32).

71. Herr Künstler's question refers to the intended visit of Annie Besant during September. Rudolf Steiner replied August 16, 1904.

To Doris and Franz Paulus in Stuttgart:

Berlin, August 11, 1904

Esteemed Frau and Herr Doctor:

You have given a beautiful poetic expression to your mood, dear Frau Doctor. I prize it very much. It is so full of the revivifying mystical powers that lie in the depths of your soul that, what I noticed in you from the beginning of our acquaintance, I find here confirmed. You possess great powers, dear lady, and you are capable of many things. And in a not too distant future your inner riches will become evident—for the good of humanity—in a way that will astonish you. You are so kind as to give me the name "leader" in your letter. I am able and allowed to be your leader only insofar as the exalted Master by whom I myself am guided gives me instruction. I follow *him* with full consciousness in everything I impart to others. And if you acknowledge that, so would I beg you to follow me in one thing— rather follow *him*: in *patience.* The right mood is that of patience. I do not say that, dear lady, to suggest that you do not possess this patience, but because it is necessary for us again and again to hold up this mood of patience before us.

You say, in an earlier letter, that you are unable to express the things that move you. I can only convey to you the assurance: the most appropriate way of expressing yourself will come to you. But once again: patience. The mood of expectancy quickens our paces.

You are of the opinion that it is of no use to repeat words during meditation that are really self-evident. This, however, is not the case. If it depended on the amount of *knowledge* we possess then this would be of no use. But it depends on the fact that we repeatedly experience *out of ourselves* what we ought to be and what we should make of ourselves through our own activity. You will find further details about this in the appendices to *The Voice of the Silence* that I promised you, and which I enclose with my letter today.

You see, my most esteemed lady, we do not accumulate inner strength by hating coercion, but by laying constraint upon ourselves freely—indeed in perfect freedom. Please interpret that form of words I gave you in Stuttgart as nothing but *advice*, and *advice* only. But it is advice that rests on the experience of esotericists throughout long periods of time.

For that reason I would beg of you, esteemed Frau Doctor, and of you too, dear Herr Doctor, to carry on with the meditation in the way you have begun. The form of words cited must pass through your mind for a *short* while, but indeed regularly, every morning over a long period. I believe that you may perhaps be continuing too long with just *this* particular formula. That is not necessary. But just consider that even adepts allow this formula to pass through their souls, even if only fleetingly, every morning as a continual reminder to themselves that life can never come to a final conclusion, but that every individual self must give birth to a higher self within it.

Accordingly the whole work of meditation should from now on consist of the following for both of you:

1. Evenings before going to sleep, retrospect of the day.
2. a) Mornings, let the meditation verse for the higher self pass through your mind.[72]
   b) Meditate on *Light on the Path*. From week to week a new sentence. But continue patiently with one verse for a whole week. (Further details enclosed).[73]
   c) Devotional mood in respect of those things that we revere as the highest, the Divine.

If, as you described, you have a special meditation that you wish to undertake, then, Frau Doctor, arrange the time in a way that appears convenient to you. But what I have suggested is effective and fruitful, and leads upward on the path of knowledge. Whether what we know seems self-evident to us or not is of no consequence; it is important that it passes through our mind.

---

72. "More radiant than the Sun," etc.
73. Unavailable; probably refers to comments in *The Voice of the Silence.*

Your feelings about what you know about me may be relied upon. I am also aware that you have a lively imagination. But a lively imagination as such is not always necessarily misleading. It may happen to be so; but it may also be the harbinger of the influx of higher experiences. And you may perceive, dearest lady, how your experiences correspond in a certain way with mine. I have written of this in a preliminary way in my letter from London; I will write further about it presently. And insofar as it concerns me, I know that all fantasizing lies as far away from me as possible; I also hold myself with all my strength as far away as possible from anything of that kind. Believe me, dear Frau and Herr Doctor, that what I say, I experience with all the strictness that mathematicians impose on themselves. And before venturing along the road to Theosophy, I turned all my attention toward ensuring that *no kind* of fantasizing in *daily life* could lead me astray. My whole life has been directed to that end for many years.

You describe young Gräser quite correctly. It is certainly not without danger to be as he is. And people like him are symptomatic of the present day. I have recommended him to you, because I know that you are different from others.

What you write about Deinhard and Bresch is certainly correct. But let us be forbearing. Neither of the two gentlemen can be any different than what their karma prescribes for them.[74] Let *us* stick by one another, let us rely on what *we* regard as important and let us overlook the failings of others.

I am very, very pleased that Mrs. Besant is coming to Stuttgart in September.

All the best for now,

From your Dr. Rudolf Steiner

Berlin W., Motzstrasse, 17

---

74. Deinhard and Bresch: see letters to Marie Steiner-von Sivers on April 18–19, 1903, *Correspondence and Documents*, p. 30 (CW 262).

Franz Paulus replied on November 30, 1904:

To begin with, I should like to inform you, on the basis of the "Rules" you sent us, of my decision to become a pupil of the EST; therefore, in eager anticipation of possible further instructions from you, I shall begin tomorrow to write down the degree of my satisfaction concerning my keeping of rules 1, 2 and 3.[75]

To Horst von Henning in Weimar:

Berlin, August 12, 1904

My esteemed, dear Herr von Henning:

Please excuse the delayed reply.[76] I am *only now* becoming gradually free of the burden of work, and in future you will certainly no longer have to wait so long. I was pleased to hear that you are visiting a spa, and hope that your recovery has made really good progress. It is not good for the sake of health or the meditation to start *practical* meditative work during convalescence. I can only advise you, when you want to practice meditation, to *begin* it *during* the time of your ordinary working life. For meditation should not steal time from other things. That, in fact, is a basic requirement if it is to prove fruitful. I shall now confide in you (that is, you personally), the contents of the meditation: Evenings before going to sleep—for a very short time—three or four minutes—retrospect of what has been done and experienced during the day. What is necessary here is to allow the most important events of the day to pass before one's mind, and during this time, to ask oneself: "Did I follow *this* event with watchful attention, so that I can learn something from it for the future?" "How should I have done it to attain such a result?" Or, concerning an action that one has accomplished: "Have I performed this deed in such a way that now—when I am no longer involved in it, but can observe myself as if I were someone else—I am satisfied with what I

---

75. Doris Paulus, on the other hand, did not join the EST until later.
76. The card to which this was a reply is unavailable.

have done?" This must all be done so that one *learns from oneself,* so that one accepts life as a means of instruction, and can thereby truly rise bit by bit to one's "higher self," which extends beyond the ordinary self. And—believe this on the grounds of esoteric experience—not only the extension of human faculties, but also the improvement of health in every way will be the result.

Then, in the morning, immediately on getting up, before eating, one spends a few minutes (longer, after awhile) on the meditation proper. If a quarter of an hour is possible, so much the better. It consists of the *raising of oneself* to one's "higher self," by repeating inwardly a certain particular form of words. I shall communicate this form of words to you *immediately,* in confidence, when you write to me that you will use it. Then a second *concentration* follows; the emptying of the mind of everything that belongs to daily life. Then, for a few minutes, everything that otherwise occupies our thoughts has to disappear out of consciousness, as well as the remembrance of the transactions and duties of our everyday life. We then allow a sentence from an inspired writing to enter this empty space in consciousness, and we surrender entirely to the impression it makes on us. We do not speculate about the sentence; we *live* with it, as we would live with a child that we love. We retain this same sentence for some weeks. For only then does it yield up its strength to us. Only then, after weeks, do we replace it with another sentence. People who meditate take, for example, *Light on the Path.* When worked with in this way, sentence by sentence, it can provide content for meditation for a long time. *Light on the Path, The Voice of the Silence, Bhagavad Gita* are among the best books for meditation.

The last part of the meditation consists of the creation of a mood of devotion within ourselves toward all that we consider to be the highest, what is divine. We are not concerned with this or that idea of the Divine, but with what—according to our subjective opinion—is of real intimate concern to us. For the Christian it can be Christ, for the Hindu the "Master," for the Moslem, Mohammed; and yes, modern scientists can immerse themselves devotionally in "divine nature." It depends on the *feeling of devotion,* not on the concept that one creates of the Divine.

My dear Herr von Henning, if you desire to move forward in the development of mystical powers, then I can inform you further on ways of doing so. I can tell you in advance that *no* kind of danger in any respect whatever is connected with it. And in relation with your question, and through my acquaintance with you, I am *allowed* to tell you that there is a "restricted circle" of people into which I may accept *you* if you *wish*. Otherwise, to begin with, there are *no* obligations except those one has *regarding oneself*, as I have already said in this letter. There is only the complete abstinence from alcohol that still obtains. That, however, has to stand, because otherwise all esoteric endeavor is of no use under normal circumstances. If then you would seek the path of meditation I will send you the "Rules" and you can make your decision. If, however, you would like to practice meditation without any attachment, I will be ready to give you advice; but the attachment to the "restricted esoteric circle" offers at the same time an esoteric connection that, in itself, is already a help and a step forward for the progress of the soul.

In this way I wish to reply to your card that gave me so much pleasure. If you do not wish to become attached, then I would beg you to remain silent about the things I have written of to you.

With cordial greetings,

From your Dr. Rudolf Steiner

Berlin W., Motzstrasse, 17

Horst von Henning's reply:

Weimar, October 24, 1904

My dear and revered Herr Doctor:

That I have not written before today—after a space of more than two months—to thank you for your kindly letter, is not because of laziness or indifference; it is merely because during this last period I have been so unusually overburdened with work that I did not find the necessary calm in which to reply to such an earnest communication as yours. Meanwhile, I found time enough in this way to test myself, and I am so much the more pleased that I can now repeat in writing what, because of special circumstances, I was only able to indicate on the occasion of your last visit; namely, that I would be very pleased if you would consider me as your pupil and, as such, would prepare me for acceptance into the "restricted circle," inasmuch as you consider me worthy of such. Your confidence in me has made me very happy, and I will sincerely strive to fulfill the duties that may be placed on me as a result of my being accepted, and will thereby contribute consciously to the welfare of my fellow human beings. It is not the desire for personal advantage, I assure you, (nor for that of a spiritual kind), that has impelled me to seek a connection to an esoteric circle; but it is an inner conviction that my innate qualities impose a duty on me to tread this path, when to this end the helping hand has been extended toward me, and the decision to advance spiritually has been taken seriously, to the degree that it lies within my powers to do so.

I would therefore heartily desire of you: take my guidance into your hands and give me whatever you deem you have the right to give me with respect to my circumstances and present ability. For my part, I shall not be lacking in good will, gratitude and patience.

With sincere greetings,

Your ever grateful,

Horst von Henning

To Eliza von Moltke in Bankau, Upper Silesia

Eliza von Moltke wrote on July 20, 1904:

My dear Doctor Steiner:

You have completely forgotten me! I know that one of the chief things for which human beings have to strive is patience, and I would have patiently waited much longer if I had not been in such great need of spiritual assistance—be so kind as to come to my aid in this matter, give me a hint as to how I must go about things to attain to my ardently desired goal one day: that of helping humankind....

But now I would so much like to work effectively on myself in the way you consider appropriate; and when you have obtained the guidance for this, which you first wanted to receive in the spiritual world, then be so good as to communicate it to me.

Rudolf Steiner replied:

Berlin, August 12, 1904

Most esteemed, gracious lady:

Please do not imagine that I shall in future treat *you* according to my custom of writing as few letters as possible. The reason this one comes so late will be explained sometime in conversation. In future I shall write to you quite regularly.

Please regard the enclosed writing [77] as entirely confidential. In such matters I am merely the tool of higher beings to whom I pay *humble homage.* Nothing is due to me; none of it is my doing. The only thing I can lay to my credit is that I have undergone a strict training to guard myself against any fantasizing. This has been my precept. For in this way what I experience in spiritual realms is free of all fabrication, of all deception, of all superstition. Nevertheless, of *that* too I rarely speak nowadays. People may regard me as a person with strange ideas; I am able to distinguish between truth and illusion. And I know that I have to go the way I do.

If you adopt the exercises indicated in the enclosed writing, most esteemed lady, then you may not commence with them before August 19, or later than September 3. That is, as the esotericist says, "written in the stars." However, if you do not wish to commence between August 19 and September 3 it would be necessary to come to an agreement with me again regarding a later date. Any day between August 19 and September 3 is possible.

---

77. Unavailable

I often think of the happy hours I spent in your house [in Berlin].
I have also become very fond of your husband, and I have great
hopes for his spiritual future. Sometimes people go their special
way; but many roads lead to knowledge.[78]

All the best to you in Silesia and may you have the inner calm that
you need.

My hearty respects to you,

Your Rudolf Steiner

Berlin W., Motzstrasse, 17

To Michael Bauer in Nuremberg

*Michael Bauer wrote to Rudolf Steiner on July 28, 1904, evidently about a
previous conversation:*

Highly esteemed, dear Herr Doctor:

Without much ado I will tell you what I would like: I wish to
become your pupil for a while and should be pleased if you would
give me a task according to my needs.

With loving greetings,

Your Michael Bauer

Rudolf Steiner noted in the margin:
"replied to with Rules, August 14, 1904."

Steiner's reply to Michael Bauer:

Berlin, August 14, 1904

Esteemed, dear Herr Bauer:

I may reply as follows to your dear lines of communication. Your
connection with the theosophical movement is such an intimate

---

78. Helmuth von Moltke was not a theosophist, but later he developed a deep interest in Rudolf Steiner's spiritual science. See commemorative words spoken for
Moltke at the beginning of the lecture given in Berlin, June 20, 1916, in *Weltwesen
und Ichheit* (*Cosmic Being and I-Being*), typescript (CW 169).

one that you will best find satisfaction for your esoteric life by join-ing the so-called "Esoteric School." But I would ask you to regard what I tell you in *this* respect as meant only for you and as com-pletely confidential. *Nobody* is *summoned* to join this esoteric School; but we are allowed to *communicate* the fact of its existence to those we find suitable. And I shall make such a communication to you. If you find that it does not suit you to join, then regard it as if the pro-posal had not been made and write to me to that effect. I will then immediately provide you with the necessary material for an esoteric training without you becoming a member of the School, and will comply with all your wishes.

To begin with, please find the Rules of the so-called Shrâvaka Order enclosed herewith.[79] One must first become a *Shrâvaka* (liter-ally, "Hearer") and obey the set rules, then later one is admitted to the higher orders.

You will see that keeping the Rules is quite easy to begin with. To be sure, the *exact* observance is necessary, as only on this condition can a true advance in spiritual life be achieved.

If you are willing to join then please write to me to this effect. I shall then send you a short "pledge," by which you will become a member, and I shall send you all further particulars on September 22 or 23.

I would only like to add something about the nature of the School. You know that the relationship of the Theosophical Society to our exalted Masters is such that the latter have imparted the theo-sophical impulse to H. P. B. [H. P. Blavatsky], and have left her to make what she would of it on the physical plane. The Theosophical Society was therefore founded by H. P. Blavatsky and Olcott in 1875. Our esoteric School has nothing officially to do with that—just for the very reason that it is "occult." It was founded by the Masters themselves, and remains under their guidance. And the truly living knowledge flows continuously from this esoteric school into the Theosophical Society. Little by little the exercises prescribed by the School will lead to the knowledge of the Masters. H. P. Blavatsky was

---

79. See the "General Rules" of this order on p. 107.

the head of this School as long as she resided on Earth. Now it is
Annie Besant. Within Germany, Austria, and the German-speaking
part of Switzerland the leadership has been placed into my hands.

As stated, this information is not meant to exert any pressure, but
is purely something based on mutual trust. Should you join there
will be *no* obligations other than adherence to the rules. If you cannot join, then return the Rules to me. Then I shall reply to your letter in another way, so that your wishes are met apart from the
School. But *within* the School one enjoys the support from above
that is so necessary.

After you have notified me of your inclination to join, I will write
to you straight away to tell you who the German members are. Also
to give you all directions for regular meditation to impart esoteric
knowledge.

In September Annie Besant will be able to give some lectures in
Germany. But because she can only stay a few days in Germany,
Munich will be the only town in Bavaria where she can lecture.
Believe me, dear Herr Bauer, if it had been possible I would have
thought of arranging a lecture by Annie Besant in Nuremberg as
well. But that is absolutely not possible because of Annie Besant's
restricted time. She will speak in Weimar on September 18, and in
Munich on September 20, and I entertain the hope that you and
your wife will be able to hear the lecture in one place or the other.

Greet your wife and the family,

I am, Yours most cordially,
Dr. Rudolf Steiner

Berlin W., Motzstrasse, 17

To Mathilde Scholl in Cologne:

Berlin, August 27, 1904

Esteemed, dear Fräulein Scholl:

First of all I should like to say something very quickly in reply to
your letter. Should Mr. Keightley come to Germany there is only one

thing we can do about it— that is to regard the whole thing as dispassionately as possible.[80] Those who know Mrs. Besant know how she will react under such circumstances. She lets things run their own course and trusts in the spiritual powers that are with her. And I will act no differently. Diplomatic thoughts must be kept very much at a distance, as we do not act according to human intellectual considerations, but follow the Masters. For this reason we do not even ask "why" in such a case. Mrs. Besant has just once written to Fräulein von Sivers that she "expects to meet Mr. Keightley in Hamburg." That is all. And I do not ask any further questions. But, dear Fräulein Scholl, one thing is necessary: that we, who are around Mrs. Besant, should stick close together in the coming time. What we are to do will be revealed in every single case. Furthermore, I would ask you not to shun Miss Link when Keightley is there, but to act as you would have done without paying attention to him, and to regard his presence as of no great consequence.[81]

Please regard these few lines as confidential. They have to be short if they are to reach you by tomorrow morning. The arrangements for the date, and so on, are *not* fixed except insofar as they have been decided on between you and Fräulein von Sivers.

More tomorrow. I must get this onto the Cologne train.

Cordially,

Dr. Rudolf Steiner

---

80. Mathilde Scholl had written on August 26 to say how worried she had been to hear from England that Keightley would accompany Annie Besant on her German tour and translate her lectures. Evidently a certain aversion existed at the time toward Keightley, presumably because, in his capacity as General Secretary of the English (formerly European) Section, he supported a move toward separating the south German Section from the German Section (as shown in his letter to Rudolf Steiner of March 7, 1906).

81. According to Mathilde Scholl's letter of August 26, Miss Link was a friend of Keightley and had been invited to stay with him.

To Mathilde Scholl in Cologne:

Berlin, August 29, 1904

Esteemed, dear Fräulein Scholl:

Your relationship to Annie Besant is absolutely right. All theosophists should have that relationship toward her. But one must remain calm, even if one finds that others do not have that relationship. Illusion is very great, and it causes some people to find themselves in a difficult position when their feeling of confidence changes to uncertain judgement. It is much less important for us to oppose what is not right, than to serve what is right. I know that *in the long run* nothing can go wrong if we do what is right in the name of Annie Besant; in the meantime, however, several things might happen that could make the situation appear difficult. Annie Besant is messenger to the Masters.[82] It is not necessary for her to employ diplomatic moves; as a true esotericist that would also not be possible for her. Believe me, dear Fräulein Scholl, that wherever diplomacy is used, a connection with the Masters is absent. I know that we are acting according to Annie Besant's wishes if we remain quite objective in the case of Keightley's arrival, and we should treat his presence as something we are quite ready to accept. We should also take the same attitude *inwardly.* Your uneasiness is quite justified. But we must remain *calm* even in the face of such unease. There is so much in Germany today that is outwardly opposed to us; but let us not undermine our positive forces by paying too much attention to such opposition.

It is an esoteric law that those accepted into the esoteric current may be subjected to strong opposition. It may be a part of their probation that they can assert themselves in the face of such obstacles. Those who become esotericists are obliged to acquit themselves speedily in things that they might otherwise have encountered only in the course of several lives. If they follow their convictions steadfastly, they will make progress. They must simply have the *complete*

---

82. Compare with what Rudolf Steiner wrote for Edouard Schuré during the Munich Congress in May 1907; see page 308.

courage of their convictions. Such absolute courage is a worthy test. Those who adhere without wavering to someone such as Annie Besant, as you do, have gained very greatly. You will advance most advantageously just through this relationship.

Those who lack this relationship toward Annie Besant make it most difficult even for themselves. But many of those who presently err in this way will come again to a correct judgement.

There are certain things that the esotericist does not even ask about. For example, I do not, therefore, even wish to occupy my thoughts much with Keightley's arrival in Germany. I have heard from Fräulein von Sivers that Annie Besant wrote: "I expect to meet Mr. Keightley in Hamburg." And then Frau Lübke also wrote of it to Fräulein von Sivers. Fräulein von Sivers then asked me as well what I thought about it. "Nothing at all," I told her.

If Annie Besant wants her lectures translated by Keightley, we shall see what happens. For myself I would have found it best if Fräulein von Sivers had done all the translating.[83]

For the moment I am unable to send you the continuation of the last letters pertaining to *Light on the Path.* But surely during this week.[84]

Greet the Künstlers heartily and cordial greetings to you too.

From your,
Rudolf Steiner

Berlin W., Motzstrassse, 17

To Günther Wagner in Lugano:

Berlin, August 29, 1904

Dear esteemed Herr Wagner:

When Fräulein Scholl recently asked me if the two speeches of Annie Besant on the Christian Question should be translated, I was unable to offer advice. Do not interpret that, dear Herr Wagner, as

---

83. The report in German was finally given by Rudolf Steiner.
84. This further commentary was evidently not forthcoming.

though I were *against* the translation. I would even welcome it with pleasure if another of Annie Besant's writings were to appear again in German. But the esotericist has to differentiate very carefully between what is a direct piece of advice and what I have just characterized. If I may be allowed to express myself in a trivial manner, I wish to "withhold my vote." But in this case, I wish my opinion to remain completely disregarded.[85] Do not misunderstand me, dear Herr Wagner. I would very much like you to hear what I have to say when I give my opinion; but I would also like to state very clearly when I do not wish my opinion to receive any consideration. Only when we, who are united in the Esoteric School, confront each other in this way is complete freedom ensured, which esotericism demands.

Presently I shall send you the Rules of the German ES. At the same time I shall give you more details about the movement concerned with the Saint John's Gospel.[86]

For the moment I would ask you to stick to your present position in the ES during the next weeks, as you have thus far.

Your sister Amalie is an ES member. Your other sister will surely also be one in a few days' time.

In Number 15 of *Lucifer-Gnosis*, I shall bring a detailed discussion of *The Four Great Religions*.[87] I hope that this book will make good headway. It is capable of winning over many hearts.

At the beginning of September there will no doubt be another ES gathering here. It will probably be a matter of speaking to the

---

85. It appears, from two of Günther Wagner's letters to Rudolf Steiner (September 1–2, 1904), that there was a plan to translate Annie Besant's brochure "Is Theosophy Anti-Christian?" from English into German and to distribute it among the clergy in Germany. Evidently, Rudolf Steiner was not enamored of this proposal.
86. This letter is unavailable. In lectures to the Berlin branch (July 1904), which Günther Wagner also attended, Rudolf Steiner mentioned that a movement was being born from the bosom of the Theosophical Society, which would introduce "a true understanding of Christianity that one does not normally possess" (July 11, 1904). And on July 18 there was talk of a "John Society," a "John's Gospel Section," the task of which was to promulgate the inexhaustible depths of Saint John's Gospel in the widest circles. Those aware of what can be sought or learned there "may join this John's Gospel Section in the fullness of their hearts."
87. Four lectures by Annie Besant at the 21st annual meeting of the Theosophical Society in Adyar, translated by Günther Wagner, published by Max Altmann, Leipzig, 1904. The discussion by Rudolf Steiner is in *Lucifer-Gnosis* (CW 34).

ES members about the nature of the Masters and about the help that they give to the ES workers. On September 12 I shall then call a meeting of the Theosophical Society to prepare for Annie Besant's visit. And then we shall go on a tour through Germany with our "Soul." I look forward to that with great satisfaction. Then on September 25, I shall speak in Dresden about "Theosophy and Modern Science." I know that this venture will be much misunderstood, but I have no other possibility than to do that. It can be misunderstood but, in a higher sense, it can never have a deleterious effect.[88]

I was very happy to have you staying with us in July, dear Herr Wagner. I hope that your wife and you are safely back in Lugano again. Give my best greetings and receive hearty greetings.

Yours faithfully,
Rudolf Steiner

Berlin W., Motzstrasse, 17

To Günther Wagner in Lugano:

Berlin, September 14, 1904

Dear Herr Wagner:

It is certainly correct to say that Annie Besant's lecture: "Is Theosophy Anti-Christian?" could not be understood in Germany in the same way as in England, because discussion about basic Christian questions in theological circles in this country, and among preachers spiritually connected with them, has taken on a quite different character here than in England during the last decades.

From the direction of our leaders we are constantly advised to make individual allowance for separate countries. What particularly concerns our Christian propaganda is that it should *not* appear

---

88. On September 29, 1904, Rudolf Steiner spoke on this subject during the third General Theosophical Congress in Dresden. This was arranged by the Hartmann supporters who were not adherents of Adyar.

under the banner "Theosophy." It should proceed from the theosophists, but nowhere should that be directly stated. Christian mysticism, interpretation of Christian symbols, and so on, should be pursued. It should certainly be our task to win over preachers—even Catholic priests—to esoteric Christianity. It will then be up to them to let esotericism flow into their teachings. It would only bring about opposition toward us if we were to approach the Christian circles *directly*.

A discussion about whether Theosophy is anti-Christian or not would only awaken new opposition against Theosophy in Germany. There is a great antipathy against anything going by the name of Theosophy, especially among the clergy. And at present it is on the increase. We cannot do anything about it if Bresch translates these things, for he always stirs up very definite opposition. He has protested against Annie Besant's visit to Leipzig, for instance. We cannot do anything about it in that instance; we must let Bresch do as he pleases. The point is that we ourselves try to do the right thing.

You see, dear Herr Wagner, on the one hand we must definitely lay the emphasis on Theosophy. On the other hand, where that is not possible, we must treat the matter as being above the mere name and outer form. "Be theosophists," we are enjoined, "in what *way* you are so is for you to decide."

I said in my previous letter that I wished "to withhold my vote." The following was the reason for this expression: I am instructed to nurture the Christian element and in this particular case I *could* only interpret my instruction as signifying that the lecture should *not* be translated. It is at this point that the work of my own reasoning commences and I come to exactly the same conclusion as is given by you. Since you have expressed it yourself I can say, too, that the same holds for me. Previously I could only say: I cannot be in favor of it. I am sure you will understand me.

Tomorrow I shall receive Mrs. Besant—in Hamburg. Then, on Friday, she will be in Berlin.

Hearty greetings to your esteemed wife.

Most cordially, wholly yours,
Dr. Rudolf Steiner

To Günther Wagner in Lugano

(Günther Wagner had written to Rudolf Steiner on October 13, 1904):

Today I come to ask you if you will accept my dear wife into the ES. For a long while she was undecided as to whether she was worthy enough for it, but the wish continually reasserted itself, that she should use this favorable opportunity to progress further along her path of life, and so she asked me to seek your advice as to whether you would encourage her to join, or (secretly) to dissuade her. Though she does not outwardly feel it so pressing to unite herself with our endeavors, nevertheless, I know that she is serious about gaining the mastery over herself. I would therefore willingly favor her being personally admitted into the restricted inner movement. She has been a member of the Theosophical Society for 5 or 6 years. We await your kind answer with expectation.

With all due respect,

Günther Wagner

Rudolf Steiner replies:

Munich-Stuttgart, November 24, 1904

Esteemed, dear Herr Wagner:

I can only write a preliminary note in the train to say that I shall very soon reply positively to your question regarding your dear wife. I am engaged in a circular tour of lecturing. I have held a series of lectures in Nuremberg, Regensburg, Munich, and now proceed to Stuttgart, Karlsruhe, Heidelberg, Cologne, and Düsseldorf. Then to Leipzig and Hamburg. I will write to you about that and other things.

I will be more and more relieved of work in Berlin and then—you shall see—all my correspondence will become more regular.

For now hearty greetings to your dear wife and you.

Yours, Dr. Rudolf Steiner

To Günther Wagner in Lugano

Berlin, January 2, 1905

My dear Herr Wagner:

Enclosed herewith I am sending the first ES letter to your dear wife. I would beg of you to tell her everything and to give her all the information you think fit. It is in the nature of things that husband and wife who both belong to the ES should support and carry one another.

I shall send you the official Rules concerning the four disciplines in a very short while.

I shall write to you too very soon concerning the ES—above all, the following should be *known* to our ES members:

The German theosophical movement is of primary importance. The German people are the vanguard of the sixth sub-race[89] and will become ever more conscious of their mission. They should do so in all humility. They should immerse themselves deeply in their own idealists.

That is the voice of the Master. Furthermore: "Study your own great idealists: J.G. Fichte, Jakob Böhme, particularly Angelus Silesius, too."

I draw your attention in particular to J. G. Fichte's *Man's Destiny*. It is available in Reclam's Universal Library edition. There are no theosophical teachings in it, but by reading such things we can shape our thought-forms in an esoteric direction and the teachings of the Masters will thereby become more alive in us.

Many thanks for translating Besant's article about mysticism. It will be very welcome for one of the coming numbers of *Lucifer*.[90]

Tomorrow I go to Stuttgart, then to Munich.

Most cordially,
Your Rudolf Steiner

My address from January 6–9:

Munich c/o Countess Kalckreuth, Adalbertstrasse, 55.

---

89. Post-Atlantean epoch.
90. It did not appear after all.

To Frau Anna Wagner in Lugano:

Berlin, January 2, 1905

My very esteemed, dear Frau Wagner:

I was only able to inform you shortly a few weeks ago that your wish to become a member of the Esoteric School can be realized. One is admitted to this School as a *Shrâvaka*, that is literally "Hearer" or "Pupil."

It is incumbent upon me now to tell you about the nature and significance of the School. You know that behind the whole theosophical movement stand highly developed beings, whom we call "Masters" or "Mahatmas." These supreme beings have already completed the path that the rest of humanity still has to tread. They are now active as the great "Teachers of Wisdom and of the Harmonization of the Feeling Life of Humanity." They are already active on higher planes (levels), to which the rest of humanity will be conditioned to ascend during the course of the next great periods of evolution, the so-called "Rounds." They work on the physical plane through the "Messengers" they have appointed, the first of whom was H. P. Blavatsky—that is, the first as far as the theosophical movement is concerned. The Masters do not found any outer organization or society, neither do they administer such an order. It is true the Theosophical Society has been established by its founders (Blavatsky and Olcott among others) to advance the work of the Masters on the physical plane, but nevertheless the Masters have *never* themselves exerted any influence over the Society itself. In its nature and leadership it is purely the work of human beings on the physical plane.

It is otherwise with the "Esoteric School." That has been founded by the Masters themselves and stands under their guidance. All that flows into the theosophical movement in the way of knowledge and power streams into it from this School. Those who belong to this School complete their probationary time and eventually arrive at direct intercourse with the exalted ones themselves. How long it takes for this to happen depends, of course, upon the person concerned. At first all that any one can do is to promote the work of the Masters in faithful devotion.

H. P. Blavatsky was the first to be appointed by the Masters as "Head of the School." The present head is our dear, greatly venerated Annie Besant.

The Shrâvakas must advance so far that, for them, reincarnation and karma are not mere theory but a life certainty, and furthermore they must recognize out of their own insight the great mission of H. P. Blavatsky. Nothing will be forced upon anyone in the School; only self-knowledge will be fostered. One can advance along the path of the Shrâvaka in four ways. You will receive further instruction concerning these four ways very soon. Then I would beg you to discuss the same very carefully with your dear husband and to tell me which of the four ways you intend to choose.

You may regard yourself as already belonging to the School if you start your meditation on the day determined by the star constellation. I will describe this to you first of all. Later it will be modified.

First of all this exercise should consist of:

I. In the early morning, before any other daily task is undertaken, if possible before breakfast, if that is in any way reconcilable with family and other duties, the following should take place:

1. We should become fully awake, inwardly perfectly calm and collected.

No outer impressions should penetrate our inner self. We should also suppress any recollections of all our everyday experiences. When we have established the complete "inner calm," then we can proceed to raise ourself to our "higher self." This comes about through holding the following formula intensively in our thoughts:

> More radiant than the Sun,
> Purer than snow,
> Is selfhood,
> The spirit within my heart.
> The selfhood am I:
> I am this self-hood.

About five minutes should be devoted to this exercise.

2. Then there follows a silent inward-looking reflection on a sentence from one of the inspired writings. This would entail that, during this part of the meditation, for four weeks to begin with, you immerse yourself reflectively with:

Steadfastness is of higher value than any success.

This sentence has been given to us by the Masters in order to impress upon us that we should never let any kind of failure deter or discourage us in our efforts. A hundred failures shall not deter us from accomplishing, on the hundred and first occasion, what we have recognized as right.

3. Then shall follow, after five minutes spent on exercise 2, another five minutes devoted to a prayer-like *surrender* to what is for us, above all else, the Divinity. It is not a question of regarding this or that as divine, but of directing all our thoughts and feelings and our whole will toward what we have always regarded as divine. That can be called one thing by one person, another by someone else. It does not matter if that to which we surrender ourselves is called God, Christ, or "The Master," but it depends upon the mood of surrender (devotion) itself.

With that the threefold morning meditation, which lasts for fifteen minutes, has been completed.

II. In the *evening* before going to sleep, pupils have to direct their thoughts backward over the course of the day. It is not important that we contemplate as many of the day's events as possible, but that we consider the most important events. We ask ourselves: What can we learn from our experiences or actions? In this way our life becomes an object lesson. We confront ourselves so that everyday we learn something of everyday value. Through this we take the past with us into the future and prepare the way for our immortality. Then, perhaps, we conclude the day with thoughts of dear fellow human beings who are in need of our good thoughts.

It does not matter if the pupil falls asleep during this evening exercise, for in that case one will go to sleep with the tendency toward an upward development. And that is also good. Only the morning meditation must be carried out from beginning to end in a completely conscious state. I would only ask of you to carry out the evening retrospect backward, that you start with the events of the evening and work backward to the morning.

You may start with the meditation on one of the days between January sixth and twentieth. After that date the meditation may not be begun. If you are prevented from starting within this period then you may only commence again between February sixth and eighteenth. Today I cannot yet tell you why this is, but a time will surely come when it will be self-evident to you.

I do not need to tell you anything further for the moment, because you have long since regulated your life as a theosophist. Wine and other alcohol hinders development.

If we carry out what I have just said, then the "Exalted Masters" will find access to our soul. They are able to help us, and under their blessed influence we shall increase in strength, knowledge, and self-reliance. Our dear Annie Besant is always stressing again and again that the Esoteric School is "the heart of the theosophical movement." And so it is. Believe me in one thing, dearest, esteemed Frau Wagner: it is not so much a question of learning and intellectual work in this School, but of faithful devotion to the theosophical ideals. Love for the life of spirit and through that a genuine great love for humanity leads us to the place to which we aspire. Study is only a means to an end. We are *obliged* to go to the limit to which anyone is able to go. But the theosophical frame of mind is what *makes* the true ES pupil.

And, for the moment, I greet you therewith in the name of the Holy Master at whose feet I lay all that I have, and against whose will I shall never knowingly transgress during life. Blessed be they, the exalted ones.

With cordial good wishes,
I am, Your Rudolf Steiner

Please note—most important: Ask me about anything that you need to know about the ES. I shall in future set aside a time especially for ES news.

To Günther Wagner in Lugano:

Berlin, May 24, 1905

My dear esteemed Herr Wagner:

I had long intended to write to you, respectively also to your dear wife; but now it must really happen very quickly. This winter it has been incumbent upon me to contribute what little I could toward consolidating the German theosophical movement. Because there is so much to do, all must suffer. I am at present occupied in completing the circular letter to ES members, which has been long in preparation.

Today I would only say that I am fully in agreement that your dear wife should do the Shrâvaka exercises with our dear, respected Annie Besant.

With hearty good wishes,

I am, Your Rudolf Steiner

To Günther Wagner in Lugano:

Berlin, July 23, 1905

Esteemed, dear Herr Wagner:

With my whole heart I participate in the destiny that has befallen your dear wife and you, though it is only today that I am in a position to express this by letter. My thoughts are often with you. We theosophists must be ready to bear even hard blows of fate in a way that we could not have done before we became theosophists. It is true that love and sympathy can never become less because of a theosophical way of life; nevertheless, the understanding and strength to endure will become greater. We cannot lose anything because of theosophy, but we gain very much. It would be a loss to us if the feelings, which are part of the finest in life, should in any way fade. Therefore I know how you must feel out of your noble and excellent love. But I know you to be a true and genuine theosophist, as well, and I know that karmic relationships are no mere piece of doctrine to you, but are alive within you. But I should like to exchange a few thoughts with you just now. It is so easy to interpret everything that is linked to our destiny as a karmic debt. But that is in nowise always the case. True though it is that karma is a real and all-embracing law, it is equally true that karmic blows can insert themselves into the chain of our relationships simply as a *primal* cause. Blows of fate that strike us are not always the result of past events, often they are new entries in our book of life that will only find their recompense in the future. Just as traders have to enter an item into their accounts for the first time, so it is also with the items in the account book of our life. These thoughts always passed through my mind during the last weeks whenever I turned my mind to your dear home in Lugano, and the character they took in my vision showed that thoughts are a reality. You understand me, dear esteemed Herr Wagner, when I write to you of this inner vision—for vision it is. And perhaps you can accept as a reality—according to your own judgement—what is a reality for me.

I desire very much to greet you both again. I hope it will surely come to pass soon.

The celebration of the London Congress, at which you were unfortunately unable to be present, is now over.[91] It is in the nature of things that such festivities, even when they are arranged by theosophists, do not go far beyond externalities. But I am of the opinion that whoever had so desired could have taken away, even from there, things to strengthen the heart and soul. Mrs. Besant, for instance, gave lectures that were full of spiritual impulse. The first of these was to the Congress on Thursday about the "Discipleship of H. P. Blavatsky" in consideration of several recent attacks on the great founder of the theosophical movement. It seems to me very important that such a spiritually advanced person as Annie Besant is

---

91. The Second Annual Congress of the Federation of European Sections of the Theosophical Society occurred in London July 8–10, 1905. Rudolf Steiner spoke July 10 on the "The Esoteric Basis of Goethe's Work" (published RSE 292).

continually pointing out so unreservedly that for her H. P. B. is not a person like other celebrities but, as she herself says, is simply the "Light Bringer." Blemishes, she says, must not be denied; but they are blemishes like sunspots, which are only there where the *Sun* is. It brought back so vividly the inner experiences of my own life during the last period. For I must say that the further I progress, the more I become aware of the immeasurable strength that radiates from H. P. B. and of how much I still have to learn in order to comprehend even a fraction of the depths of H. P. B.'s creative work.

Then, on Friday, there was the Convention of the British Section. Of the things that happened there it will interest you to know that Bertram Keightley has withdrawn from the post of General Secretary and that Miss Kate Spink has taken over from him. For the moment Keightley is going to India for four months, after that he will devote himself in some other way to the theosophical movement, which will be made possible by his being relieved of his official duties as General Secretary.

Further, the "Art and Craft Exhibition" of the Congress opened just then. Among less significant things were also some remarkable items. I would just like to mention symbolic pictures by a painter called Russell. He attempts to characterize the things that take place in the soul by symbolic colors in his pictures (stars, rays, and so on, which emanate from the figures, symbolic representations of external objects of nature, and so on). Now I can certainly say that I could never credit the pictures with any real astral perception, but, indeed, I was satisfied with the attempt that had been made by a nevertheless gifted painter.

The Congress officially opened Saturday morning with a talk by Mrs. Besant, one of those grand surveys of the tasks and aims of the theosophical movement, which she gives on such occasions. It will interest you to hear that she talked about a piece of sculpture by an Italian sculptor called Ezechiel, a Christ statue, which she said was similar in some ways to the concept that she, as a theosophist, had of the Christ-Individuality. It will also interest you to hear that Mrs. Besant drew attention to Richard Wagner on this occasion, in the tones of whose music the secrets of the astral world become audible.

That struck me as being particularly significant, for in the spring of this year, I gave four lectures to the theosophists in Berlin about the spiritual content of Richard Wagner's work.[92]

Mrs. Besant's opening talk was followed by a varied program, for the delegates of all the European theosophical districts now addressed their words of greeting in their native languages. Thus one could hear short speeches in Dutch, Swedish, French, German, Spanish, Italian, Finnish, Russian, Hungarian, and Indian, one after another.

On the previous evening Mrs. Besant gave an impressive and comprehensive speech, "The Work of Theosophy in the World," to an audience of several thousand people in the Queen's Hall. She referred to the necessity of deepening our spiritual awareness of the present day and to the work this necessitates in the most diverse parts of the world. All that she said was filled with a wonderful magnanimity and grandeur.

Then on Saturday evening there was a theatrical performance. One would have to take into account the good will that prevailed therein. This occasion certainly brought home to me how the idea behind these Congresses should be developed if they are to fulfil their task adequately. It is not a question of how the participants should be entertained but, first and foremost, of how they can be given theosophical nourishment for their soul life, which they can then take away with them to their theosophical homeland, for the advantage and benefit of those unable to take part in the gatherings themselves. The Congresses should be a center of spiritual life from which streams radiate to all parts of the world.

Now followed the meetings of the Sections. I shall send you a program, as a printed package, from which you will at least be able to see from the headings the diversity of subject matter presented there. I should like to mention in particular the lecture by Mrs. Besant on Sunday about methods of esoteric investigation. That was something quite magnificent. She explained in a most beautiful way what the requirements of esoteric investigation are, also for

---

92. Berlin, March 28, and May 5, 12, and 19, 1905, *Richard Wagner in the Light of Anthroposophy* (in *News Sheet* 5).

the West, and what precautions, and so on, have to be taken in such investigation.

I gave a small contribution myself on Monday morning on "The Esoteric Basis of Goethe's Work."

I regret that I cannot go into more detail, but the last jobs connected with *Lucifer* 24 and 25, not to mention others, are still waiting to be finished. You can imagine what demands that makes upon me. It is necessary for me to publish these esoteric-scientific writings that *Lucifer* has produced lately. The responsibility of that alone weighs me down. And I have to test each line and every turn of phrase ten times over in order to reproduce the spiritual content, as it is my duty to do, which is imparted to me in quite a different form and language.

With hearty greetings to your dear wife and you,

From your ever faithful,

Dr. Rudolf Steiner

Berlin W., Motzstrasse, 17

To Paula Stryczek in Hanover:

Berlin, June 17, 1905

Dear Fräulein Stryczek:

During these days I will write to you in detail about what you need in the near future for the ES exercises. In the meantime continue with what I gave you last time.

It gave me much pleasure to be able to visit our good Dr. Hübbe-Schleiden again last Thursday.

Hearty greetings,

Your Dr. Rudolf Steiner

I enclose herewith for you the first pages for the German Shrâvakas. The only significance they have for you is that you will thereby have copies of everything that has been sent out from here. You know it all already.[93]

---

93. Paula Stryczek had been a member of the ES in London since before 1902.

To Mathilde Scholl in Cologne
(Haubinda, Klosterheim.
Postmarked, Friedrichshall, Sachsen-Meiningen):

August 14, 1905

Dear Fräulein Scholl:

Your letter (the one before last) speaks of your present attacks of depression.[94] Do not worry about that at all. Such experiences are a necessary outcome of effective esoteric work. The main thing is that we get hold of ourselves in a conscious way. It depends, specifically, on taking care that we do not allow any interference with our harmonious relationship to our surroundings at the time. You have a very strong, but also a very sensitive nature, and *nothing* hinders you from surviving the quite harmless, but nevertheless profound changes that your astral, and even your etheric body, is going through as a result of your present exercises. Not many of the German members of the Theosophical Society follow (respectively, could follow) the same path, but all who do so have the same experiences as you are having. And I must regard these experiences as a sign of true progress. Real progress cannot be achieved without a loosening of certain centers in the etheric and the astral bodies.

A higher state of consciousness awakens when centers, formerly regulated in their interplay with one another by an unconscious organism, have their connection severed. Then the formerly unconscious organism gradually changes into a conscious one, and the disconnected centers are brought under its regulating influence. I should like to make this clear to you by means of a small sketch:

---

94. Letter unavailable.

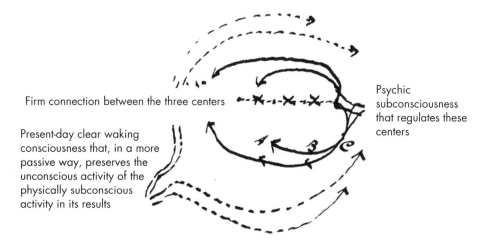

Firm connection between the three centers

Psychic subconsciousness that regulates these centers

Present-day clear waking consciousness that, in a more passive way, preserves the unconscious activity of the physically subconscious activity in its results

This depicts the present-day "normal" condition of human beings. Through the esoteric work there now begins:

1. The loosening from centers A, B and C.
2. The psychic subconscious is raised to the psychic super consciousness, and the results of the waking day-consciousness change into *things of the past.*

It looks like this:

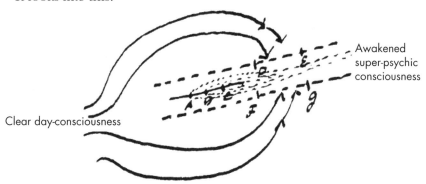

Awakened super-psychic consciousness

Clear day-consciousness

New centers are formed at D, E, F, G, which are regulated by the newly won, clear day consciousness through the fixedness that it has acquired from the senses. The centers A, B, C now stand in isolation and will later be *voluntarily* and individually regulated by the wakened higher consciousness.

The meditation "I am, It thinks, It feels, He wills"[95] brings about the loosening that has been indicated. The thinking, feeling, and willing centers divide off and unite with the original forces of the universe, which you will find characterized in Mrs. Besant's latest writing[96] as Will, Wisdom, Activity, in the following manner:

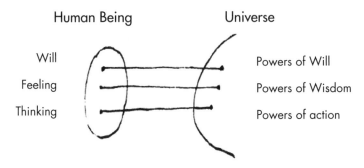

Please observe the relationship correctly: Subjective feelings, for example, correspond with objective wisdom in the universe, and subjective thinking corresponds with activity.

When the loosening occurs, certain incubatory conditions of a twilight nature appear. It is such that you are now experiencing.

During your stay in Berlin we shall also be able to speak much more about such things.

Now I would ask you to proceed strictly with the allotted exercises. If you find that it fits in better with the way you actually breathe, that is then very good. It has to go together with it later anyway. Usually, however, one allows the "spiritually-symbolic" breathing to be practiced first, but you can unite this with the actual physical breathing straightaway if you like.

I am quite in agreement with your last letter. I shall merely say, in confidence, I am aware that good old Bresch may not be judged as a healthy human being. Such a condition as appears in him may,

---

95. See *Guidance in Esoteric Training: From the Esoteric School*, (CW 242/45) This meditation is described and explained in detail as part of the "Main Exercise," pp. 35–45. It was given as "I am, It thinks, She feels, He wills."
96. Annie Besant, *A Study in Consciousness*, London and Benares, 1904.

however, develop very gradually, and it may remain hidden to the casual observer that such a person has already overstepped the limits of what is healthy. You can imagine how this complicates the whole thing and worries me, for I cannot speak openly about what I see as the truth concerning Bresch.

Most cordial greetings—also to the Künstlers.

Your Dr. Rudolf Steiner

To Adolf Kolbe in Hamburg (part of an otherwise unknown letter, which sums up the contents of the esoteric meeting that was held the same day in Berlin):

Berlin, October 4, 1905

A U M

"Seek out the way."

"Seek the way by retreating within."

"Seek the way by advancing boldly without."[97]

The last two sentences merely appear to contradict one another. The truth is that they express two perfectly correct facts.

Inner contemplation is, specifically, the first half of the path. Human beings live, at their present stage of evolution, *within* the sense impressions of the outer world. Even when they transform these sense impressions through reasoning and common sense, they still remain "on the outside."

If they now free themselves from sense impressions, if they withdraw into their inner being, they still retain their power of thought. This thinking then becomes emptied of outer content. That is the "inner contemplation." But just because the thinking has become "emptied," new content can flow into it from within.

And *this* content is of a spiritual kind, just as the former was of the senses. Just because of that, however, individuals are once more

---

97. From leading thoughts contained in *Light on the Path.*

freed from themselves. They emerge *out* of the sphere of the lower I into the "external spiritual world." That is what is indicated by the sentence "Seek the way by advancing boldly without."

And now the mystic connects all three sentences with the syllable A U M. The *A*, for a start, is the consolidation of humankind's state as they continue to be during the present stage of evolution.

The *U* is the symbol for inner contemplation, and the *M* is the emergence into the external spiritual world.

To Paula Stryczek in Hanover:

Berlin W. 30, Motzstrasse 17
December 31, 1905

Dear Fräulein Stryczek:

Regarding the sad affair that has befallen us, allow me to say the following:[98]

It is particularly important that when those dear to us pass over into the world beyond, we send them our thoughts and feelings, without allowing the thought to arise that we wish to have them back. The latter makes life more difficult for the departed in the sphere into which they must pass. We should send the *love* we give them, not the sorrow we experience, into the worlds where they are. Do not misunderstand me. We need not become hardened or indifferent. But it ought to be possible for us to view the dead with the thought "May my love go with you! You are surrounded by it." To my knowledge, a feeling such as this is like a winged garment that carries loved ones upward; whereas the feelings of many people mourning, expressed as "Ah, if only you were still with us," becomes an obstacle to them. That constitutes a general indication of how we should compose our feelings in such a case.

---

98. It concerns, as is shown by the end of the letter, the death of Günther Wagner's wife Anna.

In particular, may I now give you the following advice. I will write down for you the thoughts that I have not yet quite formulated in very good German; nevertheless, they are based on ancient esoteric tradition for such a case. Compose yourself inwardly three times a day, of which one of these times should be immediately before sleep at night, so that you take these thoughts over with you into the spiritual world. It would be best if you were to fall asleep with the thought:

> May my love be the sheaths
> That now surround you—
> Cooling all warmth,
> Warming all coldness—
> Interwoven with sacrifice!
> Live, borne by love,
> Light-endowed, upward!

It is important that you have the right feeling with regard to the words "warmth" and "coldness." Physical "warmth" and "coldness" is not what is meant, but something like "warmth of feeling" and "coldness of feeling," though it is not at all easy for a person clothed in a physical body to have any idea of what these qualities mean to a disembodied soul. Such souls have to become aware that the astral body, which they still have around them, is effective, though it cannot make use of the physical organs. Much of what humanity strives for here on Earth is given by our physical organs, which are no longer there. This lack of the physical organs is similar—but only *similar*—to a feeling of burning thirst transferred onto the soul. Those are the strong feelings of "burning thirst" experienced after a person has left the body. And it is just the same with what the will desires to do. The will is accustomed to making use of the physical organs, but no longer has them. This "privation" approximates a feeling of coldness in the soul. It is just concerning these feelings where the living can help; for these feelings do not *merely* result from a person's individual life, but are connected with the mysteries of incarnation. It is therefore possible to aid someone who has died.

Now there is something else I would ask of you. Let a few thoughts about our Herr Wagner precede the above sentences. They should contain something of the following content: "[Herr Wagner] You were surrounded by your faithful love until now; it still surrounds you unchanged; may it hold you fast in the power of the spirit, as it has previously illuminated you in the visible present."

This is everything I wanted to write to you today. I am currently burdened with so much work on the physical plane that for the moment I cannot say anything more of *special* importance—apart from the above general statements—for the physical overshadows spiritual experience. Of course, you may feel free to communicate what I have written to anyone you yourself feel it is right to do so. I would wish that the hearts of many people are turned toward this dear person.

Give my hearty regards to the dear doctor and receive the same yourself from

Your Dr. Rudolf Steiner

To Jan Lagutt in Binningen near Basel:

Berlin, January 12, 1906

Most esteemed Herr Doctor:

The correct beginning to the meditation is as follows:

One seeks to establish complete calmness of soul at that hour of *morning* when no other impressions have passed through the soul— best of all immediately on awakening. *Complete* detachment of one's attention from all outer impressions and also from all memory pictures connected with everyday affairs.

Out of this now-so-quiet soul one allows the following sentences to rise up and fill the inner space completely (lasting from 3 to 5 minutes):

In the pure rays of Light
Shines the Godhead of the World,
In pure Love for all creatures
The Divinity of my soul radiates.
I rest in the Divinity of the World.
I shall find my Self
In the Divinity of the World.

The point is that these sentences have to be conceived *quite literally*.

There then follows (during the next 3 to 5 minutes) a sentence from *Light on the Path*.[99]

In the first month—the first sentence.
In the second month—the second.
In the third month—the third.
In the fourth month—the fourth.

Then (for the next 3 to 5 minutes) devotional contemplation of one's divine ideal, to which one adds the *intensive feeling* for the *value* of a virtue one would like to implant into oneself.

In the evenings: backward review of the deeds and experiences of the day. In reverse order, from evening to morning. Without regret, with only the intention to learn from life. If one falls asleep during the exercise it does not matter. It is not a matter of completeness, but of developing a *disposition* to learn from life.

In the morning, however, one must be *fully awake* while engaged in meditation.

With heartiest greetings,
Dr. Rudolf Steiner

---

99. The four sentences are:
Before the eyes can see they must be incapable of tears.
Before the ear can hear it must have lost its sensitivity.
Before the voice can speak in the presence of the Master it must have lost the power to wound.
Before the soul can stand in the presence of the Masters its feet must be washed in the blood of the heart.

To Anna R. Minsloff in Russia:

Berlin W. 30, March 7, 1906
Motzstrasse 17

Dear Fräulein Minsloff:

Referring to your own exercises I need only tell you that you should continue with them as we discussed. If you do that you will consolidate the good powers you possess, and that is what entirely suits your nature. The result will not fail to show itself. We cannot allow a change in the exercises yet: it would be just in *your* nature that a retention of the *same* exercises leads to *rapid* progress, whereas many others must progress through change. The best spiritual beings stand protectively at your side. Your soul is preordained to be of great benefit to humanity. You are imbued with such proper feeling for the spiritual world that there is no more I need say to you today, except that I shall always beg the protective help of the "Venerable Masters" for you.

Fräulein von Sivers now tells me of the lady who has turned to you for help. With good and energetic treatment she can be helped, but just now in her present condition it will not be easy, because she is expecting a child. Nevertheless I should like to advise you to carry out a treatment with her as far as possible. This treatment will also have an effect on the child's development; however, *this* effect will be less harmful, than if the lady were to forgo psychic treatment completely.

The following is advised:

You should let the lady come to you—at first for three consecutive days, at a fixed time. Before she comes, concentrate for half an hour in the following set manner: Think first about your feet, as though the whole of your *I*-forces were in the *foot-soles*, then draw this feeling, developed in the *foot-soles*, up through the whole of your body as far as the heart, thinking the whole time the thought "I"; then think about your finger tips and say to yourself, as though you wanted to send your thoughts into your finger tips: "Through this I shall ward off evil."

Whereupon the lady may come to you. Now you should say to her the following:

"Your body is a battle ground for two opposing forces. All that shall be set to right as soon as your I-forces become ruler over your own body. We do not thereby damage either of the contestants, rather are we of service to them; but you yourself will also gain peace and firmness." When you have said that to the lady, let her stand before you and look you in the eyes. At the same time take her left hand into your right hand and say to her: "Concentrate your mind on your I." Next do the following: Concentrate your mind on your feet, so that you feel everything, to the smallest detail, *within* your feet; next draw this feeling up through the whole of your body to your heart, and think about your heart with the *single* concept of "I" in your mind. That should be continued in this way for half an hour, and during all that time the lady should never once think about her head. The latter injunction should be adhered to very strictly. Then, when that has been done, stroke the lady in two lines on either side of the backbone, from the lower extremity of the back to the head, while saying out loud: "The enemy powers are dispersing." With that, instruct the lady to think, while you are saying this, of nothing except what you are saying.

Then the lady must do the "feet-to-heart" exercise many times during the day without you. She should do it at least seven times, quite on her own and *standing*.

After this has continued for three days everything should remain as before, but the thoughts, instead of being directed toward the feet, should be directed toward the legs, from the heel to the knee, during the course of the next three days. Then:

Three days from the knee to the hips;
Three days toward the lower part of the body up to the navel;
Three days to the body, from the navel to the heart;
Three days from the heart to the shoulders;
Three days toward the upper arm;
Three days toward the lower arm;
Three days toward the hand into the fingertips.

If this is done *energetically* the lady will become calm, but if it has not quite succeeded, she should repeat everything once more.

Each time the exercise has been completed, the lady should say:

> In the pure rays of light
> Shines the Godhead of the world;
> In pure love for all creatures
> The divinity of my soul radiates;
> I rest in the divinity of the world;
> I shall find myself
> In the divinity of the world.

She should repeat this to herself seven times during the day, *after* having completed the other.

After the back has been stroked and you have spoken the aforementioned words: "The enemy powers are dispersing," call out the lady's *Christian name* very firmly while stroking the back *again* from below upward with both hands.

Until we meet again,

Heartiest greetings,
Yours, Dr. Rudolf Steiner

To Michael Bauer in Nuremberg:

Berlin W. 30, Motzstrasse, 17
July 3, 1906

My dear Herr Bauer:

I would like to have written to you long ago, but my time was fully claimed. First I was in Paris, where I gave a four-week lecture course.[100] Then I was busy with many things at home. My absence from the Nuremberg Congress will probably meet with your consent—I do not think that one could achieve very much in the short time allotted me.

---

100. *An Esoteric Cosmology*, SteinerBooks, Great Barrington, MA, 2008 (CW 94).

On the other hand, I would like to visit you and our other dear friends around August eighth, if that is all right with you. That is, in the days after the eighth. Perhaps you could get together a gathering of the Lodge. I will tell you later the date. It is specifically on another matter that I am visiting the vicinity of Nuremberg during these days.[101]

The Leadbeater affair is a serious matter. I have written a circular about it that will be posted to all the members within a few days.[102] One has to probe into the deeper causes of such a case. It happens in esotericism that through the methods that Leadbeater uses a disaster can very easily occur. Actually the thing can only be judged a-right from an esoteric point of view. I hope to be able to explain the whole thing to you in person during the next days.

[...][103]

Most hearty wishes to your wife and all members, as also to you.

Yours, Dr. Rudolf Steiner

No change has been made in the ES work as yet.

To Eugenie von Bredow in Landin, Westhavelland:

Berlin W. 30, Motzstrasse 17
August 14, 1906

Dear Frau von Bredow:

As sad as the news is that you send me about our good Mathilde Scholl, it does not surprise me at all. At the moment, however, it is not possible to help her in any way that allows her participation.

---

101. Rudolf Steiner was in Bayreuth with Marie von Sivers on August 6–7, 1906, for a performance of *Parsifal*. It is not known if he visited Nuremberg.
102. See the circulated letter of June 1906, p. 243.
103. Further remarks refer to the Cognitive-Ritual Section of Rudolf Steiner's Esoteric School; see *"Freemasonry" and Ritual Work*, SteinerBooks, Great Barrington, MA, 2007 (CW 265).

The matter is thus: she is confronted by a trial that cannot be taken from her. What you and I can do is to establish the correct inner accord with her. And the note you strike in your recent letter to me is the right one. You can best help her if you can hold strongly to this note. It would also not be quite right to account Mathilde's present frame of mind to "weakness." The esoteric stage that she has reached is not a case of inner weakness, but indicates the strength of the attacks made against her soul by certain powers. One sees it from the right angle if one regards the form expressed by her friendship as just a trial. There can be no talk of any "blame" on your part, dear lady. If you persevere in the attitude you have adopted, you will achieve the right result for you and also for Mathilde.

Both of you must find the fulcrum of your friendship in the light of the spiritual ideal. I will write to Mathilde myself in a few days. Today would not be the best time. If she emerges victorious from *this*, she will later receive all the more strength.

I could have devoted more time to you had there not been great tasks awaiting me just at this time, which have to be accomplished. However, the main thing is that you have found the possibility of following the appropriate line in your difficult situation. Much depends on such things in human progress. Security of soul is a great force toward spiritual development. You will not lose courage in the face of difficulties, even those of unimagined proportions. In your feelings you have the right relationship to your surroundings. And though it may appear that your influence is not great enough, nevertheless you will come to realize that *indirectly* this is on the right course, and will ultimately arrive at the goal.

Let the spiritual forces that you have sought be with you, by your retaining and developing of the path you have trod for some time.

Hearty greetings,

Yours, Dr. Rudolf Steiner

To A. W. Sellin in Hamburg:

Berlin W. 30, Motzstrasse, 17

August 15, 1906

Most esteemed Herr Director:
    ... [104]

Today I also have something to say to you about your exercise. It is right for you to continue it in the former way until about August 23. After that it would have to be arranged as follows:[105]

Begin your morning meditation with:

Breathing exercise. Before you begin breathing as the exercise requires, picture to yourself some well-known plant as vividly as possible. It must be familiar to you in all its details, so that the *imagination* can be quite exact. Retain this picture in your mind as the *only* object of consciousness as long as the coming eight breaths take. Do this in the following way: Inhalation—holding the breath—exhalation, so that the three stages last for intervals corresponding to 1:4:2 (according to feeling). So, for example, should the inhalation last two seconds, the breath would be held eight seconds, and the exhalation would last four seconds. (If you cannot breathe in this sequence, you may insert ordinary breaths in between, but the visualization of the plant may not be interrupted.

During inhalation and the first half of the holding of the breath meditate regarding the plant:

"*Your death—my life.*"

During the second half of the breath-holding and during exhalation meditate:

"*My death—your life.*"

(Gradually the meaning of these words will become apparent to you of its own accord.) This lasts throughout a period of seven breaths.

104. The first part of this letter concerns the Cognitive-Ritual Section of Rudolf Steiner's Esoteric School; see *"Freemasonry" and Ritual Work* (CW 265).

105. In connection with the given exercise and other breathing exercises, see the volume containing collected esoteric exercises (CW 267).

On the *eighth* breath try to project your consciousness into the plant, as far as possible, as though you are *inside* the plant, looking at yourself as the *object* from outside. (That is, as if you had emerged out of yourself and were confronting yourself); during that time meditate regarding yourself:

> During inhalation and first half of breath-holding:
> "*My death—your life*"
> During second half of breath-holding and exhalation:
> "*Your death—my life*"
> This only once, then follow with: Vivid concentration on the point between and slightly behind the eyebrows (root of the nose) while meditating:
> "*I am*"
> Vivid concentration on the inside of the larynx while meditating:
> "*It thinks*"
> Vivid concentration on arms and hands while meditating:
> "*She feels*"
> Vivid concentration on the whole of the body while meditating:
> "*He will.*"

With hearty greetings,

Yours, Dr. Rudolf Steiner

To Günther Wagner in Lugano:

Barr (Alsace)
September 8, 1906

Dear Herr Wagner:

It is certainly correct that, *in general,* the two meditations follow one another; however, in your case, it was intended that the second (written) one should immediately follow the first one every day. Should that, however, be too much, then it would be good to do in the morning what is given in the hectographed directions, and during the course of the day to undertake the written instructions as a preparation. In that way you would get on more quickly.[106]

If you perform this in the evening before going to bed, it will even provide you with what you need for a peaceful sleep.

Now, considering this peaceful sleep, the following would be best: At the moment of wanting to fall asleep and failing to do so, try to think very vividly about your feet and, as though putting all your consciousness into your feet, think into them the words "my life force." It will not be long before sleep overtakes you. It is only necessary that the whole process takes place as naturally as possible, so that at every moment the concept can lead over into the formless.

Good-bye for now,

With hearty greetings,

Yours, Dr. Rudolf Steiner

To Edouard Schuré in Barr, Alsace:

Munich, December 20, 1906

Highly respected Friend:

... I am very pleased that the exercises I wrote for you in Barr are of some value to you. They are in harmony with the Rosicrucian wisdom. And if I may make a request, it is that you should not lose patience if the appearance of an observable effect is somewhat delayed. The way is a sure one, but it requires much patience. In a short while, when the right moment has arrived, I will certainly write out the sequel to it. To begin with one learns of the effect only by quite *intimate* processes within the soul. And it actually requires great—and at the same time, more subtle—inner attention be given to perceive how the manifestations from another world present themselves. The latter are only noticeable, as it were, *between* the other happenings of one's inner life....[107]

---

106. The "hectographed directions" refer to the "Main Exercise I," which was reproduced by machine and distributed; in *Guidance in Esoteric Training: From the Esoteric School*; Rudolf Steiner Press, London, 1994, pp. 34 ff. (CW 42/245); the "written exercise" was given specially to Günther Wagner.

107. The full letter is in *Nachrichten der Rudolf Steiner-Nachlassverwaltung*, No.6.

To Alfred Meebold in Heidenheim an der Brenz:[108]

Dear Herr Meebold:

I wish to deal in summary with the questions you raised—respectively with the points you touched on.

Your question about the Masters I have only implicitly referred to by my indication that not I is meant when I say I. I know that you understand me aright, for I value very highly the experience you have made during your lifetime, and I so spoke to you in full confidence.

I know that you are familiar with the auxiliary exercises. Nevertheless, it is necessary that they be practiced systematically at some time. What you describe as an "inner experience" is a result of the previous exercises. And the other part of the description I have given you will also become experience for you in time to come and, indeed, from each separate exercise a separate feeling will arise. I beg of you not to think of that as trying to influence you by "suggestion!" With such notions one only strews stones in one's path.

The meaning of "holding one's breath" will become apparent to you if you guide your thoughts in the following direction: the process of earthly incarnation is conditional upon "breathing through the lungs." Therefore, as a matter of practice, the ascent to the spirit must cancel out this process, and so on and so forth. With that I only broach the thought that I ask you to carry further.[109]

Please do not regard the matter of "secrecy" as a duty *in principle,* but only a *temporary* injunction owing to the present chaotic situation in the ES and TS. I do not impose upon you a pledge of silence in *principle,* in the case of intimate friends in whom you have *absolute* trust. *For the moment,* however, regard this "silence" only as though one friend were saying to another: "Please do not speak about that to anyone." The time will certainly come when we shall be able to agree that, in the case of *such* friends, the pledge of silence will not be necessary any more. Therefore, regard the confidentiality as

---

108. 1906; no further information.
109. In CW 266. *Esoteric Lessons 1913 and 1914, 1920-1923, Volume III,* Steiner-Books, Great Barrington, 2010.

being confidential only in *this* sense. I would be happy myself if this, too, did not have to be as it is. I am very pleased myself with those of my pupils who are beginning to understand my relationship to occultism in the same light as that of a mathematician to his mathematics. Therewith the painful question of authority has been exhaustively dealt with.

It would please me very much to see you at the Congress.[110] It gives me great pleasure that you are going to start with the exercises so soon. In important matters I will *always* be ready to help you through letters.

Heartiest greetings,

Yours, Dr. Rudolf Steiner

To Michael Bauer in Nuremberg:

Berlin, August 4, 1907

My dear Herr Bauer:

Herewith I am sending you the "auxiliary exercises," which also cover the last three periods. You wrote to me some time ago that the people in Nuremberg do not have these. I am sending them to you so that you can give them to the esoteric pupils when you think it appropriate. That could be after the holidays, of course, for it is always good if those who are practicing continue with it as long as possible.

For you personally I am sending seven verses apportioned to the seven days of the week.[111] They are to be practiced in a way that one contemplates the Saturday on Friday, the Sunday on Saturday, and so on. You may do this several times a day and try to grasp the whole

---

110. The letter bears no exact date, so it could refer to either the Paris Congress in May 1906, or the Munich Congress in May 1907.

111. Michael Bauer was Sub-Warden for Nuremberg (leader of a regional Esoteric Group), just as, for example, Adolf Arenson was for Stuttgart and Sophie Stinde for Munich. The "auxiliary exercises" and the "seven verses" are contained in *Guidance in Esoteric Training: From the Esoteric School.*

meaning in 20 to 30 minutes. You will gain very much toward establishing a connection with the mysteries of the all-pervading sevenfoldness.

At the same time I am sending you esoteric leaflets that will provide you with a means of experiencing more deeply the innate power of the four verses that you know.[112]

Extend the practice time at your leisure, as far as it is compatible with your strength. But, at any rate, not beyond measure.

You will surely send me the copy of your Munich lecture soon. I must complete the "Federation Yearbook" and your lecture should appear in that.[113]

Greet your dear wife cordially. She should continue her exercises in the same way.

With hearty greetings,

Yours, Dr. Rudolf Steiner

To Eugenie von Bredow in Landin, Westhavelland:

Berlin, August 4, 1907

My dear Eugenie von Bredow:

It will be best to leave it wholly to your sister's discretion as to whether she wants to proceed with the more intimate theosophical activity, or not. The doubts and scruples that she experiences because of her belief that she is not doing the right thing are certainly also a cause of the disturbance. Occult development is possible only when *such* doubts and scruples are energetically repelled. It would not be good, however, to use persuasion on her. Therefore the only thing to be recommended is that her doubts about her complete inability to do anything should be taken away from her— to tell her that her lack of courage goes too far; but also, to place

---

112. The "esoteric leaflets" are unavailable. This may possibly refer to explanations in *Light on the Path.*
113. Lecture given at the Munich Congress in May 1907, on "The Fostering of Esotericism within the Society." The Federation Yearbook did not appear, however.

everything into her own hands. One must not believe that theosophy, as such, is not going to help a person forward. And to this your sister will remain faithful.

Let yourself look upon it in that way, then there will be no cause for you to be sad about it either.

To you personally I send my best thoughts and remain as ever.
Yours cordially,

Dr. Rudolf Steiner

Only today are we now able to travel.[114]

To Mathilde Scholl in Cologne:

Berlin, August 4, 1907

My dear Mathilde Scholl:

Your letter proves well that you are searching for the central core of your being within yourself; continue in this direction, bring to realization the goals you have set for yourself. The light that springs from spiritual science is such that it can illuminate all our actions and thoughts as well as all our dealings with other people. It is only when we place our relationship to others in this light that we find the right attitude toward them. Then, whatever form this or that may assume outwardly, nothing can harm us. Our relationships in life do not become colder when we allow this light to fall upon them. But we easily get onto the wrong track if we have once placed ourselves in this light and then do not let *everything* be illuminated by it. Look at the thing in this way and continue thus. Your niece is on the right path. Give her the enclosed few words.[115]

Accept my most cordial greetings and my best thoughts.
Ever yours,

Dr. Rudolf Steiner

---

114. Rudolf Steiner and Marie von Sivers spent August in Italy.
115. Unavailable.

To Anna R. Minsloff in Russia:

Berlin, March 23, 1908

My dear Fräulein Minsloff:

First of all a hearty greeting. The exercises were not intended to be dropped occasionally, but practiced continuously until you receive fresh ones. It will be good for now if you continue with the morning and evening exercises in exactly the way they were described to you on your last visit here. Many mysteries lie hidden in these exercises that will be revealed to you after years of energetically identifying yourself with their content. You, in particular, will achieve true inner revelations by patiently continued practice. Should you at present occasionally feel an ebbing of your forces, it is but a transient phenomenon of no further significance, and will transform into further energy again. Of special importance for the morning exercise are:

1. The seven sentences known to you.
2. The four meditations: "I am," "It thinks," "She feels," "He wills," in connection with the breathing described to you.
3. The "Word of Might" that was given to you.
4. Devotion toward divine ideal.

Between 2 and 3 insert the vivid picturing of a plant (imagination) and try to submerge yourself into the concept that humankind owes its life to the plant. It is done like this:

Inhale with inner vision of the plant and the thought:
　　"*Your* (the plant's) death—*my* life."
Then hold the breath with the imaginative perception of one's picture of the plant; then exhale with the thought:
　　"*My death—your* life."
One repeats this *three* times; then there follows:
Inhale again with the thought:
　　"*Your death—my life.*"

Then exhale
 "My death—your life."
Then retain the breath again (three times as long as for the inhalation). Repeat this another three times.
Then one changes place with the plant; one identifies oneself with it in thought and looks at oneself in thought as if one were a quite different being.
At the same time: Inhale with the thought:
 "My death—your life"
Exhale with the thought:
 "Your death—my life."
Then hold the breath again for a while.
This is done *once*.
All the while one keeps the concept of the plant in mind.

Evenings: the exercises as described to you.

The subsidiary exercises: Concentration of thoughts, acting from initiative; overcoming of desire and pain, positivity, impartiality.

This is repeated, so that having completed it, one begins again at the beginning; one month for concentration of thoughts, then one month for acting from initiative, and so on, as described on your sheet.

If you do these exercises everything will be all right.

And if you, my dear Fräulein Minsloff, do not overstrain yourself, then I shall be quite in agreement with all that you are doing for other people. You will work in a beneficial way. Everything is all right the way you do it.

———————

Now something more about the founding of the Russian Section. Nothing much will result from the founding of this Section insofar as it concerns our *great spiritual cause*, which is the only thing of benefit and importance. The German Section is already a stumbling block in many respects, but one that is necessary, and that cannot be disregarded. We *had* to have the Section in this case. The Section would be even less productive where you are concerned. In your country, and especially among your people, you have the greatest theosophical asset in that what you have become acquainted with here as true Theosophy and as genuine, life-giving, enduring Christianity, is destined to attain to the acme of its spiritual unfoldment only in eastern Europe. In the un-theosophical spiritual life of the West there is a science that, from a *spiritual* point of view, is only of value for the future through its all-embracing *technique of thinking*. This technique of thinking must become a part of spiritual life for all future times. But in the East the content of the Folk-Soul must be developed for the salvation of all humanity. This content of the Folk-Soul makes it possible that, for many things coming from the East, great wisdom can be expressed in a few sentences that the West could not fully express in whole books. The sufferings in your country are the birth pangs of the content of this Folk-Soul. To one who truly knows the situation, this germ within the Folk-Soul appears as a breath of magic. Very much spiritual work must be accomplished here. What was spoken of by Miss Kamensky in Munich, when she lectured at the Congress, has nothing to do with *this* spiritual outlook, for the views of Miss Kamensky are in essence mere theoretical reflexes from the West; the Folk-Soul lies much deeper. Much of this Folk-Soul comes to expression in Tolstoy; nevertheless, this must all combine with genuine Theosophy if something real is to grow out of it.

Compared to what I know permeates your aims—compared to that, dear Fräulein Minsloff, the founding of the Section is a childish and primitive work, the innocent game of a few theorizing folk, obsessed by the kind of Theosophy with which they have become acquainted. And in the face of that it would be best to let them get on with the founding of the Section and to say to oneself that they can do as they like about it. Our purpose will be served with the founding of the Section only by what is "poured into the vessel" of the Section. For this reason it would also not be quite right for me to hold lectures there just now. Let the Section be founded first. Section or no Section, we shall not deviate from the course we have set for ourselves. And to *this* serious end, this Section of yours will be of no benefit, but neither will it be of any great detriment. Thus, it appears best that we should wait a little while for my lectures, though not *so* long either; let the founding of the Section run its own course. Continue with your own work, my dear Fräulein Minsloff, as you have until now. It is better for you to carry out this valuable work in a positive manner and let the Section be formed without more ado. Whether you and the few members of the German Section should join the Russian Section or not need not be decided at all at the moment. That can come about *when* the Russian Section has been founded, should that ever take place.

This letter is written *only* for you, and I would beg you to reveal its contents to *none* of the other theosophists, with the single exception, should the opportunity occur, of Fräulein Olga von Sivers. And yet, nevertheless, she should also regard the matter only as a guideline for herself and not tell it to others.

As ever,

Yours, Dr. Rudolf Steiner

To Sophie Stinde in Munich:

Cologne, June 10, 1908

My dear Fräulein Stinde:

Our fixed program for the ES to take place on Sunday mornings and the Lodge meetings on Sunday evenings still holds good, does it not? I would like to give a philosophical talk on Sunday at about five o'clock for the audience of the previous philosophical talk, and for those you think suitable. But this should be arranged exactly as you think fit. Stockmeyer is to be accepted into the FM on this occasion.[116] It will not be possible after all for a *short* preliminary celebration on Monday for the FM. Stockmeyer has the most urgent desire to become a member precisely on his 50th birthday. The admittance can, of course, only take place on Tuesday, one day after his birthday,

---

116. *Free Masonry* is abbreviated as "FM," and is a reference to the "Cognitive-Ritual Section" of Rudolf Steiner's Esoteric School.

but one might perform a short, specially arranged, preliminary cele-bration of admittance on Monday—perhaps *without* the Lodge rega-lia. But if it causes you too much trouble, then Stockmeyer will have to be content to wait till Tuesday. I would also very much like to hold a class for advanced esoteric pupils during the Monday course.

Cordial greetings to the Countess and to you,

Your,

Dr. Rudolf Steiner

I will arrive at the earliest on Saturday evening, coming from Eisen-ach where the Lodge is to be opened.

To Maria Kili in Strasbourg, August 1908:

The exercises must not be spoken about to anyone.
Make a written copy of this and return to me.

Dear Fräulein Kili:

The exercises I promised to you on my visit to Strasbourg are as follows:

Early morning: as soon as possible after waking, before any other thoughts have passed through your mind, try to divert your atten-tion from your surroundings and all mundane thoughts, and give yourself up completely for five minutes to the following seven sen-tences (not according to your watch, but according to estimate):

> In the pure rays of the light
> Shines the Godhead of the World,
> In pure love for all creatures
> The divinity of my soul radiates.
> I rest in the divinity of the world,
> I shall find myself
> In the divinity of the world.

When this has been done take a deep breath, as though you were breathing the sound "*Y.*" After having inhaled in this way, add to the

"*Y*" the sound "*CH*," so that "*ICH*" is within you as the force pervading the breath. Allow this force (the "*ICH*" within the breath) to penetrate the rest of your body through your thoughts; during this process keep the thought that "*Y*" signifies "Jesus" and "*CH*" the "Christ." This breathing should be repeated three times.

After this you should picture to yourself how a plant grows from a seed, blossoms, comes to fruition, withers, and dies. This should fill your mind for about five minutes (not according to the clock but according to your estimate of the time).

Evenings: reading seven or eight sentences of Dr. Steiner's *Theosophy*, and afterward, for about fifteen minutes, create your own thoughts.

After this, *retrospect* of the day's experiences; that is, beginning with evening and ending with morning.

These exercises should be continued day by day until I give you new ones to replace them.

One must be patient, doing the exercises for months, perhaps for years. The fruits will ripen eventually.

Heartfelt theosophical greetings,
Dr. Rudolf Steiner

To Wilhelm Hübbe-Schleiden in Hanover:

Berlin, November 15, 1908

Esteemed, dear Herr Doctor:

To my knowledge, my introduction to *Goethe's Scientific Writings* in Kürschner's *National Literature* has not been published separately.[117] If the publishers brought this out separately at the time, it was without my knowledge. But that will not have been the case.

---

117. This and other writings by Rudolf Steiner on Goethe are available as *Goethean Science*, Mercury Press, 1988; also edited and with an extensive introduction by John Barnes as *Nature's Open Secret: Rudolf Steiner and Goethe's Scientific Method*, Anthroposophic Press, Hudson, NY, 2000.

The publication I mentioned in Hanover is *The Construction of the Atom and Life* by Dr. Adolf Drescher (published by Emil Roth, Giessen, 1908). In the preface to this book you will also find a mention of the earlier book by the same author you spoke about. Drescher has not taken occultism into consideration in dealing with the construction of the atom. That is why I referred to him only by way of general comparison.[118]

With reference to the colors of the pentagram! The coloring of the enclosed pentagram figure that was made for individual esoteric pupils will also be the best for you. This concept, however, is complicated. If a *single* color is used, then the most effective will be the one used in the point of the pentagram where the Moon is situated (reddish violet).

The serpent is best thought of in the yellow of the pentagram and hexagram where Mercury is situated.[119]

The Rose-Cross seal; blue background—black cross—seven-pointed star. (In Munich the exoteric *eight* stands in place of esoteric *seven*.)[120]

Arrangement:

Please excuse the brevity; it is time for departure.

In affectionate friendship,

always yours,

Dr. Rudolf Steiner

---

118. Rudolf Steiner was giving lectures in Hanover on November 4–5, 1908, and must have had a conversation with Hübbe-Schleiden, who was much occupied with the composition of the atom.

119. See "Pentagram and Hexagram Exercise on pp. 159-167.

120. This refers to the Rosy-Cross seal that Rudolf Steiner introduced for the first time at the Munich Congress. Compare *Rosicrucianism Renewed: The Theosophical Congress of Whitsun 1907* (CW 284).

To Anna R. Minsloff in Russia:

Berlin, November 16, 1908

My dear Fräulein Minsloff:

It is evident from your dear letters that you regard my visit to Russia as important just at this moment. Now you can rest assured that I am ready at any time to do everything possible in your affairs to promote the tasks we are serving. Even now I would be willing to overcome the difficulties if my journey to Russia would do any good. But the situation is such that, not only would it not help, but would *damage* our work if it were set out as it would presently have to be arranged. And the damage would be even greater because, at a later time, my journey would bring much advantage. We would deprive ourselves of this advantage, however, if we were to do now what would amount to no more than "splashing around in the water." There are many reasons that confirm this—first, and most essential: *The powers who watch over our spiritual movement indicate that it is the theosophical mission that has to commence its activities with you at a later date.* For in Russia this has to be founded on a well-proved scientific basis if it is not to remain unfruitful.

Secondly, my journey would only cause misunderstandings at the present time. It would cause misunderstandings especially in the Theosophical Society—where we have misunderstandings enough. It is true that in a not-too-distant future the Theosophical Society will be faced with a quite new situation. This situation would be adversely affected if my journey were arranged so that I gave lectures to those opposed to the founding of the Theosophical Section in Russia. We would then have everyone, even those in Adyar, against us. But for us it is the *thing itself* that matters, and we would harm this if we were to be regarded as opponents of the Russian Section. It would be necessary *now, even before* my arrival in Russia, for me to *insist* upon *all* the German members joining the Russian Section, to prevent damage being done to it. Then, if I were called upon by a group of members from the Russian Section, there would be no *outward* objection to my coming; *inwardly*, however, the present moment would remain the most unfavorable ever. Whether or not you join the Russian Section is something about which I shall *never* influence you. The relationship of you and your companions toward me will not be altered whether you are members of the German or the Russian Section. It is only of concern that you find the path appropriate to you, the thing *of importance.* And that consists in your case of preparing your theosophical affairs so they stand on a well-founded basis that avoids all theosophical dilettantism, and takes into consideration historical human development. In these matters you, my dear Fräulein Minsloff, have been led by all that you have done until now. It must, of course, be left to you as to how you stand toward the newly-founded Russian Section. The people in Adyar seem to think that I have been influencing you in your decisions, whereas you yourself discovered that *this* Section with *these* arrangements was incompatible with the Russian situation.

But, Section or no Section, things will run their course in the way they *must,* out of spiritual necessity. In all of your decisions you will always have to ask yourself: Does this course of action agree with the spiritual requirements? The times are too serious today for the mere abstractions presently favored in some theosophical circles.

Therefore, as stated, let the situation of the Theosophical Society be set straight also in Russia. Several things about to happen in the Theosophical Society will contribute to such a straightening out. Everything will turn out all right. This letter is for you *only.*

Most cordially and faithfully,

Yours, Dr. Rudolf Steiner

To (recipient and date unknown):

Most esteemed Herr Doctor:

With this I have copied for you what you can use, to begin with, for the purposes we spoke about. I would mention that a description of such exercises serves only to give a kind of direction; in following the exercises one gains a kind of practice out of oneself.

Under this supposition I may assume also that the sketchy outline will suffice, and that I leave nothing unclear.

With theosophical greetings,

Dr. Rudolf Steiner

Berlin W., Motzstrasse, 17

Enclosure.

Most esteemed Herr Doctor:

The following is to be advised for the aims we spoke of:

Evening: after completing all the day's work, so that no daily worries, and so on, intrude between these exercises and falling asleep; let the whole horizon of your consciousness be filled with a serious thought taken from your philosophy of life, summed up in a few syllables. For example, consider for several minutes the indwelling of the World-Soul in the human soul, so that concrete thoughts on the subject pass through your mind, and the whole contemplation has a devotional character. You do not just think the truths; you *sense* them, *feel* them. You sum it up in this way:

"World-Soul within the I."

You concentrate your whole mind on such a concept—which is thus the final result of a chain of thoughts and feelings; you fill yourself with this concept to the exclusion of all other thoughts, feelings, and perceptions.

Then allow your whole bodily frame to be filled with the concept by letting it slip down in thoughts from the head, through the body, into the feet and hands. (The whole to occupy about 10 minutes, not by the clock, but according to judgement.)

Position of the body, and so on, is not, in itself, important. It depends only on your assuming a position so that nothing can divert your attention.

The longer you can retain the aftereffects of the exercise in your mind—without any other thoughts (but within reason)—the better it is.

Morning: on waking, repeat the whole process.

You may continue the same exercise over many days—the best results are obtained if one has the patience to work on the same concept for weeks—then one varies it.

THE GENERAL RULES OF THE SCHOOL

In addition to these Rules see also: "General Demands (Subsidiary Exercises)" in *Guidance in Esoteric Training* to be included in CW 267

The Rules of the English School[121]

The Esoteric School

While the "three objects" of the TS are before the world, it has yet another object not thus proclaimed—to offer assistance in the development of the inner life to the more earnest and devoted of its members, to point out to them the road to the entrance of the "narrow, ancient way," and to give them such help as is congenial to their varying temperaments, when they deliberately elect to enter on a life devoted to life's higher purposes.

There is, in the long life of each individual, a point that is the turning point; at which the man turns aside from the ordinary prizes of earthly life, wealth, fame, power, and aspires to find himself. These things may still interest him, may still even attract him, but they no longer come first, and, if a conflict should arise, they would be sacrificed to the higher aim. To know, or to love, or to serve, to tread one of the three paths of Knowledge, Devotion, Service, has become the imperious necessity of the life to which all else must yield. The man is resolute to seek *first* "The Kingdom of God and Righteousness."

---

121. The "Rules" are from the original in English by Annie Besant.

To such earnest and sincere seekers the Esoteric School of Theosophy opens its gates, and it endeavors to suit its methods to their needs. To this end it offers at present three special methods, suited to fundamentally different temperaments, to which more can be added should the need arise, as well as a general method, which may be adopted by any who do not wish to specialize at the beginning, and which serves as a basis, on which a specialized discipline may later be built. There are, then, four ways before him: the General Discipline; the Christian Gnostic or Devotional Discipline; the Pythagorean or Intellectual and Artistic Discipline; the Karma or Action Discipline. The methods of seeking differ in each, but the end and object of each is the same—the realization of the Inner God. This is the true Wisdom, the true Gnosis; it is the direct knowledge of the Eternal by the unveiling of our own eternal nature, and that humankind *can* thus know is the essence of theosophy. By this unity of purpose they are bound into one Esoteric School, and the variety of method is intended to subserve the unity of purpose. The preservation of this unity is essential to the usefulness of the School; hence every member is expected, while naturally preferring his own method as being suited to his own temperament, to show respect and fraternal feeling to his fellow-worker in whom the Inner God is equally seeking manifestation. Only by such wide-minded tolerance can the unity of the School be maintained, while by its inclusiveness it adapts itself to the ever-extending area of the Theosophical Society.

The Esoteric School has two divisions. The first of these consists of a Probationary Order, the Hearers; the second of pledged members. Passage from one grade to the other depends on the progress made, and is decided by the Corresponding Secretary of the Division, aided by a report from the candidate's Sub-Warden.

No pledge is taken from the newcomer, beyond a promise to return his papers if required, and to regard them as private while in his possession and afterwards. A breach of this promise, if known on the physical plane, entails his exclusion, and, if not so known, bars his inner progress.

After two years in the Probationary Order, and after having shown himself to be sufficiently familiar with theosophic teaching, the member may be allowed to take the Pledge of the School. To gain this privilege the member must have shown earnestness and devotion in study and in practice, rendering him worthy to become a pledged member; and he must be recommended by his Sub-Warden to the Corresponding Secretary.

The Pledge must not be taken until the member has been in the Probationary Order for at least two years, but he may remain in the Order after taking it, and must remain in it unless he is ready for the studies of the next grade. Permission to take the Pledge implies a standard of character, as well as attainment in knowledge and in meditation, and pledged members are allowed to attend certain meetings of the School from which the unpledged are excluded.

Each Discipline is entered by way of a probation intended to enable the candidate to judge of the suitability of one of the methods to his temperament. The details of methods are to be found in the following pages, which give the directions for each. These papers are left in the hands of candidates for six months, during which time they can study the general and specialized methods, examine the courses of reading and meditation, and decide on the path they desire to follow. The candidate should devote a month to the steady daily practice of each Discipline, and carefully note its reaction on himself, mentally, emotionally, and physically. This will occupy four months of his candidature. The fifth and sixth should be spent in the polishing of the rough work of the preceding months, and the careful deciding on the method to be followed.

During this time applicants are regarded as enrolled in the Class of Candidates in the Probationary Order. They may participate in the meeting of any Group the Sub-Warden of which is willing to admit them. Information as to Group Meetings may be obtained from the corresponding Secretary.

At the end of six months the candidate may select the Discipline he wishes to enter, and may apply to the Corresponding Secretary for admission. He will then be called on to write out and sign the following promise:

I promise to show to no one outside the ES any of the papers of the Probationary Order of Hearers of the ES, and to observe the Rules of the ... Discipline, which I now enter. I further promise to return to the Outer Head of the School, or her agent, on demand, any papers I have received or shall receive.

Name..
Address..
Date..

This candidate must state:
Age..
Religion..
Caste, Church or Sect (if any).............................
Married or Single..

The papers of the Order are in common, but the student must follow in his meditation that given for his Discipline, and must observe its proper rules. He may add to these any that suit himself, but he may not omit any.

At the end of his two years in the Probationary Order, he may change his Discipline; but in that case he must begin again, and spend another twelve months in his newly selected Discipline, before he can pass into the First Degree, or be eligible to take the pledge of the School; he must also obtain a recommendation from the Secretary of the Discipline he is leaving.

The general outlines of method will be found in the Rules of the respective probationary Disciplines, each following the path indicated in its Rules, with additional details and amplifications as progress is made. Speaking very generally: the General Discipline follows the old Hindu and Buddhist method of a discipline of the body by rules of diet, of the emotions by deliberate culture, of the mind by stated organized meditation, leading on to the practice of yoga; the Christian Gnostic or devotional Discipline guides its Disciples to illumination by prayer, devotional meditation, self-examination, study and occasional fasting; the Pythagorean Discipline educates by silence, brooding meditation, contemplation of the Good and the Beautiful, deep study of Ideas, the true "mathematics and music"; the Karma or Action Discipline demands regularized self-sacrifice and strenuous, unselfish work, training the will to subordination and co-operation and the body to alert service. They all form a single Path in main principles, with difference in details. Needless to say that the deep teaching is only given by the individual Teacher to the individual pupil, and that the help to be given in the School prepares for the Probationary Path.

Rules of the General (Raja-Yoga) Discipline[122]

1. Every pupil should rise at a fixed hour (consistent with health and with family obligations), and, after bathing, should sit for meditation, before taking any food.

2. Every pupil must give a quarter of an hour to meditation on the lines laid down; he must recite at noon the sentence that will be taught him; and he must spend ten minutes, ere retiring to rest, in reviewing the day.

3. Every pupil must spend half an hour a day in the study of a book selected from the appended list.

4. Every pupil must belong to a local Group, or must be attached to such a Group by correspondence. The Group is in the charge of a Sub-Warden.

5. The Groups shall meet at fixed times, and local members must attend regularly, and in case of unavoidable absence must send a written excuse. A record of attendances shall be kept by the Sub-Warden. Corresponding members must be put in touch with a member attending the local Group.

6. Every pupil must keep a daily note of his observance of Rules 2 and 3, and must send or hand to the Sub-Warden on the first

---

122. Copy of Annie Besant's original in English.

Group meeting of the month a written statement that he has observed the rules, or, in case of any failure, that he has fallen into such and such an omission, with the reason thereof. Negligent pupils, after three warnings, will be required to return their papers, and will cease to be members of the School.

7. As to diet: The use of wines, spirits, liquors of any kind, or any narcotic or intoxicating drug, is prohibited, unless ordered by a doctor. If indulged in, progress is hindered and the efforts of teacher and pupil alike are rendered useless. All such substances have a directly pernicious action on the brain, and especially upon the pineal gland.

8. The eating of meat is not prohibited, but if the student can maintain health without it, he is recommended to do so. The eating of meat strengthens the passional nature, and the desire to acquire possessions, and therefore increases the difficulty of the struggle with the lower nature. Changes in diet must be made with caution.

9. The Hearer must satisfy his Sub-Warden of his adequate knowledge of two of the books laid down for study, before he can pass into pledged membership.

Business Rules

1. The receipt of all papers must be promptly acknowledged. The word "received" on a postcard, with initials of pupil subjoined, is sufficient.

2. *Pupils should keep all papers in a locked box used for no other purpose, and should make provision for the forwarding of this box to the Secretary of their Discipline in case of death; they must notify the Sub-Warden of their Group of the arrangements made.*

3. Anyone who wishes to retire from the Discipline can have his name removed from the list of members by applying in writing to the Secretary of the Discipline, and signifying the Discipline to which he wishes to be transferred.

4. Any member who leaves the Order must notify the Secretary of the Discipline, and return all papers relating thereto.

5. Any change of address must be at once sent to the Secretary of the Discipline, and notified to the Sub-Warden of the local Group.

Daily Practice

The Hearer should remind himself daily that he is setting before himself as his immediate object in life the entering on the Probationary Path. To this end he aims at gaining control of his mind and purifying his life. Thrice a day at least he should call in the inconstant mind and fix it on his ideal; these fixed points should be: Morning meditation, noon, ere retiring to rest.

Meditation: Sit cross-legged on the floor, or sit on a low chair with the two hands palms downwards on the two knees. The back should be erect, not sloped; the eyes closed. Recite slowly the verse committed to memory the previous evening; think over it, trying to reach its full meaning, and do not let the mind wander away to something else; if it runs away, bring it back and fix it again on the verse. Spend five minutes in this practice. Then turn your thoughts to the Supreme Self, as God around you and within you, and think intensely that you are one with Him; say:

> More radiant than the Sun,
> Purer than the Snow,
> Subtler than the Ether is the Self,
> The Spirit within my heart.
> I am that Self.
> That Self am I.

Five minutes should be given to this. Then think of the Perfect Human being, the Master, as showing forth the love and beauty of God; think of him as embodying the virtue of the month. Suppose the virtue be Compassion, think how this would show itself in conduct, and conclude this by the earnest wish: "May I, by becoming compassionate to all, prepare myself to be a disciple of Him who is Compassion." Five minutes should be spent in this part of meditation. If half an hour can be given to meditation, each of these periods can be doubled.

Noon: Collect your thoughts at noon, and fix your mind on the idea that you are not your body nor your mind, but the Spiritual Human being. Repeat: "More radiant than the Sun," etc.

Before retiring to rest: Review the day, especially with regard to your thoughts, your desires, and the effect of your conduct on the welfare of those around you. Commit to memory the verse for the following morning's meditation.

Pledge of the School

I pledge myself to endeavor to make theosophy a living power in my life, and to support the theosophical movement before the world.

I pledge myself to maintain a constant struggle against my lower nature, to abstain from untruthful and injurious speech, and to be charitable to the weaknesses of others.

I pledge myself to do all in my power, by study and otherwise, to fit myself to help and teach others.

To all this I pledge my word of honor, invoking my Higher Self.

Name..

. . . . . .

The First Rules Given by Rudolf Steiner in 1904

An enclosure from a letter sent to Amalie Wagner on August 2, 1904
(The original handwritten document is not available.):

Confidential
EST [Esoteric School of Theosophy]
Order of the Shrâvakas
Meditation by instruction of the Outer Head of the School

I. *Rules*

1. Every morning, if possible before partaking of a meal, a meditation should be taken up. The way it is done should be determined by the Arch-Warden.

2. In the evening before retiring to rest, a sentence prescribed by the Arch-Warden should be inwardly repeated in one's thoughts, and thereafter a short retrospect of the day's events should be taken up.

3. Every day a quarter of an hour should be devoted to the study of a book chosen by the Directors of the School.

4. Every fourteen days a short report should be given to the Arch-Warden to confirm that the daily exercises have been accomplished and, in cases where this has not happened, to state the reasons.

5. The Shrâvaka should possess a notebook where one notes daily fulfillment of the exercises.

6. The partaking of any kind of alcoholic drink is forbidden to the Shrâvakas, because this would be harmful to the brain, and especially to the organ connected with spiritual insight. The contravention of this rule would render all the efforts of both teacher and pupil ineffective. The only exception to this rule is when the taking of alcohol is prescribed by a doctor.

7. Abstention from the eating of meat is not compulsory, but it is pointed out that a vegetarian diet will help in the struggle against one's lower nature. Changes of diet must be undertaken with the greatest caution.

II. *Business Rules*

1. Receipt of papers, and so on, to be notified.
2. Papers to be kept in a locked chest, and so on.
3. To be returned on resignation from ES.
4. Change of address to be notified.

III. *Pledge*

(This pledge must be copied by hand, signed with the full name and address and forwarded to the Arch-Warden.)

I give my word of honor that I have carefully read the Rules of the Order and shall endeavor to keep to them strictly. I also promise that I will not divulge the contents of any books or papers marked "Confidential" by the Head of the EST to anyone who does not belong to the School.

Furthermore, I promise to return all papers to the Directors of the School on demand.

Age _____ Name _____

Religion _____ Address _____

. . . . . .

Handwritten enclosure from a letter to Michael Bauer August 14, 1904.
The title page bore the inscription:

Confidential
By instruction of the Head of the School EST

Rules of the Shrâvaka Order

1. Every member must undertake a *meditation* at a certain time during the morning (insofar as this is compatible with the member's state of health and duties), and this should take place before any nourishment has been taken.

2. Every member should spend a quarter of an hour in meditation before retiring to rest. This should be done in the following way: a) Thoughts should be raised to one's Higher Self by quietly bringing to mind a certain definite sentence; b) A review of the experiences and events of the day should be made in retrospect.

3. Every member should spend half an hour a day in studying a serious book chosen by the school.

4. Every member should acquire a notebook in which to note— quite briefly—that meditation has been taken up and, should this have been neglected, to state the reason why. A progress report should be made every fourteen days to the leader of the Group concerned. Negligent members will be excluded from the Group after being warned three times and they will be required to return their papers.

5. Members must abstain from all alcoholic beverages, except where these are ordered by a doctor. Such beverages have a harmful effect on the brain, and especially on the organs that promote the development of spiritual life.

   The eating of meat is not prohibited, but one is advised to abstain from eating meat, because the struggle against one's lower nature is thereby made easier.

*Draft of what was presumably used for the first hectographed copy of Rules
1904. Taken from two handwritten pages with a cover. Archive number
3023-25. The cover bears the inscription:*

Confidential. In the name of the Head of the School. Shrâvaka
Order of the EST Rules. Communicated by Dr. Rudolf Steiner,
Arch-Warden of the EST for Germany, Austria and German-speaking Switzerland.

1. Each pupil is obliged, upon rising, to accomplish a meditation,
   at a time (determined by himself) consistent with his health and
   family commitments, after first washing and before taking nourishment.
2. The pupil must devote as much time to this meditation as necessary to accomplish it intensively and without disturbance (about
   15 minutes on average).
3. The pupil must devote a few minutes to a review of the day,
   before falling asleep.
4. The pupil must work with study material as prescribed by the
   School.
5. The pupil must keep a diary in which is noted day by day the satisfaction felt concerning adherence to rules 1, 2, and 3.
6. The pupil must become attached to a group, along with other
   members of the School, when required by the Leader of the
   School.[123]
7. The taking of alcohol is strictly forbidden, since, according to
   occult experience, to partake of alcohol damages the spiritual
   organs and renders the efforts of pupil and teacher of no avail.
   An exception could be made only on the orders of a doctor.
8. The eating of meat is not forbidden; nevertheless the pupil will
   find that a meat-free diet will make the struggle against one's
   lower principles easier.

---

123. Regional Groups, under the leadership of a Sub-Warden, also existed while
Rudolf Steiner was in charge. For example, in Nuremberg under the guidance
of Michael Bauer (see Steiner's letter to him on August 4, 1907, p. 93), and in
Stuttgart under Adolf Arenson, who, according to his certificate, was appointed
by Steiner in 1906, and also held meetings.

Vertraulich.

Im Namen der Häupter der Schule.

Shrâvaka - Orden

der

E. S. T.

Regeln.

Herrn Dr. Unger übergeben durch

Dr. Rudolf Steiner

Arch-Warden der E. S. T. für

Deutschland, Oesterr. Ungarn und

die deutsche Schweiz.

Facsimile of first page of the handwritten rules sent personally to Carl Unger in Stuttgart. Archive number 6851-53. The text is followed by the meditation (as in the circular letter of June 5, 1905) with the instructions "beginning on December 14, 1904."

First reproduced circular letter sent out on June 5, 1905.[124]
On seven undated handwritten pages (Archive Number 4407.13).
The title page bears the following inscription:

Confidential. First Rules of the Esoteric School of the TS.
By Instruction of the Head of the School.

The Esoteric School of Theosophy

While the "three objects" of the Theosophical Society are before the world, it has another object not thus proclaimed: to offer assistance in the development of the inner life to the more earnest and devoted of its members; to point out to them the road to the entrance onto the "narrow, ancient way," which leads them to the higher regions of existence.

Because of this aim, the Esoteric School constitutes the heart of the Theosophical Society.

The Esoteric School is divided into separate classes. The first consists of a Probationary Order, the Hearers; the next is the First Class, after that the Second Class, and so on.

A new member is accepted into the Probationary Order. To begin with, no pledge is taken beyond a promise to return any papers as required, and to regard them as private, only to be spoken of to members of the School.

A description of further arrangements within the School will be imparted to the new entrants in the course of the next three weeks.

Only the immediate tasks confronting candidates on the pathway of their trials leading to the goal can be discussed here. Initially, these instructions are valid for the first couple of months. After that period further instruction will be sent. One must spend at least twelve months in the Probationary Order. After that the candidate may be admitted into the First Class.

---

124. Entry in notebook (Archive Number 124): "June 5, 1905 Esoteric News 1 sent to eight members."

The goal of the Probationary Order can be attained, to begin with, through the observation of a "daily rule." It consists of the following:

The School Member shall rise at a fixed time and undertake a meditation before having eaten. The time that this takes place is not fixed by the School. It must be determined by each person separately, but must then be strictly adhered to. Only by means of a regular (rhythmic) ordering of this life can members adapt to the rhythm of the cosmos and thus reproduce within themselves the divine laws of the universe. In this reproduction of the universal laws, however, lies the possibility of attaining to higher existence.

1. The morning meditation commences with the probationary candidate seeking to establish complete inner control, so that during the time one is thus engaged, nothing in the surroundings is seen or heard, and nothing pertaining to everyday life remains in the thinking. To begin with, during such a time of inner quiet, one should direct thoughts toward the Divine in the universe. And then one must come to an inner understanding that one's own inner being is at one with this universe. To this end one should inwardly repeat the following words in complete inner concentration of soul. These words should not merely appeal to the understanding, but to the whole human being; they must become a thoroughgoing inner experience:[125]

> More radiant than the Sun,
> Purer than snow,
> Finer than the ether
> Is the Self,
> The Spirit in my heart.
> This Self am I.
> I am this Self.

---

125. The explanation for this meditation given in the Esoteric Class in Berlin on October 24, 1905 can be found in *Guidance in Esoteric Training: From the Esoteric School*, pp. 83–86.

2. After concluding the foregoing one concentrates on a sentence from *Light on the Path,* namely, during the first fourteen days, on the sentence:

> *"Before the eyes can see they must be incapable of tears."*

During the following fourteen days:

> *"Before the ear can hear it must have lost its sensitiveness."*[126]

The following fourteen days:

> *"Before the voice can speak in the presence of the Masters it must have lost the power to wound."*

During the following fourteen days:

> *"Before the soul can stand in the presence of the Masters its feet must be washed in the blood of the heart."*

It is not a matter here of speculating about these sentences, but of *living* with them for a few minutes, immersing oneself in them in a loving way.

3. After this has been accomplished, pupils should direct their thoughts to what each holds as Divine. They must devote themselves in *complete reverence* to this Divinity. This third section should constitute a kind of devotional *mood of soul,* toward what one acknowledges as God.

The whole meditation should last about 15 minutes. It must be strictly observed that one remains completely *awake* during the meditation and does not fall into a hazy state of consciousness.

---

126. In a communication of January 29 contained in the section, "Individually-given Exercises," Rudolf Steiner points out that "sensitiveness" here means "touchiness," or "to take things personally."

---

4. In the evening, before retiring to rest, a review should be made of the day's events. One asks oneself what *experiences* have been made and what has been gained thereby, and if one could have done better in one's actions. Thus one becomes an objective *judge* of oneself. One must not have regrets. That would be of no value for oneself or for the world. But one should *learn* every day from past events and make use of it for the future, thus making an object lesson of life. All evolution consists of this. The review is conducted in such a way that one starts with the events that happened last in the evening and progresses backwards to the events of the morning.

---

5. One should keep a diary where one enters each day a few words concerning the progress of the morning and evening meditations, and which can provide information about this to the Leader of the School when required.

6. The partaking of alcohol is incompatible with the aims of meditation.

7. The abstention from eating meat is *not* statutory but is recommended, because it works beneficially toward furthering the aims of the Esoteric School.

Further information in the next three weeks.[127]

---

127. Nothing is known about this.

Second circular letter of Rules sent to all esoteric pupils from a handwritten original:

Berlin, October 17, 1906

Confidential!

The following is transmitted with the best of greetings, "in spirit and in truth" to all who have come to me for guidance in esoteric training.[128]

This communication contains things that everyone intent on undergoing esoteric training should observe as a matter of duty. These are not part of the actual meditation, but should be practiced in addition. The matter is to be interpreted in such a way that the esoteric schooling is *justified* only for pupils who take these obligations upon themselves. Only then can success be assured.

At the same time it must be pointed out that patience is required for esoteric training. No one need imagine that success will be greater if one yearns for or demands new exercises. Everyone should stay energetically with the exercises given, and practice these again and again until new ones are received. No one who *really* needs something will be passed over at the appropriate time. Much depends on whether or not such patience is practiced.

Whatever irregularities pupils imagine—or think they imagine— in their state of body or soul as a result of these exercises, they should report to me at once. The same is true of anything they require as advice or moral support.

Further necessary dispatches will follow at the correct time. If everything is observed in the right way the Masters of Truth will guide the pupil on his path.

In this sense

Dr. Rudolf Steiner

Berlin, Motzstrasse, 17

---

128. The so-called "subsidiary exercises," see *Guidance in Esoteric Training.*

Supplement

The following documents seem to be drafts of a tract relating to the Esoteric School that, however, was never completed:

Undated handwritten copy—Archive number 3220:

1. The School speaks: Alluding to the fact that human beings can*not* discover the self in the world of the senses.
2. The School speaks of the world of perception as a world made visible through a spirit messenger.
3. The School speaks of words that have been forged by the Spirit.
4. The School shows how human beings have to overcome the opponents of knowledge within the self.

Undated handwritten copy. Archive number 3196/97:

Before the Gates of the School

Teacher: What do you want from me?

Pupil: I wish to test everything and retain the best.

Teacher: Then there is nothing for you to seek in *this* School, for you are already aware of the standard of what is best.

In the Preparatory School

I.

Teacher: What do you want from me?

Pupil: I strive after truth.

Teacher: Then let yourself be tested by the truth. It will retain what is best in you.

II.

Teacher. What have you learned?

Pupil: I have learned to let myself be judged by truth.

Teacher. Then you know what humility is: practice it until it is entirely yours.

Question:

You are striving after self-knowledge? Will your so-called Self be of any greater significance to the world tomorrow when you have gained knowledge of it?

First Answer:

No: if you are no different tomorrow than you are today, and if tomorrow your knowledge only recapitulates the state in which you find yourself today.

Second Answer:

Yes: if you are a different person tomorrow than you are today, and if that new state in which you find yourself tomorrow is the result of your knowledge of today.

Theosophy is the knowledge of the divine Self in humankind; but many believe themselves to be theosophists who regard their own small ego as divine.

Self-knowledge is in many cases no more than egoistic self-reflection. Many theosophists imagine they can recognize the divine Self within themselves; they merely confuse their own small human self, however, with the divine Self.

———————————

You merely seek the *Master* within yourself, not in the other person; how deeply you are steeped in separateness! Do you not know that the Leader's self is *your* self?

———————————

It is said that the Masters are to be found *everywhere*, that is certainly correct—if you, however, are *nowhere* then you cannot find them in the "everywhere."

Concerning the Hierarchy of the Adepts

Undated handwritten copy. Archive number 3207/08:

Since the Root-Race of the Hierarchy of the Adepts came down to Earth, and the Sons of the Fire-Mists descended to Earth as the teachers of human beings, there was never a time when the Earth lacked teachers, nor was there ever a link missing in the sacred chain beginning with the One who is Nameless—the Great Initiator—and ending with the lowliest of pupils who pay allegiance to the Great Lodge in one of the prescribed ways. The last section of the Hierarchy, which started from the Great Initiates, came from the ranks of the scholars of the sacred science. And these are recognized as pupils when they enter the School and are admitted to the path of trial. Then they receive the initial instructions whereby they can take the first steps.

Today as you enter a School such as this as an enrolled member, the gateway leading to the path of trial hovers over you and closes; we welcome you here within in the name of the Masters who have vouchsafed the way that you may enter this Temple where true initiation is imparted, and to which you must direct your heart and your thoughts daily. For your entry here would be of no avail if this in itself did not constitute the first step along the path of trial. And of what use is it to tread a path that one does not then follow to the end? There is no difficulty in such circumstances that you yourself do not cause; there is no obstacle that the God within you is unable to surmount.

Listen to what our Master says:

Behold the Truth before you: A clean life, an open mind, a pure heart, an eager intellect, an unveiled spiritual perception, a brotherliness for one's co-disciple, a readiness to give and receive advice and instruction, a loyal sense of duty to the Teacher, a willing obedience to the behests of *Truth*, once we have placed our confidence in, and believe that Teacher to be in possession of it; a courageous endurance of personal injustice, a brave declaration of principles, a valiant defense of those who are unjustly attacked, and a constant eye to the ideal of human progression and perfection that the secret science (*Guptâ Vidyâ*) depicts—these are the golden stairs up which the student may climb to the Temple of Divine Wisdom. Say this to those who have volunteered to be taught by you.

Conversation between Master and Pupil[129]

Sketch from a Notebook from 1906. Archive number 488:

The pupil addresses the *Master:*

What is the way to life in the realms of the supersensible where spirits are creative and souls have awareness?

The *Master* speaks:

If you can remain for a while in the place where you are untouched by any dependent being, then do you stand within spirit-creation; if you can remain awhile where no perceptual senses speak to you, then you become aware through the power of the soul.

---

129. Among notes left by a participant of the ES Class in Berlin on June 5, 1908, is this conversation that derives from *The Original Book of the Rosicrucian School.* See *Guidance in Esoteric Training.*

The pupil addresses the *Master:*

Where then is the place to which I am directed?

The *Master* speaks:

The place is within your I; but you will discover it only if you abandon *your* I, if *your* willing becomes silent, and *your* contemplation extinguished; the "I will" speaks and the "I think" awakens to life.

The pupil addresses the *Master:*

How may I speak the "I will" if my willing is silent; how may I awaken the "I think" if my contemplation is extinguished?

The *Master* speaks:

Only the willing that *you* do not will reveals the I; only the thought that *you* do not think proclaims the Spirit.

INDIVIDUALLY-GIVEN EXERCISES

A FEW EXAMPLES

Most of the numerous personal exercises can be put into matching categories, the most basic of which have already been included in *Guidance in Esoteric Training: From the Esoteric School.* Exercises of a different character can be found in the following Section.

Concerning the Essential Purpose of the Exercises

Written for Professor Dr. Hans Wohlbold, Munich, in 1917.
(The handwritten original is not available):

The essential purpose of the exercises is to develop an activity of imagination capable of converting spiritual reality into knowledge. The essential thing is that this imaginative activity be experienced independently of the physical organism. Experience will teach us how we have to think, and so on, without allowing the ordinary requirements of bodily-conceived notions to interfere in it. The moment this comes about will be revealed while doing the exercises. I would particularly advise:

1. In the evening a retrospective review of the day's events. Through this a first step is made toward forming concepts not commensurable with how concepts are ordinarily formed. Concept-forming becomes freer.

2. Concentration, with complete self-composure, on a short theme for contemplation. The latter should be *entirely comprehensible,* so that no unconscious or semiconscious associated ideas are allowed

to mix with it, but one remains wrapped in constant awareness of one's own spiritual activity. Then one drops the thought content from consciousness and seeks to retain the energy and maintain consciousness without a thought content for a short time. In this way one converts the ability to know into that calm energy needed if one would grasp the spirit that would otherwise escape, so to speak, through the mesh of ordinary thinking, thereby eluding consciousness.

I suggest exercises 1 and 2 for the evening:
In the morning it would be good to perform an exercise of thought concentration similar to exercise number 2. For this a pictured concept such as the Rosicrucian exercise described in principle in the second part of my book, *An Outline of Esoteric Science*, would serve admirably.

To acquire the necessary self-composure for the concentration of one's thoughts, it would be good to perform the six exercises (as auxiliary exercises) described in the second part of *An Outline of Esoteric Science*.

The reason for doing these exercises is partly to develop a stronger soul-activity than is normal. As the quantitative value in the world of physics can turn into a qualitative one by a natural process at a critical stage, so also the enhancement of the normal cognitive faculties can turn them into a faculty directed toward the spiritual world.

Exercise for Adolf Arenson, given at the beginning of April 1904
in Stuttgart. Handwritten document. Archive Numbers 5299, 5300, 5301:

1. Take up a daily review of what one's personality has encountered during the day. Place before oneself the most important happenings of the day and one's response to them. This must all take place from the viewpoint of wanting to *learn* from life: How can I improve on what I did today? These are the sort of questions to ask oneself. One does not thereby blunt one's reactions toward joy and

sorrow. On the contrary. One's sensitivity increases. But one does not cling to worry and remorse over what has been done, but transforms it into a resolution to do better in the future. One becomes the architect of one's own soul. Just as architects do not sit down and lament ruefully that the houses they have built are not better than they are, but make use of the experience they have gained in building the inferior houses in the possible construction of others—so also must people act toward themselves. Our personality perishes through worry and remorse, it is raised up by learning. Worry and remorse serve no purpose. The time we spend on them should be used to advance ourselves. The whole exercise need only take three to four minutes. Then one falls asleep, having acquired a portion of Manas, which possesses within itself a power to lead the soul upward. If one can add to this a good resolution for one's life or a good thought for a fellow human being, that would be particularly favorable. Thereby one becomes gradually changed, because during sleep one has added to the Manas a worthy content, free of all restrictions of one's personality, a content that will benefit human evolution.

2. In the morning, as one's first piece of mental activity:
 a) One rises to one's own higher self through complete surrender to the words:
>   *"I am the living impulse within my sheaths.*
>   *My higher self is as pure as the purest crystal."*

 b) One concentrates with complete absorption on an elevated thought. Best of all would be the meditation occurring in the third chapter of the *Bhagavad-Gita*, Karma Yoga, from the third verse on:
>   *"As I told thee before..."*

Always just *one verse*. One stays with one verse for fourteen days, after which one takes the next, and so on. In this exercise—as in the previous one where one rises to one's higher being—the field of vision that presents itself to our consciousness must be absolutely *pure*. *All* other thoughts must be *completely* banished from the mind. If any other thought arises it must be rejected powerfully.

c) One creates a devotional mood toward all that one considers most holy (The All-Creative Principle, God, and so on, according to one's personal attitude, and what one has learned to call and to value as the highest.)
For the morning meditation 8–10 minutes.

Patience and persistence and complete seriousness are absolutely necessary. One must place oneself in a frame of mind where the need for meditation is just as naturally acute as are physical needs to the body. One then waits to receive—everyone will receive at the right time.

The commencement can begin immediately, on April 16 (not earlier), then again on May 16.

Handwritten exercise. Number 3105/06 in the Archive:

Morning Meditation

1. More radiant than the Sun,
   Purer than Snow,
   Finer than the Ether
   Is Selfhood   *5 minutes*
   The Spirit in my Heart.
   This Selfhood am *I*.
   I *am* this Selfhood.

2. Inhalation: *Seek out the way* (deep and calm) — 1 length

   Holding the breath: *Seek the way by retreating within* — 3 lengths

   Exhalation: *Seek the way by advancing boldly without* (not in jerks) — 2 lengths

   3 times — 5 min.

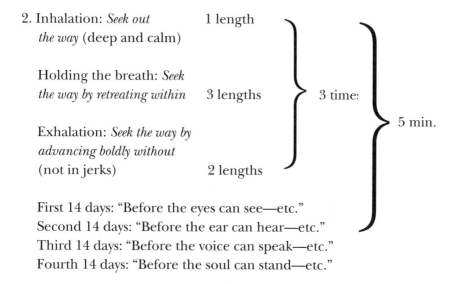

First 14 days: "Before the eyes can see—etc."
Second 14 days: "Before the ear can hear—etc."
Third 14 days: "Before the voice can speak—etc."
Fourth 14 days: "Before the soul can stand—etc."

3. Devotional surrender to one's own divine ideal. 5 minutes.

   To finish:
   > First Month: self-confidence
   > Second Month: self-control
   > Third Month: presence of mind
   > Fourth Month: inner activity

Evenings

Retrospect of the day:
> Regarding an experience:
> Have I learned sufficiently from it?
> Regarding an action:
> How can I improve on it?

Without regret. Merely with the intention of learning from life, backward from evening to morning.

With no alcohol.

Handwritten exercise, Archive number 3107:

Mornings

I.

More radiant than the Sun,
Purer than Snow,
Finer than the Ether
Is Selfhood,
The Spirit in my Heart.
This Selfhood am I.
I am this Selfhood.

Complete alertness.

II.

Direct the thoughts to the left hand and the heart and form the concept:
Seek out the way.

Next pause at the heart and think:
Seek the way by retreating within.

Next think about the right hand and lay it over the left, while conceiving in one's mind:
Seek out the way by advancing boldly without.

III.

Immerse oneself in devotion into what one conceives of as a divine ideal.

Evenings

Retrospect of the day.
No regrets.
From evening till morning, in reverse.
During this one may fall asleep!

Exercise from a notebook Archive number 105, February 16, 1906:

1. More radiant, etc.

2. Inhalation, exhalation, holding the breath.
   I am, permeating the whole body.
   This must be performed *3 times* in succession, whereby the *I am* actually accompanies the whole process.

   Inhalation, exhalation, holding the breath.
   It—in which   is really I —
   This also

   Inhalation, holding the breath, exhalation.
   Inwardness is

3. The currents within the body —

Then, after the meditation, a lapsing into contemplation and allowing the following figures to work upon one:

Fig. 1: What is "disappearing into oneself" and out of this "disappearing" to arise anew?

Fig. 2: How does the point become a circle, and how does the circle become a point?

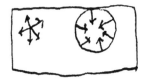

Fig. 3: What is interior, what is exterior? What is above, what is below? What is matter, what is Spirit? What is physical matter, what is ether?

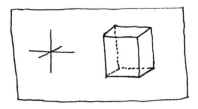

Fig. 4: What is the Astral?

Fig. 5: How do the spirits who create sensitivity act upon what manifests in matter?

Fig. 6: How does the "turning point" of evolution come about (Involution-Evolution)? Picture to yourself that the lines represented here are made of fish-bone, but under such tension, that at every moment the power they exert resists their position.

Exercise: Handwritten Archive document number 3187/88

Evenings

Begin with a retrospective review of the day's events; bring to mind single episodes of these events. In reverse order, from evening to morning. This only need last 5–7 minutes.

Then, with the experience "Out of the Spirit-World my self flows down to me" concentrate one's thoughts on the center between the eyebrows and direct toward it the words:

"I am"

Then, with the experience "The Spirit-World ensouls the silent Word" concentrate one's thoughts on the larynx, and toward it direct the words:

"It thinks"

Then, with the experience "The Spirit-World creates its own wisdom" concentrate one's thoughts on the heart, arms and hands and direct toward this part of the body the words:

"She feels"

Then, with experience "In me the Spirit-World comes to the realization of itself" concentrate one's thoughts on the aura, which can be thought of as enclosing the body in an oval sheath, and into this region direct the words:

"He will"

The meditation should last 10–15 minutes.

Mornings

The meditation on the Rose-Cross as described in An Outline of Esoteric Science.

Apart from the foregoing the 6 auxiliary exercises.

Exercise: Handwritten Archive Document number 6860/62:
With note from end of August 1906, Stuttgart:

One immerses oneself completely in the concept:
"Impersonal Higher Self"

It does not depend on visualizing ideas formed by someone else, but on producing the best concept of the "higher self" one is presently capable of doing.

One regards the concept as though placing it into the inner part of the head, near to where the pineal gland is situated. One centers consciousness here for awhile and completely fills it with the concept "Impersonal higher self." For awhile, therefore, one imagines one's whole being concentrated in the pineal gland and identifies oneself with this concept. Everything else is banished from consciousness.

After continuing in this way for a while, the above concept is transferred slowly from the region of the pineal gland in a line toward the top of the spinal column, near its connection to the brain. Then it is transferred again downward in line with the spinal column to a point that is designated *kundalini*. After visualizing the *kundalini fire* (spiritual fire) permeating the above concept, it is transferred slowly upward again along the spinal column to a point in the inner part of the head near to the cerebellum. Next, one transfers the concept "Impersonal higher self" in two lines toward the two eyes, and it is allowed to stream out from there into infinite space. It is then drawn back through the eyes and into the point near the cerebellum again. This is repeated while the concept is caused to flow from there to the two ears, allowing it to stream through them into infinite space. It is then withdrawn again through the ears to the original point near the cerebellum.

When one has imagined in this way that one has twice directed the concept "Impersonal higher self" through space, and has filled it with the content pertaining to it, one then leads it back, thus enriched, from the cerebellum along the spinal column to the kundalini, permeating it there with spiritual fire in imagination, and directing it *very slowly* to the point in the neck level with the larynx (indeed, so slowly that the transit from the kundalini to this point in the neck takes about 20 minutes). From this point one now thinks intensively:

"I am not you."

I, the concept of the higher self, according to all the processes it has undergone in the above manner.

You, the ordinary self, with which one does not identify at the present moment.

Exercise: Handwritten Archive Document number 3192:

Christian Gnostic Meditation

1. In the early morning, immediately upon waking, before any other impressions have passed through the soul, one attempts to clear the mind of all memories connected with daily life. One seeks to divert one's attention from all outward perceptions. Then, when one has attained this inner calm, one allows one's whole inner being to be completely filled with:

    The first 5 verses of the Gospel of Saint John —

2. Following this, every day during the next fourteen days, one attempts to portray to oneself the whole of one's past life, in order to gain a complete self-knowledge.

    At the end fourteen days, one goes through the whole of Saint John's Gospel, so that every day for a week one dwells on one chapter.

    Therefore, during the first seven days:
    John 1: 6 to the end.

    And during the second week:
    Chapter 2, and so on.

When one has arrived at the 13th chapter, one tries to experience:

The washing of the feet — how every higher being is indebted to lower beings for its existence, and is obliged to bow in humility to them.

The scourging — how one must stand erect in face of the scourgings of life—that is, in the face of all sorrow and pain.

The crowning with thorns — how one must stand erect even in the face of scorn and derision.

The crucifixion — how one's own body is something alien needing to be borne, and to which one is bound fast.

The mystic death — one experiences the veil that shrouds the spirit world, but then how it is torn asunder, allowing one to catch a glimpse of the spirit world.

At the same time one makes the acquaintance of the basis of wickedness and evil and experiences the descent into hell.

The laying in the grave — one identifies with all beings on Earth and with the Earth itself. One is immersed in the Earth.

The resurrection — can only come as an experience, because ordinary spoken words cannot adequately express it.

3. Then one pictures to oneself the figure of Christ Jesus, and proceeds to ponder at length the concept:
I Within Your Spirit

Evenings: Retrospect of the whole day's events.

1 and 3 are the same every day; only 2 changes every week, as has been described.

When the complete sequence of exercise 2 has been accomplished one starts again at the beginning, and so on indefinitely. After a longer period one is able to experience the inner and outer *symptoms* which are described in accounts of the development of Christianity.

Outwardly	*Inwardly*
One feels as if the feet were immersed in water.	One has the vision of oneself performing the washing of the feet.
One experiences a burning over the whole of one's skin.	One sees oneself scourged.
One experiences a feeling of pain in one's head.	One sees oneself crowned with thorns.
The stigmata redden during meditation.	One sees oneself crucified.

Exercise with the image of the Rose-Cross.
Handwritten document. Archive number 3229:

Evenings:

1. Retrospect. Vivid. In reverse.

2. Seek thou, my soul,
   Pondering musingly in thy depths;
   On thy foundation rests thy spirit;
   Within thy spirit stirs the World Spirit.
   I am in all of this
   thinking   feeling
        living.

   (peace of soul).

Mornings:

> In you, rune of worlds
> I view
> The sevenfold weaving of the spirit
> In the seven rose-stars
> Of life's dark pathways
> In the Cross's blackened wood
> I am in all this.
>
> (peace of soul).

Exercise. Handwritten document. Archive number 3236/37/38:

Mornings:
Concentrate on a line
running through the body thus:

The line does not
go down the spinal cord,
but runs through the body
somewhat in *front* of it.

Next meditate the content of the following words:

> *Warming light streams into me from above*
> *Heaviness of Earth spreads warming light within me*
> *and gives me form*

Then for a long time retain the concept: I AM.
Then do not form *any* concept, but *await* what comes with an empty consciousness.

Evenings:

Try to concentrate your thoughts on your own bodily sensations in the following stages:

> I am my head
> I am my neck
> I am my arms
> I am my rib-cage
> I am my heart
> I am the blood that circulates within me
> I am my lungs.

Then concentrate on your breathing in the following way:

Concentrate on inhalation and experience the in-flowing breath as
> *I [ee]*

Concentrate on the inhaled air filling your body, and experience it as
> *A [ah]*

Concentrate upon exhalation and experience the out-flowing air as
> *O [oh]*

Do this in *seven* consecutive breathing processes; then focus the mind in contemplation of the inner part of the head (point a).

Feel therein as though the word *IAO* was resounding; retain this sound for 1 to 2 minutes, then do not form *any* images, but await what is to come with an empty consciousness.

A current of light from
between the eyebrows to the neck: I

The current of light follows
alongside the spinal column: A

The current of light returns
inside the spinal column to the
point between the eyebrows. O

Seven times
every 2 minutes
(14 minutes)

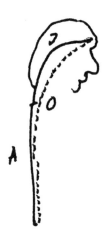

I A O penetrates into me through me out of me
I A O produces powers within me through me out of me
I A O lives in me weaving in me through me out of me
(as often as possible)

Mood:

I A O as the name of Christ
This is connected with the secret
of how Christ works within human beings.

Exercise: Handwritten document. Archive number 5273:

1. *Evenings*: Retrospect of the day's events, in reverse order.
   (4-5 minutes).

2. *Evenings*: The following meditation (4–5 minutes):

> I feel myself in light-filled space
>> (along with the concept of the world around
>> filled with light).
>
> Light weaves the garment of my ether body
>> (concept of one's own body created out of
>> light).
>
> I feel myself in the world of color
>> (concept of a sea of color in which one is
>> immersed).
>
> The color-world of the spirit endows me with my own soul
>> (concept of one's own soul).

> In light and color
> Thinks, feels and wills
> Myself

3. *Mornings:* Inner picture of a black cross
   with seven shining stars:

> To this the meditation (4–5 minutes):
>> My Self
>>
>> thinks, feels and wills
>> Through light and color
>> I rest quietly
>> In my Higher Self
>> My I
>> In Christ

To be accompanied by the 6 exercises: Control of thought, and so
on, as they are given in *An Outline of Esoteric Science*.

Exercise. Handwritten document. Archive number 3233:

Day I:

Evenings: Summary of a truth in a short sentence. Conversion into a symbol drawn from mathematics or physics (10 minutes).
Breathing:
>Inhalation: Ingest the symbol into the head.
>Hold the breath: Keep the symbol in the head.
>Exhalation: Picture to oneself that one retains the symbol, but allows the air to be exhaled without it.

Mornings: Repetition of the same exercise. Persist therein with a tranquil mind, with no outer impressions and with no memories of life on the physical plane (15 minutes).

Day II:

Evenings: Summary of a truth in a sentence. Transformation into a symbol drawn from the plant world.
Breathing:
>Inhalation: Ingestion of the symbol through the heart.
>Holding the breath: Retention of the symbol.
>Exhalation: Picture to oneself that one retains the symbol, but exhales the air without it.

Mornings: Repetition of the exercise and persistence with the thoughts as on the first day.

Day III:

Evenings: Summary of a truth in a short sentence. Transformation into a symbol drawn from the animal world.
Breathing:
>Inhalation of the symbol through the larynx.
>Holding the breath: retention of the symbol.
>Exhalation: Picture to oneself that the symbol remains and the empty breath is exhaled.

Mornings: Repeat as on previous days.

No alcohol. No lentils, beans, peas.

Exercise: Handwritten document. Archive number 5269:

Evenings:

1. Retrospect of the day's events in reverse order (4-5 minutes).

2. At first concentration on the thought: *I think things and facts.*
   Retention of this thought in the mind for about a minute with exclusion of other thoughts.
   Next concentration on the thought: *My thinking flows through time.*
   Again retention of this thought for a minute.
   After this preparation, concentration on the following in succession (3–4 minutes):

   > *I follow the flowing thinking*
   > *I shall recognize my will in my thinking*
   > *I shall find my I in my thought-will*
   > *I shall live as I in my thought-will*
   > *I await release of the I from the I*
   > *Then peaceful inner soul-mood.*

Mornings:
Concept of a *blue* circular disc with red surrounding.
Then transformation into a red disc with blue surround.
Reconversion into original state.

Do this seven consecutive times.

Conceive through inner observation how the thinking thereby becomes mobile and free in itself and ultimately is raised to a condition free from the body.

With your mind thus conditioned, concentrate on some simple object and observe how your inner soul-activity has now become different from what it was before being thus conditioned.

The whole to last 4-5 minutes.

The 6 exercises as given in 2nd part of *An Outline of Esoteric Science.*[130]
Indications of time, of course, according to judgement.

---

130. Chapter 5, "Cognition of the Higher Worlds. Initiation."

Morning–Midday–Evening–Exercise, Handwritten. Archive number 3230:

In the morning:

        I recognize the thought-picture
        Of my inner being
        In my head;
        I think the rhythmic feeling life
        Animating my inner being
        In my heart;
        I feel the power of will
        Consolidating my limbs
        In the whole of my body.

At midday:

        Let stream forth
        The power of my right eye
        Into my left arm
        And the power of my left arm
        Into my right leg —

        Let stream forth
        The power of my left eye
        Into my right arm
        And the power of my right arm
        Into my left leg —

Before going to sleep:

        I will
        Leave my body —
        My feeling follows after me
        My will enters the spirit land
        May strength permeate it
        May it take hold of all my
        limbs on waking....

SUPPLEMENT

End part of an exercise to which the beginning part is missing.
Archive No. 1704:

With all your strength, review your life very *concretely* as far as memory serves you, and feel your responsibility for having descended into your *present* incarnation; say to yourself that you are deserving of every part of your destiny—then make clear to yourself the disparity that exists between a life burdened in this way with unfulfilled karma, and one that confronts a purified human being, who has settled all accounts with life (Karma).

Look up to the idea of an immaculate Master.

Thus shall I become, thus *will* I become. —

Explanations of Light on the Path. *From a 1906 notebook. Archive number 105. It is not known to what the separate dates refer:*

Meditation from January 11 concerns the following:

When the higher self has taken complete command over the human being, when the sheath of personality has therefore fallen away then the whole choir of higher spirits can speak through a human being, just as previously the sense world spoke through a human being.... To prepare for this moment one must develop the capacity to no longer defend what belongs to oneself, what is separate. One ceases to be a warrior; one becomes a tool in the hands of the warrior.

The saying does not refer to the higher fact itself, but gives instruction for the development of the faculty whereby the higher fact may be obtained.

Meditation of January 12:
Instead of "king" read "kings," for (one) has to do with whole ranks of higher beings; one can, however, only speak about a single warrior because, at this level of existence, what is manifold sounds together in complete harmony and thus expresses itself as a unity.

Meditation of January 13:
Nothing—at least, nothing important—sinks back in evolution, but it will be *redeemed* in the course of time, that is to say, it will be accepted back into what is higher. Over the course of time, what is higher (the good) takes back into itself even what is evil, and changes it into what is good through its own strength.

To begin with we are concerned with the Divine Spirit. This Spirit could not develop to certain heights if it did not cast out from itself what is evil and, in this way, first attain a certain level *without* this evil.

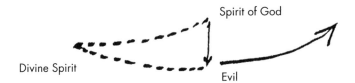

With the evil inside, it would not have attained to the heights; but now, from the heights, it can take up the evil again and accompany it on its further path.

The Saint redeems the criminal
God redeems Satan.

Of January 16:
Wherever *intuitive* knowledge is referred to here, it should be understood to mean "imaginative" knowledge.

Intuitive knowledge will be made accessible by means of the second sentence: Losing of sensitiveness.[131]

---

131. *Light on the Path*: "Before the ear can hear it must have lost its sensitiveness."

1. Knowledge based on the senses: Everyday knowledge.
2. Imaginative knowledge: Spiritual insight (picture vision).
3. Intuitive knowledge: Spiritual hearing (inner word).
4. Divine knowledge: Complete identification with the Absolute.

Knowledge concerning [person's name] is quite correct, and the more you attain in this direction, the more quickly you will achieve progress. We must only ensure that with every such thought we combine the proper spiritual gravity, that we act in such a way that we could nevertheless do everything from the opposite assumption.

1. It is clear to me in my *feelings* that the destiny of [name] is the right one.
2. It is clear to me in my *will* that I must nevertheless act as though I could prolong the life of [the person named] indefinitely.

Feeling and *will* must always go in opposite directions. Otherwise knowledge is not spiritual but abstract.

Apart from the meditation: reflect
    In the meditation: *live* in contemplative thought.

Of January 19:
In the case of such concepts, the opposite thought must always be kept in mind: Inner peace must never be bought at the price of *turning away* from the outer world, but always after coming into harmony with the outer world. That is exactly the same as, for example, the case of two other polar opposite thoughts: the esoteric student *never* thinks or speaks the one or other thought without having the corresponding opposite, at least faintly, in the background of the mind. If I say, for example:

"God is within me."

I should at least subtly think:

"I am within God."

Thereby the one-sided thought-form is constantly immobilized, as it were, by its corresponding opposite, as is, for example, the physical body by the etheric body.

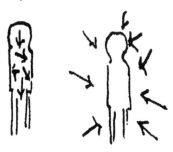

The forces (↗) are active within the body and would cause it to disintegrate if the polar opposite force did not hold it together from outside. From a dynamic aspect the ether body is the positive, the physical is the negative pole.

Of January 20:

Too much emphasis on the inner life can easily lead to a hardening of *Ahamkara* [I-organization]. One may rise to great heights and yet remain within it. To express this fact all esoteric training has an important saying:

Everything that is *not* done for the sake of your immortality contributes to that immortality.

For example:

If I take up a course of training, I will improve myself—yet not completely effectively. However, if I incorporate this training into a Gothic cathedral, or into the soul of another human being, or just into my interactions with other people, then what I have implanted into my surroundings will become part of my immortal being.

Building plan as such:

  : Architect dies

The effects produced by the cathedral become the building stones out of which the immortal soul of the architect is constructed. This is the basis of the saying:

Pray and work.

In beholding what is absolute, that which is relative loses all power over you.

Polar opposite thought:

You are unable to recognize what has absolute value

unless you irradiate what is relative by its light.

A criminal can only be recognized in a relative sense when one can see how the divine is revealed in the criminal.

Such a dream can be quite a good indicator: The tired swallow—the insight into evolution, symbolized by the development of the swallow out of the reptile—tires at first and does not allow the wings to develop as they would through independent progress in dullness of soul. Seen at a deeper level, however, the former leads more surely to the goal. It is just those who are most profoundly wise who appear to be worthless to the furtherance of evolution in the eyes of those concerned only with outer life. Such thought-forms weave in your surroundings and occasionally break forth in dreams.

The dream of the 24th is important. All such dreams are symbols for higher truths. The first part—hovering in the plant world—represents more or less the picture of humankind during the Fifth Round (minerals will no longer be present). All visions that have a foundation are in a certain sense prophetic, for no one who is more highly developed can have a vision of anything that will not later be shared by all humankind.

Continuity of consciousness will be achieved only when both the experiences of *dreams* and those of dreamless sleep are present.

Dream experiences are *pictures* analogous to the picture that is seen.

Experiences out of dreamless sleep are, in every case

Audible experiences and, if they are of any actual value,

spoken audible experiences—that is, words.

One does not have to understand the words in every case, for in recalling them they may appear to be in a language we do not understand.

Of January 25:

All forms are at the same time an expression of what is eternal.

If we search for the eternal *in* the form we shall find it; if we search for it by avoiding the form we cut ourselves off from it still further.

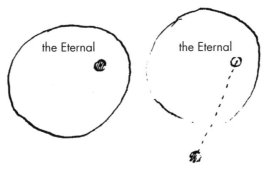

To January 26:

Sensitivity toward the outside world is conditioned by the fineness of one's vibrations. A heavy drinker is immune to the vibrations of another drinker. That is why a teetotaler finds those who drink unpleasant. It is this way with everything. Evolution, through refinement of its vibrations, uncovers all the impurity, baseness, and so on, of the surrounding world and thus achieves only a heightening of the crucifixion in matter. The ability to bear pain for the sake of fellow creatures increases during the course of evolution. Only when one has overcome *oneself*—that is, when one has progressed beyond refinement of one's vibrations—will peace come about. Then, however, one will not possess more acute vibrations, but rather, *simpler* ones. Not refinement of vibrations, but simplification of vibrations is what is in question.

I. Two undeveloped human beings.

The vibrations correspond with one another, therefore they will fit together; the one is not aware of the other.

II. An undeveloped and a developed human being.

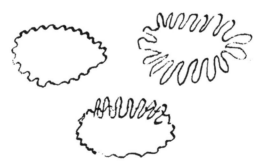

Every single "out-growth" of the second form is aware of those of the first, but cannot immobilize them.

III. An undeveloped and a still higher developed human being.

The simple vibrations of the second form are certainly aware of the deviations of the first, and have sufficient strength to immobilize them.

Of January 27:
Just this would have to be seen in the light of the foregoing rule of simplification. A person becomes greater when he becomes more simple.

Of January 29:
It is rather important that we interpret *sensitiveness* as "*Empfindlichkeit*" [sensitivity] and not as "*Empfindsamkeit*" [touchiness, sentimentality].[132] It therefore reads:

Before the ear can hear, it must have replaced its *sensitivity* with a simplified, receptive sensing into others. When a person is easily offended it is the personality that reacts to the outer world. In a receptive person, it is the eternal part of that person that acts upon the outer world with the simple rhythms of the eternal.

Of January 30: Everything in the sense of I, II, and III.

---

132. This refers to the translating into German of Mabel Collins's *Light on the Path*, which was written originally in English.

Of February 3:

The Masters are not a rampart against evil, but the leaders in absorbing evil. We should not cast out evil, but just take it up and use it in the service of the good. The rage of the lion remains evil only as long as it is used by the lion in an egoistic fashion; if some conqueror could use the rage of the lion to accomplish social service, then it would be beneficial. Therefore, what is *evil* can be recognized as *un*-real. There is no evil. Evil is only a misplaced *good.* Only when one recognizes this fact is spiritual alchemy possible.

Of February 6:

Precisely the progress achieved by Christianity is that the personality is included on the way to the eternal.

Therefore the Christian principle is correct: You will rise again with your *glorified body*—that is, according to Christian belief, the *personality* is *eternal.*

Pentagram and Hexagram Exercise

Supplement to the letter addressed to Wilhelm Hübbe-Schleiden
on November 15, 1908

Notes from memory of the Esoteric Lessons in Berlin
November 29, 1907 and January 7, 1908

Berlin, November 29, 1907. Notes from memory by Günther Wagner:

A current passes through the ether-body in the form of a pentagram: From the point of the I in the forehead to both feet, from there to the antipodal hands and from one hand to the other via the heart. When the body and the limbs are bent the currents bend too. To the various sections of the currents the various planets belong as shown. One must conceive of the planets more as principles, which are really always active in all Globes, but in a special way in certain ones.

Pentagram and Hexagram Exercise

The Ether Body

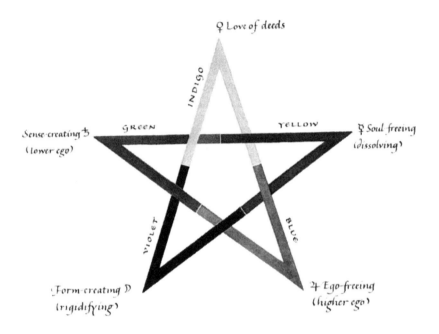

For the pentagram and hexagram exercise of the Esoteric School,
Berlin, November 29, 1907.

The Astral Body

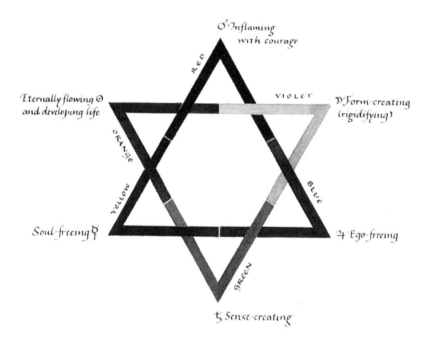

Rudolf Steiner arranged for the two colored figures to be drawn on either side of a piece of stiff paper so that they overlay one another exactly. See letter to Hübbe-Schleiden of November 15, 1908 on pp. 101-102.

Principle of Saturn   physical basis
     of Sun   continual growth, continual progress
     of Moon   holding fast, retarding, making rigid
     of Mars   courage, introducing aggressiveness into
                sense life, red blood
     of Mercury   release from sense life
     of Jupiter   freeing of the I
     of Venus   consummation of love

The colors as here given correspond to the planets, alternatively to the principles:[133]

Saturn	green
Sun	orange
Moon	violet
Mars	red
Mercury	yellow
Jupiter	blue
Venus	indigo

The hexagram corresponds to currents in the astral body; however, this double triangle exists merely as a section and is not to be understood as a linear figure. (Whereas the currents within the ether body form the lines of a pentagram, the hexagram is an expression of the astral body in quite a different way—not as linear, but as essentially *bodily, planar.*) When the figure is rotated on its vertical axis the true figure is made evident, even though the horizontal section does not reveal a true circle (oval). The horizontal

---

133. In other connections different correspondences are sometimes given; for example, for eurythmy or in the color sketch "The Human Being in Relation to the Planets," which should not be understood as a contradiction, but as the expression of different aspects. See, for example, Rudolf Steiner's *Macrocosm and Microcosm*, Rudolf Steiner Press, London, 1985; *Planetary Spheres and Their Influence on Man's Life on Earth and in Spiritual Worlds*, Rudolf Steiner Press, London, 1982; and *The Spiritual Hierarchies and the Physical World* (CW 110), SteinerBooks, Great Barrington, MA, 2008.

lines actually form planes; the upper one at the height of the arms, the other at the height of the knees.

The triangle that points downward is connected with the bodies: astral body (Moon), ether body (Sun), physical body (Saturn-principle). The other triangle has to do with the higher parts: Sentient soul (Mars), Intellectual soul (Mercury) and Consciousness soul, only at the beginning of its development (Jupiter). The colors are accordingly.

One should meditate on these figures and the meaning of their details, in order to become conscious of one's own true inner life and one's connection to the cosmos. One will then awaken unusual inner sensations.

Notes by Alice Kinkel from memory of the same lesson:

The Saturn principle: (Oriphiel. Green—Lead) is the physical basis, yet spiritual.

Life: (Michael. Sun. Orange—Gold) Eternal growth, eternal progress.

Appearance in Maja: (Gabriel. Moon. Violet — Silver) Holding fast, retarding, making rigid.

Consciousness: (Samael. Mars. Red—Iron) Courage, aggressiveness, incorporation into sense life through the red blood.

Divine Intelligence / Holy Spirit: (Raphael. Mercury. Yellow — Quicksilver) Leading out of the sense-life.

Power / The Father: (Zachariel. Jupiter. Blue—Tin) Release of the I.

Love. Son / Transition from God to Human being / Mediator: (Anael. Venus. Indigo — Copper) Consummation in pure love.

Diagrams of pentagram and hexagram (see pp. 160-161).

The hexagram corresponds to currents in the astral body. But it is only a section. If the figure were rotated around its vertical axis it would reveal its true shape; its horizontal section would not be a perfect circle. The upper plane should be experienced as level with the arms, the lower with the knees.

The triangle that points downward relates to the physical body, Saturn; astral body to Moon; ether body to Sun. The triangle that points upward relates to the higher parts. Sentient soul, Mars; Intellectual soul, Mercury; Consciousness soul, Jupiter.

Through intense meditation on these figures we become aware of ourselves and our relationship to the macrocosmos. The pentagram represents the currents of the ether body and their connection with the planets.

The physical body is connected with all the forces of the universe. It is the center into which all the forces of the zodiac stream.

The ether body is connected primarily with the center of Earth.

The astral body with the Moon's center.

The I is not just a point that has become attached to the root of the nose through a gradual enlargement of the forehead and shrinking of the ether body; there is another point in front of it. The line of connection to this is variable; it points to the center of the Sun. The more a person develops, the closer these two points come together. People who undergo development have to transfer themselves into this second point—that is, outwardly—and they have to learn to look upon their bodies as they would any other external physical object. (*Tat tvam asi,* "that is you!"—from the Veda); this releases people from egoism. An intensive after-experience of the Mystery of Golgotha, and the fact that the superfluous, egoistic blood of humankind flowed there, helps in this respect.

The meditation shall be as sacrificial smoke rising to the gods.

———————————

Berlin, January 7, 1908 (continued from November 29, 1907); notes from memory by an unknown hand:

If we are to benefit from observation, as in the last lesson, of this kind of occult figure (the hexagram), then it will not suffice to continually stare at it. It would be better if we paint it in our minds again and again during quiet hours, and meditate on the meaning of the various colors. Only in this manner do we acquire the advantage and benefit that such an occult sign can have when observed in the proper way. For the whole wisdom of the world is provided for us in a few occult figures such as this. And by pondering them deeply we can gradually gain an insight into the spiritual connections of the higher worlds.

Let us consider two colors from the hexagram that stand opposite one another: red and green. It is fully intentional that these two colors are opposite one another. What might the red color signify, and what the green? We find the green color externally in the plant world, which covers the Earth with its mantle. And what is the human being's relationship to the plant? We know that humankind's existence on Saturn corresponds in a certain way to our minerals. Not that humankind was ever a mineral! Our present-day mineral kingdom is actually the youngest of the kingdoms of nature. We know, furthermore, that humankind led a plant-like existence on the Sun. Today a greenish sap flows in the plants. A similar fluid flowed in the human beings of that time. If, by magic, we could force astral components into the plant today, it would turn red! Because human beings received their astral body on the Moon, their inner fluid turned red—changed into red blood.

Just reflect: the plant is chaste, it has no desires or passions—anger, fear, dread. Through the fact that people in a certain way became baser than the plant, they received into themselves something that raised them above the plant: the alert, ordinary consciousness. The plant world of today is sleeping. A plant is the upside-down human being. With its roots it points to the center of the Earth, where its I can be found. Exactly the same force that works downward in the plant, works just the opposite way upward in human beings. The fact that blood was acquired by human beings expresses the taking up of the I. The expression of I-being is the red blood.

If you look with spiritual eyes at the inner surface of a green leaf it will appear red. This red force is, so to speak, spiritual. If one looks at a red patch against a white background, scrutinizes it well and then looks at the white surface, a green patch will appear. And the same happens the opposite way round. These colors are considered complementary. Thus, also in such physical appearances the inner spiritual connection comes to expression.

Or let us take two other colors: blue and orange, which stand opposite to one another. You must know that orange has two aspects: orange and gold.

Where do we find blue in nature? When we look up into the limitless distances of the domed heavens! And where gold? On paintings by Old Masters we find golden backgrounds. These Old Masters painted according to a tradition that had some knowledge of the appearance and beings of higher worlds. If we look with spiritual eyes into heavenly space it appears out of gold-based depths. That is why we see angelic heads on a golden background in old paintings, because, if you look with spiritual eyes into heavenly space it appears to you to be golden.

Thus we must try to collect, to build up our soul, what, in reality, is spread out over the whole cosmos. Consider for a moment how scattered over the Earth are all the foodstuffs we require to build up our bodies. Consider this vividly! It is just the same in spiritual matters. The soul also has to collect out of chaos all it needs to upbuild itself.

If a soul begins to meditate in this way, then an organ in the physical body begins to develop: the mucous [pituitary] gland, an organ that, in a normal, average human being, is hardly the size of a cherry stone, situated beneath the pineal gland, but contains disproportionately large forces within it—specifically, those that regulate the body's build, with respect to size. The so-called giants that are exhibited are cases of an illness of the mucous gland. When these forces have been unleashed they have to find an outlet in some way or other. When someone who meditates begins to work upon the self, forces of the mucous gland are awakened. It is from this mucous gland that, out of the chaos of emotions, the structuring of the astral body is effected. When the pineal gland becomes swathed in golden threads from the mucous gland, the moment has arrived when the transformation of the astral body into *Manas*, or Spirit-Self, has progressed far enough for the ether body to be converted into *Buddhi*.

One who meditates in this way upon such occult signs will be working to good effect on the structuring of the higher bodies.

Sometimes the soul develops quietly in a very short time. One could say: It is not in any way a matter of time in development, but only deep inward peace.

Concerning the same. Notes from memory by Günther Wagner:

Meditate on the hexagram. Apex pointing upward—red; apex pointing downward—green. Opposites: complementary colors. Green, the color of plants. Red, the color of human blood.

People can progress only if they consider desires and passions. The part of Earth's astral body that belongs to the plant world is red—that is, physically green, spiritually red: the plant. In the case of plants, their red astral forces point downward to the center of the Earth, whereas the same forces in human beings have turned upside down and point upward.

Green and red: opposites. Blue and orange likewise, at least in one of their two aspects: golden (added by another hand: violet and golden). These are also complementary colors. Physically the sky is blue; from the aspect of Devachan it is golden, as painted in early medieval pictures. The same with other opposites.

Through observing such symbols given to us by the Masters, we regulate and transform our astral body, especially the aura, into Manas. All sorts of unimportant outward experiences can point to these color connections, and so our spiritual body is formed, built up and developed, when we make use of all kinds of widely dispersed experiences, in the same way that our physical body is built up and developed assimilating various foodstuffs gathered from all over the world.

By regulating and organizing itself the astral body produces an effect that works especially on the mucous or pituitary gland (hypophysis), which is a small organ, hardly the size of a cherry stone, and mainly has to do with bodily growth. As a result of such structuring of the astral body, the pituitary gland begins to grow continually more radiant; it sends out rays, and eventually envelops the pineal gland as well, which lies above and activates it; as a result the effects spread to the astral body which it begins to impress and reorganize.

FROM THE TEACHINGS ABOUT THE MASTERS
OF WISDOM AND OF THE HARMONY
OF SENSATIONS AND FEELINGS

This section comprises only those accounts by Rudolf Steiner and notes from memory by participants of esoteric lessons concerning the nature of the Masters.

The Twelvefoldness of the Masters

Written answer to a written question asked in Dornach. The question was handed to Rudolf Steiner on May 29, 1915 by Alma von Brandis, a Berlin member then living in Dornach. His answer was later given by Alma von Brandis to Marie Steiner-von Sivers. Alma von Brandis was a so-called "old" member, conversant with ideas about the Masters then current in the TS as represented by Sinnett in his Occult World *and* Esoteric Buddhism. *Sinnett had, for example, already touched on the question of the connection between the Mahatmas and the twelve parts of the human being in* Esoteric Buddhism *as follows:*

Intricacies concerning the nature of the adept may be noticed here, ones that will hardly be quite intelligible without reference to some later chapters of this book, but have such important bearing on any attempt to understand what adeptship is really like, that it may be convenient to deal with them immediately. The dual nature of the Mahatma is so complete that some of his influence or wisdom on the higher planes of nature may actually be drawn upon by those in peculiar psychic relations with him, without the Mahatma-man being at the moment even conscious that such an appeal has been made to him. In this way it becomes open to us to speculate on the possibility that the relation between the spiritual Mahatma and the Mahatma-man may sometimes be rather in the nature of what is sometimes spoken of in esoteric writing as an overshadowing, than as an incarnation in the complete sense of the word.

Furthermore, as another independent complication of the matter we reach this fact, that each Mahatma is not merely a human I in a very exalted state, but belongs, so to speak, to some specific department in the great economy of nature. Every adept must belong to one or other of seven great types of adeptship, but although we may almost certainly infer that correspondences might be traced between these various types and the seven principles in man, I should shrink myself from attempting a complete elucidation of this hypothesis. It will be enough to apply the idea to what we know vaguely of the occult organization in its higher regions. For some time past it has been affirmed in esoteric writing that there are five great Chohans or superior Mahatmas presiding over the whole body of the adept fraternity. When the foregoing chapter of this book was written, I was under the impression that one supreme chief on a different level again exercised authority over these five Chohans, but it now appears to me that this personage may rather be regarded as a sixth Chohan, himself the head of the sixth type of Mahatmas, and this conjecture leads at once to the further inference that there must be a seventh Chohan to complete the correspondences that we thus discern. But just as the seventh principle in Nature or in man is a conception of the most intangible order eluding the grasp of any intellectual thinking, and only describable in shadowy phrases of metaphysical non-significance, so we may be quite sure that the seventh Chohan is very unapproachable by untrained imaginations. But even he no doubt plays a part in what may be called the higher economy of spiritual nature, and that there is such a personage visible occasionally to some of the other Mahatmas I take to be the case. But speculation concerning him is valuable chiefly as helping to give consistency to the idea above thrown out, according to which the Mahatmas may be comprehended in their true aspect as necessary phenomena of nature without whom the evolution of humanity could hardly be imagined as advancing, not as merely exceptional men who have attained great spiritual exaltation. (pp. 14–15)

Question: Do the various Masters constitute "parts," so to speak, of a single being, so that this being contains twelve different Masters within itself, seven of which are physically incarnated and five remain in the spiritual world?

Answer: Yes.

Question: Does one of them, for example, possess to perfection the qualities of the physical body, so that he represents the harmony of the physical organs; another express the harmony of the temperaments within the physical body (that is to say etheric body); another the harmony of knowledge (astral body); a fourth the above-mentioned qualities expressed in terms of the feelings; a fifth the above-mentioned qualities expressed in a way comprehensible to the understanding; a sixth these qualities expressed in a completely conscious form; and [a seventh] in command of the other six? (The words: "in command of the other six" were corrected by Rudolf Steiner to "commanded *by* the other six.") Manas as 8th, Buddhi as 9th, Atma as 10th, Holy Spirit as 11th, the Son as 12th—are these five individuals invisible at the present time?

Answer. The seventh is the servant of the other six and is ruled by them. He also holds sway over the other five—that is to say, brings them into incarnation. There are always seven in incarnation. If the eighth incarnates, the first becomes discarnate.[134]

Rudolf Steiner drew the following diagram:

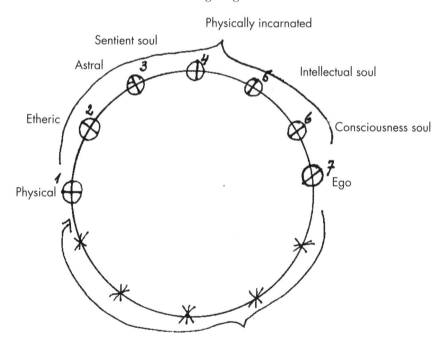

134. See concerning a letter to Marie Steiner, Berlin, July 3, 1904, page 211.

Diagram illustrating the activity of the Masters in cultural history.
Drawn for Elise Wolfram, Leipzig, between 1906 and 1908.[135]

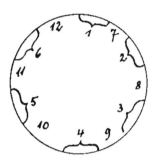

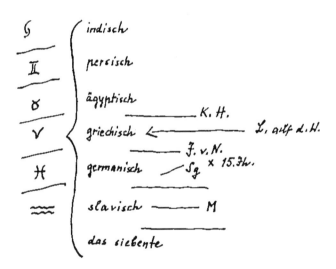

Explanations by Rudolf Steiner, provided by Elise Wolfram:

On the upper diagram:

  1, 2, 3, 4, 5, 6 signify post-Atlantean cultural epochs.

---

135. The original is not available. Reproduced from an authentic copy. The seven cultural epochs are Indian, Persian, Egyptian, Greek, Germanic, Slavic, and the seventh.

On the lower diagram:

K.H.   Kut Hoomi, *inspirer of transition* period from Egyptian to Greek epoch.[136]

L, auf d.W.   Inspirer of *Light on the Path* (his occult name Hilarion) inspirer of Greek epoch.[137]

J.v.N.   Jesus of Nazareth, inspirer of transition period from Greek to Germanic epoch.

S.G   Saint-Germain, inspirer of Germanic culture.

M.   Morya, inspirer of Slav culture.

---

136. Rudolf Steiner elaborated on the term *inspirer of transition period*:
"One says of the Master that he is born in the same body. He makes use of it for centuries, even millennia. That is so in the case of nearly all leading individualities. Certain of the Masters form an exception. They are the ones who have a very special mission. In their case the physical body is preserved, so that death does not occur at all for them. Those are the masters who have the task of being responsible for the transition from one epoch to the next." (*Theosophy of the Rosicrucians*, Rudolf Steiner Press, London, 1981, p. 54; current edition is titled *Rosicrucian Wisdom*, Rudolf Steiner Press, London, 2000)
"We are not concerned here with physical death, but with the following: Physical death is only an apparent occurrence for those who have understood the Philosopher's Stone for themselves, and have learned to isolate it. For others it is a real happening, which signifies a great division in their life. For those who understand how to use the Philosopher's Stone, death occurs in appearance only. It does not constitute even a decisive turning point in life, but is, in fact, only there for the others who can observe the adept and say that he or she is dying. The adept, however, does not really die. It is much truer to say that the person concerned has learned to live without the physical body—has, during the course of life, learned to let all those things gradually take place within that happen suddenly in the physical body at the moment of death. In the body of the person concerned, everything has already taken place that otherwise occurs at death. Death is then no longer possible, for this person has long ago learned to live without the physical body. The adept lays aside the physical body in the same way that one takes off a raincoat, and puts on a new body just as one puts on a new raincoat" (*The Temple Legend: Freemasonry & Related Occult Movements*, Rudolf Steiner Press, 1985, pp. 103–104).
137. It was generally acknowledged in the TS that Master Hilarion inspired Mabel Collins's *Light on the Path*. Rudolf Steiner told Oskar von Hoffman's daughter that her father, who translated *Light on the Path* into German, had received inspiration from the Master Hilarion while translating this work. He was greek, which is said to account for the beauty of his translation that was considered more effective mantrically than the original English text.

References in Esoteric Lessons concerning the nature and activity of the Masters
The supposed first two Esoteric Lessons in Berlin

I.

Berlin, July 9, 1904

First there was a prayer spoken by Dr. Steiner, then an indication to state that through him it is the Masters who speak, and that he is only the medium through which the ideas of the Masters are expressed.

The Master Morya informs us about the goal of human development. It is he who guides humanity toward that goal. The Master Kut Hoomi is the one who points to the goal.

Description of the lower ego and the higher I. There is a lower ego in each human being that has to be brought under control.

After that the transitoriness of bodies was considered. My body will perish and your bodies will also disintegrate into their finest particles, but the words now being spoken will not disappear, because we ourselves will turn into what we now speak of. That is the seed from which we shall one day rise anew.

Thoughts and feelings are realities, and they will provide the material for the forthcoming building. We must therefore be intent on cultivating thoughts and feelings of the highest and purest order. Through such thoughts and feelings we become attached to what is similar to them, and thereby create many thousands of connections.

There are four degrees, divisions or paths of development.

There are also seven senses; five senses that are also known from life on the physical plane and two senses that await development.[138] There are ten foci of forces within the human being:

1. Prana — in the chest.
2. Apan — in the region of the organs of secretion.
3. Saman — in the navel.
4. Udan — in the center of the throat.
5. Vayu — permeates the whole of the body.
6. Kurm — in the eye. Assists in opening the eye.

---

138. Further details in *Foundations of Esotericism* (CW 93a).

7. Krikala — in the stomach. The cause of hunger.

8. Nag — causes vomiting.

9. Devatta — causes yawning.

10. Dhananjaya — what remains with the body, even beyond death.[139]

Prana corresponds to the eight-petaled lotus flower. Udan corresponds to the sixteen-petalled lotus flower. The two-petaled lotus flower is situated between the brows.

It is said of death: As one must learn to die, so one learns to let one's feelings die. But the first thing we must learn is to stand firm. That is to say, we gain a firm hold amid the confusions of life, we lose all fear and anxiety and can look with confidence and calm at any situation with which we may be faced.

Thus there are four steps to be taken:

1) First we must search for the I, the center of our being, so we can recognize what is not I. We have to search for the innermost core of our being, for it is something inherent in every single being. The center is everywhere. Everywhere is periphery. You must imagine yourself removed to the furthest bounds of existence. Wherever you are you will be able to discover the center. Earth rotates around the Sun; the Sun rotates with the Earth through space. Every single heavenly body forms a center of its own. No human beings like ourselves are living on these heavenly bodies. There certainly are beings dwelling on these bodies, but no human beings. Human beings have no connection with them. A connection with them does not exist. You can attain this connection only by inwardly raising yourself to a level where all these beings have a common basis of existence.

2) We must activate our astral body, that is, to experience I in the ocean of astrality.

3) We must gain control over the ocean of astrality and attain profound silence.

4) We have to become aware of the Voice of the Silence. It is to be found where the Master calls to us, as if from without. *That is you!*

---

139. Taken from *Die Wissenschaft des Atems*, translated from Sanskrit by Pandit Rama Prasad Kasyapa, B.A.; F.T.S. Published Leipzig (n.d.)

The best picture we have of such development is the following: When one has discovered the central core of one's being, one's I, then one has to think that one has set sail on the great ocean. Nothing can be descried on the surface of the ocean. As far as sight can penetrate there is only water and sky. The limits of the ocean are bounded by the horizon. We think of ourselves as a wave on the surface of the moving ocean; as a single wave among many. Then, when we feel completely at one with our surroundings, we have the task of bringing tranquility to the waves. A deep calm must ensue. No sound is audible, nothing is visible. The water in which we are submerged is completely calm. No movement is discernible. In this complete silence, in this complete isolation, the Voice of the Master will be able to resound. It will no longer be drowned by the sounds of everyday life. The exercise concludes with this and the practical part is added. We all practiced this picture by immersing ourselves in thoughts of the I, then in the lapping of the waves, then in the tranquility of the ocean.

II.

Berlin, July 14, 1904

1. Today the Mahatmas will have something to say to us.
2. Three duties of the occult pupil will be named: To overcome pride and vanity. To practice Theosophy in daily life. To stand up for theosophy.

[3.]
[4.]   } [Introduced in the notes, but not elaborated]
[5.]
[6.]

7. Now the Master Morya will speak.
8. The Masters can be regarded by us as Ideal. They have attained what we must attain in the future. We can therefore question them about our future development.
9. Within us lie germinal forces, which have fully blossomed in the Masters.
10. To comprehend evolution, the progress from plant to animal, and then to human being may be observed.

11. As a symbol for the development of the plant the following sign is shown us: ⊥

12. As the symbol for the development of the animal: T

13. As the symbol for the development of humankind: ✝ [140]

14. (Not stated).

15. There are three steps in evolution, and accordingly three virtues.

16. Furthermore there are two currents in every human being: *Manas* and *Kama*, the good and the evil current; the evil current is Kama.

17. The way of redemption is shown to us in Saint John's Gospel. There we find 1) The Washing of the Feet. 2) The Slapping of the Cheek. 3) The Scourging. 4) The Crowning with Thorns. 5) The Bearing of the Cross. 6) The Crucifixion. 7) The Wounding.[141]

18. That can lead to a complete transformation.

Munich, November 10 or 11, 1905.

Notes written from memory by Eugenie von Bredow:

There is a need for the esoteric pupil to understand the plan being worked out unconsciously by humanity under the guidance of the White Lodge.

Humankind is the part of Earth that is of central and crucial importance to it. In many other worlds other beings are active and the "humans" of those worlds are similar to our higher animals. Humanity has received the Earth-planet already formed by the Gods, and reshapes it, so to speak, for itself. To begin with, human development takes place on the physical plane—in the widest sense of the word. For this it was necessary for human beings to develop intelligence, so that a *singular* logical thinking can unite everyone into a single humanity.

---

140. For the symbols see: *The Temple Legend*, Rudolf Steiner Press, London, 1985, p. 311.
141. Rudolf Steiner usually enumerated the seven stages of Christian initiation as follows: 1) Washing of the feet; 2) Scourging; 3) Crowning with thorns; 4) Bearing of the cross; 5) Mystic death; 6) Laying in the grave; 7) Resurrection. See *Founding a Science of the Spirit*, Rudolf Steiner Press, London, 1999. (Previously, *At the Gates of Spiritual Science*) (CW 95).

The Atlanteans could not yet think; they were guided by the Gods. The Aryans are obliged to become masters of their world through their own efforts. On an intellectual level humankind has attained to unity that does away with differences of opinion. There can be no difference of opinion about the construction of a steam engine, or things of that nature. The products of natural science, the exploitation of natural forces, the means of transport have welded the various races and nations into a unity. Five thousand years ago—what a difference, for example, between what was produced by the Chinese and by the Europeans. Today a kind of bridge has been formed between the East and the West. A Bishop of Bremen, writing about the customs in "The March" [of Brandenburg] in the eleventh and twelfth centuries, speaks of how animals were slaughtered and the blood of horses was drunk during religious ceremonies. That was in eastern Germany, whereas in the West the founding of towns was going forward. Such contrasts existing side by side would be impossible today.

But then humanity had just begun to make use of the forces of nature. In times to come and into the next millennium things will be quite different. Humankind will extract the forces from flowing water and use them. They will gather the mighty power from the Sun's rays in huge mirrors and will know how to make use of them. They will learn to handle the forces inside the Earth that derive from a mighty spiritual being, and are presently displayed as volcanic eruptions. People will invent the most wonderful machines to channel all these released energies into the service of humanity. They will even gain control over the forces of magnetism of the whole Earth-planet, for the Earth is only a large magnet having its south pole where the North Pole is and its north pole at the South Pole. At present human beings can only steer ships with this force. When, in primeval times, changes in the Earth became necessary, it was through the power of the Gods that the Earth's axis was set at an angle; in times to come it will be possible for human beings to make the Earth rotate on its axis. The development of human intelligence and logic will continue to grow and bring about the unity of all humankind on the physical plane.

Moral evolution was first made possible by the Gods through the ethical teachings of all great religions. A time must come, however, when humankind will have grasped the moral law as clearly as they comprehend the rules of logic today. What is good and true on a moral level will then no longer be a matter of opinion, as expressed today by various religions and through the creation of parliaments to decide one or another legal point. When human beings become aware of the fact that the good and the moral can be something as clear and definite as a mathematical formula, then they will have united on this level as a humanity that will bear a very different physiognomy than the humanity of our day.

To lead humankind to a knowledge of such a moral order, to reveal its laws to human beings, so that a group of people may arise who consciously work toward these aims, that was the object of the Fourth Master, Christian Rosenkreutz, in founding the Rosicrucian Order. The development of other intellectual capacities in the West is the task of other teachers. In the East the spiritual teachings given to the Indian race by the ancient Rishis still work strongly in the people. Christian Rosenkreutz and his seven pupils laid the foundation for the recognition of the moral law, so that this would not continue to reverberate in what was given by the different religions, but could be grasped as it was, and awaken to life in each individual. The truth with regard to morality and goodness will arise within people as something acknowledged and experienced.

To open the way for uniting people into the wholeness of all humanity is the task of the Esoteric Schools.

Berlin, December 13, 1905.
Notes written from memory by Eugenie von Bredow:

After a few introductory remarks for a member about to be admitted, he spoke in a most beautiful way, so that I believe I actually felt more than I did on October 13.

He spoke about the most important event of our time: the conquest of Tibet by the English, the nation of egoism, whereby the last remnants of spirituality would disappear from the Earth. He spoke about the religion of the Tibetans, about their inner purity of comprehension, about the Buddhism taught by the Buddha in intimate converse with his disciples. He said that the incarnated teacher on Earth represented the female element, that which is to be fructified by the Divine or male element. From this union the Bodhisattva was created, whom the Tibetans speak of as *Avalokidishvara*, the Wisdom of God. He spoke about the Dalai Lama and his selection from among children who were born at the time of special events in nature. He spoke about the Spirits of the Fire-Mist, of whom our Masters were the pupils. He spoke of the rhythms of nature, of the stars and of the whole universe—that only the astral bodies of human beings were still chaotic, and that human beings must also bring rhythm into this, otherwise they would disturb evolution.

He next began speaking about Christmas and about the importance of festivals. He said that during Christmas the Sun stood at its lowest point, that on the 25th it began to climb higher, and that during that night the Masters of the White Lodge held a meeting from which they sent forth the Sun forces of the coming year to *those* on Earth who yielded completely to them, who were ready to render up their personality completely and beg for strength from them. If a person celebrates Christmas in this way, entreats the Masters in this fashion, then they will send down their strength to human beings on this December 25, and the strength of the Masters will work through them.

He then spoke about the last incarnation of the Master Kut Hoomi and his visits to universities so that he could express the high wisdom in other languages and the modern idiom; but, he said that this incarnation did not occur *in a particular individual*, but that his *power* was active first in one place, then in another.[142]

---

142. From fragmentary notes by Eugenie von Bredow on an esoteric lesson in Munich December 14 or 15, 1905: "Doubt about Kut Hoomi having been at universities in Europe. Need of this in order to acquire European concepts. Similar need to learn Chinese to make himself understood to Chinese people."

Berlin, December 28, 1905.
Notes written from memory by Eugenie von Bredow:

There were two things he wished to tell us today about mantrams and the most important of the precepts the exalted Master Morya gave to his pupils.

There are nine attributes pertaining to the Master:

1. Truth
2. Wisdom
3. Immeasurableness
4. Goodness
5. Endlessness
6. Beauty
7. Peace
8. Blessing
9. Uniformity

From us he demands five:

1. Refinement of one's disposition
2. Purification of one's love
3. Emptying of one's memory
4. Clarity of understanding
5. Extinguishing or kindling of the will

One's disposition must become purified. Love must lose all unchastity and become divine. It must not hold fast to anything that might breed prejudice. It must become objective. The mind must be clear and the will must be extinguished where there is selfishness, but must become inflamed with zeal where it can serve as a tool of the Masters.

Mantrams produce vibrations of the word, and these accord with the vibrations of thoughts in the akashic substance.

Regarding the Christmas verse "*Gloria in excelsis Deo et pax hominibus bonae voluntatis*": It has a *mantric* effect in Latin. Then he gave us an Indian mantram of similar content, with which he closed the lesson.

The festivals are nodal points established by the Masters. New Year also; therefore, elevation of mind is necessary.

Cologne, February 12, 1906.
Notes from memory by Mathilde Scholl:

John the Baptist prophesied the coming of Christ Jesus during the middle of the fourth Sub-Race. Now, however, the individuality of the Master Jesus leads humanity from the fifth to the sixth Sub-Race—again to John the Baptist—Waterman [Aquarius].[143]

Christ Jesus is the living Word. All beings in nature come together in human beings, and form the Word in them. That is the human I—Christ Jesus. Humankind becomes Christ when it inwardly experiences that the whole world comes together within, unites inwardly. The time when Christ first appeared to humanity was the time when He, as first among humankind, revealed the I in a bodily incarnation. That was the seed from which all self-consciousness, all I-consciousness, everything personal has its origin.

But He gave back His I to the world and thereby showed humanity the path of self-denial.

At the Day of Judgement, when everyone shall rise from the dead, it will become evident whether individuals have developed their I only to the point of egoism or to selflessness. Then the dividing of the human race will take place. Those who have developed their I to the stage of selflessness will bear the seeds of future humanity within their awakened I. They will be the sixth Sub-Race from which the sixth Root-Race will evolve. Those who have developed their I only as far as selfishness will not undergo any real resurrection; they will bear the seed of death within themselves. They will form the seventh Sub-Race, destined for the realm of evil, turning into dross. They are the chaff that will be cast into the fire; the sixth Sub-Race are the wheat grains from which will spring forth what is new.

This division of humankind is being prepared now. Through the principle of brotherly love, represented by the Master Jesus, the unification of humankind to become the sixth Sub-Race is taking place and, founded on this principle, it will lead into the future.

---

143. For a full explanation of "sub-races" and "root-races" and the epochs of human evolution to which they refer, see Chapter Four in *An Outline of Esoteric Science.*

When the sixth Sub-Race has been perfected, then the Word, Christ, will not rest in an *individual* human being, but will apply to all humankind, and the individual human beings will together form the letters of this word, the new Christ, who will then, in quite a new fashion, become the resurrected one. As an *I,* His life had already submerged itself into humanity during the third Root-Race. In its full development it will appear during the sixth Root-Race in the whole of humankind.

Berlin, June 26, 1906.
Notes from memory by Eugenie von Bredow:

Introductory remarks concerning the four Masters who work with us in our movement:

The Master Morya: Strength

The Master Kut Hoomi: Wisdom

The Master Saint-Germain: We turn to him with our ordinary
   difficulties.

The Master Jesus: The more intimate side of humankind's character.

Berlin, October 22, 1906.
Notes from memory by Amalie Wagner:

Sublime, exquisite, there are no words to describe what we received. The Masters of Wisdom, and so on, were surely in our midst. The strength that issued from our beloved Teacher was great. In the end I saw him beaming and youthfully transfigured. And then the solemn words:

A — The past.

U — The present, the whole of the world around us.

M — The still unknown future, for which we desire to live.

We must be pioneers, the elite of humanity. We must feel exalted, not conceited, but we must prove ourselves worthy of such a status, not haughty, but with humility.

Of the four Masters it was once more stated: The Master Jesus was the "Friend of God from the Highlands"[144] who visited Tauler, the teacher of the Gnostics.

We should learn to know more and more about the nature of the Masters. For that it is necessary to transfer ourselves back into the past.

On the Moon there were no creatures that breathed through lungs. They inhaled warmth, or imbibed it, and gave out coldness. Thereby they deprived the Moon of warmth. Just as for us breathing creatures the air is rendered usable by the plants, which inhale the poisonous carbon dioxide exhaled by human beings and animals and make use of it, breathing out pure oxygen in its place, so were there also beings on the Moon that performed a similar function as our present-day plants by exhaling warmth, which prevented the too-rapid cooling process. These creatures were called "Fire Spirits." They had not yet achieved the human stage. Furthermore, there were spiritual beings on the Moon that had already progressed beyond the human stage and they assisted in the preparation of the respiration of air. It is true they were obliged to incarnate into bodies that were not endowed with lungs, but they yearned for oxygen. The latter was only made available on Earth by the developing plant world. Only by the middle of the Lemurian age had humankind's being progressed so far that the "living breath" could be breathed into him. With the first breath oxygen was inhaled. That was of great importance. The spiritual beings who brought that about are called "Spirits of Air."

The fire-breathing dragon is the symbol for the "Fire Spirits."

Jesus was a *Chela* of the third degree. When he was thirty years old the following happened to him. He withdrew from his body and Christ took possession of this pure and noble body—physical, etheric and astral. Jesus himself withdrew to the astral plane, where he remained united with the Brothers of the White Lodge and achieved the rank of Master—and so on.

---

144. See *Mystics after Modernism*, SteinerBooks, Great Barrington, MA, 2008. Also see Wilhelm Rath, *The Friend of God from The High Lands*, Hawthorn Press, Stroud, UK, 1991.

Morya—his true name is revealed only to the more advanced pupils—strengthens the will.

Kut Hoomi is the real Master of Truth.

Jesus, The Leader of his Church, influences most of all the heart forces.

We can call upon them when we need their help.

The twelve Masters of the White Lodge have all taken part in the whole Earth evolution. They cannot work directly onto the physical plane. We have to raise ourselves to their level. They work on us, into us, and through us by means of the School. The Leader, the Teacher of the School, holds no responsibility toward anyone other than the one in whose name he or she speaks.

Another participant in this lesson, Ludwig Kleeberg,[145] reports:

As though through direct knowledge and acquaintanceship he spoke about the Great Masters, who guide our lives and aims from above: Kut Hoomi, Morya, Jesus, and Christian Rosenkreutz—the Masters of Wisdom and of the Harmony of Sensations and Feelings.

Basel, November 23, 1907.
Notes taken down from memory by Alice Kinkel:

Who are the Masters? They are human beings who have merely progressed more quickly along the path of human development than others have done; human beings who have made experiences in advance of others and can therefore become leaders. Such a personality was the "Unknown One from *Oberland*" who worked in various ways. He was said to be from the *Oberland*, because he came from the Highlands. It was Jesus of Nazareth who worked there and

---

145. In *Wege and Worte. Erinnerungen an Rudolf Steiner aus Tagebüchern und aus Briefen*, Stuttgart 1961.

lived by the name "*der große Unbekannte aus dem Oberland*" ["The Great Unknown One from the Highlands"] in the thirteenth and fourteenth centuries. Johannes Tauler was taught by him.

The esoteric pupil must enter into an actual relationship with the Masters.

Düsseldorf, April 15, 1909.
Notes from memory by Mathilde Scholl:

Today we would like to bring to mind that, as in every esoteric lesson, what is revealed in these lessons emanates from the Masters of Wisdom and of the Harmony of Sensations and Feelings.

We wish to develop ourselves, not because of any egoistic desire for development, but to become helpers of the development of humankind, whose karma is linked to ours. If we receive benefit from the instructions given us for our daily work in esotericism, we should go away from these lessons as human beings, different from what we were when we came in. To accomplish these most intimate affairs of the soul in the right frame of mind is the most important task. This cannot be stressed too often.

Our meditations take into consideration, in the first instance, the division within present-day humanity into sleeping and waking consciousness. We were endowed with these since primeval pre-Atlantean times and they have been adjusted to fit this division within human beings. Why is it necessary that human beings withdraw their I's and astral bodies out of their physical and etheric bodies during the night? Because, the divine beings, who fashioned the physical and etheric bodies into such a magnificent and perfect temple, take up their residence within it during the night, while the I's and astral bodies of human beings likewise proceed into heavenly realms. If they did not do this, then they would completely spoil the physical and etheric bodies, since, apart from the spiritual-divine beings who have created them, luciferic beings can also exert an influence over the astral body. For it was the latter that caused the astral body to become free and independent. Because of this, human beings fall into error and guilt when they return to their physical bodies during the day. It is not the physical and etheric bodies that are prey to these aberrations, but the astral body, which was seduced by the I, after it yielded to the insinuations of luciferic beings. The ordinary human being is protected against the more profound and dangerous influences of these luciferic beings by the spiritual-divine creators who endowed them with strong powers, which the esoteric pupil can make use of to rise to higher stages of development.

On going to sleep, esoteric pupils should say inwardly, "I return to my Creators," and on waking "I come from where I resided before my body was created." And in this meditation they should rest for a moment consciously within these realms. If this is accomplished in this frame of mind, they will enkindle within themselves the sacred flame, the inner warmth they need. And before falling asleep in the evening they should evolve the same feelings in the esoteric exercises that is done at night, even though this might amount only to the daily retrospect. By reviewing the events of the day in reverse order esoteric pupils create inner spiritual images that can be taken with them as an extract over into the spiritual world. Daily review must occur in reverse order, because that is how things happen in the spiritual world; a bridge is thereby created leading from the one realm to the other, so that things from the spiritual realm flow more easily into our world, and we can enter more easily into it. When we take ordinary forward thinking with us into the spiritual world we create opposition to it, thrust it away from us, and set restrictions on ourselves and further development.

Just as at night the luciferic beings work on human beings from within, as it were, so during the day the ahrimanic-mephistophelian powers work from without. What then have these powers achieved in humankind by means of their influence? The luciferic beings brought to human beings, along with independence and I-con-sciousness, the most extreme form of this—*hate*. People would never have had the capacity for hating if they had not separated them-selves more and more in their I. And the ahrimanic beings veiled the divine spiritual beings from the eye of humanity in the mists of maya, so that what lay behind the things of the sense world could no longer be seen. And *fear* arose as the result. Human beings would never have known fear if they could have beheld the divine creator instead of being confronted with objects in space. Small children first learn to be afraid when they come into contact with matter—when they bump against material objects.

To advance successfully, esoteric pupils must endeavor to set aside the tendencies of both hate and fear, even in their most intricate manifestations. Zarathustra, one of our greatest teachers, has therefore handed down words that will be a help us to achieve fearlessness, if we follow them in the right spirit. These are his words:

> Behold, I will speak! Come now and listen, all those from afar and those nearby who wish to hear me. Of Him will I speak who shall be revealed in Spirit to those who seek. I will speak to you of Him who is the First and the Greatest, and of that which was revealed to me by Him, the Great Spirit who is Ahura Mazda. Anyone who therefore will not listen to my words according to my meaning and intent, to that person will befall much evil when Earth shall have run its course to the end."[146]

With these words Zarathustra wanted to make humanity aware that the visible Sun is only the covering behind which dwell the powerful rulers of the Fire-Spirits, just as everything physical is merely a vessel for something spiritual, and if we concentrate our minds on the mighty Ahura Mazda who stands behind the life-giving Sun, then fearlessness will be our portion.

And to gain freedom from hate, the great Zarathustra bequeathed to us another symbol at a much later time. He had two pupils. In one of them he so conditioned the astral body that it became clairvoyant, thus enabling this pupil in a following life to unite his own prepared astral body with that of Zarathustra, who offered it to him for that purpose. This pupil became the great Hermes, leader of the Egyptian Mysteries.

---

146. *Zend-Avest*, Yasna 45. Free translation.

Another sacrifice made by Zarathustra was of his etheric body, which he bequeathed to his second pupil, whose own etheric body had likewise been carefully prepared to receive it. This latter pupil returned to Earth as Moses, and the fact that Moses was endowed with a very special etheric body is made evident from the story in the Bible about the little box of rushes in which he had to remain enclosed for a while as a small child, shut off from the world in the water, so that his I and his astral body should not bring confusion to these subtle processes through outer influence.

The I of Zarathustra was sufficiently powerful to create for himself a new etheric and astral body for his succeeding incarnation. After having passed through an incarnation as Nazarathos, the teacher of Pythagoras, he finally incarnated as Jesus of Nazareth, who was now able to sacrifice his three bodies, including his physical body, to Ahura Mazda, whom he had always proclaimed. Ahura Mazda now descended and dwelt within him, and thus, in this sense, Jesus could pronounce the words: "I am the Light of the World." (Saint John's Gospel).

And the sign that Zarathustra left behind—of being without hate—is the blood that flowed at Golgotha. Hate is the most extreme expression of the I. And where is the I to be found? In the blood. Even our physical blood undergoes a change when this hate—this hardening process of the I, this becoming wooden—is transformed into hatelessness, and this, in turn, is transformed into love. If chemists only had sufficiently fine instruments they could, for example, detect the difference in the blood of, say, an ancient Indian and a Francis of Assisi. This spiritualization is expressed even in the physical. In the blood that flowed for humankind at Golgotha we have a symbol of "hatelessness," through which we are able to transform every feeling of hate into love and offer it at the altar of the creative powers. The magical breath that emanates from Golgotha brings about the transformation of hate and fear, which are brothers to one another just as Lucifer and the ahrimanic-mephistophelian powers are also brothers to one another.

Düsseldorf, April 19, 1909.

Notes from memory by Mathilde Scholl:

On entering the School, esoteric pupils have only one obligation to fulfill—namely, to apply their common sense and intellectual capacities completely to the teachings that come to them, so that in listening to them they ask themselves: Is it reasonable for me to tread this path? In this way, with understanding and common sense, they can recognize and grasp what is being offered them. This is absolutely necessary if esoteric exercises are to produce the right effect. Our esoteric work can bring forth the proper fruits only on this condition. On the other hand, the School has to fulfill its own obligation: that everything flowing through it must emanate only from the great Teachers we call the Masters of Wisdom and of the Harmony of Sensations and Feelings.

What then is the aim they attach to this Esoteric School? It must train a small group of people, endowing them with a knowledge of world and human evolution, so they will carry away with them the true attitude toward the great spiritual truths that stand behind earthly occurrences. They will then allow these truths to flow into and benefit human evolution. How does it happen that such a spiritual movement should come into existence just now? Through important happenings in the spiritual world, because all that happens on Earth is merely a reflection of that realm. We have seen that it is the great spiritual hierarchies that carry out the commands of the Godhead, and guide human destiny. It was necessary, 800 years before our era, to send the hindering forces into earthly evolution to prepare, from a certain aspect, for the Mystery of Golgotha. The hosts of a leader, known in occult circles as Mammon, were unleashed for this purpose. They increasingly darkened human awareness of the divine. The ancient clairvoyance was lost to human beings, and western science and philosophy grew and blossomed. Ancient Eastern philosophy still arises out of the old clairvoyance, whereas that of Greece springs up entirely from what is material. The saying of Thales: "All things are created from water," was gradually interpreted more in a purely materialistic way. Human beings forgot what stood spiritually behind water. But the great teachers were nevertheless at work even during this time of darkened consciousness to make human beings aware once more of their spiritual origin. Let us suppose that a person of that time had never had a chance to hear the teachings of a Buddha, a Zarathustra, and so on. What would have happened to such a person after death? You know that the time between two Earth lives is just as much subject to change as is the historical life in the physical world.

The darkening of human consciousness came about only gradually, as does everything that happens in evolution. These spirits of Mammon could make their influence felt only gradually. The children were always less clairvoyant than their parents, the grandparents even more clairvoyant, and so on. If a person died, whose awareness of the spirit was quite darkened, then that person took this darkened consciousness into the spiritual world, and was obliged to work out of it little by little—that is, figuratively speaking, that person had to work upward through the line of that individual's ancestors, from one to another, until coming to the original ancestor who still fully possessed the ancient clairvoyance. In this way, the cloud obscuring that individual's vision was dispersed. Of course, this took a long while, and it could happen that someone in this position could not find that original ancestor because the latter had incarnated again in the meantime. Then this person was obliged to return to Earth prematurely. In Eastern wisdom this path was called "the way of the fathers," or "*Pitri* (fathers)—*yana*." One, however, who absorbed the teachings of a Zarathustra, or a Buddha, or followed some great teacher, was received in the other world by the hand of this teacher who shortened the *Pitriyana* for this individual, and dispersed the cloud that obscured vision leading to that individual's divine origin. This path was called the "*Devayana*" ("the way of the Gods"), according to Eastern wisdom.

The light of the Mystery of Golgotha shone into the time of deepest darkness. It is known to esoteric pupils—or should be known—that it was at the moment when the blood flowed from the wounds, when Christ started His journey into the spiritual world, that He appeared in Devachan. That was the spiritual mirroring in the heavenly world of the physical events in the world below. What has been accomplished for humankind by the Mystery of Golgotha has already taken place, but the understanding of it can only gradually light up in human hearts; truly, in general, it is not even possible for it to do so today. At the time of the Mystery of Golgotha the leadership over human destiny was taken out of the hand of Michael by Oriphiel, one of those served by the hosts of Mammon, the power whose task it is to create hindrances and difficulties for human evolution.

Michael took over his office from Gabriel, who returned to power in the sixteenth century after four other archangels had meanwhile succeeded Oriphiel. The regulating of human births came under the jurisdiction of Gabriel. That is why, for instance, he announced the birth of John and the Christ. He was the one who, in the sixteenth century, prepared the human brain through selected births so that an organ was formed therein (to be sure, not perceptible to investigation by natural science), which nevertheless makes the present-day brain appear different from that of a person, for example, of the thirteenth or fourteenth centuries.

The human brain has thus undergone a distinct change since the sixteenth century, perceptible to the seer, and has the purpose of enabling humankind eventually to understand Christianity in its full significance.

We have seen that from the fourth to fourteenth centuries, copies of Christ's etheric and astral bodies were made available to individuals who were thereby enlivened by the spirit of true Christianity. Saint Augustine, who received an imprint of Christ's etheric body, acquired, after many blunders, an insight into the mystic knowledge that has so much similarity to our theosophical teachings. The division of the human being into seven parts was, for example, for him a known fact, even though he used a quite different nomenclature for it. All those endowed with this etheric or astral body were distinguished by a deep humility, because they were aware that the consciousness they bore within them, the great truths they had to impart, were inspired, were filled with a grace they could not comprehend through their I. The occurrence of a cosmic event, such as a person's endowment with the etheric or astral body of Christ, is usually accompanied by some natural phenomenon—which we are inclined to regard as mere coincidence—that is deeply connected, however, with the spiritual event. To cite just one example: when Thomas Aquinas received the astral body of Christ as a small child, lightning struck and killed his little sister, who was lying in a cradle in the same room, but the boy's astral body was thus made elastic so that it could receive the higher astral body into itself.

As a result of the preparation—accomplished by Gabriel in the sixteenth century—of a new organ in the frontal lobe of the human brain, it became possible during the last third of the nineteenth century, after Gabriel had again handed over his leadership to Michael, for what we call theosophy to be infused into people by the great Masters of Wisdom and of the Harmony of Sensations and Feelings, so that the significance of the Mystery of Golgotha could be brought home to humanity in all its implications. When a person now crosses the threshold at death it is possible for each human being to discover his or her own great Master, now available to anyone in a living physical body who seeks him.

The Connection of the Masters
with the Raising of the Dead in the Gospels

Notes from memory by Elisabeth Vreede.
Esoteric Lesson possibly held in Karlsruhe, January 21 or 23, 1911:

Saint Matthew's Gospel tells us how three Magi came from the East bringing their incense, gold, and myrrh to the newborn Jesus Child, the reincarnated Zarathustra. They pay homage to their re-born Master, who, in his various incarnations, had been active in the past three cultural epochs. They are at the same time the guardians of the ancient store of wisdom from the Old Indian, the Old Persian, and the Egypto-Babylonian epochs. And by laying this in the symbolic form of incense, gold and myrrh at the feet of the Jesus Child, they also demonstrate what was active in those epochs as a germ of future cultures that can be rescued for the future of humankind only through being penetrated by the power of Christ, which would one day ensoul this Child. They themselves would not experience the rebirth of the wisdom of their cultural epochs. "They departed into their own country another way."

But we can ask ourselves the following question: "Where did these three Wise Men subsequently stay? What will become of their wisdom?" And we should remind ourselves that cultures rising and passing away here on Earth bear a seed that can be fructified by the Christ Impulse, and will come to a new blossoming in the epochs following the Mystery of Golgotha. What was offered to the Jesus Child by the three Magi from the East as the germ of a new culture will be reawakened by Christ. It contains the forces that will truly permeate these later epochs with the Christ Spirit. Everything pertaining to the store of wisdom contained in the third post-Atlantean epoch will be reawakened by the Christ to fructify our fifth epoch. The second epoch—that of Zarathustra—will be reawakened to bring a true understanding of the Christ in the sixth epoch. And the first epoch—the Ancient Indian epoch—will experience a reawakening in the seventh epoch with the help of the Christ power.

And in every instance Christ must be the Awakener of a *particular* individual, a human soul whose destiny it is to be chosen as the special vehicle to convey this seed of culture from ancient times, and who, at the same time, is the soul best suited to ensure that what has been brought to humankind as a gift by Christ will be led on into the future, so that the understanding of Christ and for his mission may also be imparted to future ages of humankind.

We shall now consider these awakenings one after another.

FIRST: In Saint Luke's Gospel (chapter 7) the awakening of the Young Man of Nain is described to us in stirring words. Every word is important in this account, which indicates that in the Young Man of Nain lives all of the third epoch—the Egypto-Chaldean cultural epoch—as it was able to develop under the influence of those powers then active.

The Young Man of Nain of Saint Luke's Gospel is no other than the Young Man of Sais—the difference in the spiritual background of the third and fourth cultural epochs is hidden in the very name. The Young Man of Sais wanted to delve into the secrets of the world without preparation; he wanted to be like the other initiates, a "Son of the Widow" Isis, who mourned her lost husband, Osiris. But because he was not prepared, because he wanted to unveil the statue of Isis himself here on the physical plane and glimpse the heavenly secrets, he died. No human mortal could at *that* time lift the veil of Isis. The powerlessness of the Egyptian wisdom is symbolized in the Young Man of Sais.

Again, he was born and grew up as the Young Man of Nain. Again he was the "Son of the Widow." Again he died in his youth. And Christ approached as the dead one was carried out through the city gates. And "many people of the city were with her" (his mother). It was the host of the Egyptian initiates, all of them dead, who bury the dead. "And when the Lord saw her he had compassion on her." He felt compassion for the mother, who stood there in the manner of Isis, the sister and wife of Osiris. And He spoke: "Young Man, I say to you, Arise! And he who was dead sat up and began to speak. And He delivered him to his mother." The former Isis has descended to Earth. Her powers can be experienced even here on Earth. The son has been given back to his mother and it now rests with him to unite himself completely with her. "And those who were present glorified God saying: A great prophet is risen up among us." For, through the kind of initiation represented in this awakening, the Christ had sown a seed that will only come to blossom in the young man's next life on Earth.

A great prophet, a great religious teacher, has developed in the Young Man of Nain! In the third century A.D. Mani, or Manes, the founder of Manicheism, made his appearance in Babylon. A strange legend relates the following story about him:

Skythianos and Terebinthus—or Buddha—were his predecessors. The latter was the pupil of the former. After the violent death of Skythianos, Terebinthus took the books of Skythianos and fled with them to Babylon. It went badly with him too; only one old widow accepted his teaching. She inherited his books and left them to her foster child—a boy of twelve years, whom she adopted when he was seven years old (as a slave) in place of her own son. Her adopted son, who can also be called the "Son of a Widow," appeared at the age of twenty-four as Manes, the founder of Manicheism.

In his teachings all the wisdom of the ancient religions is gathered together and illumined by him with a Christian Gnosticism that enabled the devotees of the Egypto-Babylonian star wisdom, the followers of the ancient Persian religion—even the Buddhists of India—to absorb an understanding of the Christ Impulse in this form.

This soul that formerly lived in the Young Man of Nain was engaged in preparation; he was initiated in this way by Christ for a future when the contents of Manicheism, which have not yet fully developed, will arise for the salvation of the people of the ancient East. During his life as Manes this soul worked to prepare for his real future mission: to bring about the true reconciliation of all religions.

To achieve this he had to be born again as a soul with a very special relationship to the Christ. All that had arisen in this soul as ancient and new knowledge during its lifetime as Manes had to become submerged again. As the "innocent fool" it inevitably had to confront the external knowledge of the world and the working of Christ in the depths of its being. He was born again as Parsifal, the son of Herzeleide, the tragic personality deserted by her husband. As the son of this widow, Parsifal again left his mother and set out into the world. After straying in many different directions he succeeded in being chosen as the Guardian of the Holy Grail. And the continuation of the Parsifal legend tells us how he again set out toward the East, how he discovered his brother among the people of the dark race, and how these people will one day also receive the blessings from the Holy Grail. Thus he prepared himself in his life as Parsifal to become a future teacher of Christianity, whose task it will be to penetrate Christianity itself more and more with the teachings of Karma and Reincarnation when the time is ripe.

SECOND: The second post-Atlantean epoch was that of Zarathustra. This has a special connection to Christ, because Zarathustra directed people's attention to Ahura Mazda, the Sun God, who was drawing nearer to Earth, and was none other than the future Jesus. And the whole mission of Zarathustra was to prepare the way for Christ by teaching people to work for and value the world, and not flee from evil, but to conquer and redeem it. And so the individuality of Zarathustra, the most highly developed human entelechy, was fit to be chosen to dwell for eighteen years within the sheaths that were later to take up the Christ. His I withdrew from these sheaths shortly before the Baptism by John in the Jordan. So it was that he was not present in the flesh as Christ walked the Earth. He himself took up incarnation very soon after leaving the three sheaths of the Nathan Jesus. His I united with the etheric body of the Solomon Jesus, which, at the latter's death, had been taken up into the spiritual world by the mother of the Nathan Jesus.

Therefore it was not possible for Christ Jesus to choose Zarathustra as the representative of the second post-Atlantean epoch when the raising from death took place; but there was living at that time another individuality whose development, and the importance of whose mission for humanity, ran strangely parallel to that of Zarathustra. This was Lazarus, the reincarnated Hiram Abiff, the most important of the Sons of Cain, who had similarly worked upon his earthly mission out of the forces of the I, just as Zarathustra had done in Ancient Persia. He became "ill" and "died" and was laid in the grave. Christ Jesus heard of his illness and spoke to His Disciples of Lazarus' death. "Then spoke Thomas, called the Twin, to the other Disciples: Let us go that we may die with him." (John 11: 16)

In this awakening Lazarus was to undergo, Thomas, the "Twin," represented the souls belonging to the second post-Atlantean epoch—just as at the awakening of the Young Man of Nain the "people of the city" represented the third post-Atlantean epoch. The second post-Atlantean epoch was the epoch of the Twins. The words of Thomas, which are otherwise completely incomprehensible, signify that the second post-Atlantean epoch is willing to be awakened by Christ. What lived as a seed of culture in the Ancient Persian epoch is *not* dead. It is *not* a matter of the awakening of a dead person, but of the initiation of someone who is alive. That is the great difference in the account of this awakening and that of the other two. Therefore Christ spoke the words: "I am the Resurrection and the Life, he that believeth in me, though he were dead, yet shall he live."

And Christ Jesus approached the grave in which the supposed dead man had been placed and spoke the sacramental words before the crowd: "Lazarus come forth!" And he that was dead came forth, bound hand and foot with grave clothes and his face bound about with a napkin. And Christ Jesus spoke the words—at the same time indicating that from this time on this initiate would commence his task: "Loosen him and let him go."

He is not a youth, like the Young Man of Nain, he is a man in the full possession of his spiritual powers. The awakened Lazarus is the one who wrote the Saint John's Gospel. He is the one who stood beneath the Cross and to whom Christ Jesus spoke from the Cross, indicating the Mother Sophia-Mary: "Behold thy mother!" So, proclaimed once more is his strange vicarious relationship to the I of Zarathustra who, as the Solomon Jesus Child, was really born as the son of this mother.

Endowed with this strength he can already unfold his activity before the sixth post-Atlantean epoch. Even during the fifth cultural epoch he is making preparation for the sixth, which is that epoch that is to reveal the deepest understanding for the Christ Impulse and which will best understand the Gospel of Saint John.

(Among the twelve Apostles Lazarus-John is similarly also represented by another. John, the brother of James and the son of Zebedee, is not an Apostle in the real sense. James and John are in a way a single person. They represent, in the intimate circle around Christ, the powers of the Intellectual- or Mind-Soul, which plays a dual role in the human being but is nevertheless a unity. That is why these two are called "Sons of Thunder," for thunder is in the outer world what thought is for the inner life of human beings. But when Lazarus becomes John, he takes the place of the one who is Zebedee's son, and as such he is the one who lay on the breast of Jesus at the Last Supper.)

THIRD: When Christ Jesus walked the Earth only the last dwindling descendants remained of the third post-Atlantean epoch. The second cultural epoch had almost entirely disappeared as a bearer of civilization, and only a few of the adherents of the largely degenerate Zarathustra religion could still be found scattered here and there. But the first epoch—the Ancient Indian cultural epoch—the oldest and most spiritual of them all, had successors, both at the time of Christ Jesus and during our own epoch, even though it had become degenerate by being infected with materialism. This epoch will be the last to be renewed, the one that will have to wait longest.

This awakening is mysteriously revealed in the story of the raising of the twelve-year-old daughter of Jairus and in the preceding account of the healing of the woman who had suffered for twelve years from an issue of blood (Luke 8: 40–56). The girl is very near death when Christ comes to heal her. But the woman is there too, whose illness started at the birth of this child. The blood, which is the life force, flows from her. She typifies the once-flourishing spiritual culture of Ancient India, which cannot be healed by any doctor—for no Yoga methods, no Vedanta philosophy, however sublime, can rescue the Indian cultural epoch from destruction.

The woman is karmically related to this girl who has reached the age of twelve years. That means that the development of the etheric body is coming to an end. The ancient Indian cultural epoch was when the etheric body was being developed. What was sown as a seed in the etheric body during the ancient Indian Epoch will be quickened to life and preserved for the last, the seventh epoch.

But this awakening can only take place when the woman has been healed. This woman approached Christ from the crowd, "From behind" (Luke 8:44), touched the border of His garment and was healed; for "your faith has made you whole" (Luke 8:48; Mark 5:4). She was healed because she had a faith within herself that the spirit is incarnated on Earth. And after she was healed of the issue of blood through her free decision to touch Christ's garment, what was once within her as a living force and is beginning to die—and could even be regarded as dead—could be brought to life again: It is the daughter of Jairus, the "ruler of the synagogue"—for the first cultural epoch was that of the Brahmins, the priests. There was a great multitude about the dead girl "that wept and wailed greatly"— again, it was those belonging to the first post-Atlantean epoch who were bewailing what was past. Saint Matthew alludes to the "pipers" (minstrels) (Matthew 9:23) who played beside the dead. Krishna also played upon the pipe and the people followed the sound of it.

Christ Jesus, however, evicted them all. A great Mystery is about to unfold, for the awakening to life of just this first cultural epoch, connected with the development of the etheric body, is related to the deep secrets of human nature. Jesus takes with him only Peter, John, and James, and the father and mother of the child. All together, with Christ and the child herself, there were thus seven people present: the three Spirit Powers, the three Soul Powers, and Christ as the Cosmic I. Thus the epoch of the ancient Holy Rishis was mirrored in these seven people. Just as the Rishis could only function when all seven of them were present, so could the maiden only be raised from the dead when the sevenfold powers were gathered together. And she was healed and Christ Jesus commanded that she should be given something to eat. For the Ancient Indian civilization had previously not needed to "eat," it had received its knowledge directly from the spiritual world through the wonderful development of the etheric body alone. But this source of nourishment had come to an end. From now on the people inevitably had to eat what could be supplied from their surroundings. And Christ Jesus "charged them directly that no one should know it," a command that it is impossible to interpret in the sense of a physical reality. But the secrets that were enacted in this resurrection must remain hidden and unknown for a long time to come.

Alongside these three awakenings belonging to the three pre-Christian epochs, several strange accounts from the Gospels can be connected with the entering of the Christ impulse into humanity's development.

FOURTH: In Saint John's Gospel (4:47–54) we are told of the nobleman's son—that is the son of the Roman—who was at the point of death. Portrayed in him is the languishing of the fourth post-Atlantean epoch, the Greco-Roman period. Christ healed him because of the father's plea, because the father believed even without "signs and wonders." The son was not raised from the dead, for he had not died. The fourth post-Atlantean epoch was still living at the time of Christ Jesus; it was merely ill and could be healed only through faith. For only in the form of faith could the Greco-Roman epoch take the Christ-Power into itself.

FIFTH: The account of the healing of the sick man at Bethesda, the pool with the five porches, immediately follows this account in Saint John's Gospel. These indicate the fifth post-Atlantean epoch with all that lives within it of the forces of the previous epoch. The people lying there are ill. They do not have the right attitude toward the spiritual world, and have sunk too deeply into matter. From time to time an Angel descends and moves the water. A fresh revelation from the spiritual worlds heals those nearest to it, but it does not cure those who come later. And so there was a man there who had waited for thirty-eight years without being able to get near the water. Thirty-eight is twice nineteen, which is the time it takes for Sun, Moon and Earth to return to the same relative positions to one another—or in other words, it is the time it takes a human being's thinking, feeling and willing to go through all possible phases in their relationship to one another. Thus the period of nineteen years represents a *single* Earth life, and the thirty-eight years denote two incarnations, which is about the average number of lives human beings have experienced since the coming of Christ, and brings us to our own day, when a new revelation of Christ will be revealed out of the spiritual world. Christ Jesus did not heal this man by lowering him into the pool when the Angel appeared, but said to him: "Rise, take up your bed, and walk!" That is to say, He strengthens in human beings the power that can overcome illness. But the man did not know who had healed him, "for Christ had vanished from sight, a multitude being in that place." (John 5:13). Christ had indeed been active within him, but the man knew nothing about it in his ordinary consciousness. Thus it has been since the Mystery of Golgotha, right up to our own time. But afterward "Jesus found him in the temple" and "the man departed and told the Jews that it was Jesus who had made him whole."

Now he knew that the word is true that Christ Jesus spoke to the Jews: "My Father has worked until now, and now I work." And again Christ said: "The hour is coming, and now is, when the dead shall hear the voice of the Son of God; and they that hear shall live," the hour that will strike in our presence, the hour when Christ will come to judge the dead and become the Lord of Destiny. Thus in many ways this account of the healing of the sick man of Bethesda bears reference to our own time.

SIXTH: In Saint Luke's Gospel a parable that points to the spiritual situation of the sixth post-Atlantean epoch has been secretly introduced. As we have seen, this epoch, which signifies the reawakening of the second post-Atlantean epoch, is prepared by Christ Jesus through the raising of Lazarus. And in Saint Luke's Gospel, Christ Jesus related a parable just after having spoken about good and evil, and about "the servants of God and the servants of Mammon." In the sixteenth chapter He told of a certain poor man named Lazarus who had, while on Earth, had a bad time, but after his death he was received into Abraham's bosom—whereas the rich man, who had fared sumptuously on Earth, was received into hell.

So will the good and the bad split off from one another in the sixth cultural epoch, and the true picture of events is staged in the spiritual world. The naming of the poor man connects the parable to Lazarus of Saint John's Gospel; and the sixth post-Atlantean epoch is expressed in the figure of the rich man, who says, "I have five brethren" still unconverted. They represent that part of humanity that has not taken the Christ into itself in the sixth epoch, and so must succumb to the evil forces.

SEVENTH: The seventh cultural epoch is not mentioned again specifically, since this has already been given in the relationship existing between the woman with the issue of blood and the twelve-year-old girl. The woman has already been healed when the maiden is restored to life. The one event cannot take place without the other.

In this and other ways the Gospel writers have secretly introduced into their writings the course of the historical development of humankind.[147]

Notes from Personal Conversations with Rudolf Steiner
Regarding the Master Jesus and Christian Rosenkreutz

Rudolf Steiner replied to a question concerning the Friend of God from the Highland, that he was the Master Jesus who, since the Mystery of Golgotha, has incarnated during every century. To another question about whether he was currently incarnated, Rudolf Steiner said that he was living at the time in the Carpathians, and indicated that they were in spiritual contact.

(Recorded by Friedrich Rittelmeyer, no date)

To a question about the significance of the assembly of twelve leading Friends of God with their aged leader, (the "Friend of God from the Highlands") as described in the leader's last letter, written at Easter 1380, Rudolf Steiner replied:

"You see, this is where you have the change to Rosicrucianism. It is the same thing that is pointed to in 'The Mysteries', a Christmas and Easter poem by Goethe." Since that time Christian Rosenkreutz has become the leading personality in the spiritual life of the West. Both he and the Master Jesus, the Friend of God from the Highlands, have been incarnated in every century since then. They incarnate in turns every century, and from that time on the Master Jesus has worked along with Christian Rosenkreutz.

(Recorded by Wilhelm Rath from his conversation with
Rudolf Steiner in Stuttgart, October 16, 1922)

---

147. See the lecture given in Munich, August 31, 1909, *The East in the Light of the West*, Spiritual Science Library, Blauvelt, NY, 1986, lecture 9 (GA 113); also the November 11, 1904 lecture in Berlin, *The Temple Legend*, Rudolf Steiner Press, London, 1985, lecture 6 (CW 93); and April 19, 1917 in Berlin, *Building Stones for an Understanding of the Mystery of Golgotha*, Rudolf Steiner Press, London, 1985, lecture 7 (CW 175).

To the question as to whether the Friend of God from the Highlands was Christian Rosenkreutz, Rudolf Steiner replied: "No! But Christian Rosenkreutz was among the twelve Friends of God whose secret meeting was reported by the Friend of God from the Highlands." To the further question as to whether the Friend of God was Zarathustra, Rudolf Steiner answered "Yes."

To the question: Is he who is called John in the first three Gospels the same as Lazarus? Rudolf Steiner answered: "The writer of Saint John's Gospel is Lazarus. He is only called 'John' in the same way that many were called 'John' in his day. What was the name 'John' at that time?"

Question: Is Lazarus the same as the son of Zebedee?

Counter question: Do the sons of Zebedee belong anyway to the intimate circle of the Twelve? To the starry circle where Christ saw himself mirrored? "It must be a mistake if it is written thus in the Gospels. We must not be surprised if mistakes do occur, because the Apostles were able to exchange their physical bodies with one another under the prevailing, very different soul conditions of that time. The three Disciples in the Garden of Gethsemane belonged, at any rate, to the most intimate circle of the twelve and Lazarus belonged to it too."

(Recorded conversations of the Christian Community priests Werner Klein and Emil Bock with Rudolf Steiner, February 1924)

The Master Jesus is in continual incarnation, with intervals that never exceed twelve years.

(Recorded by Emmy von Gummppenberg, no date)

With Regard to Mani

The Young Man of Nain became a pupil and follower of Christ after he had been raised from the dead. He did not belong to the Twelve.

Question: Is he not named as a pupil of Christ in the apocryphal Gospels?

Answer: "In his following incarnation he was Mani. His further incarnations can be recognized by legends similar to that of the Lazarus awakening.

(Recorded from conversations of the Christian Community priests
Werner Klein and Emil Bock with Rudolf Steiner, February 1924)

Mani will not incarnate during this century, but intends to do so in the next century, if he can find a suitable body. The ordinary kind of education does not provide any possibility for Mani to develop; only Waldorf education would do so. If the right conditions are provided he will appear as a teacher of humankind and take up leadership in matters of art and religion. He will act from the power of the Grail Mysteries, and he will instruct humankind so that they may decide even about good and evil.

(Recorded by Ehrenfried Pfeiffer from his conversations
with Rudolf Steiner between 1919 and 1921)

SUPPLEMENT

BY HELLA WIESBERGER

The Masters of Wisdom and of the Harmony
of Sensations and Feelings in the Work of Rudolf Steiner

At the first General Meeting of the German Section in October
1903 Rudolf Steiner outlined his future program as "esoteric historical research," a part of which was to comprise the teaching of great
spiritual leaders of humankind. Esoteric historical research from
the three aspects of body, soul, and spirit shows how bodily existence is determined by the great cosmic natural forces, how the personal element plays a part in history, and how the universal spirit of
the cosmos interweaves in human destiny by directing its life into
the higher self of a great leader of humanity, thus influencing the
whole of humankind:

> For that is the path followed by the life of the spirit: it flows into
> the higher selves of the leading personalities, who then impart
> it to their brothers and sisters. From one incarnation to the
> next the higher selves of men and women are progressing and
> thereby continue to learn in ever greater degree how to make
> the inner self into a missionary for the divine world-plan.
> Through esoteric historical research one will become aware of
> how the leaders of humanity develop to such a height that they
> can take over a divine mission; one will comprehend how Bud-
> dha, Zarathustra, and Christ came to their missions.[148]

---

148. "Esoteric Historical Research," by Rudolf Steiner in *Lucifer-Gnosis* (CW 34).

At the next General Meeting in October 1904 the theme of world leaders was taken up again with many references to the fact that, to understand the subject properly, one must differentiate between Masters of the past, present and future.

The Masters of the Past, Present, and Future

After references such as those in the lectures of October 7 and 24, 1904, this fact was again dealt with in detail on October 28 with the justification that, although it was already known to most people, one should nevertheless continually remind oneself that

> During the course of our fifth Great—that is, post-Atlantean— Epoch, a very important step will be made for the whole of evolution—specifically, that the leaders of humanity, or Manus, will arise from the ranks of humankind itself.
>
> All the great leaders, the Manus, who helped humankind in its progress during the preceding Great Epochs, who gave the great impulses, did not undergo their development on the Earth alone, but in part on other heavenly bodies, and thereby they have brought down to Earth from other worlds the impulses they wished to impart to humankind. The Manus of the Lemurian race and also those of Atlantis, as well as the principal Manu assigned to our fifth Great Epoch, are superhuman individuals who have undergone special training on other planets so that they can become the leaders of humanity.
>
> On the other hand, such highly evolved individuals are developing among humanity itself during our fifth Great Epoch that they can become leaders of humanity from the time of the sixth Great Epoch onward. In particular, the chief leader of the sixth Great Epoch will be a human being, just as we ourselves are human beings, only he will be one of the most advanced— indeed the most advanced of all. It will be a being that began its development during the middle of the Lemurian epoch, when humanity was only just coming into existence. This being was always a human being among other human beings, but could

develop more quickly and went through all the stages of human development. That will be the basic characteristic of the Manu of the sixth Great Epoch. Such beings have to undergo the most manifold initiations. They have to be initiated again and again.

It was for that reason that in the fifth Great Epoch there have always been initiates right from the beginning, those who were initiated in such a way that they could, as it were, go their own independent way. That had not been the case throughout the whole of the Lemurian epoch, nor during the whole of the Atlantean epoch. During those epochs, those who assisted human progress, the rulers and leaders of the State and of the great religious communities, stood under the influence of higher beings. During the course of the Lemurian and Atlantean epochs they depended entirely on those exalted beings who had undergone their training on other planets. Humanity will only be given its freedom during the fifth Great Epoch. During this epoch we will have initiates who are certainly in contact with higher beings, but who have not received their comprehensive instructions worked out in such detail. The initiates of the fifth Great Epoch will be given more and more freedom as regards the details. Directions will be given in general, not only to the initiates, but also to those who receive their inspiration from them. They will receive the impulses in such a way that they will have to work from their own initiative.

(Berlin, October 28, 1904)

A few months after this exposition we again find an emphasis laid on the fact that the leaders of humanity and Masters of the fifth Great Epoch—the post-Atlantean epoch—will arise from the ranks of human beings:

Now he will become one of the Masters who is able to pass through all the phases of humanity but in more rapid succession, and is able to raise himself to become a leader of humankind.

(Berlin, May 5, 1905)

Such human beings will then become the "true" Masters of Wisdom and of the Harmony of Sensations and Feelings. The direction of this endeavor is revealed in the following:

> The task we have today is to grasp the esoteric in the purest element of thought, in Manas. To comprehend what is spiritual in the finest distillation of the brain is the true mission of our age. To make this thought so powerful that it acquires something of an esoteric strength itself—that is the task that has been set us in order that we may assume our rightful position in the future.
> (Düsseldorf, March 7, 1907)

The same is expressed in the answer to a question once asked as to where the initiates of humankind are to be found today, when a life's work such as theirs is at stake:

> Spiritual truths have now to be grasped by human *thought*. If you were to meet these initiates today you might not find in them anything of what you are seeking. They had their tasks more in earlier incarnations. Today human *thinking* must be spiritualized.[149]

Of the Twelvefold, Sevenfold, and Fourfold Activity of the Master

Until the separation of the first Esoteric Study Group from the Esoteric School of Theosophy in the year 1907, Rudolf Steiner gave the names of four Masters who were especially connected with the theosophical movement: the two Masters from the East, Kut Hoomi and Morya, and the two Masters from the West, Christian Rosenkreutz and the Master Jesus. After the separation he only spoke of the two Masters from the West.

If one asks why only four Masters—respectively two—are named, whereas according to other statements, twelve constitute the Great

---

149. Friedrich Rittelmeyer, *Rudolf Steiner Enters My Life*, Floris Books, Edinburgh, 1982.

White Lodge,[150] and if it is further stated that never more than seven of these are incarnated at any one time,[151] then it will be evident that certain rules are connected with the numbers 12, 7, and 4. To begin with there is a fixed relationship between 12 and 7, expressed thus in notes of a privately held class lesson of Marie von Sivers in Berlin on July 3, 1904:

1						
2	2					
3	3	3				
4	4	4	4			
5	5	5	5	5		
6	6	6	6	6	6	
7	7	7	7	7	7	7
	8	8	8	8	8	8
		9	9	9	9	9
			10	10	10	10
				11	11	11
					12	12
						13

I	II	III	IV	V	VI	VII

When we contemplate the development of a planetary system, the following has to be taken into account: Such development proceeds so that two things always interchange with one another: *evolution* and *involution*. And now we have to contemplate the seven from the point of view of evolution and involution.

When it comes to the turn of the next planet each of the ruling planets has to move on one stage further. Eight is the further development of seven. When a planet develops further, it turns into the next one. When it arrives at the seventh stage no

---

150. Lecture in Cologne, December 3, 1905, "Parzival and Lohengrin" (typescript).
151. Lecture in Berlin, October 10, 1905, *Foundations of Esotericism* (CW 93a).

further step is possible. If seven were to become eight, it would present a stage already attained, and it would be merely a repetition of the first; it is the seven on another level. In moving forward we find that the leaders themselves have undergone a change. We have twelve rulers and a thirteenth who is superfluous. This thirteenth causes the whole planet to change into its first condition, but on a higher level.

With twelve it finishes. So it is that in every sequence of a planetary chain we have twelve exalted leading spirits, not seven. In the first of these the eighth is not active, and so on. (Our concepts are a part of lower Devachan. These beings are beyond our conception and therefore it is not a question of something proceeding out of something else, but of their relationship to one another—it is beyond time.)[152]

These beings have been designated the twelve Rulers through certain symbols—for example, the signs of the zodiac, through which the Sun passes. Corresponding to the macrocosmic stages is the enhancement of consciousness occurring in the microcosmic development. Thus the number twelve has always been a decisive factor and there have always been twelve universal leading spirits: the twelve Tribes of Israel, the twelve Apostles, the twelve Knights of the Grail.

Twelve is therefore the sacred number underlying all things, both in the macrocosm and the microcosm. Seven of these are actively engaged and five of them have other tasks to perform. For the physical planet only the number seven comes into question and that is the reason why, of the twelve principles, only seven principles of humankind are taught.[153]

---

152. Concerning space and time in connection with the numbers seven and twelve, compare the lecture "The Bodhisattvas and the Christ" (Munich, August 31, 1909), *The East in the Light of the West/Children of Lucifer*, Spiritual Science Library, Blauvelt, NY, 1986.

153. See *Cosmic Memory*, SteinerBooks, Great Barrington, MA (CW 11); it is indicated that there are twelve stages of consciousness, of which, however, only seven can be described. The eye of the seer can perceive five further stages, but it is impossible to describe them.

These stated facts—that only seven of the twelve leading spirits are of importance for the physical realm—and also the replies to questions on May 29, 1915 make it clear why, within the Theosophical Society, one speaks of seven Masters: Kut Hoomi, Morya, Jesus, Christian Rosenkreutz (called the Count of Saint Germain since his incarnation in the eighteenth century), Hilarion, Serapis, and the so-called Venetian Master.[154] These seven were regarded as the seven rays of the Logos, and to each was ascribed a special way of working according to the kind of ray that was attributed to him. Of Christian Rosenkreutz, for instance, it was said that, as representing the seventh ray, he worked by means of ceremonial magic. Rudolf Steiner apparently rejected this idea, for in the lecture given in Berlin on June 20, 1912, he stated that the individuality of Christian Rosenkreutz; "whom we acknowledge as the leader of the occult movement leading into the future," is often misunderstood, even by occultists, and that he would certainly never transmit his authority by means of an exoteric cult.[155]

However, as shown by the lecture of July 3, 1904 in Berlin and the answers to questions on May 29, 1915 in Dornach quoted above, Rudolf Steiner also spoke about the sevenfold activity of the Masters. To a question regarding this sevenfoldness, asked by another member, he answered: "Two are active in the East, two in the West, two in the Center, but one moves about." The expression "in the Center" does not refer to Central Europe, but to the region of the Mediterranean, as being the center of the world. Central Europe belongs to the western half of the world considered from a global point of view; that is why Rudolf Steiner always spoke about the two Masters of the West in reference to those who were representative of Central Europe.

The various references to the reincarnations of the Masters may also appear controversial at first glance since we are told that such highly developed individualities are already released from earthly incarnations, but are also told of actual incarnations of certain Masters having a special mission, even to the extent that their physical

---

154. See "From the Teachings about the Masters of Wisdom..." pp. 169 ff.
155. Recorded by Friedrich Rittelmeyer.

bodies are preserved, and that death does not occur.[156] This apparent contradiction, however, only shows that the work of the Masters is varied and complicated, and that their office comprises many different ranks—for example, Bodhisattva and Buddha—as described often by Rudolf Steiner.[157] This double possibility of being incarnated or not is exemplified, for instance, in *The Temple Legend*:

> … the Masters, as a rule, are not personages known to history; they sometimes incarnate, when necessary, in historical personalities, but this is, in a certain respect, a personal sacrifice. The level of their consciousness is no longer compatible with any work for themselves—and preservation of a name does after all involve work for oneself. (p. 120)

When the present day "leaders of humanity" go about in the world in their human guise, they are not recognized by what they are in the outer world. When from the theosophical standpoint we speak of the "Masters of Wisdom and of the Harmony of Sensations and Feelings," people would often be surprised to see in what simple, unpretentious human form these "Masters of Wisdom and of the Harmony of Sensations and Feelings" pass through all countries. They are present on the physical plane, but do not give their most important teachings there, but they impart them on the spiritual plane. Those who wish to hear them, to receive their teachings, must have access to them not only in their physical body of flesh, but in their spiritual form.[158]

The foregoing passage also illustrates clearly how necessary it is to be wary when judging and reflecting on statements made by Rudolf Steiner concerning the incarnations of the Masters—especially

---

156. See quotes from Rudolf Steiner in the footnote on page 173.
157. See, for example, the lecture in Berlin on October 25, 1909, in *The Christ-Impulse and the Development of I-Consciousness* (CW 116).
158. Munich, August 24, 1911, "The Dionysian Mysteries," in *Wonders of the World, Ordeals of the Soul and Revelations of the Spirit*, Rudolf Steiner Press, London, 1983.

where these are defective or not authentically transmitted. For the fact must also be considered that the Masters do not appear only in physical incarnation, but also by means of incorporation, inspiration, or also by means of astral appearance. This is indicated in the report by Eugenie von Bredow of an Esoteric Class lesson where the Master Kut Hoomi was being discussed and it was said that "this incarnation did not occur in a particular individual, but his power was active first in one place, then in another![159] It is evident that occult phenomena are at work here that are difficult or impossible to grasp with the ordinary intelligence, wherefore, no doubt, the manifold guises in which the Mahatmas appeared to H. P. Blavatsky and other TS members, were necessarily the cause of such great misunderstandings. The possibility, however, of materialization was never doubted by Rudolf Steiner; Friedrich Rittlemeyer records a conversation with him:

> A conversation, particularly fresh in my memory, took place after a Group Meeting. Dr. Steiner spoke about the previous incorporations of the Master. "Someone in the room approaches you," he said. "You give him your hand and speak with him. He leaves the room again, but you do not observe that he leaves the house." However readily Rudolf Steiner replied to such questions, he nevertheless gradually steered the conversation away in two different directions: first toward the side of the most important present-day task, namely, the spiritualization of thinking, and second, in the direction of historical connections.

The Seven Great Life-Secrets and the Masters

If we now proceed in our inquiry regarding the activity of the Masters in human affairs, from a consideration of the relationship of twelve to seven to the question of the relationship of seven to four, we are faced with a still more complicated problem. To elucidate this we must start with the letter to Günther Wagner on December

---

159. Berlin, December 13, 1905.

24, 1903, contained in the first part of this book. This letter was in reply to a request for a fuller explanation of the indication given at the first General Meeting of the German Section in Berlin, in October 1903. There it was stated that each of the seven Races had a Mystery to solve. The reply to Günther Wagner commenced with the following sentence quoted from *The Secret Doctrine* by H. P. Blavatsky: "Out of the Seven Truths and Revelations, or rather revealed secrets, four only have been handed to us, as we are still in the Fourth Round."[160]

This sentence is from Blavatsky's commentary to the ten Stanzas of the so-called "Dzyan" book, which, as the basic source of theosophical knowledge of the universe, forms the main part of *An Outline of Esoteric Science*. The remaining content consists solely of the commentary thereto. In general Rudolf Steiner was very critical of the commentaries by H. P. Blavatsky, but of the Dzyan Stanzas themselves he has always spoken with great esteem—for example, in the lecture given in Düsseldorf, April 12, 1909.[161]

The following is the first stanza, which Rudolf Steiner translated into German:[162]

1. The Eternal Parent, wrapped in her ever invisible robes, had slumbered once again for seven eternities.
2. Time was not, for it lay asleep in the infinite bosom of duration.
3. Universal mind was not, for there were no *Ah-hi* to contain it.
4. The seven ways to bliss were not. The great causes of misery were not, for there was no one to produce and get ensnared by them.
5. Darkness alone filled the boundless All, for Father (Law, Necessity), Mother (World-Substance) and Son (Ordered World, Substance, Cosmos) had not awakened yet for the new wheel and his pilgrimage thereon.

---

160. *The Secret Doctrine*, Vol. 1, Stanza 1, verse 6.
161. *The Spiritual Hierarchies and the Physical World*, SteinerBooks, Great Barrington, MA, 2008 (CW 110).
162. From a notebook of 1903. Archive No.427, pp. 580–581

6. The seven sublime Lords and seven Truths had ceased to be, and the universe, the son of necessity, was immersed in *Paranishpanna* to be out-breathed by that which is, and yet is not. Naught (super-existence) was.

7. The causes of existence had been done away with; The visible that was, and the invisible that is, rested in eternal non-being, the one being (Super-Existence).

8. Alone, the one form of existence (Super-Existence) stretched boundless, infinite, causeless, in dreamless sleep; and life pulsated unconsciously (blissfully) in universal space, throughout that All-Presence sensed by the "Open Eye" of the *Dangma*.

9. But where was the *Dangma* when the *A-laya* of the Universe was in *Paramartha* and the great wheel was *Anupudaka?*

> *Ah-hi* = Soul of the Dhyan-Chohans.
> *Paranishpanna* = Perfection.
> *Dangma* = Seer.
> *A-laya* = World-Soul.
> *Paramartha* = Perfection.
>   (*Parama* = above all things,   *artha* = comprehend).
> *Anupadaka* = Without parents.

The full text of the commentary by H. P. Blavatsky to the sixth verse of the above first Dzyan-stanza to which Rudolf Steiner refers in his letter to Günther Wagner, December 24, 1903, is as follows:

The seven sublime Lords are the seven Creative Spirits, the Dhyan-Chohans, who correspond to the Hebrew Elohim. It is the same hierarchy of Archangels to which Saint Michael, Saint Gabriel, and others in Christian theology belong. Only, while Saint Michael, for instance, is allowed in dogmatic Latin theology to watch over all the promontories and gulfs, in the esoteric system, the Dhyanis watch successively over one of the Rounds and the great Root-Races of our planetary chain. They are, moreover, said to send their Bodhisattvas, the human correspondents of the Dhyani-Buddhas, during every Round and

Race. Out of seven Truths and Revelations, or rather revealed secrets, four only have been handed to us, as we are still in the Fourth Round, and the world also has only had four Buddhas, so far. This is a very complicated question, and will receive ampler treatment later on.

So far "There are only four Truths, and four Vedas"—say the Hindus and Buddhists. For a similar reason Irenaeus insisted on the necessity of four Gospels. But as every new Root-Race as the head of a Round must have its revelation and revealers, the next Round will bring the fifth, the following the sixth, and so on."

According to H. P. Blavatsky—and confirmed in Rudolf Steiner's (December 24, 1903) letter to Günther Wagner—only four of the seven Truths, or Revelations, have as yet been bestowed on the world. Whereas each revelation needs someone to reveal it, there must have been only four Buddhas. It must remain an open question as to whether, and in what way, these four Buddhas are identical with the four Masters spoken of by Rudolf Steiner within the Esoteric School; he once equated, however, the ranks "Master" and "Buddha."

We are here directly confronted with the question of the relationship of the Masters to the Buddhas or, respectively, to the Bodhisattvas; for Rudolf Steiner refers to both as "great spiritual leaders of humanity," and he says of both that they form a unity of twelve whose task it is to regulate the further evolution of the world, and to teach humankind the importance of the Christ-Impulse for human progress. A condition for the closer study of this question is, undoubtedly, an acceptance of the fact that the designations "Master," "Buddha," "Bodhisattva" are not personal names but denote stages or titles in the hierarchy of the initiates, attainable by a human being who goes through the necessary development. In the lecture given in Berlin on October 1, 1905, the concept *Bodhisattva* means: "one who has absorbed all earthly experiences into oneself so that one knows how to use everything and has thus become a creator." The sages of this world, therefore, are not yet Bodhisattvas, because a sage is still unfamiliar with some things. After working for a long time as a teacher of humankind within the rank of Bodhisattva, one ascends to the degree of Buddha; one no longer needs to incarnate, but works in a purely spiritual way to further evolution.

As Rudolf Steiner sometimes uses the term *Bodhisattva* and sometimes *Master* when speaking of the same personality—for example, Zarathustra—and once equates the rank of Buddha with Master, the term "the Masters of Wisdom and of the Harmony of Sensations and Feelings" may be assumed to refer to the same rank that goes by the name *Bodhisattva* or *Buddha* in the Eastern tradition.[163] But Rudolf Steiner has often stated that, for an understanding of the actual relationships, we are presented with very complicated structure, the outcome of the intervention of beings of the higher hierarchies.

An understanding of what even H. P. Blavatsky calls "a very complicated question" concerning the relationship of seven to four is elucidated only through Rudolf Steiner's description of what he calls "the seven great Life-Secrets." They are the same as what H. P. Blavatsky calls "The Seven Truths and Revelations, or rather Revealed Secrets." In the letter by Rudolf Steiner already referred to, he calls them "The seven esoteric Root-Truths." In the notes of a lecture it is stated:

We speak of seven great Secrets. There are seven great Mysteries that reveal the seven great phases of life. Their name is the "Unutterable." (Berlin, October 28, 1903)

During the General Meeting, which had taken place ten days earlier, Rudolf Steiner had already referred to this "in the sense of a certain occult tradition." This tradition had then already appeared in a literary form through the work of the English occultist C. G. Harrison. In his book *The Transcendental Universe*,[164] which contains six lectures, Harrison took a stand against the Theosophy of H. P. Blavatsky from the standpoint of traditional European-Christian occultism. He had to admit, however, that *The Secret Doctrine* "affords

---

163. See "The Christ Impulse in Historical Development," lecture 1, *Esoteric Christianity and the Mission of Christian Rosenkreutz*, Rudolf Steiner Press, London, 1984.
164. *The Transcendental Universe*, Lindisfarne Press, Hudson, NY, 1993.

most valuable information in regard to prehistoric civilizations and religions, and hints at certain secrets, the very existence of which was unsuspected and some of which have been tested by a process known to occultists and found correct" (lecture 1). In the sixth lecture Harrison dealt with the "Seven Great Mysteries." These Mysteries, it is said, are valid for all stages of consciousness and cannot be explained in words, "but necessitate the employment of a symbolic system, the nature of which the writer is not at liberty to explain." In a footnote thereto they are enumerated as follows: 1) Abyss; 2) Number; 3) Affinity; 4) Birth and Death; 5) Evil; 6) The Word; and 7) Godliness.

In the very fragmentary notes from the first years of Rudolf Steiner's lecturing activity in spiritual science, these seven Mysteries are usually mentioned only in part, and the name of Harrison is never alluded to. Also in later, even more concrete statements, they are only partially dealt with, so that it is not possible to recognize that a sevenfold unity is under discussion.[165] Only one single reference alludes to all seven Mysteries as they are enumerated by Harrison. This is in the Paris lectures, May and June, 1906. The reference in the June 13 lecture follows:

> There are seven Life-Secrets of which no one, outside of the Occult Brotherhoods, has ever spoken. Only in the present epoch has it become possible to speak about them exoterically. They are also known as the "unutterable" secrets.[166]

These are the Seven Mysteries:

1. The Mystery of the Abyss.
2. The Mystery of Number. (This can be studied in the Pythagorean philosophy.)
3. The Mystery of Alchemy. (This can be understood through the writings of Paracelsus and Jakob Böhme.)

---

165. See: *Secrets of the Threshold*, Anthroposophic Press, Hudson, NY, 1987 (CW 147); *Esoteric Reading and Esoteric Hearing*, SteinerBooks, MA, 2008 (CW 156); *The Problem of Faust*, November 3–4, 1917, typescript (CW 273).
166. This report by Schuré was originally in French.

4. The Mystery of Birth and Death.
5. The Mystery of Evil, dealt with in the Apocalypse.
6. The Mystery of the Word, the Logos.
7. The Mystery of Godliness; it is the most hidden of all.

From the notes by Marie von Sivers of her private lessons (Berlin, July 2, 1904) it follows that in the case of these seven great Mysteries or esoteric Root-Truths we are not dealing just with concepts in general, that "run like a red thread through the whole esoteric movement,"[167] but that behind these concepts high spiritual beings are standing. Accordingly, the seven possible relationships that the Trinity of Father, Son, and Spirit enters into can be understood as actual beings, and the names by which these seven possible "Relationship-Beings" are designated relate again to the names of the seven Life-Mysteries. In the first lecture cycle about spiritual-scientific cosmology we find described in a basic way how the whole of evolution is controlled according to three principles: Consciousness, Life, and Form, and how each of these three principles passes through seven stages or phases.[168] The stages or phases of Life therein named correspond furthermore with the Seven Great Mysteries of Life. Knowledge about them and the soul experiences that accompany them form the two integral halves of initiation and consequently the content of Anthroposophy as the modern science of initiation.[169]

Whereas one constantly hears in Rudolf Steiner's spiritual science of the seven stages of Consciousness and of Form, referred to as the seven principles of the human frame and of the Earth's structure, this is not to the same extent true in the case of the seven stages of Cosmic Life. This is evidently connected with the fact that the Planetary Spirit does not reveal its inner reaction.[170] And that is proba-

---

167. Paris, May 5, 1913, *Die Welt des Geistes und ihr Hereinragen in das physische Dasein* (CW 150).

168. October 17–November 10, 1904, *Beiträge zur Rudolf Steiner Gesamtausgabe* (Nr. 67/68, 69/70, 78).

169. Dornach, December 30, 1914, *Art as Seen in the Light of Mystery Wisdom.* Rudolf Steiner Press, 1996 (CW 275).

170. Berlin, 3 November 1904, "Planetary and Human Evolution."

bly why the seven Life-Secrets are called "unutterable," which must be extremely difficult to describe—as indicated in the lectures in Munich, December 4, 1907, and Dornach, December 30, 1914.

The notes of a lecture in Berlin, November 1, 1904, provide the most decisive indication that the relationship of *seven* to *four* concerns both the seven Mysteries themselves, and also the revealers of the Mysteries, the Masters. According to this, the main characteristic of the seven Life-Secrets is their application to all cycles of evolution because of their constant recurrence; and, indeed, they do recur "in every Round and Epoch of Earth evolution, and likewise in all cyclic developments within human beings themselves." This indication explains for the first time the statement in the letter to Günther Wagner on December 24, 1903 that "... number four of the above-mentioned Seven Truths is derived from the seven esoteric Root-Truths, and that of these seven partial truths (the fourth being considered as complete), one is divulged (as a rule) to each Race [Epoch]."

From this we can draw the following threefold conclusion:

1. The seven Root-Truths or Secrets are relevant in the first place to the great evolutionary cycles of the planetary chain: Saturn–Sun–Moon–Earth–Jupiter–Venus–Vulcan.

2. For the whole of Earth evolution the fourth Mystery, that of birth and death, applies.

3. Because the seven Mysteries always recur, they also apply to every sevenfold division within the total Earth evolution—however, only as partial truths within the much larger fourth Mystery.[171]

The question arises from all of this: How does the present time and the work of Rudolf Steiner stand in relationship to the seven great Mysteries of Life?

---

171. Dornach, November 3–4, 1917, *Geisteswissenschaftliche Erläuterungen zu Goethes Faust*, vol. 1, untranslated (CW 273).

The Work of Rudolf Steiner in Relationship to the
Fifth of the Seven Great Life-Secrets

As the seven great Mysteries of Life hold good for all cycles of development having a sevenfold nature, it must follow that the time of our immediate present, that of the fifth post-Atlantean cultural epoch, must be influenced by the fifth of the Mysteries, *Evil.* This, indeed, does not apply in its entirety, but only as partial truth belonging to the future, for the more comprehensive principle is the fourth Mystery that still prevails and holds sway throughout the whole of Earth evolution. The fifth Mystery will be revealed in a much more powerful way during the fifth planetary stage of the Earth than it is today during the fifth cultural epoch. In the fifth epoch it will attain to its full strength when the Earth shall have developed to the Jupiter stage of consciousness.[172]

We are told in the letter to Günther Wagner (on page page 51) that theosophy—the part of theosophy you might find in Blavatsky's *Secret Doctrine,* or her *Esotericism*[173]—consists of a sum total of partial truths from the fifth Mystery, and we are inclined to ask: What has Evil got to do with Theosophy?

This question is partly answered by the view spiritual science takes toward Good and Evil. According to this view, knowledge of good and evil in our cultural epoch is bound up with knowledge concerning the spiritual impulses underlying human and cosmic evolution.[174] Evil appears when people, either individually or collectively, deviate from conformity to progressive cosmic impulses. There is no evil as such; evil is not an absolute reality, but arises when something that is good in some aspects, is used improperly in the world. Through this fact, something good is turned into something evil.[175]

---

172. Munich, January 16, 1908, *Anweisungen für eine esoterische Schulung* (CW 245).

173. Volume 3 of *The Secret Doctrine.*

174. Dornach, September 28, 1918, *Geisteswissenschaftliche Erläuterungen zu Goethes «Faust,»* vol. 2 (GA 273).

175. *Secrets of the Threshold,* Anthroposophic Press, Hudson, NY, and Rudolf Steiner Press, London, 1987, lecture 2, Munich, August 25, 1913 (CW 147).

Another view of evil was the determining factor in the previous cultural epoch, the Greco-Latin age, for, being the fourth epoch, it was ruled by the fourth Mystery, the Mystery of Birth and Death. This can be seen from the following modification of the seven steps to initiation. The Christian-Gnostic way of initiation that was customary for the fourth epoch had the following seven steps: 1) the Washing of the Feet; 2) the Scourging; 3) the Crowning with Thorns; 4) the Crucifixion; 5) the Mystic Death; 6) the Laying in the Grave; and 7) the Ascension. The Christian-Rosicrucian way of initiation appropriate to the fifth cultural epoch has the following seven steps: 1) Study toward true Self-knowledge; 2) Imagination; 3) Learning of the Occult Script, or Inspired Knowledge; 4) Creating Rhythm in Life (preparation of the Philosopher's Stone); 5) Correspondence of Microcosm and Macrocosm (knowledge of the connection between human being and the universe); 6) Resting or Immersing Oneself in the Macrocosm; and 7) Godliness. Now the experience of evil in both ways of initiation certainly lies at the fifth step, but in the Christian-Gnostic way of the fourth epoch it was connected with the experience of the Mystic Death as the so-called "Descent into Hell." In the way of initiation of our fifth epoch, however, we become acquainted with the true *good* in the correspondence of the microcosm to the macrocosm, and *evil* as the deviation from this correspondence in either direction. Since the way of initiation appropriate to a particular epoch is always bound up with the powers that epoch must develop in connection with the seven Life-Secrets, Anthroposophy must, therefore, necessarily become the science of correspondence—or even the non-correspondence of microcosm to macrocosm. The question regarding good and evil, according to that, must be solved today by means of a knowledge of the proper correspondence.

Seen in this light, the passage from the letter of December 24, 1903 stating that Theosophy is the sum of the partial truths of the fifth Mystery is explained, in that this statement refers only to the double aspect of the fifth step in the modern way of initiation: the correspondence between microcosm and macrocosm on the one hand, and on the other hand, the deviation from this expressed as evil. Through this, a knowledge of good and evil that shows a more fixed character (a character, so to speak, more "spatial") during the fourth epoch, receives a more "flowing" character during the fifth epoch. It becomes more and more a question of the knowledge of the true impulse of the age, or, expressed in another way, the knowledge of the true impulses behind the cosmic evolutionary history. There is a certain law and order about this step from the more "spatial" to the more "temporal" kind of knowledge, which Rudolf Steiner once pointed to when he spoke about the relationship of the first four cultural epochs to the three following ones:

> When what is of a spatial nature changes into something temporal then the process comes about through the relationship of four to seven, the fourfoldness extends to become a sevenfoldness.... The relationship of four to seven depends upon a certain definite law. (Berlin, October 28, 1904)

It is also evident from the following notebook entry that the stand toward the question of good and evil must be very different from what was right during the previous epoch:

> The Masters are not a rampart against evil, but the leaders in absorbing evil. We should not cast out evil, but just take it up and use it in the service of the good. The rage of the lion remains evil only as long as it is used by the lion in an egoistic fashion; if some conqueror could use the rage of the lion to accomplish social service, then it would be beneficial. Therefore, what is *evil* can be recognized as *un*-real. There is no evil. Evil is only a misplaced *good*. Only when one recognizes this fact is spiritual alchemy possible.

In connection with the seven great Mysteries of Life and in the sense H. P. Blavatsky expresses in the words, "every new Root-Race [Great Epoch] has to receive its Mystery and its revealer of Mysteries at the beginning of a new Round of Evolution," we can only infer that Rudolf Steiner, as revealed in his work, is the *first* revealer of the fifth esoteric Root-Truth, the fifth of the great Life-Mysteries, and that, indeed, in its double sense: on the one hand, that of the correspondence of macrocosm to microcosm; on the other, that of its deviation, expressing itself as evil.

In the collection of notes referring to the early years of Rudolf Steiner's lecturing activity on behalf of spiritual science, the truth about the Mystery of Evil is only hinted at, but it is nevertheless already touched upon in its full depth. For instance, in the report of what Rudolf Steiner said at the First General Meeting of the German Section of the TS states that one of the most important of the many reasons leading to the founding of the theosophical movement as a "powerful occult necessity" was that every Race [epoch] was given a "Mystery," and that we, as representatives of the fifth epoch, had arrived at the stage of the fifth Mystery, which, however, could not yet be revealed at the present day. It then proceeds as follows:

We are, however, at the point where we shall gradually move toward it. Its nature is hinted at by Saint Paul, who was an initiate. It will be revealed to us only during the course of the epoch. A premature speculation about this Mystery through purely intellectual ability would pose an indescribable danger to humankind. Since a speculation of this sort has already twice nearly succeeded[176] and is about to happen again within a short time, the great teachers of humankind have brought the theosophical movement into being. Humanity is to be prepared for the great truth. Theosophy is working toward a particular moment in time. A core of people are to be prepared who will understand this Mystery when the time comes for its revelation—a core of people who understand it correctly and will make use of it for good ends, and not allow it to become a curse on humanity. Earlier epochs formed such a core of people from those already appointed, and from suitable individuals and families who were particularly chosen; they were led by

176. No further details are known about this.

the Manu into suitably remote districts. Because of the universal spread of traffic over the whole globe this method is no longer appropriate, but also no longer necessary. In place of this procedure, education through the worldwide international Theosophical Society is to form this core of people.

(Berlin, October 18, 1903)

If at that time the fifth Mystery of Life was characterized more in a general way, later it was described more concretely as the unjustified use of the sacred forces of transmutation.

Profound insight into the secret of existence arises when we know the source of injustice, evil, crime, and sin that occur in the world. They happen because the best and most holy powers that exist in humankind—the powers of transformation—are applied improperly. There would be no evil in the world if there were not also these *most holy powers of transformation*.[177]

With greater and greater emphasis and with ever greater clearness Rudolf Steiner spoke about the dominance of evil, above all of its predominance in history as retrogression from the progressive stream of evolution, especially since the outbreak of the First World War. The great importance that is attached to a knowledge of evil as the root Mystery of our epoch makes it understandable why the visible sign of the anthroposophical movement, the Goetheanum building, was connected with this. At the laying of the Foundation Stone, Rudolf Steiner spoke for the first time "from esoteric obligation" about the Fifth Gospel, the Gospel of Knowledge, of which the central message was the macrocosmic Lord's Prayer:[178]

---

177. *Esoteric Reading and Esoteric Hearing*, SteinerBooks, Great Barrington, MA, 2008, lecture 3 (CW 156).
178. Trans. Dorothy Osmond with M. Cotterell. Also contained in "The Laying of the Foundation Stone of the First Goetheanum at Dornach, September 20, 1913," *Guidance in Esoteric Training: From the Esoteric School*, Rudolf Steiner Press, London, 1994, p. 120.

AUM, Amen!
The Evils hold sway
Witness of Egoity becoming free,
Selfhood's guilt incurred through others
Experienced in Daily Bread
Wherein the Will of the Heavens does not rule,
In that we severed ourselves from Your Kingdom
And forgot Your Names,
You Fathers in the Heavens.

And during the next ten years of intensive work on the building, in cooperation with many voluntary helpers, the central motif, the carved group, "The Representative of Humanity between Lucifer and Ahriman," was created as visible artistic expression of the double nature of the fifth Life-Secret. "The Representative of Humanity"—Christ—acknowledged by Rudolf Steiner as the Master of all Masters—personified the full correspondence of microcosm to macrocosm, and gained the mastery, through His radiating love, over the powers of opposition, of evil: Lucifer and Ahriman. When the building, almost completed, was destroyed by fire on New Year's Eve, 1922–1923, this wooden carving was all that was saved—a legacy and a warning by its creator to remind us to be aware of the deepest Life-Secret belonging to our fifth epoch.

PART II

THE HISTORY OF THE SEPARATION
OF THE ESOTERIC SCHOOL INTO AN
EASTERN AND A WESTERN SCHOOL
IN 1907

This part contains letters and documents from the years 1906 and 1907, which provide the background for insight into the splitting-off from the Esoteric School of Annie Besant. In addition to this, notes are included from Esoteric Classes from 1912–1913 when the underlying reasons for the separation from the Theosophical Society were again investigated.

For the new edition of 1966, the material from the archive relating to this section was checked again. Through that it became possible to extend the notes and to correct one of the dates. The letter that was numbered in the first edition as XII now becomes letter IV with the corresponding corrections for the letters following it.

FOREWORD

BY HELLA WIESBERGER

The strictness with which Rudolf Steiner adhered to the two most important rules of esoteric life, the observance of truthfulness and continuity, is exemplified particularly clearly in the deeper causes that underlay the separation of his First Class of the Esoteric School from the Esoteric School of Theosophy. That the connection was severed again after a period of only three years of working together shows that, with all his willingness to cooperate, he was not prepared to compromise in spiritual matters. Above all, the rule of absolute truthfulness held good for him—a rule without which all esoteric endeavor would prove futile, and true brotherhood could not be achieved. He expressed this very succinctly during the time of the greatest controversy between him and Annie Besant. At that time he alleged as his "ideal" to have a theosophical-occult movement inaugurated and strictly followed, "to be founded solely and exclusively on truthfulness." Even if no stone were to remain standing out of all that had been built until then, nevertheless, his ideal would have been fulfilled if one could say of it: Here the attempt had been made to found an occult movement that was completely and utterly directed toward truthfulness.

During this same time he warned that if occultism were not followed correctly, humankind's powers of judgement would be impaired instead of developed.[179] This had shown itself in the TS at that time—not only in the changed attitude of Annie Besant toward the running of the society, but also in that she had reconstituted

---

179. Berlin, June 20, 1912, in *Earthly and Cosmic Man*, Rudolf Steiner Publishing Co., London, 1948 (CW 133).

therules of the Esoteric School and had demanded a pledge of obedience from the members.[180]

This tendency of development was already evident to Rudolf Steiner when he initiated the separation from the Esoteric School in 1907. This was the result of a personal agreement between him and Annie Besant concerning her presence at the Theosophical Congress in Munich during Whit-week 1907. The separation as such had been mentioned several times by Rudolf Steiner.[181] However, the actual underlying reasons will be revealed only by the pertinent manuscripts reproduced in this volume. They make it clear that he regarded certain actions perpetrated by leading personalities of the TS as no longer tolerable. He later characterized them as "the beginning of the end of the Theosophical Society."[182]

This relates to events connected with the Masters who, from the beginning, had held a position of fundamental importance in the TS and the Esoteric School. The term *Meister* [Master], the same as the Sanskrit *Mahatma*—literally "Great Soul," is a generally accepted title of honor in India for spiritually advanced personalities; this title received special significance for the Theosophical Society at the transfer of its headquarters in 1879 from America to India, because its founding and teachings rest upon the Tibetan Mahatmas who possessed superhuman wisdom and capacities and who communicated with H. P. Blavatsky. During the first years of the society's existence the Mahatmas, who otherwise live in the greatest seclusion, appear to have been seen many times—sometimes in astral form, sometimes materialized, and sometimes in a physical body. They

---

180. The pledge follows: "I pledge myself to support the Theosophical Society before the world and in particular to submit myself unreservedly and instantly to the commands of the supreme head of the Esoteric Section in everything pertaining to my relationship with the theosophical movement and to co-operate in the policies that she defines in order to prepare for the advent of the World Teacher and to render the Society every support that I can, regarding time, money and work." Quoted from the article "A New Spiritual Slavery" in *News of the Anthroposophical (Theosophical) Society,*" April 1914.

181. See *Autobiography,* Chapter 32; and the quote at the beginning of Hella Wiesberger's introduction, p. 3.

182. Dornach, June 15, 1923, "The Emergence of the Anthroposophic Movement," in *The Anthroposophic Movement,* Rudolf Steiner Press, London, 1993 (CW 258).

imparted teachings, gave commands, and sometimes left objects behind, particularly letters, the so-called "Mahatma Letters." After the deception practiced on H. P. Blavatsky with forged Mahatma letters, the Masters withdrew from the society and became the "inner" Head of the Esoteric School; the "outer" Head referred to H. P. Blavatsky, and later her successor, Annie Besant.

News of the Mahatmas initially reached Europe through sensational writings of the English journalist Alfred Percy Sinnett, who lived in India. Blavatsky had put him in touch with one of her Tibetan teachers who answered his various questions. As a result of this correspondence, in 1881 Sinnett published his book, *The Occult World*, which included a number of Mahatma Letters.[183] His *Esoteric Buddhism* followed in 1883. These two writings provided the first systematic statement of the theosophical philosophy of life. In 1885 Mabel Collins published the much-read booklet, *Light on the Path*, which included talk of the Masters, and to which Rudolf Steiner wrote a commentary. Also, the foreword of the main theosophical work, *The Secret Doctrine*, states that the book's contents are derived from the teachings of the Masters, but that any deficiencies in transmission are to be attributed solely to the author.

Whereas Sinnett's publications were encumbered by a kind of sensationally directed and over-simplified journalism, Blavatsky's intention was to emphasize the varied and complicated connections existing in the hierarchy of the Adepts, whereby all the great Adepts and historically known Initiates could be traced back, like the branches of a tree, to a great primal leader of early humankind— the Initiate, known as the *Mahaguru*. Rudolf Steiner referred to this personality in the manuscript, *Concerning the Hierarchy of the Adepts*, quoted in this book.[184] Marie von Sivers referred to this in a personal statement:

When the individuality of the Mahaguru incarnated as Buddha, the teachings of the latter led to misunderstandings and

---

183. A complete collection of the Mahatma letters to Sinnett and others was published by Trevor Barker in 1923. The originals are in the British Museum.
184. See Archive number 3207/08, 149.

differences of opinion. He had given too much. Buddha had to incarnate once more as Shankarasharya; he trained the Tibetan teachers, the *Mathams* [Schools of Shankarasharya Philosophy], who have revealed in part the teachings of Theosophy, to convey to the various religions the esoteric content inherent in each of them, and to raise the sunken spiritual level of humanity." (1903, no date)

These "Tibetan Mahatmas" chiefly refer to the two who were H. P. Blavatsky's teachers. They were also spoken of as the leadership of the Esoteric School, the "Masters." They have long been known in theosophical literature by the names "K" (Kut Hoomi) and "M" (Morya). Their portraits are also familiar to theosophist, and were painted by a German theosophist, Hermann Schmiechen, from sketches by H. P. Blavatsky; the origin of these are described in A. P. Sinnett's *The Occult World* (p. 176 ff). The painter later joined the German Section, and also made copies of this portrait for Rudolf Steiner that were exhibited initially in the Esoteric Classes. Marie Steiner remembered that these pictures had an important part to play and produced a striking effect:

I personally experienced how several people lost their powers of speech and temporarily became quite absent and confused. But on earlier occasions the pictures were shown very obscurely, or during Esoteric Classes; now they are often printed.[185]

Since the history of the TS was determined by its connection to the Masters, we can see now that it was because of the wrong development of this connection that the TS foundered. For as it was originally conceived as an institution founded by the Masters in three sections—the third directed by the Masters themselves; encounters with them—as well as the instructions and tasks they gave—were constantly referred to when the credibility of the teachings or the conduct of the affairs of the society were called into

185. From a letter of September 29, 1948.

question. Such an appeal to invisible authorities is an anachronism for our stage of consciousness, and inevitably leads to misunderstandings and embarrassing situations. Two great scandals developed out of this, and they undermined the further effectiveness and importance of the Theosophical Society in the eyes of competent and critical personalities.

The first scandal arose in the early 1880s. H. P. Blavatsky was publicly denounced as an imposter through the supposed discovery of forged letters from the Masters. According to Rudolf Steiner's account, however, she was not the deceiver, but was herself the victim of an occult deception. He once pointed out that she had been deceived because the "Exalted Powers" present at the birth of the theosophical movement had been impersonated—for it is possible for occultists, following their own private concerns, "to take on the form of those who had previously been the inspirers of genuine impulses."[186] This apparently applies also to the authorship of the letters from the Masters. For this reason it is also not a contradiction when Rudolf Steiner spoke at one time of these letters as being important documents,[187] and on another occasion described them as the result of a swindle.[188] In the first instance, he was referring to the original, genuine letters, as published by Sinnett; on the second occasion to the forged ones.

How was it that a person such as H. P. Blavatsky, immersed to such a degree in practical occultism, could be deceived in this way? Rudolf Steiner, who often illuminated the riddle of Blavatsky, once explained that we must seek within the background of our present-day conditions of life for an explanation of why the Masters were obliged to make use of H. P. Blavatsky as a tool to bring about the cultural "miracle" of much-needed occult revelations. Blavatsky possessed a "greatness of soul" and unreserved devotion toward the

---

186. Helsingfors [Helsinki], April 11, 1912 "Humankind's Connection with the Elemental World," (GA 158).
187. Berlin, June 21, 1909, *Mitteilungen für die Mitglieder der deutschen Section der Theosophischen Gesellschaft*, No. 10, January, 1910.
188. Dornach, June 12, 1923, "The Opposition to Spiritual Revelations," *The Anthroposophical Movement*, Rudolf Steiner Press, London, 1993.

aims of the Masters, which, because of their scholarly reserve, could never have come from the scientific celebrities of the last third of the nineteenth century. Blavatsky, however, was lacking in the scientific training, and she did not always need to depend on the Masters, but could take personal responsibility for her stance.[189]

For the TS, the scandal concerning the forged letters from the Masters caused the main body of the members to see themselves as confronted with the choice of either continuing to believe in the invisible authorities, or considering them a hoax. The discussions about it in the society and amongst the interested public were numerous. Many members left the society then because they could no longer believe that Blavatsky was an ambassador of true Masters. She was obliged to give up her post in the society and leave the headquarters in India. She insisted on the society's support so that the Masters could remain in contact with it—if she were to leave the society, the Masters would go with her. Apparently she did not receive enough support from the society, for, although she was soon asked officially to resume her post in the society, she remained in Europe and never again returned to India.

These events occurred around 1885–1886; in 1887 she established her own newspaper in London, called *Lucifer*[190] and, connected with this, the "Blavatsky Lodge," whose members regarded her as their spiritual teacher and received esoteric instructions from her. In 1888—the year the *Secret Doctrine* appeared—the "Esoteric Section" of the Theosophical Society evolved from this, and brought with it the obligation to remain faithful to the Masters under all circumstances. Originally the Esoteric Section was part of the TS, but soon disputes arose about the leadership, which led Blavatsky in 1889 to change the Esoteric Section of the society to

---

189. Berlin, May 5, 1909, *Rosicrucianism Renewed* (GA 284); Helsingfors, April 11, 1912, "Humankind's Connection with the Elemental World" (CW 158); Dornach, October 11, 1915, *The Occult Movement in the Nineteenth Century*, Rudolf Steiner Press, London, 1973 (CW 254).

190. Rudolf Steiner also called his first theosophical periodical *Lucifer* because the name indicated the principle of *independence*. "That is why Blavatsky called her periodical by this name, and that is why ours is also thus called—to bear witness to this principle." Stuttgart, April 29, 1906, *The Mystery of Christ* (CW 97).

the fully independent "Eastern School of Theosophy" (commonly abbreviated to EST or ES). Thereafter, the School remained under her sole leadership. During the same year, Blavatsky's *The Key to Theosophy* appeared—"an explanation, by way of question and answer, of ethics, science, and philosophy, for the study of which the Theosophical Society has been founded." The question of the Masters was discussed in the chapter, "The Theosophical Mahatmas."[191] The Masters had relinquished their direct dealings with the society and became the "Inner Head" of the Esoteric School, whereas Blavatsky—and after her death, Annie Besant, whom she had elected as her successor—personally became the leader of the School as its "Outer Head."

The society had become a democratically administered fellowship. Thus, a new configuration and inner consolidation had been effected through a scandal staged by opponents of Theosophy, to which H. P. Blavatsky had fallen prey.

This was the situation when, after the turn of the century, Rudolf Steiner joined the Theosophical Society and its Esoteric School; this is the basis, for instance, of his letter to Amalie Wagner on January 2, 1905 regarding the polarity of the movement and the society, respectively the Esoteric School and the society.

The second scandal in the society, also in connection with the Masters, occurred in 1906–1907. In May 1906, C. W. Leadbeater, who was a prominent theosophical author due to his own clairvoyant investigations, had to withdraw from the TS because he had been accused of certain moral transgressions. It was made known in January 1907 that the Masters K. H. and M. had appeared several times at the deathbed of Founder-President H. S. Olcott in Adyar and had confirmed him in his wish to appoint Annie Besant as his successor, and had urged him to purge the affair connected with

---

191. According to correspondence (preserved in the Archive of the Rudolf Steiner *Nachlaßverwaltung*) between Rudolf Steiner and Leipzig editor Max Altmann, the "new and only authorized version" of this book in Germany was translated and published by Rudolf Steiner. It is noteworthy that this occurred in 1907 when, because of the events in Adyar concerning the Masters, Steiner found it necessary to separate from the Esoteric School of the TS.

Leadbeater, which had been too hastily dealt with. Olcott informed the General Secretary accordingly.

After Olcott's death on February 17, 1907, A. P. Sinnett—acting as Vice-President until the May election of a new President—first expressed his doubt about the authenticity of those who claimed to be the Masters; this led to great discussions in the society. Since the matter had been published abroad, not only among theosophists, but also in the public press, Rudolf Steiner found it necessary to publicly express his opinion about it through his periodical *Lucifer-Gnosis*. (See "About the Impending Presidential Election" on page 278.) He had also written personal notes about this to Olcott and other various authorities. At the end of one letter to a TS functionary he wrote that he "naturally considers it quite impossible for the President of our society to be the head of an Esoteric School." He expressed himself particularly freely and clearly in his letter to the Russian, Anna Minsloff, on 26 March 1907, (see 263). On this basis he came to an agreement with Annie Besant—who had come to the May 1907 Theosophical Congress in Munich (during the presidential election)—that he would separate his Esoteric Study Group from its former connection with the Esoteric School. In the first Esoteric Group meeting that he held after the Congress in Munich, June 1, 1907, he characterized this separation as a decisive change. The final words—that the questions probably being asked by many were answered "because of the latest developments"—refer apparently to the questionable circumstances surrounding Olcott's death. After that Rudolf Steiner spoke only about the Masters of the West.

Annie Besant also voiced her opinion at that time about the division of the Esoteric School into an Eastern and a Western School as introduced by Rudolf Steiner. After returning to London from Munich she wrote about it to Wilhelm Hübbe-Schleiden, a leading German theosophist prior to the turn of the century. He had probably approached her with a question about this matter—for he was also a member of Rudolf Steiner's first Esoteric Section.

He thereupon received the following answer from her on June 7, 1907:

31, St. James' Place,
London, S. W.
June 7, 1907

Dear Dr. Hübbe-Schleiden,
Dr. Steiner's occult training is very different from ours. He does not know the Eastern way, so cannot, of course, teach it. He teaches the Christian and Rosicrucian way, and this is very helpful to some, but is different from ours. He has his own School, on his own responsibility. I regard him as a very fine teacher on his own lines, and also a man of real knowledge. He and I work in thorough friendship and harmony, but along different lines.

Always sincerely yours,
Annie Besant[192]

In addition to this, she also officially informed the members of the EST of this through one of the so-called Esoteric Papers, "Membership in the ES" (1908), where it is stated that there is now a School in Germany, whose head is her "good colleague" Dr. Steiner. She had talked with him the previous year (1907) and told him that it would be better "if his pupils were to form a separate organization under his care, instead of remaining as a merely nominal part of the EST, which nevertheless looked to him as their head." The truth of the matter was, however, that the initiative for this came from Rudolf Steiner, and the causes were as previously stated and quite different from the above.

These causes then led further to the separation from the Theosophical Society. The stone that started this avalanche was the Leadbeater case. Annie Besant had still been one of those who, in 1906, had condemned Leadbeater most stringently by demanding that "the Theosophical Society must eschew all teachings that defile and

---

192. Facsimile in Emil Bock, *Rudolf Steiner. Studien zu seinem Lebenswerk.* Stuttgart, 1961.

degrade."[193] However, after her election as President of the TS, she engineered his reinstatement in a way that evoked much criticism and dissent. Among other things, R. G. Mead left the society at that time. Rudolf Steiner, who had already clearly proclaimed his views to Annie Besant in a personal letter at the beginning of November, 1906 (see p. 246), refused to approve the reinstatement of Leadbeater. He reserved his vote, which Annie Besant interpreted favorably, regarding it as not negative. Whereupon Rudolf Steiner felt himself obliged to send a long despatch to Adyar, to ensure that his vote was not interpreted in the meeting as being in favor of reinstatement.

This problem was summarized by Edouard Schuré in his May 1, 1913 letter to the President of the Theosophical Society in France, in which he explained his withdrawal:

> ...The distinguished personality of the President, Mrs. Annie Besant, and her exalted past record should have provided sufficient guarantee that the TS would adhere to the broad principles of tolerance, impartiality, and truthfulness, which form the essence of its program.
>
> Unfortunately, it turned out differently. The original cause of this deviation is the close connection between Mrs. Besant and Mr. Leadbeater, a learned occultist, but a shady character of doubtful morality. Since Mr. Leadbeater was condemned by the General Council of the TS, Mrs. Besant has publicly announced her condemnation of the educational principles of which he was accused. Her verdict about the theosophist whose unworthiness has been recognized was most severe. Through an unbelievably sudden change of mind, she later soon declared her intention to allow Mr. Leadbeater to be readmitted to the TS, and she

---

193. Quoted from Eugenie Lévy: *Mrs. Besant and the Crisis in the Theosophical Society.* Berlin 1913. After the withdrawal of Leadbeater in 1906 Annie Besant could still write: "If I should one day also transgress I would ask of those who love me that they should not hesitate to condemn my failings, that they do not try to gloss them over or to say that black is white; rather they should seek to alleviate my heavy destiny—as I would try to alleviate the destiny of my friends and brothers—by proclaiming the inviolable purity of the ideal.... Leadbeater has come to grief, Judge has come to grief, I too shall probably come to grief."

successfully—though not without some difficulty—won the majority vote from her associates. Her excuse for this change of mind
was compassion and forgiveness. The actual reason was that the
President needed Leadbeater in her occult research, and that this
co-operation appeared necessary for her to maintain her authority. It is clear to those who have followed her words and deeds
since then, that Mrs. Besant has succumbed to the fatal suggestion
of her dangerous companion, in that only under the spell of his
absolute authority would she be able to see, think, and act.

The personality who now speaks through her mouth is no
longer the author of the ancient wisdom, but is the dubious
visionary, the skilled user of suggestion, who no longer dares to
show himself either in London, Paris, or America, but who, hidden in a summer house in Adyar, directs the TS from there
through its President.

The unhappy result of this influence will soon become evident
in broad daylight through the Alcyone affair, and the founding of
The Order of the Star in the East. By coincidence I have inadvertently
had the opportunity to become aware of the secret motivation
and, as it were, the psychological trigger of this deplorable undertaking. I begin with the fact that, at that moment, no one even
mentioned a new teacher who would come from India—or spoke
about an imminent incarnation of Christ—and that probably no
one had thought of such a thing. No one had yet discovered Alcyone in 1908. I had just brought out the translation of Rudolf
Steiner's book *Christianity as Mystical Fact.* This book had drawn
the attention of the European public to the resurgence of Western esotericism through the splendid writings and the achievement of this German theosophist. While I was staying in Stuttgart,
I met around ten English, Dutch, French, and Swiss theosophists.
The question was raised, "Will the two Schools—that of Adyar
and the one belonging to Dr. Steiner—be able to get along with
one another?" We all had the opinion that an understanding
could be achieved in spite of the different outlooks, and that this
would be very desirable for the higher interest of Theosophy,
which did not represent any separatist or national movement, but

was a universal current of present-day culture. Only one of those asking questions protested. He was a Dutch theosophist, a very intelligent person with a sceptical and caustic wit, and an intimate friend of Leadbeater and those in Adyar. He explained quite plainly that the two Schools would never come to an understanding with one another, and he explained that "India alone was in possession of the tradition, and there had never existed a scientific esotericism of the West."

I was surprised by this definite assertion. I soon comprehended its meaning and import when, like a bomb—or rather, like a fabricated firework—the Alcyone affair burst upon us. For this affair is truly nothing but the answer of Adyar to the resurgence of Christian esotericism in the West, and I am convinced that, without the latter, we would have never heard a word about the future prophet Krishnamurti....

In Munich Annie Besant had declared to Rudolf Steiner in 1907 her incompetence with respect to Christianity; and, to the degree that this was to penetrate the society, she was willing to leave this matter to him. Thus, at the turn of the year 1909/10 she and Leadbeater proclaimed that the imminent reappearance of Christ was to be reckoned with, and that to this end Jiddu Krishnamurti had been chosen as the vessel.[194] Christ was spoken of as a *Bodhisattva-Being*, as a world teacher similar to other great spiritual teachers, whereas Rudolf Steiner had always taught that in Christ is a Cosmic Being, who only incarnated once in a physical body. He felt it necessary to defend his concept of Christ against the confused beliefs of Annie Besant, which ran counter to all Western feelings, and consequently, Mrs. Besant in March 1913 officially excluded the German Section with its 2,400 members from the TS; this followed the founding of the independent Anthroposophical Society at Christmas 1912, which had taken place in anticipation of these events.

---

194. In order to prepare for this event "The Order of the Star in the East" was founded in January, 1911. Jiddu Krishnamurti (1895–1986) dissolved the order in 1929 and resigned completely from the role allotted him and from the Theosophical Society. He became a spiritual teacher and began a school in Ojai, California.

THREE LETTERS

THE SO-CALLED "LEADBEATER CASE"

that introduced the separation from the Esoteric School of Theosophy

I

To the Members of the German Section
of the Theosophical Society

[Berlin, June 1906]

Dear Friends!

The Founder-President of the Theosophical Society sent the following executive notice to me, as General Secretary of the German Section, and asked me to convey its contents to the members.

The serious accusations[195] which have been raised by the Executive Committee of the American Section of the Theosophical Society against Mr. C. W. Leadbeater caused the Founder-President to call a meeting for 16 May in London, at which were present the whole of the Executive Committee of the British Section and delegates from the American and French Sections. A consultation of the Presidents was to have discussed what action to take.

After careful consideration of the accusations and after taking Mr. Leadbeater's oral explanations into account the following resolution was adopted:

---

195. Concerning accusations toward Leadbeater, see Gregory Tillet's biography of Leadbeater, *The Elder Brother*. London, 1982.

"After taking cognizance of the accusations made against Mr. C. W. Leadbeater, and after hearing his explanations the Committee unanimously recommends to the President to accept the resignation of Leadbeater that he handed in prior to any decision by the Committee.

Mr. Leadbeater's membership of the Theosophical Society is hereby made null and void, as are also his rights as presiding delegate."

H. S. Olcott
President of the Theosophical Society

Dear Friends!

An important statement reached the members of the Theosophical Society in a somewhat brief form through the above document. Mr. Leadbeater is not only a member of the society, he is one of the most notable propagators of the teachings of the theosophical world outlook. His books have provided an introduction and guide to Theosophy for many people. He has very many pupils who follow his path. He has just completed a lengthy lecturing tour through which he has accomplished many important things for the theosophical movement in America and Australia. And directly following this he is faced with "serious accusations" made by the American Section—by that Section, that is, for which he has done so much.

Faced with this situation, I have to acknowledge that, as their General Secretary, I owe the members of the German Section an explanation about this. Some often stressed that the Theosophical Society is composed of the work of its individual members, and it is not a matter of indifference when one's faith in prominent works is shattered by facts such as those communicated in this circular issued by the President. For along with this faith in those who work, there must also be faith in their actions, and what is accomplished is what composes the real living content of the society. It is through this that the society is to fulfill a great task, from which its members will draw spiritual nourishment. The society will certainly not survive by endlessly reiterating the "three basic principles" that should stand above all efforts of the individual.

Now, however, there are reasons why one should not speak in a circulated letter about things that have caused some of our American members to bring serious accusations against Mr. Leadbeater, and have moved some members of the Executive Committee of the British Section, as well as some delegates of the French and American Sections, to give their assent to the acceptance of Mr. Leadbeater's resignation.

I myself can speak all the more freely about the Leadbeater case because, from the point of view of that occultism I am obliged to represent, I have to reject the methods by which he arrives at his occult knowledge and what he recommends to others as a useful method of working. With that I do not express any views, either to affirm or deny the accuracy of the occult truths to which Leadbeater subscribes in his books. In occultism a person is meant to be able to arrive at some true insight in spite of the fact that the methods employed are dangerous and apt to mislead. Therefore I find it necessary to trace the Leadbeater case back to much more fundamental causes. At the same time, however, I have to explain that hardly anyone is guaranteed not to fall into serious error if Leadbeater's methods are employed in one's work. For this reason, because I take this attitude, the case of Leadbeater came as no surprise to me. But I do not believe that anyone who agrees with Leadbeater's occult research has any reason now to condemn him. A clear indication should have been made in the circular sent to the members that either the accusations refer to things that have absolutely nothing to do with occultism, or that, with the condemnation of Leadbeater, his whole occult system falls to the ground. I am quite clear regarding the latter; therefore, instead of an official explanation lacking in the executive notice, here I have given my viewpoint to the members of the German Section.

As for a judgement of Mr. Leadbeater on a human level, which might be important to some, it might be added that in his explanations he always stressed his good intentions in all those things of which he has been accused. And no one has a legitimate reason for doubting this assertion by Leadbeater. Another point to consider in this matter is that right now a great many American members of the Theosophical Society have circulated a letter vigorously protesting against the action taken against Mr. Leadbeater, and strongly demanding his restitution along with all his rights. The conclusion can be drawn from this that one can have a different view than the one brought against Leadbeater by the American Executive Committee and those who have simply adopted the views of this committee.

I would ask the respected members of the German Section not to allow themselves to be shaken in their adherence to Theosophy, whatever the consequences of the Leadbeater affair might be. Herewith I send all friends my heartfelt theosophical greetings.

Dr. Rudolf Steiner
General Secretary of the German Section

For further verbal clarification of the matter I am always willing to put myself at the disposal of any member as the opportunity arises.

II

To Annie Besant, beginning of July 1906[196]

Dear Mrs. Besant:

I have received your communication of June 9, 1906 from Simla, India, addressed to the Wardens and Sub-Wardens of the ES. I thank you very much for it. Allow me the following reply. Since you have granted me complete freedom in the running of the ES affairs in Germany, I was reluctant until now to take up your precious time with letters; but the present case—that of Leadbeater—is urgent enough to warrant this letter. To begin with, I would like to mention

---

196. Text according to the handwritten original intended for translation into English by Marie von Sivers. Annie Besant apparently never answered this letter (at least, no answer was found among the fairly complete collection of her letters).

that, to make the deciphering of this letter easier for you, I have asked Marie von Sivers to translate it. In my opinion this is certainly not a mistake, for my colleague will not become more confused by what I have to say; and as far as the ultimate issues are concerned, I will not fully express them. I think that *you* will be able to read between the lines.

And now, just a word in advance. I shall speak quite openly. And I would beg of you to accept the following in that sense, dear Mrs. Besant.

What has been brought against Mr. Leadbeater has not caused me a moment's surprise. And neither was I surprised by what the gentlemen Mead and Keightley, who were present at the meeting of the Executive Committee, could report from Paris; nor has the report sent from that meeting to the General Secretaries ultimately succeeded in making me change my opinion from what it was *before* the whole affair was made public in this way.

The whole thing appears to me from a much more profound aspect and in a deeper connection. I *have* to see the cause of all this misfortune in the peculiarity of Mr. Leadbeater's occult methods. These occult methods *necessarily* lead, in certain cases, to this or other mistakes similar to those evinced in Mr. Leadbeater's case, because such methods are no longer appropriate to the current stage of Western humanity. It need not always be the same mistake, but it can amount to similar things just as serious. These methods can only lead to a positive result if, standing behind everyone who enters on the path of development, there is the absolute authority of a *guru*—which is impossible in the West due to the general cultural situation. Western people can be led to the stage of psychic development where Leadbeater stood only if the part of their guidance that can no longer proceed from the *guru* is replaced by a *mental* development that has reached a certain stage. And Mr. Leadbeater lacks this stage of development. In this case I do not refer merely to an intellectual philosophical training, but to the development of a stage of consciousness that consists of inwardly contemplative insight, which simply demands the stage of brain development that must be the prerequisite of the Westerner. In Germany, for example, the way to this kind of learning must be taken from the thought-mysticism of Fichte, Schelling and Hegel, which is not at all understood according to its true underlying occult basis.

All this occurs because thought is the same on all planes. Whenever *thought* is developed—whether on the physical or on a higher plane—it will be a guide in everything if it is free from the senses and grasped in I-consciousness. If it is first developed on the physical level—in accordance with the Western brain formation—it will then continue to be a reliable guide throughout all stages of sensible and supersensible knowledge. If this is missing, Western people wander about *without a rudder*, regardless of whether they are moving on the physical or on a higher plane. At the present time when all higher human powers are so closely linked with the powers belonging to the lower levels of the sexual realm, a slip, such as Mr. Leadbeater's, can occur at any time. His "case" is certainly not an isolated one, but something that belongs in the region where such things are customary now among many occult groups with a policy that more or less tends to the left. With good foresight into the peculiarities of the fifth-cultural epoch, the Masters of the Rosicrucian School have elaborated the "path" that is the only one appropriate for a Western person in the current cycle of development. As far as it can be presented to the public, I have communicated this "path" in the periodical *Lucifer-Gnosis*.[197]

One should not, therefore, reflect on the isolated case of Mr. Leadbeater, but on the danger of his method of working. This danger is inherent to it, and one should never speculate that it may not lead to such mistakes. Something is wrong with it that starts not at the point where a person is led to such things as these, but at the point where, in the sense of such *methods*, one arrives at conclusions such as those that appear in Mr. Leadbeater's writings.

Had I been on my own, I would have *never* recommended the writings of Mr. Leadbeater as suitable theosophical reading material.

---

197. This refers to the articles: "How Can One Attain Knowledge of Higher Worlds?" which appeared as a book in 1909, and is currently published as *How to Know Higher Worlds: A Modern Path of Initiation*, Anthroposophic Press, 1994.

Once I had—because of deeper underlying causes—joined the Theosophical Society, I could not, of course, reject the books of a recognized leader.

Therefore, the "case" is stated here according to its merits. However, the handling it received at the hands of the Committee of the British Section is very inappropriate from an occult point of view. Why is it not obvious that through a judgement such as this, one has sawed off the branch one sits upon, so to speak.

The difficulty certainly lies in the fact that the esoteric character of the TS must necessarily clash with its occult aspect when it concerns a serious matter derived from spiritual realms. Under all circumstances it must be observed that Mr. Leadbeater is not morally judged in the accepted sense; and everyone who hears of the matter should also be informed that Leadbeater has *not* "had a moral lapse" in the ordinary sense of the word, but has fallen prey to his own method of working. What the public condemns here should be judged according to the principle; "Where there is a bright light there must be deep shadow." One can overcome the shock of it only by such an interpretation; otherwise the society will succumb to it.

The point is not that we should pass judgement on Mr. Leadbeater, who is now being condemned by so many people, but only that we should find the right way to continue working together fruitfully. And this way can only consist in recognizing that the Rosicrucian path is the right one within European conditions. If we do not do that, cases such as the Leadbeater case will crop up again, and the society will disintegrate into its atoms. In the current phase of human development, occultism must be publicly spelled out—with, of course, all the limitations that are imposed on us by the sacred Masters; but one will have to speak from a truly occult point of view when imparting such instruction. It would be contradictory to the demands of our time if we limited ourselves to the mere course of events that might come under the control of so-called "common sense." This term *common sense*, specifically played a fatal role at the Paris Congress.

I do not wish to elaborate to you, dear Mrs. Besant, the various propositions about what should be done in Germany to heal our major concern, because, in any case, it is only possible for me to exercise the complete freedom I am also entitled to in this case. In Middle Europe the direction of occult endeavor has been determined since the fourteenth century, and we, of strict necessity, are obliged to follow this direction. Those in Germany who still follow the path that was set up *prior* to the founding of our section have often said to me at my lectures: "Yes, but Leadbeater speaks differently…" Mainly it was foreigners, however, who were visiting Germany who said such things. I was aware that I *had* to speak differently.

Finally, I only need say that I am conscious of my devotion to the Masters in every word of this letter, and therefore I can also be aware that you, dear Mrs. Besant, will not take my frankness amiss.

In constancy and faithfulness

Yours truly
Dr. Rudolf Steiner

III

To Annie Besant (November, 1, 1908)[198]

… It can fill one with genuine sadness that the case of Mr. Leadbeater, who has deserved so much from the society, should have caused such an uproar. In this case it happens as with so much in the world. In essence it is very simple, but because of all the things built up around it, both at the outset and especially during the last years, it has become complicated. For my part there was never any unclearness about the matter, and my view of it today is the same as it was when it first arose. My whole attitude toward Mr. Leadbeater is not altered in the least by the whole affair. The case has been torn away from the sphere of occultism and placed into a field of

---

198. Text according to handwritten original intended for translation into English by Marie von Sivers. The beginning of the letter deals with the theosophical activities in Germany. Annie Besant gave a formal answer to this on November 23 from Adyar without, however, discussing its content.

influence where it does not in principle belong, into the field of influence where the standards set by the TS prevail. It is not permissible for anyone to interfere in an exoteric way in the field of responsibility of an occultist. One might be allowed to declare a disagreement with another person's views and standards of behavior, but there is no province in the exoteric society where it is permissible to pass judgement thereon. For example, I would never, myself, have permitted a discussion of the affair in a general assembly of the German Section, and I would only have taken part in such a discussion myself if it had been under the auspices of a purely occult committee. But this is my own individual opinion, which has never changed. I endeavored from the very start to work in a clarifying and conciliatory way to the best of my ability. But as General Secretary of the German Section I would like to fully express myself officially concerning the present situation of the case. The situation in our Section makes it inappropriate, especially now, to follow in any way the examples set by other Sections, and to direct the plea to you as President, dear Mrs. Besant, to reinstate Mr. Leadbeater. When the Committee was called to London two years ago to deal with the matter, the German Section was entirely ignored. Now, of course, I do not say this because there is anyone belonging to the German Section who might feel slighted in any way, but because the German Section has never been in the position where it could pass judgement. My endeavor was, therefore, to prevent the surging waves this case had stirred up from flooding over into the German Section in any way. This was definitely successful. Now, however, it is inappropriate to engage the German Section in the reinstatement, when it was not in any way involved in the dismissal.

Now, there is something important to be said against this line of argument—namely, that the society is one complete whole and that therefore an occurrence such as this affects *all* of its members. This would undoubtedly come into consideration if the reinstatement of Mr. Leadbeater would depend on a general vote. That, however, is not the case. Mr. Leadbeater resigned voluntarily and can therefore be readmitted any time by any section. The German Section would, of course, have no objection to such a readmittance.

As things stand in our Section, you, dear Mrs. Besant, will have no objection to my having absented myself from a discussion of the affair at our last general meeting.

Added to the direction this matter has taken in the English Section, is the attitude that Mr. van Hook in America takes toward it.[199] Along with this may I say that you can always count on my loyal support in this respect? In reply to the statement that one or another piece of information relates back to spiritual sources, I would always stress that no one can be denied the right to base an opinion on spiritual sources and adhere to such sources in one's dealings, although, on the other hand, everyone else is also entitled to value such a claim in the way thought best. I would myself dispute my own right to do many of the things I do if, for example, I were now to censure Dr. W. van Hook.[200]

---

199. Around May 1908, Dr. Weller van Hook, the American General Secretary, sent a letter in defence of Leadbeater, and he wrote in a private note that this letter had been dictated to him by a Master. Through an indiscretion of one of the recipients, its contents became general knowledge. The General Meeting of the English Section, angered by this, called on the President, the General Council, and the members to end the scandal. Annie Besant took the opportunity to answer on September 7, 1908 with a letter to members of the TS (printed in England in November), where she turned the argument as follows: "Leadbeater withdrew in 1906 in order to spare the Society any argument to preserve its good name. As both failed and as he is an honorable person, we should ask him to rejoin the Society. Only in this way can the argument be settled."
200. The end of the letter is about Hugo von Vollrath.

ELEVEN LETTERS AND AN ARTICLE

*Regarding the Choice of Annie Besant, Leader of the Esoteric School,
To Be the President of the Theosophical Society, Which Led to
the Separation from the Esoteric School*

I

*To the Founder-President of the Theosophical Society
H. S. Olcott in Adyar:*[201]

With deepest respect the undersigned, in his capacity as General Secretary of the German Section and as a member of the General Council of the Theosophical Society, ventures to offer the following points regarding the communication from the Founder-President of January 1907 and the resolutions of a part of the General Council, as well as the letters of Mrs. Besant.

1. It seems inappropriate to declare a member unsuitable for inclusion in the society because he or she subscribes to one or another philosophy, and applies the consequences of such views to his or her teaching methods. The society can only be an administrative body, in the sense of its present constitution, and no judging body can preside over it to decide whether any particular point of view is right or wrong. One could only diverge from this principle if, at the inception of a member, he or she were obliged to accept a particular view. That, however, would not be in the spirit of the society.

---

201. According to an undated handwritten document (January 1907). The document was sent after Olcott's death (February 17, 1907) to the General Council and the General Secretary, dated March 1, 1906.

2. In the case of Mr. Jinarajadasa, nothing can be found to warrant his exclusion from the society, if one disregards misunderstandings. His expulsion would only be legal if one were to acknowledge that a member could be excluded if his or her opinions did not agree with those of another section of the society. Accordingly, the exclusion of Mr. Jinarajadasa should be unconditionally *revoked.* If this does not take place it will be in disregard of what has been stated above in Point 1. *The undersigned therefore strongly recommends that Mr. Jinarajadasa should continue to be regarded as a member of the society.*

3. The undersigned wholeheartedly welcomes the nomination of Mrs. Besant to be successor to the most esteemed Founder-President. He would only add that he hopes the esteemed Founder-President will be allowed to continue to reside in a physical body for many years to come. He therefore sends his best wishes and thoughts for the President's recovery.

4. The undersigned, in his capacity as General Secretary of the German Section, cannot pay any attention to the fact that the nomination of Mrs. Besant took place on the orders of the exalted Masters. However important the manifestation of the exalted Masters may be, even for the *esotericist,* the administration of the Theosophical Society is no concern of theirs and they should regard the nomination of Mrs. Besant as merely proceeding from the resolve of the Founder-President. Whether the latter is advised by the exalted Masters or by someone else is merely a *private* matter of the Founder-President himself as far as the exoteric society is concerned. The undersigned is, therefore, not in any position to officially communicate to his Section the reason for Mrs. Besant's appointment. He can only treat it as something esoteric. On the other hand, he would strongly advocate to the German Section the nomination of Mrs. Besant to the presidency out of the resolve of the President, and he does not doubt for a moment that the great universal respect that Mrs. Besant commands would win the almost unanimous support of the German Section. The wishes and thoughts of the undersigned will

continue to accompany Mrs. Besant as President in all respects, as was the case in her former capacity.

With the most sincere good wishes and theosophical greetings,

Dr. Rudolf Steiner
General Secretary of the German Section

II

To Marie von Sivers in Berlin

Budapest, February 25, 1907

… I only wanted to add to the letter to the General Secretary the following sentences on a specially included page:

"The undersigned General Secretary of the German Section of the TS replied to the letters of the General Council, of the Founder-President and Mrs. Besant from January 1907 as follows: He takes the liberty of expressing his opinion concerning the impending questions, even to the General Secretaries. With theosophical greetings, Dr. Rudolf Steiner." It can still be sent off today. Only the passage referring to Olcott's survival would simply have to be cut. However things may turn out, everything will prove calamitous for the TS, but not unfavorable for the spiritual movement. Even the collapse of the TS as such ought not to alarm us in any way. You must realize that I have to be content with hints about the affair of the Masters in Adyar in my letters to you. But you will have to concede that there is *now* something more than "blindness" if one supposes that one could establish an administrative action in the society under the authority of the Masters. Mrs. Besant could do nothing worse, in her present situation, than to incorporate this authority into her own impulses. It would thereby compromise just those who are her supporters. For if we were to vote for her we would have to vote for her for reasons that are not hers. Can there be anything more absurd than that? One ought not to misuse the sacred authority of the Masters to support something that exposes one to the danger of vulgar ideas. For the Masters have nothing to do with the "humanitarianism" that merely disguises inner aspect of narrow-minded present-day egoism. If one turns this egoism the opposite way round, nothing will be revealed as a result of the sense of shame that rightly belongs to it, except the revelling in pity and the "philanthropy" of the left! The Masters are concerned with spiritual knowledge and not with preaching morals.

You will understand me. Whether it is Sinnett or whether it is Olcott—that will change nothing in other respects. We have to go forward.

III

Draft of a circulated letter, end of February 1907, presumably to the General Secretary of the German Section. Page 1 of the typed text and the signature are missing.:

It is granted to the Founder-President, by virtue of his office, that from his personal decision, he is allowed to suggest his successor. Meanwhile the Vice-President should take over the business responsibilities and conduct the voting procedure. Anyone may vote for whomever he or she wishes. The President's suggestion is not binding. The voting should not take place before the first of May. Any voting card handed in before May 1 is therefore not valid. During the month of May all members are to vote for the new President of the Theosophical Society. Sinnett is the acting Vice-President until the new vote has taken place.

I shall not make any use of what I am about to say. I shall not talk about it, even though it has been talked about in other Sections.

If the suggestion had been put forward by Olcott that he proposes Annie Besant, then we would all have voted for Annie Besant. Colonel Olcott's suggestion, however, was linked to psychic phenomena. It has been conveyed in a communique, sent to all General Secretaries, that on the last day of his life, the two Masters appeared at his deathbed and expressed a wish that Mrs. Besant should succeed Colonel Olcott.

You must forgive me for discussing this matter, if only for the simple reason that I believe I have exact knowledge about these things. I am, nevertheless, in the peculiar position of not being able to discuss them further. We would be in a difficult position if we were to place our confidence in this communiqué. We must treat it, therefore, as if it did not exist. We must interpret it as if only the personal wish of Colonel Olcott were involved. We should overlook its contents and only discuss its outward implication.

It must be a matter of indifference to us whether Olcott has been advised by a Schulz or a Müller or by a Mahatma. Maybe the advice was given him by a Mahatma. We are concerned here with an administrative procedure, and it is a fact that the Masters are not concerned with administrative matters on the physical level. On the other hand, we could be in a peculiar position if we found ourselves disagreeing with a pronouncement of the Masters. Therefore, all we have to do is simply write the desired name on the voting slip. For those of us who are practicing occultists the word of the Masters should be absolutely binding. Olcott may have let himself be advised. That concerns him as an esotericist, but it does not concern the society. If we were to regard it as the wish of one of the Masters we would be placed in a most difficult situation as theosophists. If the communique from Adyar were correct then the President would have been chosen already and there would be no need of a vote.

I would most earnestly ask you to make sure that, as far as is in your power, little or nothing is said about the matter. One should recognize, however, that at least in the German Section, it is understood that these matters are not for the general public and that, when they have to be discussed, they are regarded as the intimate family concern of the society. We can only act beneficially in the great cause if we not only try to remain silent about the matter, but also try to be so quiet about it that it never receives public attention and so cannot even get into our papers. Just think what a shock it would be for our society if the world got to know that the President of the Theosophical Society was elected by supernatural means! This decision is to be regarded as non-existent. This is somewhat difficult because it can be read everywhere and it is being discussed on all sides as to whether it is of value or not. The only thing to do is not to bother about it. The exalted Masters of Wisdom have nothing to do with the administrative side of the society. The content of the society furnishes us with wisdom, the framework thereto must be supplied and built up by human beings.

My advice to you, which not only arises out of my conscience, but out of my whole personality, is to ignore this communiqué.

IV

To George R. S. Mead, who sent a letter to Rudolf Steiner on March 3, 1907, begging him to make known to the German Sections the contents of Mead's circular letter to the Branches of the TS, written on March 1, 1907, opposed to the candidature of A. Besant.
Taken from a typed preface in German and English.

Munich, March 6, 1907

My dear Colleague,

Many thanks for your March 3 letter with its enclosure concerning the presidential election.

I quite openly admit that I regard as the worst thing of all in the whole affair that within the society the idea could ever arise that such an occasion as the presidential election could become mixed up with any kind of manifestation from the spiritual world. Even the fact that such a matter could be published is bad enough—for whatever happens now, the confusion it has caused is difficult to correct. I would, therefore, much rather have kept silent about the whole Mahatma affair within the German Section, and have ignored the word "Appointment." I would have proclaimed Mrs. Besant's nomination to be a personal decision of our dear Olcott. With that we could have progressed from the calamitous manifestations in Adyar to the rest of the agenda. To me, that did not appear to be unjustified, for the revelations concerning Olcott can be attributed merely to the weak state caused by his illness.

All that is, of course, said with respect to the German Section. But now, because the matter has been made known and has been discussed in the other Sections, a policy of that kind has caused an impossible situation, and whoever has to work, as I have to do, in a young and growing Section that has made great progress lately, is now faced with a deplorable situation.

This has come about in the following way:

1) We may not place our members in a position to be influenced by any supersensible revelations where a free election is being held according to the Statutes.

2) We would become the laughingstock of the non-theosophical world if *these* revelations became known at all. I would not hesitate for a moment to accept this scorn and ridicule if a pertinent principle were at stake. In this instance, not only is this not the case, but rather, one would forfeit the right of ever again calling on the experiences of higher worlds if one were to pretend to support one's claim by a dependence on the Mahatma revelations. And in the whole way that the German theosophical movement has so far been guided by me, it would be almost impossible merely to shrug off the question of what this involves. Finally, the members have the right to hear an opinion about it. The moment, however, that I give my opinion, I destroy something of what I have built up here.

For all these reasons I must also withhold my consent for you to publish your valuable communications, just as previously I have refrained from publishing anything concerning supersensible things. I have informed Mr. Sinnett that I shall not institute the election before the first of May. Perhaps we may still have a chance before then to correct the unfortunate situation caused by Adyar.

I would like to add a personal comment to one of the points in your circular—that I consider it to be inappropriate for the President of our society to be head of an Esoteric School.

Yours very sincerely
Rudolf Steiner

V

To all Members of the German Section
of the Theosophical Society

Berlin, March 12, 1907

Dear Friends:

Certain events now taking place in the Theosophical Society make it necessary to address the following lines to the members of the German Section. Until now, these events have not affected the German Section—and justifiably so. But now, unfortunately, they are creating a great stir among other Sections—alas, much to the detriment of the society—and it can hardly be avoided that the matter will play into our Section from outside and create a disturbance among the people here. That is why this letter is necessary. The events in question concern the choosing of a successor to our dear esteemed Founder-President H. S. Olcott. According to the Statutes the choosing of a new President should have been the easiest and simplest thing in the world.

It has now become confused without the least reason.

The Statutes say:

The Founder-President, Colonel H. S. Olcott, holds the office of President during his lifetime and has the right of proposing his successor. This proposal is subject to acceptance by the society. The voting is to take place in the following manner:

The President is elected for seven years.

Six months previous to the expiry of the President's time of office his successor should be nominated by the General Council at a meeting convened by them and the nomination should be made known to the General Secretaries and the General Secretary of the society. Each of the General Secretaries collects the votes of his Section according to its Statutes, and the General

Secretary of the society those of the other members of the society. A majority of two-thirds of the total number of voters is required for the election.

It is clear from this that the Founder-President enjoyed special rights that will no longer obtain in future.

In accordance with these rights we now have to vote. That is to say, the General Secretary of a Section has to inform the members of the proposal that the Founder-President has put forward about his successor. In addition to this the General Secretary has to hand out or send to every member in his Section a ballot paper for the member to fill in according to free choice.

Naturally members do not need to limit their choice to that of the Founder-President, but may set down on the ballot whatever name one finds appropriate. The ballot, when completed, must be returned to the General Secretary.

In the case of the German Section everything has basically been done in accordance with the Statutes, apart from the actual voting. This must take place according to the instructions of the Vice-President, who is to fulfill all the functions of the President until his office is taken over by the new President. This functioning Vice-President is now Mr. Sinnett. In our Section the voting will take place at the correct time and in the correct manner.

As far as this goes all is perfectly in order.

Disarray in this matter has been caused by the following:

Before his death our esteemed Founder-President distributed to the General Secretaries and to others all kinds of circulars in which he stated that he had been directed by "higher worlds" to nominate a certain person—namely, Mrs. Besant—to be his successor.

The Founder-President maintained that certain Masters, who go by the names M. and K. H. in theosophical circles, had appeared to him and had given him the above instructions.

Whether these instructions are genuine or not is a matter for discussion by occultists. It would have been necessary for the administrative body to completely ignore the whole matter. For who it was who advised Olcott about his successor need concern no one except

Olcott himself. It also does not matter in the least whether Olcott allowed himself to be instructed by an ordinary human being or by a supersensible power.

One can be of the opinion that Olcott should not have communicated any of this to others. But this revelation can probably be ascribed to weakness of his last periods from severe illness. It can also be ascribed to this weakness that he acted contrary to the Statutes in appointing his successor, for the Statutes do not give him the prerogative to appoint his successor, but only to propose one.

The right thing, therefore, would have been to extract what was right from Olcott's circular, and ignore the rest.

This, however, has not happened in some of the Sections.

It is just the things that do not concern an election that are being so widely discussed. Through this there is a danger that a purely administrative affair might become mixed up with esoteric matters. It is just when we adopt the right esoteric attitude in attributing our *teachings* to supersensible sources, that we should carefully guard against bringing a matter that only concerns the society, such as the election of a President, into any kind of connection with supersensible powers. It would contradict all esoteric principles if one were to introduce the subject of the supersensible into the sort of discussions that one has on the occasion of a presidential election. It must be emphatically stated here that it should not in principle be necessary to state the following and that it is only mentioned here to prevent misunderstandings that might arise through discussions, concerning which the one in charge of the German Section is innocent, but which unfortunately have already come up.

None of the individualities who are recognizable to supersensible vision would ever get involved in a concern such as the present presidential election. That would amount to restricting our will; these individualities intend only to free our will, through the whole way they relate to us, so that the will can express itself rightly in every detail. That is why the spiritual life-currents that proceed from them never reach us in a form that can inhibit our freedom of choice. With that I already make a statement that goes beyond the authority of the

General Secretary, but yet I have to say it as a friend of the members.

The time will also come when I shall be able to tell you how it stands with regard to the announcements issued from Adyar. I would not be doing the right thing to speak about it now.

I would now beg the members just at this time to make a careful distinction between what is officially announced and what is not. For example, the message Mr. Mead sent out to the groups is a totally private message. It is not to be understood in any other way, except as the personal opinion of Mr. Mead. All official notices can reach the members only through the General Secretary of a Section. Also the Deputy President, Mr. Sinnett, will only communicate through me and I will dutifully forward everything to the members.

This is toward the clarification of the case.

More will follow soon.

With heartfelt theosophical greetings

> Dr. Rudolf Steiner
> General Secretary of the German Section
> of the Theosophical Society

VI

To Anna Minsloff in Russia

Berlin, March 26, 1907

Private and confidential!

My dear Fräulein Minsloff:

Your feelings about what has been issued from Adyar about occult happenings are guiding you correctly. Right now, however, we are experiencing a difficult time, not only with respect to the further progress of the Theosophical Society, but spiritual life in general. Many dark powers are at work to destroy just the most sincere occult endeavor that is so much needed for the healing of humankind today. At the present moment my lips must remain sealed about the real deeper causes of the struggle that is being waged behind the scenes. It can turn into a terrible strife and we must face what is to come with open eyes. The time may soon come when I may be able to speak about the events taking place in Adyar. For the present, the best course will be to simply ignore what comes from Adyar, or is otherwise spread abroad about occult events, if it runs along the same lines as what has previously been published. It surely signifies blindfolding oneself if one acts like Miss Kamensky, and is happy to find a straw to cling to somewhere to lift a weight off one's mind. One must ignore everything that comes from this quarter.

Now the important thing at the moment is not who is to be chosen; the main thing is that the sacred affairs of the Masters are not lumped together with something like voting. Whether Mrs. Besant is voted for or not does not matter, but that she does not find it wrong to bring voting into connection with the exalted Masters does matter. That is what must create the greatest imaginable confusion, and in future may lead to the last remaining link being broken between the Masters and the society. For it may be that the Masters will no longer bother themselves about a society that assigns to them a role such as the one presently upheld by Adyar.

Much more important than whether Mrs. Besant is chosen or not is that she herself is brought back to the right course. If no particular complications arise, then Mrs. Besant must necessarily be chosen. Of all the older members of the society, she appears until now to be the most suitable. Please do not mention to a single human being that you are considering me [in that capacity], for, apart from it being the most hopeless suggestion, my task lies in quite a different sphere than that of running the society. We must work toward making the office of President more and more into a merely administrative one. The best President will be one who keeps the records in good order, attends to the correspondence from Adyar, and beyond that does not voice an opinion about occult things. The fact that Mrs. Besant will not regard her office in that light is the strongest argument against her being appointed. But such a view of the President's office will only prevail after many years. Therefore it will be best for the moment to appoint Mrs. Besant. How we

shall handle that in practice, how we shall proceed in strictly reject-
ing any occult opinions like the present ones spread abroad, and
whether the society is able in future to be a bearer of the spiritual
life, will depend upon that. But for the moment no member
should make a decision. The vote will only be taken on May 1 in
the German Section, and until then many things can happen that
might sway the voting one way or the other. But by then you will
have heard from me what I consider best.

Your inner life proceeds along the right course as we discussed it
here. As you are doing everything correctly I have no further
instructions for you, except just to send you my thoughts from afar,
but in spiritual proximity, as far as I am able to do so,

In this sense I am truly yours
Dr. Rudolf Steiner

VII

To the Members of the Executive Committee
of the German Section of the Theosophical Society

Berlin, April 28, 1907

Dear Friends:

The letter I sent to each member and to the Group Leaders has
made known the duty that will shortly be laid upon us of choosing a
successor to our dear late Founder-President. The circumstances of
this election have also been discussed in this letter in a general way.
Through my present writing I am appealing to the dear friends of
the Executive Committee in this matter. I emphasize once more that
there is *at present* no *unclarity* as far as the purely external side of it is
concerned. The *unclarity* could only come later through the incom-
pleteness of the Statutes, of which I shall speak later.

I shall set down here those parts of the Statutes that have a bearing on the election and, of course, in the wording, established since
April 1905. They are as follows:

§ 9. The Founder-President, H. S. Olcott, holds the office of President during his lifetime and has the right to nominate his successor. This nomination is subject to acceptance by the society. Voting should take place in the following way:

§ 10. Six months previous to the expiration of the President's time in office, his or her successor should be nominated by the General Council at a meeting convened by them, and the nomination should be made known to the General Secretaries and the Registrar. Each of the General Secretaries should collect the votes according to the regulations of their Section, and the Registrar should collect the votes from the other members of the society. A majority of two thirds of the total number of votes is required for the election.

Now I shall add the names of the Members of the General Council:

Ex officio: A. P. Sinnett, Hon. Sir S. Subramamia Aiyer, W. A. English, Alexander Fullerton, Upendra Nath Basu, Bertram Keightley, W. G. John, Arvid Knös, C. W. Sanders, W. B. Fricke, Dr. Theodore Pascal, Decio Calvaria, Dr. Rudolf Steiner, and Jose M. Masso.

Also, the following Committee Members: Annie Besant, G. R. S. Mead, Khan Bahadur Kaoroji Khandalwala, Dinshaw Jivaji Edal Behram, Francesca Arundale, Tumachendra Row, and Charles Blech.

Now it is immediately clear that these statements contain unfortunate obscurities—Yes, that unless the outcome of the election is positive on the first occasion, we would in that case not have a decision, unless—as some people seem to take for granted, the General Council were in a position to make a further nomination. But that is not thus expressed in the Statutes—at least, not in the above-quoted extracts. In addition to this, however, there is the problem that, in a literal interpretation of the Statutes—and we must undoubtedly abide by a literal interpretation—the member cannot in any way do anything beyond either voting in favor of the person nominated by the Founder-President, or indicating on the ballot sheet that one does not accept this. It would not, therefore, be of the least use to write another name on the ballot. To describe what is to take place as a ballot seems, to say the least, questionable. For one is allowed only to say "Yes" or "No."

But in the present instance we can, of course, do nothing but abide by the Statutes.

In January the Founder-President sent me a circular letter in which he mentioned that, while he was confined to his bed because of illness, the Masters approached him and persuaded him to appoint Mrs. Besant as his successor. Through this and other letters nothing more was achieved than to establish that the Founder-President wished to nominate Mrs. Besant to succeed him. Officially no attention must be paid to the fact that the President received advice about it from the Masters. For in such a consideration we would be conjuring up esoteric questions—such as what concerns the Masters and the validity of their appearance at Olcott's bedside—while dealing with a purely administrative affair such as the election of a President. And through bitter enough experience we have learned what that leads to. In other Sections, what I take to be the only right course has not been carried out—namely, to simply keep quiet about the appearance of the Masters, as one has to with regard to esoteric questions in a business context—but they have been talked about. And this has brought a flood of letters, both for and against, and an unfortunate discussion, where things were talked about that can be mentioned only during quiet esoteric study, and certainly not in connection with the election of a President. Nothing whatever should have come under official discussion except the Founder-President's nomination of Mrs. Besant. Nothing else concerned us officially—for whoever influenced Olcott in his decision, whether an ordinary mortal or one of the Masters, is his affair. The members were only concerned with the nomination and had to decide whether they considered Mrs. Besant the most suitable person or not. This does not mean, of course, that the appearance of the Masters could not have been made known unofficially, so that the advice, in which Olcott had faith, and the appearance of the Masters in Adyar in which Olcott believed, could not also have been believed in by the other voters. Thus it was logically quite clear what I, as General Secretary, had to do. Primarily, to announce officially that it was Olcott's wish to choose Mrs. Besant. Then, after Olcott's demise, to organize the election and, at the same time, as a friend, to make known to the Members, unofficially, the confidential information regarding the appearance of the Masters. To have instituted the election before Olcott's demise would have seemed quite absurd to me. For although one might have been able to talk as an occultist about Olcott's impending death, to have instituted an administrative course of action upon such a consideration would not ever have entered my head. For, theoretically, Olcott might have lived for another ten years. At present, according to the Statutes, the period of office of a new President may only last for seven years, and if Olcott had lived another ten years, we would have had two Presidents, the second of which would never have been able to take office. Now, I must confess that I find it quite inexplicable how some Sections have considered instituting an election while Olcott was still alive.

Immediately after the demise of the dear Founder-President I received an official document from the Vice-President, Mr. Sinnett, dated February 22, which decreed that the election was to take place during May. I was issued a definite and indisputable directive. I was to arrange the vote for the month of May—for Mr. Sinnett had rightly taken charge of the business matters and it is therefore his duty to conduct the voting.

In the sense of this communication from Mr. Sinnett the proceedings will be undertaken in the German Section.

Every member will receive a ballot at the appropriate time with the necessary information.

If nothing else had happened I would not have had to send this letter to dear theosophical friends, for everything is essentially clear. But now extensive discussions have occurred as a result of these unusual statements. In other sections some have queried the authenticity of the Masters's appearance. Even some of the oldest members of the Theosophical Society have been involved. There has been tremendous opposition to Mrs. Besant in some cases. People have said that Mrs. Besant already fills too many offices. She should not be given any more, and so on. Finally Mrs. Besant was violently attacked because of an article she wrote in the February issue of the *Theosoph-ical Review.* It is not possible, of course, to recapitulate the contents of this article in detail, and a short resumé of its contents could be all too easily misconstrued as a subjective rendering. Therefore, I do not wish, within my capacity as General Secretary, to recapitulate what I said in issue number 33 of *Lucifer-Gnosis*,[202] but as friend of the members. This article could be interpreted as containing only the following: "The Theosophical Society requires that its members acknowledge a universal brotherhood of humankind. Whoever acknowledges that the society is obligated to carry out tasks in accor-dance with the creation of such a brotherhood is acceptable for membership of the society. One should not say that a member may be excluded because of behavior that might give offence to one or another person, provided that such a member abides by the above society rules. For the Theosophical Society does not possess any code of moral behavior, and one can discover actions by the greatest of human spirits that might give offence to one or another person according to their time and country."

I must confess that I considered this article as a true, even obvious, expression of occult opinion, and I presumed that other theosophists would regard it in the same light, until I obtained a copy of the April issue of the *Theosophical Review,* where it was repeatedly expressed from many quarters that such an opinion was the height of immoral-ity and would inevitably undermine all good moral behavior. And the explicit, or implicit, refrain, constantly reiterated: Is it possible for such a person who can preach such immorality to be President of the society? Perhaps it is not yet the right time to discreetly ask: What becomes of the realization within life of the teaching of karma, which shows us that people are dependent on their karma for present actions—that future actions are dependent on present thoughts? Should we, as theosophists, make judgements just as people who know nothing about karma, or should we regard the actions of oth-ers to be the result of former lives? Do we not know that thoughts are facts, and that whoever strives for true thoughts is working directly to

---

202. See p. 278.

overcome what still encumbers people from earlier times? What Mrs. Besant has described in this article is no less than an ancient occult precept that is expressed thus in the otherwise questionable novel, *Zanoni*: "Our opinions are the angel part of us; our acts the earthly."[203] In more peaceful times Mrs. Besant's article would have been accepted in the same way that an occultist speaks about current morals. From all this and from some other things it has appeared that there has been opposition toward Mrs. Besant for a long time in the society. This fact, however, has long been known to those who had the opportunity to observe certain occurrences. It has only appeared on the surface, since Mrs. Besant is to be elevated to the office of President as a result of Olcott's expected information. However, it will strike many as strange that even Mrs. Besant's old friends have now deserted her or respectively taken sides against her.

Just in this case, I now wish to be as far removed as possible from influencing anyone in the very slightest. But I hold myself responsible, nevertheless, for saying something that might prove useful in helping people to make up their minds.

Mrs. Besant has been accused of acting on the advice of the Masters—or even according to their commands. That is indeed confusing. Some have pointed out with much force that the presence of the Masters does not constitute a dogma of the society, and that one can remain quite a good member of the society without believing in the Masters. It was further stated that one can in principle be convinced of the existence of the Masters, but can on that account take the revelations at Olcott's sickbed as illusions or things of that sort. It has been further emphasized that, on an occasion such as a ballot where everything is left entirely to the discretion of each individual Member, if anything like an authoritative order from the Masters is published, it is bound to lead to psychic tyranny.

These things have been voiced by opponents. Now the things that she herself says about this main contention will be written down. In a letter dated Benares, March 24 she said:

---

203. Bulwer-Lytton, Sir Edward, *Zanoni*, Part I, Book 2, Chap. 5, p. 93, Garber Communications, Blauvelt, NY, 1989.

In connection with Colonel Olcott's statement in his informative letter,[204] that his Master had instructed him to make me his successor, I declare categorically—in view of letters from several dear friends, who just for this reason would like to vote against me—that Colonel Olcott has made this communication truly while of sound mind, and that I myself have personally received this order to be accomplished as if I had been in his presence. I would rather be rejected because of my Master's word, than be successful through disavowal of what, in my opinion, leads to higher honor than that from any choice due to the multitude's acclaim. Whereas many members do not believe in the Masters and others do not believe in this particular revelation, the Theosophical Society draws its substance, its life, its strength, from the Masters and I am their servant, just as H. P. Blavatsky and Colonel Olcott were, and I only carry out my work in the society as their servant. I do not demand belief from anyone, but I must assert my own belief. If one separates the society from the Masters it will become dead. Those who do not want the second president to hold this faith must vote against me.

These sentences clearly express, first, that whatever Mrs. Besant does is intended to be done according to the wishes of the Masters. Secondly, however, it is expressed that she accepts the present revelation of the Masters as being absolutely authoritative.

One can be very much in agreement with the first point and not, however, with the second. I can only assure you at this point that I am not yet permitted to reveal what I know about the appearances in Adyar. The time will certainly come, however, when I will be able to speak openly to theosophical friends about this matter. The ballot will not therefore depend on what I know of this.

Now, I have to state immediately and openly that, just because of things that, to my distress, have to do with Annie Besant's attitude toward occult matters, and with other things connected with her, I

---

204. This refers to the January letter quoted above about the Master's appearance.

can foresee difficulties due to her, which might affect even our work in the German Section. I do not therefore make a secret of the fact that I also have great misgivings. And few people know how difficult it is for me to speak here of such things.

Now I would like to say something that could help some. One might desire to be a servant of the Masters. One might maintain that the society only has meaning when carrying out the work of the Masters, and yet one does not need to take the revelations now issuing from Adyar as one's guideline. It is especially incorrect, as many seem to believe, that these revelations either emanate from the Masters, whom one must obey, or that they are an illusion. There is, as every occultist should know, a third possibility. But as I said before, because I am not allowed to speak about these revelations, it must still remain only an indication. At any rate, the matter is this: One does not necessarily have to agree with Mrs. Besant's particular spiritual bent, but one can, nevertheless, acknowledge that, under the present circumstances, she is the only candidate under consideration for the presidency; for one must consider that Mrs. Besant's personality is not the cause of such opposition, but those who now turn against her are turning against spiritual life in general. The latter will certainly not admit this without more fuss, but it is nevertheless a fact. There is a current within the society that, if it succeeds in its aims, will gradually extinguish the spiritual life. Through it the society will perhaps become an association for comparative religion, for philosophical musings, for ethical culture or the like; it would not remain a spiritual brotherhood. One may therefore adopt the attitude that one cannot go along with Mrs. Besant's spiritual tendency; one wants, however, to preserve the spirituality as such of the society, and therefore one is obliged to vote for Mrs. Besant under present circumstances, even though it might lead later to spiritual conflict regarding her spiritual pathway. We simply have to accept this fact as something that is conditional on the circumstances within the society.

I shall immediately send to every member a ballot with the information, and I will thus prepare the voting in the corresponding manner.

If you care to write anything to me concerning these explanations, I would be very grateful if you could do so very soon so that it reaches me before the election.

With heartfelt sincere theosophical greetings

Dr. Rudolf Steiner
General Secretary
of the German Section of the TS

VIII

To Wilhelm Selling in Berlin

Munich, May 4, 1907 [205]

My dear Herr Selling:

Herewith I am sending you the necessary documents pertaining to the election and I would ask you to have them copied.

1. A confidential report to all my esoteric pupils. I would ask you to have 250 copies made of this. It is to be sent separately—that is, with nothing else enclosed—in a sealed envelope to the addresses that I shall send you by express mail no later than *tomorrow morning* (Sunday). You may therefore have this letter copied tomorrow, Sunday, and Fräulein Boesé can write the addresses on the envelopes and send them off on *Monday.* You may charge the postage to me.

2. Voting slips and information belonging thereto. These are to be sent together in a sealed envelope to *every* member of the German Section. According to the rules, we may not do it any differently—that is, a letter containing voting slip and information to be sent to every member of the German Section.

The circular to the esoteric pupils must be sent *at least* 24 hours before posting the voting slips. If you are, therefore, in a position to send off the letter to the esoteric pupils by Monday, then the voting

---

205. Steiner was in Munich at the time preparing for the Theosophical Congress.

slips may be sent on Tuesday or, if it needs to be postponed, then correspondingly later.

Fräulein Boesé will in any case help you with all the things and I beg of you to do everything very exactly, for, naturally, no (non)-esoteric pupil should receive a copy of the confidential letter.

With heartiest greetings
Your Dr. Rudolf Steiner

IX

To Wilhelm Selling in Berlin

Munich, May 4, 1907

My dear Herr Selling:

These are the names of the esoteric pupils, to whom the circular must be addressed. A few will arrive tomorrow by express post. Then the thing will be concluded by Monday and can be sent off on Monday evening, followed by the voting slips on Tuesday.

The rest of the circulars are to be *sent here to me* please. I shall need them. With this we shall have completed the voting arrangements for the present.

With hearty greetings
Dr. Rudolf Steiner

Please *send me* the addresses of the esoteric pupils immediately, as soon as the envelopes have been addressed. I would ask Fräulein Boesé to write the addresses—also those of the esoteric pupils.

X

Munich, May 5, 1907

My dear Herr Selling:

Herewith are the remaining addresses of the esoteric pupils. Please let Fräulein Boesé copy them and send them off and send me what remains of them.

With hearty greetings
Dr. Rudolf Steiner

XI

Letter circulated to all esoteric pupils

Confidential

Munich, May 4, 1907

The Impending Election of the President of the Theosophical Society

To all those members of the German Section
who look to me for esoteric training:

It is incumbent upon me to address particularly all who belong to the esoteric current at a time when the choice of the future President of the Theosophical Society is to be made by the German Section.

The esoteric pupil has a different relationship toward spiritual life than the one observed by the members of the Exoteric Society. The only thing that concerns the members of the Exoteric Society are the Statutes and, according to these, Colonel Olcott's nomination of Mrs. Besant to the presidency is at issue. A member will therefore have to decide only whether Mrs. Besant is considered the most suitable candidate or not, and to vote accordingly. With that, all exoteric matters have been dealt with.

The matter is different in the case of the esoteric pupil. Here we have the situation where a message has come from Adyar that Colonel Olcott made the nomination at the request of his Masters who appeared at his sickbed shortly before he died. Mrs. Besant, on the other hand, has emphasized very clearly that she is determined to accept the decision, because her Master has told her to do so.

In the present letter I am only addressing those who have confidence in me, for only such have turned to me for esoteric advice. If they had not had this confidence in me they would not have asked me for advice, and I hereby specifically demand that only those who have such confidence in me should attend to what I am now saying. Others may ignore it.

Occult relationships are very involved and no one should think that it is easy to discuss them. The time will come when I shall be able to talk about the events in Adyar more easily than today.

Until now it has been my principle not to divulge anything within the theosophical movement that cannot be corroborated by my own knowledge. This must still remain my principle. Having said this, I do not mean that others should not teach what they have received in good faith. I specifically emphasize that they have the right to do so. The above principle applies only *for me*. It is this principle alone that allows me to feel justified in thus addressing theosophists esoterically and in taking up the attitude I do toward people in general.

After these preliminaries I will now, according to my duty, speak about Mrs. Besant's nomination.

Through all the discussions about the appearance of the Masters in Adyar, the following alternatives have been shown to exist: either they are genuine, in which case it would be a denial of the Masters to disregard them; or they are spurious, and a consideration of them is out of the question, and everything to do with Mrs. Besant's leadership must be doubted. There is no such alternative as *this*, however. Within truly occult circles no allusion should be made to the eventual falsity of the Adyar visions. To question their *authenticity* would never occur to a true occultist.

I am *obligated* to hold a different opinion about these things than that of Mrs. Besant. That, however, does not alter the following facts:

Mrs. Besant stands firmly within the spiritual life, which issues forth from the Masters. For those within the Theosophical Society who desire to have this spiritual life, Mrs. Besant appears to be the most suitable candidate for the presidency just now.

Mrs. Besant and I have different experiences of many important things. I have to accept that through her many difficulties could occur in the leadership of the esoteric life of Middle Europe. And my attitude toward those who trust me will never be other than what I can hold myself responsible for through my own knowledge toward those we call the Masters. Once more I emphasize: Whoever has no faith in me in these matters should pay no attention to me. I will impart the message to whomever I can, but I do not desire that anyone accept what I say in any way other than heartfelt conviction.

Just because I feel so completely independent of any belief in authority regarding Mrs. Besant—just because I find other paths marked out for me by the exalted individualities we call the Masters—for that reason I can say that I am completely of *one mind* with Mrs. Besant when she says that the Theosophical Society receives its strength, power—and yes, even its content—from the Masters, and it would inevitably forfeit its very existence if it were to renounce its belief in the Masters and thus deny spiritual life itself.

Even though, under Mrs. Besant's presidency, I shall have to part ways with her, nevertheless, I must acknowledge that Mrs. Besant is perfectly right in her appeal to the Masters.

All of this is alone decisive for me, even though I would make it equally clear and candid to an esoteric pupil that I hold it appropriate for Mrs. Besant to be President; and, on the other hand, for all who trust in me there will *never* be anyone who will exert a "psychic tyranny over others."

However, the discussions about whether the Adyar visions are genuine or not, can only be regarded as un-esoteric by occultists who do not, therefore, pay any attention to them.

In view of the responsibility toward the "Wise Ones of Humankind" that I take upon myself in writing this letter, I send you my greetings.

Rudolf Steiner

XII

Article from Lucifer-Gnosis, *No. 33, 1907 (GA 34):*

About the Impending Presidential Election
of the Theosophical Society

I would gladly avoid any lengthy discussions of this matter in this paper, and merely report what is of interest for Theosophy in general. We are concerned here with the internal affairs of the society, and this periodical only devotes itself to practical theosophical work and administrative questions in so far as these are connected with Theosophy.

However, I cannot apply this principle completely under the present circumstances. The matter of the election has a bearing on so much and has caused so many discussions that it would be taken as deficient by many if I were to say nothing about it at all.

The late Founder-President had the right, according to the Statutes, to nominate his successor. This nomination is subject to ratification by the society, and for the nomination to become valid the nominated candidate must gain two thirds of the total number of votes. Now, the late Founder-President has put forward Mrs. Besant's name. The currently authorized Vice-President has asked the General Secretary to institute the election during May. That will occur in the German Section according to the rules. With that—if nothing else had happened—there would have been nothing else to correct.

Exactly! If nothing else had happened, but unfortunately, several things did happen and complicated what was simple.

First of all, I will relate what occurred. The late President Olcott did not simply report that he had nominated Mrs. Besant to be his successor, but allowed the report to reach the General Secretaries by the most diverse circulars, which then found their way into the theosophical press—and, unfortunately, not just the latter—that the exalted individualities, whom we call "the Masters," and, indeed, the ones who are especially connected with Theosophy, appeared at his deathbed and instructed him to appoint Mrs.

Besant as his successor. Not only that, but these exalted beings imparted to him an important message concerning Mr. Leadbeater, who had recently withdrawn from the Theosophical Society. Now one should have simply ignored this addition to the nomination of Mrs. Besant. For, whether one believed in the authenticity of this apparition of the Masters or not, why should a member voting according to the Statutes be concerned about the source of Olcott's council? Whether he was instructed by the Masters or by some other ordinary mortal is entirely his affair. The voters only need to adhere to the Statutes and not question further than whether Mrs. Besant is the right person or not. But a difficulty arose immediately because Mrs. Besant let it be known that she had been called by her Master to accept the choice, and for *this* reason to accept the burden—yes, she even regarded the command of her Master as a decisive factor in the election. This presents us with a serious practical difficulty, for Mrs. Besant enjoys the confidence of many members in esoteric matters. Because of her behavior, a purely administrative affair has been turned into a matter of conscience for those members—if they adhere to the Statutes according to their feelings, they would then be in opposition to the personality who should enjoy their confidence in esoteric matters. Many also asked: Can Mrs. Besant be elected if, even before she takes office, she mixes up a purely administrative concern with something esoteric, such as a message from the Masters? Would we not, in future, be in danger of receiving orders from the Mahatmas in Adyar, instead of getting simple presidential messages? The resulting confusion in such a case is unthinkable. Within our German Section the danger of this has certainly not been very great, for our work during the last years has succeeded in keeping at bay many storms that have swept through the rest of the society. Even the Leadbeater affair has passed over us without creating too much unnecessary contention. Later there will be time to speak about the revelations from Adyar. That would have happened, and will happen; for one such as the present writer—adhering firmly to the opinion that, after all, higher wisdom is simply the emanation of more highly developed spiritual individualities—would never impart anything through his teachings for which he could not take responsibility in relation to those individualities. Such a one would feel obligated to speak openly about what the revelations from Adyar pretend to be. But one is not allowed to speak about such things at an inappropriate time.

To all this, something else is added. What has been spoken of above has led to discussions in the non-German part of the society, and amounts to a vote of opposition to Mrs. Besant; the extent of these discussions was increased even more by her article in the March issue of *The Theosophical Review* concerning the basis of our society. This article could have been interpreted in a way that it would appear to contain nothing but the following: The Theosophical Society requires its Members to acknowledge a universal brotherhood of humankind. Whoever acknowledges that the society exists for the purpose of acting in accord with the creation of such a brotherhood is eligible for membership in the society. One also should not say that a member may be excluded because of behavior that might offend one or another person, provided that the person concerned acknowledges the above rule of the society. The Theosophical Society possesses no code of moral behavior, and one observes, in the greatest spirits among humankind, behavior that might offend one or another person according to the conditions of their time and country. The present writer must acknowledge that he regarded the article of Mrs. Besant as a true, even self-evident, expression of occult opinion, and assumed that other theosophists would think likewise, until he acquired the April issue of *The Theosophical Review,* where it was repeatedly reported from many quarters that such a view was an expression of the greatest immorality, and will inevitably undermine all good behavior in the society. And it was constantly expressed or implied: How is it possible for anyone who preaches such immorality to be the President of a decent society? It is probably not the time just yet to discreetly broach the question: How the teaching of karma applied, which shows that people are dependent on their karma for what they do at the present moment, but that their future actions will depend on what they think now. Shall we, as theosophists, judge people in the same way as those who know nothing of Theosophy? Or shall we regard the actions of others as conditioned by their earlier life? Are we still aware of the fact that thoughts arc facts, and that any of our Members who strives after true thoughts is laying the foundation for the work of overcoming what still encumbers us from earlier lives? What has Mrs. Besant done by means of this article beyond explain an ancient occult precept properly expressed in the otherwise rather doubtful novel *Zanoni*: "Our opinions are the angel part of us; our acts the earthly." In more peaceful times Mrs. Besant's article would have been accepted in the sense that an occultist often has to point to current moral behavior. That shows us that the presidential election is threatening to remove discussion from the realm of quiet practical opinion. The question of whether one should allow purely administrative things to become involved in esoteric considerations can easily turn to the fundamental question of how the society should continue in its attitude toward occultism. And, if that were the case, those who consider the preservation of our occult basis to be a fundamental condition of the life of the society, cannot have a moment's doubt that the choice of a personality who is guided by an occult view is the right one, even though they regard that personality as presently in error about the Statutes and Constitution. Such an error cannot be corrected, however, if the society becomes estranged from occultism through the present election of a President. That is sufficient for today. We shall still have something to say about what concerns the election itself. Whether that will be through this periodical or only within the circle of members will depend on circumstances. It will have to be done.[206]

It would not have been necessary to write this if people outside Germany had not talked so much about it. But now the readers of this periodical can say that what is talked about so much elsewhere is not completely hushed up.

---

206. It did not appear in *Lucifer-Gnosis*.

FROM ESOTERIC LESSONS
ON EASTERN AND WESTERN OCCULTISM

*The first Esoteric Class after the separation from the Esoteric School
of Theosophy, on the separation of the Eastern and Western Schools:*

Munich, June 1, 1907 [207]

My dear Sisters and Brothers:

To a greater or lesser extent, all of you have progressed in occult training. Today we intend to become clear about the essence of such a training. Esoteric students must be quite clear about the fact that they are constantly surrounded by invisible (to ordinary people) beings. Just as we walk through air, we also constantly walk through countless invisible beings wherever we turn. Every single thing that surrounds us is the expression of such beings. When we breathe we inhale not only air, but, at the same time, a high spiritual being, whose physical body is composed of air, which streams into us and entirely fills our organism. When we exhale, this being flows out of us again. We should be aware that with every breath we take, a divine spiritual being takes up residence within us, and we should realize that we shall one day become such a being ourselves. This being that incarnates into the air is at a much higher stage of development than we are today, but at one time it was at our present stage, and there will come a time when we shall have progressed as far as it has.

Now, when we belong to an Esoteric School, the exercises, however they are given, are arranged so that we gain a living consciousness of the in-streaming spirit. So what is it that says "I" in us? It is the stream

---

207. Text according to handwritten notes by Anna Weissmann.

of the inhaled air. It creates the red blood within us, and only after the red blood started to flow in our bodies could we learn to say "I" to ourselves. But it is not only within the in-streaming air that a spiritual being works in upon us. Spiritual beings are at work in every part of our body—in muscles, nerves, and bones. Knowledge of this, however, does not yet make us into esotericists. If I say to myself: "the air penetrates my body," I am a materialist. If I know and recognize the fact that a spiritual being penetrates me when I inhale, that makes me a "knower" but not yet an esotericist. But when, full of awe and filled with the deepest reverence toward the divine being that penetrates my organism, I allow the in-streaming breath to flow into me, when a living consciousness of this higher being entirely fills me, then I am an esotericist.

What is this air-embodied spirit doing in me? It enters my blood, penetrating my whole organism, so that a body composed of air is formed within me, surrounded by bones, muscles, sinews, and so on. Through the exercises I have to become quite conscious of this airy body. It is the same as what says "I" within me. If one carries out one's exercises in this way, one becomes more and more free. It is as though a quite different human being were born within one. One then no longer says "I" to one's bones, muscles and sinews. One feels entirely united with this body built of air. One discovers one's self in the spirit of this God incorporated into the air.

What are we actually doing when we perform exercises? We have to be quite clear about this. When we do exercises we are living the way everyone will live at some time in the future. During the time of such exercises, esoteric pupils find themselves in a future state of humankind. In the future everyone will only do this conditionally. Only in a very far distant future will it be the natural thing for all human beings to breathe in this way. But when that time comes, human bodies will have become quite different. They will have developed so that it will be quite natural to breathe as esotericists sometimes do today. An esoteric pupil is actually doing something in anticipation of what will happen later. It is, in a certain sense, not yet quite timely. The physical body is not yet adapted for it. Esotericists thus live ahead of their time and work into the future.

But only in this way can progress occur. Our Earth could never develop further if it were not inhabited by people who live as all of humanity will live in a far distant future. If no one on Earth was willing to do esoteric exercises, Earth would become more and more rigid. It is true that everyone shares in the transformation of Earth during Devachan, but if those incarnated on Earth merely tried to preserve everything as it is now, and, at the same time, those in Devachan tried to transform the Earth, then there would be no harmony in their respective efforts. The human beings on Earth would cause Earth to become quite bone-like and rigid, whereas, through the efforts of those in Devachan who wish to transform the rigid Earth, the Earth would finally split up and disintegrate. For that reason esotericists must be quite clear about the sacred duty they have to fulfill for the progress of humankind when they do esoteric exercises.

In itself, it is quite a contradiction of present circumstances if the esotericist lives in a way that can be natural only in the future. But only in this way can progress be achieved. Human beings always find it necessary to make use of the bodies that are the natural and possible ones for their stage of evolution. A being that ought to belong to Jupiter or Venus [epochs] according to its stage of development must, nevertheless, make use of the physical bodies available to all humankind if it would live among us. But in spirit, it leads a life belonging to a far distant future, and through this it gradually carries this future down into us and enables us to attain it.

Now, someone might say: Would it not also be possible for one to go through such development on one's own, without any Esoteric School? Certainly it would. Everyone will, for example, undergo a transformation of the breathing process during the course of development. But that is like saying: I would like to study mathematics completely on my own without a teacher. One would then, of course, also have to forego the use of any textbooks. Certainly one could also learn mathematics in this way, but it would take about 3,000 years to learn what could be picked up in about five months with the aid of a teacher.

In itself it would be quite possible—yes, certainly it would—for one to find out for oneself all that can now be learned through esoteric exercises. For all the exercises are basically a part of human nature. But it would not be 3,000 years, but many hundreds of thousands of years that would be needed. The way can be shortened by means of esoteric training. It has no other purpose than this. By undertaking such esoteric exercises a person grows spiritually toward the future, and experiences within what will come to pass in the future, and what one thus experiences is what is known to us as "the higher worlds." The higher worlds represent future human conditions. At every moment, therefore, we must be conscious of our sacred duty. With every breath we must experience the Divine that pours into us. The Godhead flows into us with every inhalation, but with every exhalation we kill His body by making the air unusable. But, ultimately, our exercises will gradually teach us how to exhale the air in the same purity as we inhaled it. Anyone not inclined to learn this through exercises will, of course, eventually attain it by natural means, but will have to wait until, in the future, the human body has been so transformed that this kind of breathing comes as naturally as, through our present constitution, the way we now breathe.

The air flows in and out of us today and transforms the used-up blood into blood that can be reused. Was that always so? No! There was a time when everything that today constitutes the warmth of our blood was not within us, but streamed in and out of our organism as air does today. Just as the air-spirits flow into us today, so it was the fire-spirits at that time. Then human beings inhaled and exhaled warmth. And just as warm blood could be formed through the influence of the air-spirits, so another kind of substance flowed through us when the fire-spirits were at work on our organism: milk. What flows in all beings who suckle their young is a remnant of that time; but the functions within the human body connected with milk are directed by other spirits.

During the time when a young humanity was developing on Earth—for example, at the time of Atlantis and the first epochs following—the leaders of humanity were not yet human, but fire-spirits. It is to them, therefore, that we must first turn when we try to advance.

Today not all people advance at the same rate; some remain behind, so it was then as well. A number of the fire-spirits remained behind the others and created a resistance to new development. The spirits of the air and wind had already commenced their activity among humankind, having succeeded the fire-spirits, when the retarded fire-spirits obstructed their way. The Northern Sagas give people a notion of what these retarded spirits were like in the myth of the God Loki. He represents such a retarded fire-spirit and opposes the Aesir. He was the cause of Baldur's death. Wotan, the One who lives in the flowing air, is a God of the winds. He was experienced by the ancient Northern peoples when they heard the storm brewing, and when they drew breath into their bodies.

These Northern peoples were not without their Mysteries. We know how the peoples of our post-Atlantean Epoch poured out of the West toward the East from ancient Atlantis. As the Mysteries had flourished in Atlantis, so they also remained in the new Epoch being formed. Four cultural epochs have formed our fifth Root-Race [Great Epoch]: 1) the Indian, 2) the Persian, 3) the Chaldean-Babylonian-Egypto-Semitic, and 4) the Greco-Roman Epoch. But not all the multitudes coming from Atlantis reached the regions in the East: some of them stayed in the Western areas belonging to modern Europe. This group also had its Mysteries, which developed later into what we know as the Druidic and Drottic Mysteries. But this Western culture did not remain isolated from what grew up in the East. What eventually blossomed in the East culminated in the foundation of Old and New Testament wisdom. It reached the West and united with what had developed quietly there with great impact. This impact brought untold blessings.

We must clearly see that Atlantis is the source of all Eastern and Western wisdom.

Atlantis was a land thickly shrouded in mists. These mists had a very special connection to humanity. Human beings of that time experienced something through the mists; their souls were made receptive toward the speech of the Gods. In the bubbling springs, in the rustle of leaves, the people of Atlantis heard the voice of God speaking to them. And when they were alone and sunk into their own inner beings, they could perceive a sound that was the Voice of God speaking to them. They did not need laws and commandments. God told them what they had to do. And the sound reverberating throughout Atlantis and echoing out of the hearts of those people during silent hours of communion, was later fixed in Egypt into the *Tau* symbol: "T." This is also the original form of the Cross.

If we are now clear about the way these mists provided a link with the Divine—so that people could take up into themselves and understand divine wisdom in a direct way—we shall turn our attention to the water that flows in our country. If we look at a drop of dew glistening on the grass in the morning sunlight, then our hearts are filled with piety. This tiny glistening dewdrop is a reminder for us—a reminder of those times in Atlantis—when fogs covered the land and when people had an inkling of the Divine wisdom that enveloped them.

The wisdom of Atlantis was embodied in the water, in a drop of dew. And the word "dew" [*Tau* in German] is nothing other than the ancient Atlantean sound. Thus we should view with awe and reverence every drop of dew that glistens on a blade of grass, and regard it as a sacred legacy of the time when the link between human beings and the gods was not yet broken. The Tau symbol, the ancient sign of the Cross, is *Crux* in Latin. And what is the name for dew in Latin? *Ros*; *Ros-Crux* is our "Rose-Cross." Now we recognize its true significance. It is the *Tao* of Atlantis, the wisdom of Atlantis, that twinkles at us today from every dewdrop. The Rose-Cross conveys exactly this to us. It is the symbol for the new life that will blossom forth in spirit in the future.

Thus our Northern Race remained in intimate connection with ancient Atlantis. It was different in the case of those Races that wandered toward the East and formed the four epochs of India, Persia, Egypt, and Greco-Roman. They developed independently. But it is a rule of the spiritual world that every culture that has evolved independently through its own effort must also perish if it cannot receive a new impulse from the regions from which it sprang, from its mother country. So it was necessary for the exalted culture of the East to receive an impulse from our territories, to merge itself with the spiritual culture that had grown up quietly in our lands.

The exalted spiritual individuality who recognized this fact was Christian Rosenkreutz. In the thirteenth and fourteenth centuries, he took up the great task of uniting the Eastern and Western cultures. He has always lived among us and he is still with us today as the leader of the spiritual life. He brought the spiritual culture of the East—revealed in its greatest blossoming in the Old and New Testaments—into intimate harmony with the ancient wisdom of Atlantis.

Thus he gave us the form of Christianity that had already been prepared and introduced through that mysterious "Unknown One from the Highlands" who visited Johannes Tauler. "Highlands" is the name for the spiritual world, the Kingdom of Heaven. That spiritual individual who was concealed in the "Unknown One from the Highland" was none other than the Master Jesus himself, in whose body the Christ had lived on Earth. He is also still with us today.

The Master Jesus and the Master Christian Rosenkreutz have prepared two paths of initiation for us: the Christian-Esoteric path and the Christian-Rosicrucian one. These two paths have existed ever since the Middle Ages. But spiritual life disappeared more and more from human consciousness when materialism arose. At the end of the last century, materialism had reached such a degree that a new spiritual impulse was required if humankind were not to perish.

A single personality, through her psychic capacities, could perceive the Voice of the Masters. This was H. P. Blavatsky. Not all occult traditions had been lost by the time she began her work. Rather, the Eastern brotherhoods had received occult knowledge, but in a rigid, ossified form, without any life in them. When Blavatsky wrote *Isis Unveiled,* these brotherhoods assumed that this was their knowledge, for they were familiar with many symbols and teachings, and they tried in every way to put obstacles in her way.

So H. P. Blavatsky was hindered in the worst possible way in accomplishing her work in the sense of Christian esotericism as she originally intended. She really had to suffer terrible things at that time. And those occult brotherhoods actually succeeded in forcing her to present what she had to offer in her second work, *The Secret Doctrine*, in an Eastern guise. We are still accustomed to receiving most of our occult terminology in Eastern language. But this Eastern form of truth is not for us Western peoples. It can only restrict us and divert us from our goal. Here in the West are the people who will form the nucleus for the coming epochs.

That should be the true answer to what was proclaimed recently as the voice of the Masters from the East. Our Western Masters have also spoken, even though it was accompanied by less fanfare. And we would inscribe what they have said deep into our hearts. They summoned us to share in the future development of humankind, and to remain steadfast and endure in all the battles that remain ahead of us; to hold on to what we possess of the sacred living tradition. This summons will continue to sound in our souls. But no one should believe that there is disharmony between the Masters of the East and West. However, an incisive change has occurred lately regarding the Esoteric Schools of the East and of the West.

Until now, both Schools have been united in a large circle under the combined leadership of the Masters. Now, however, the Western School has become independent, and there are two comparable Schools: one in the East, the other in the West—two smaller circles instead of the one large one. The Eastern School is being led by Mrs. Annie Besant, and those who feel more attracted to her in their hearts can no longer remain in our School. People should sound exactly their hearts' longing to discover which way they are being led. At the head of our Western School there are two Masters: the Master Jesus and the Master Christian Rosenkreutz. And they lead us along two paths: the Christian and the Christian-Rosicrucian way. The Great White Lodge leads all spiritual movements, and the Master Jesus and the Master Christian Rosenkreutz belong to this Lodge. Let that be the answer—the true, factual answer—to the question that many of you must have been asking because of the most recent events.

We stand at the dawning of the Sixth Day of Creation. We have to develop the sixth and seventh cultural epochs out of ourselves. The future in its rising light is already present within us. Apprehending this, receive into yourselves what the Master Christian Rosenkreutz has spoken. (The reading of the Master's words followed.)[208]

Notes from memory relating to the final part of the same lesson on June 1, 1907:

… In 1459 Christian Rosenkreutz saw it was necessary for the wisdom of the *Tau* to unite with Christianity so that it could be led into the new evolution. He brought to the people of Middle Europe the wisdom of the *Tau* or *Ros-Crux* that united with the wisdom of the Old and New Testaments.

At the time of Johannes Tauler, a personality lived who was called "the Unknown One from the Highland." This person instructed Johannes Tauler, who then preached so powerfully that some of his audience remained as if dead. The individuality that appeared in this personality was the individuality of the Master Jesus, who has always been the leader of the development of the West—although this has been concealed. Together with this individuality there was another Master-Individual at work in the West: Christian Rosenkreutz. They are still the Masters of the West, who guide the development of Middle Europe. A brotherhood is formed by the Lodge of the Masters, but the work they perform for human progress is nevertheless varied. Just as the other two Masters are working for the East, so these two Masters work for the West.

Of all the learned ones living in the West during the last third of the nineteenth century, none were suited to the task of introducing the new spiritual impulse, which the Great White Lodge found necessary to protect the Western world from destruction by materialism. But in H. P. B. the Masters found the desired tool to introduce the new teachings to the world—the wisdom that would bring in the future. H. P. B. incorporated the Western wisdom, given her at that time, in *Isis Unveiled.* This is an important work, containing great treasures of the highest truth, but in part they are portrayed

---

208. These words were not written down.

in a distorted way. That is why H. P. B. was not understood in the West then.

There are also great occult brotherhoods in the West. Many of them were not in agreement with what H. P. B. was doing. Among these brotherhoods, a strong persecution arose against her, causing H. P. B. to suffer immensely, in a way of which no one has any inkling. These occult brotherhoods were anxious to propagate occult knowledge only in an orthodox sense. They therefore joined together to oppose H. P. B. who merely wanted to bring future knowledge to the West, but because she was not understood she turned to the East and allowed herself to be inspired by Eastern wisdom, which she wrote down in *The Secret Doctrine.* That is Eastern wisdom. At first she just wanted to bring Western future knowledge.

The questions that have arisen concerning the appearances (of the Masters) in Adyar must be answered. It is not for occultists to decide whether these appearances are genuine or not. The voice of the Western Masters is less clamorous than that of the Eastern Masters. The call of the Western Masters goes out to all those in the West, to know if they wish to unite themselves with the two Masters of the West. If we want to introduce the Eastern wisdom here and follow the Eastern teachings, this would indicate the decline of the West. We need the Western teaching given to us by these two Masters.

Previously the Western School was only an appendage to the Eastern one, was subordinate to it; now, however, both are simply linked by a bond of brotherhood, each going its separate way, independent of one another. The Western School is no longer subordinate to the Eastern School, but they are coordinated. What is given through me by order of the Masters of the West goes alongside what is given through Mrs. Besant on the orders of the Masters of the East, quite independently of it.

The Christian teaching and the Christian-Rosicrucian teaching now exist in the West. The former educates through feelings, the latter through understanding. The dying cultures of the East still need the Eastern teachings. The Western teachings are for future cultures.

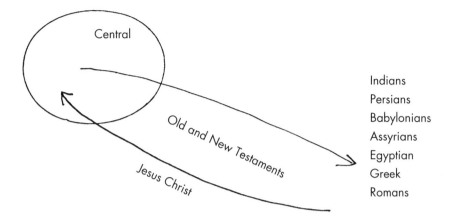

From the end of other notes from memory of the same lesson:

... The Masters also must incarnate physically to aid development. The Master of the "Sixth Dawning" is Christian Rosenkreutz. Jesus of Nazareth—Christian Rosenkreutz. If we try to take that into our feelings and allow it to become perception, we will understand why there must be an Esoteric School of the West and an Esoteric School of the East. They stand side by side, of equal value. Each possesses its two Masters: Mahatma K [Kut Hoomi] and Mahatma M [Morya]; Master Jesus of Nazareth and Master Christian Rosenkreutz. One of these schools is led by Mrs. Besant, the other by Dr. Steiner. But we have to decide which one to follow.

Further commentaries on Eastern and Western Occultism in Esoteric Classes concerning the separation from the Theosophical Society 1912–1913:

Basel, September 20, 1912
Notes from memory by Mathilde Scholl

It is understandable that esotericists think their esoteric life is now threatened by all that is presently happening in the exoteric theosophical movement. For all that we undergo and experience now is *certain* to invite criticism, even though one of our most important exercises is *positivity*—to see the positive and good side of everything. It must be said also that esotericists must understand what this is about—what is meant by *positivity*. We will consider for a moment what an esotericist ultimately is in relation to the world. You will all remember a time in your childhood when you indulged in childish games with complete seriousness, when these games were a purpose for existence. When, as a grown-up, you watch children play and join in their games, you will quickly note the difference in the way you feel when you play now, and when you played then. Perhaps you will play better than the children do, but the reason for this is that now you stand *above* it, you do not lavish your whole interest on it. The esotericist must take the same stance toward everyday life that the grown-up takes toward children's games. Our earnestness, our dignity, must be bestowed upon our esoteric life and we must always clearly distinguish the boundary that separates us from our exoteric activity, otherwise we are not true esotericists. For that reason we must attend to our exoteric affairs just as well as we did before, perhaps even better, but we must always perform them so that we stand *above* them. We will gradually come to observe that our state of mind changes because of our meditations. If we do *not* notice this, it rests entirely with ourselves for not having looked carefully enough in the right direction. Let us suppose for a moment that an esotericist has carried out the morning meditation with true love, devotion and ardor; he or she has also succeeded, furthermore, in becoming empty and opening to the spiritual world, but this person has to admit that no inner experience has been received. Now, it may happen that, during the succeeding exoteric activity—this may be as ordinary as tidying up a room, folding laundry, and so on—there suddenly comes the feeling that one ought to remember something, to reflect upon something. If one does not comply with this urge, an opportunity to make progress will have been missed. If one yields to this impulse, one will observe, flashing through the mind, thoughts that are sometimes very beautiful—they may sometimes appear grotesque—and often, almost always, quickly disappear again from memory. The point is that we should perceive, independently of our reasoning, that something is thinking in us, about which we can say: Not *I* think, but *it* thinks in me. Though such thoughts may not mean much at first, nevertheless there is a feeling by which they may be strengthened and reinforced: the feeling of gratitude toward the higher powers. If, after every moment of this kind—it may be as fleeting as the flickering of an eyelash; it suffices for us to have merely become aware of it—if we say to ourselves after such a moment as this: I give you my thanks, O powers of the higher hierarchies, for having allowed me to notice such a thing—then, as a result of such feelings of gratitude and awe, these moments will increase in number when the higher worlds wish to reveal themselves to us. We can then retain in our memory what was formerly dark, drifting through our minds like dreams. Eventually we shall be able to induce such conditions arbitrarily, and ultimately it will gradually become clear that this kind of thinking is always there within us, independent of our reasoning and anything that approaches us from outer life. Therefore, esotericists can never say that outer existence hinders them from properly conducting their esoteric lives. That always rests with them, with the mood they create for themselves. If we call to mind this feeling of gratitude and reverence—a feeling we could call the mood of prayer—after every meditation, and become conscious of the grace of which we partake when we experience the true beauty underlying every natural pleasure—the vision of a rose, the sound of a symphony—then, one day, the heavenly worlds will unfold before us.

The way you sit here beside one another as an Esoteric School would never previously have been possible in human history, and the powers that oppose the Masters of Wisdom and of the Harmony of Sensations and Feelings—the luciferic and ahrimanic powers—go to great pains, of course, to tackle esotericists in their weak points. You will notice how at the beginning and during your meditation, the sympathies and antipathies you foster toward other people rise up with exceptional strength, that desires and passions that previously might have caused shame do not seem unjustified, such qualities that previously manifested only weakly toward the outside—particularly by well-mannered people—now break out with elementary power. There is only one remedy against this: self-control.

We would like to speak further on these matters on Sunday; for now we shall see how to apply what we have heard to what is presently happening in the Theosophical Society. Everything now allowed to flow down from the spiritual worlds with the permission of the Masters of Wisdom and of the Harmony of Sensations and Feelings comes in abundance; what is granted to us as interpretations of the Gospels and the Mystery of Golgotha is so profound and extensive that esotericists are obliged to sacrifice time, ardor, energy and strength, and several other things as well, if they want to absorb everything and arrive at an understanding. And it is understandable that some people fall away and say they cannot continue, for we have to learn, learn, and always learn afresh to plumb these depths, and it is merely a probation for the soul when we think that we cannot continue.

There are, however, sluggish souls who do not *want* to learn; of these the luciferic powers take control and suggest to them that, instead of studying, instead of seeking the direct path—and the way to find this leads through constant study, from Krishna on the one hand, from Elijah on the other and by way of Buddha and Socrates to Christ—they would rather wait for a world leader who will give to them with both hands, so that they do not have to exert themselves.

So that we do not have to give in to such mistaken ideas we must always cultivate truth as our highest, most sacred possession, and never make concessions that are contrary to truth, for esotericists *must never* offend truth. It is a terrible thing and a grave offence for esotericists to twist the truth round out of brotherly considerations, to cloud the truth, even very slightly, in order not to give offence to someone, for that person will also be harmed thereby. And if we, with bleeding hearts, are forced to witness the way someone—perhaps someone we love—offends truth, we should, nevertheless, stick to what we know is right regardless of the consequences for us. We can do one thing, however, and that should give us the answer to the question we asked at the beginning: Though we may have to condemn what people *do*, we should never criticize the people *themselves*, but love them. Whether or not we really love them will be revealed to us in the moments of our meditation. To take nothing at all of our sympathies and antipathies and our little worries into the spiritual worlds with us—that will open up these worlds to us and enable us to enter into them in the right way.

Basel, September 25, 1912 [209]
Notes from memory by Elisabeth Vreede

What should be understood here is that this esoteric movement cannot be compared with any other in the world. Many occult or semi-occult movements are produced today, but one should be aware that this movement of ours is not in the same category with other movements, and those who become members of our movement should feel a sense of responsibility toward the tasks it presents.

One should become aware that an Eastern view can never take root in European soil. A case such as that of the Japanese General Nogi, who committed suicide at the grave side of his Emperor, can show Westerners how strange the soul-life of Eastern peoples must remain for us. At the time General Nogi had conquered the Europeans (Russians), aided by the weapons of modern culture; but the fact that the Eastern peoples have gained complete command over Western mechanical equipment does not establish the basis for a mutual understanding on a soul level. When I spoke about Ram Mohan Roy in the first lecture of the cycle on Saint Mark's Gospel, I intended it as an example of the attitude of an enlightened Eastern person toward Christianity. One of Ram Mohan Roy's successors who lectured about "Christ and Christianity" could, in turn, only imagine spiritual redemption as being derived from *Avatars*.[210] He maintained that the efforts at reformation by Ram Mohan Roy in India would have no success if there were no Avatar who could back

---

209. These notes refer to the Second Section of Rudolf Steiner's Esoteric School, The Cognitive-Ritual Section.
210. *Avatar*, or "divine embodiment," is one who has descended to Earth, a divine being, beyond the necessity of reincarnation.

his claims, for in India one would have no success with natural means. Count Björnstjerna, the Swedish Ambassador (in London) at the time, took a negative attitude toward the teachings about the Avatars, which the East wanted to force on the West.[211]

So began, even at that time [1840s], the rejection of Eastern beliefs by the West. Such events, which pass almost unnoticed, should be regarded as prophecies. The future was already foretold at that time (the rejection of the "Alcyone-fraud" by Dr. Steiner). In Ram Mohan Roy and Björnstjerna the whole conflict between East and West, which we are experiencing today in the Theosophical Society, already existed in embryo. The whole preliminary history of the Theosophical Society is contained in this little incident, for Ram Mohan Roy was the founder of the Bramo Samaj, the genuine theistic sect—or rather union. This gave rise to the Arya-Samaj. Expecting this to provide them with every blessing, H. P. Blavatsky and Olcott moved to India in 1878 to join this union. The pioneers of this movement met them when the ship arrived, negotiated with them and finally left them in the lurch.

The last thing remaining from the East is Greek culture—carried over for a time into East-Asian territory by Alexander the Great; this represents the last manifestation of genuine Eastern thinking. Greece always kept its eye on Asia and was looked upon, spiritually, as a remote corner of Asia. Today there is a tendency to eliminate the study of classical antiquity from higher education, and there is a certain justification in our time for being opposed to an education that draws its strength from Greek wisdom, which is no longer understood.

Some of the Greek culture was at first adopted by Rome, but as soon as the Romans started to spread across Europe, by founding cities—that is, by means of outer conquest—culture was reduced to

---

211. In Rudolf Steiner's library was a German translation of Magnus Count Björnstjerna's book, *Theogony, Philosophy and Cosmogony of the Hindus,* which stated: "What the teachings of Brahma in their present decadent state need is a reformer, like Luther, who could restore them to their original pristine state. Ram Mohan Roy made the attempt, but this failed and no one will succeed unless he or she assumes the form of an Avatar; for by natural means one acquires no converts."

an individual level. The origin of this Roman culture is still mythical and is difficult for Western people to understand. The time of the seven Kings—which are no longer regarded as historical personages—Numa Pompilius and the Sibyls, indicate the transference of ancient Eastern wisdom to Europe. With this a boundary was drawn between what came from the East and the Latin wisdom, which was destined to penetrate European culture completely. Then came the time of the Republic, and later the Caesars. We can already comprehend what these Emperors did, whereas an Alcibiades is truly a fairytale prince to us. Roman justice developed during this period, and later penetrated the administration of all legal matters. Then followed the Papacy, which governed the European world from Rome and reached its zenith at the time of Michelangelo and Raphael. The Papacy can be regarded as the last out-flowing of Eastern responsibility (for human spiritual life). But then Rome came to an end. (What one still meets in Italy is not much more than a kind of museum). The responsibility now devolves on Europe. Every one of us present in this temple should have the feeling: Until the nineteenth century the East held responsibility for the West; now that is past and done with.

The task we have undertaken through our acceptance into this temple is an enormous one. Compared to people in everyday life, to people in the profane world, we can experience ourselves in the position of those who have put their personal worries on one side and can regard them as small compared to the concern that the Gods bear toward human beings, and the concern they show for the transference of responsibility from the East to the West (we should experience that as the concern of the Gods for human beings, and the share we take in that).

Supplementary remarks by Hella Wiesberger to the foregoing notes:

Ram Mohan Roy, founder of Brahma-Samaj, who died in 1836 in London, made a great stir in Western spiritual life in the 1830s by attempting to free Hinduism of its crassest idolatry and to show it the way to the true theism of the Vedanta philosophy. His follower, who gave a lecture on "Christ and Christianity" (1870) was Keshub Chandra Sen who died in 1884. The Ârya-Samâj Union, which was derived from Ram Mohan Roy's Brahma-Samaj, was founded in the same year (1877) as the appearance of Blavatsky's *Isis Unveiled*, which caused such a sensation that the first edition was sold out within ten days. There the Ârya-Samâj was founded in Lahore by Swâmi Dayânand with the aim of ending idolatry by means of true theism. A correspondence was introduced by the leader of the Ârya-Samâj-Group in Bombay between Olcott and the founder of the Ârya-Samâj, Swâmi Dayânand Sarasvati. Olcott wrote to Sarasvati in May 1878 to say that a group of American and other serious spiritual researchers wanted to seek for light in the East, since they did not find what they wanted in Christianity and had thus publicly announced themselves as the enemies of Christianity. After that, through the suggestion of Sarasvati, the American Theosophical Society united with the Ârya-Samâj in May 1878 and the English Theosophical Society did likewise a month later as, "The Theosophical Society of the *Ârya-Samâj* of India"; it was decided that the Theosophical Society itself and all its branches in America, Europe, and so on, should recognize Swâmi Dayânand Sarasvati as their teacher. The prominent people mentioned by Rudolf Steiner, who met Blavatsky and Olcott in Bombay, belonged to the Ârya-Samâj-Group in Bombay (according to Josephine Ransom in *A Short History of the Theosophical Society*, Adyar 1938).

Introductory words to two Esoteric Lessons:

Cologne, January 2, 1913

On the esoteric path, a person's downfall can be caused by deceit, pride, and so on. Even larger communities or a whole esoteric current can be misled and get entangled in error in this way. Just as we know how easily an individual person can come to grief in this way, so we must understand the aberrations of larger groups of people.

Evidence of this bears witness to an egoistic love where a person wished to remain faithful to someone known to be misguided. In the same way it would also provide evidence for an egoistic love toward Mrs. Besant if one were to ignore the fact that she is moving in the wrong direction, which, if persisted in, can only cause mischief. And Mrs. Besant herself once pleaded—when she was writing about the Leadbeater case—that one should draw her attention to it and give her a warning if her "downfall was threatened." We are, therefore, only doing our duty by drawing Mrs. Besant's attention to it, but one must be quite clear that this is how it is with the course she is following and that, from the moment we recognize this, the portals of our temple must remain closed to the followers of such an esoteric course.

Cologne, January 4, 1913

When talking about the esoteric conditions under which we live, it is often said that *our* (Western) course has cut itself off from the Eastern one. This, however, is quite incorrect, especially today. For a long time it has not been a question of being of the West or of the East, but of being true or untrue. As long as it only concerns differences in supersensible matters one could say, if one really wants to, "That is something I cannot judge." In *that* case one may speak about there being two directions. But now the differences have descended to the physical plane, and the question no longer has anything to do with Eastern or Western occultism; the world has now gotten what it so much cherishes when it must make decisions—"physical documents" to prove its case. Everyone can see in material documents that what Mrs. Besant said in 1909 completely contradicts what she maintained in 1912. The question, however, is whether the world will approve of *those* things to which she otherwise clings. When it happens that a General Secretary (of the English Theosophical Society) can write that Mrs. Besant must have forgotten the letter of 1909, then humanity must have arrived at a pretty state of affairs. If we call the other current (the esoteric one of Mrs. Besant) the Eastern current, then one offends genuine Eastern esotericism and philosophy. In the beginning stages of the theosophical movement, when there was still an authentic Eastern impulse in the Theosophical Society, H. P. Blavatsky, for example, still had a correct view of what an *Avatar* is. Mrs. Besant never had that, and therefore we need not be surprised that she never had any understanding of the Christ. The course she takes is motivated only by the desire to carry out personal wishes and views. It would be disastrous for the world if what Leadbeater saw as the truth were to be disseminated throughout the world.

PART III

THE RELATIONSHIP BETWEEN THE MOVEMENT, THE ESOTERIC SCHOOL, AND THE SOCIETY

This section contains notes and jottings of lectures that were given not to the Esoteric School but to the society; they are included here because their content was certainly discussed in the Esoteric School, although there is no record of this. Three of these lectures have already appeared in other volumes of the comprehensive edition of Rudolf Steiner's works, but they are, nevertheless, included here so that all the material pertaining to this problem, of such importance to Rudolf Steiner, can be surveyed together.

PRELIMINARY REMARKS

BY HELLA WIESBERGER

During the formative years of the society and the Esoteric School Rudolf Steiner indicated seven times that we must be aware of the difference in character between the movement and the society, and also between the Esoteric School and the society.

The *movement* signified for him the new spiritual revelation that the "Masters of Wisdom and of the Harmony of Sensations and Feelings" and their earthly messengers could impart to humanity since the last third of the nineteenth century. He once characterized the relationship between the messengers and the Masters in the following way:

> Initiates have the duty to instruct humanity; they, in their turn, have received their instruction from the higher beings who have already progressed beyond human development—that is from the Masters of Wisdom and of the Harmony of Sensations and Feelings, the exalted beings who truly influence every spiritual current that exists on the Earth, and who gradually infiltrate their wisdom little by little as human beings rise higher and higher in their development. (Vienna, June 14, 1909)[212]

Rudolf Steiner named H. P. Blavatsky as the first messenger of the theosophical movement (in a letter, January 2, 1905). The second messenger he named was Annie Besant (in a letter to Mathilde Scholl on August 29, 1905); however, this was meant in a limited sense, as he expressed two years later, since it was a short episode in which she had been drawn into the current of the initiators because

---

212. *Das Prinzip der spirituellen Ökonomie*, untranslated (GA 109).

of her pure and elevated mentality (in a written statement to Edouard Schuré in 1907). The third messenger, looked at historically, was Rudolf Steiner, who was, in fact, the first one who could establish and elaborate the *science* of the spirit, as demanded by the consciousness of the age. With the method of training described in *How to Know Higher Worlds: A Modern Path of Initiation,* he made it possible for everyone to follow the path to supersensible knowledge through their own spiritual responsibility, so that every aspirant might meet their Master in their own time. Steiner described how he understood this initial act of "leading the aspirant to the path of progress," and how an inaugural act or appointment to the office of spiritual teacher requires just as much sense of vocation as would a corresponding post in public life. In the introduction to his first book on supersensible knowledge of the world and human destiny, he wrote:

> In order to be a "teacher" in these higher regions of existence, however, having acquired the faculty for perceiving them is not enough. Systematic knowledge belongs here as much as it does to the profession of teaching on the level of ordinary reality. "Higher seeing" does not make a person a "knower" in the spirit any more than healthy senses make a "scholar" in sense-perceptible reality. But in truth, *all* reality is one; since the lower reality and the higher spiritual reality are merely two sides of one and the same fundamental unity of being, a person who is ignorant with regard to lower knowledge will probably remain similarly ignorant of higher things. This basic fact calls up a feeling of boundless responsibility in those who, through a spiritual calling, feel obliged to speak out about spiritual regions of existence. [213]

As spiritual teacher, what Rudolf Steiner had to give the world in public, and through the society and Esoteric School, was recognized as the theosophical movement. He considered the movement and

---

213. *Theosophy: An Introduction to the Spiritual Processes in Human Life and in the Cosmos,* Anthroposophic Press, Hudson, NY, 1994, p. 17.

the Esoteric School (as its most direct organ) to be an endowment of the Masters, which could only be accountable to those into whose care it was entrusted; the democratically-organized society, on the other hand, was a foundation created by human beings, to whom it was accountable, and who administered its affairs. Through this the latter became the first institution concerned with occult matters that "worked to combine organization with freedom."[214] It was destined, as it were, to act as a bridge connecting occultism proper with what was fully public. At the same time it provided the opportunity, when communities were threatened with greater and greater division, for people working toward similar intellectual ends to meet together in brotherhood. This attitude of brotherliness was expressed during the founding of the Theosophical Society in the following three principles:

1) To form a nucleus of the universal human brotherhood, without distinction of race, creed, sex, caste, or color.
2) To encourage the study of comparative religion, philosophy and science.
3) To investigate unexplained laws of nature, and the powers latent in human beings.

Rudolf Steiner always adhered to these principles, and they were part of the rules of the Anthroposophical Society. It is in this spirit that humankind is to prepare the universal Christian Brotherhood-consciousness of our succeeding cultural epoch. He alluded to this as early as 1904:

In occult schools, three words describe the coming epoch, the epoch of a later human race... brotherly love, pneumatology [spiritual science], and freedom to rely on one's own authority in religious matters. (Berlin, October 10, 1904)[215]

---

214. From a handwritten note to the address given at the General Meeting of the German Section in Berlin, October 21, 1906.
215. *On Apocalyptic Writings, with Special Reference to the Apocalypse of St. John* (typescript).

This brotherhood ideal at the foundation of the society was strongly emphasized by Rudolf Steiner not just during the years when the society was being built up, but he expressed the fact that this came about at the instigation of the Masters (Berlin, January 2, 1905). A new direction in accordance with this ideal was necessary then because it could not occur through the Theosophical Society; for soon after the founding of the society the more restricted interest in ancient Eastern teachings began to take precedence over the spirit of universal and, therefore, truly Christian occultism. Light is shed on the background of this development by what Steiner wrote as personal guidance for Edouard Schuré on September 9, a few weeks after having reached agreement with Annie Besant at the Munich Congress in May 1907 about the separation of the Esoteric School.

This communication therefore appears under the heading: "For information only; cannot be directly communicated in this form at this time":

The Theosophical Society was founded by H. P. Blavatsky and H. S. Olcott in New York in 1875. This first foundation had an expressly Western character about it. Also the book *Isis Unveiled*, where Blavatsky published a great many occult truths, possesses such a Western character. Concerning this writing, however, it must be said that the great truths that were granted to her were reproduced in a very distorted, often caricatured form. It is as though a harmonious countenance were to be completely dis-torted in a convex mirror. Things that are spoken of in *Isis* are true; but the *way* they are spoken about is an irregular reflection of the truth. This occurs because the truths themselves are *inspired by the great initiates of the West*, who are at the same time the initiators of Rosicrucian wisdom. The distortion arises because of the inadequate way that they are taken up by H. P. Blavatsky's *soul*; for those who are educated, *this* fact should have proved the exalted source of these truths. For no one who reproduced these truths in such a distorted way could have arrived at them *of their own accord*. Because the Western initiators saw what little possibility they had of insinuating into humankind in this way the flow of spiritual knowledge, they decided to drop the whole thing completely for the time being *in this form.*

The gateway was now open, however: Blavatsky's soul had been so prepared that the spiritual truths could pour into her. *Eastern* initiators were able to control her. These Eastern initiators had the best of intentions. They were able to perceive how humankind was being driven by Anglo-Americanism into the most dreadful danger of acquiring a thoroughly materialistic way of seeing things. They—the Eastern initiators—wanted to inject into the Western world *their* form of spiritual insight, which had been preserved from ancient times. Under the influence of this current, the Theosophical Society acquired an Eastern character; and, under this same influence, inspired Sinnett's *Esoteric Buddhism* and Blavatsky's *Secret Doctrine.* But again, these were both distortions of the truth. Sinnett's work distorted the exalted message of the initiators by introducing an inadequate philosophical intellectuality and Blavatsky's *Secret Doctrine* was distorted by her own chaotic soul.

The result of this was that the initiators withdrew their influence more and more from the official Theosophical Society, and this became an arena for all kinds of occult powers to distort its high purpose. A short episode was inserted here when Annie Besant entered the stream of initiators, owing to her pure and elevated mentality. But this short episode came to an end when she came to be influenced by certain Indians who had developed a grotesque intellectualism inspired, in particular, by a German philosophical system that they had misinterpreted. This was the situation when I was faced with the necessity of joining the Theosophical Society. Initially, true initiators stood behind it, and because of *that*, it is *presently* an instrument for the spiritual life of today, even though later events gave it a certain imperfection. Its favorable progress in Western countries depends entirely on how well it can adopt the principle of Western initiation into its sphere of influence. For the Eastern initiations must necessarily ignore the *Christ-principle* as the central *cosmic* factor of evolution. Without this principle, however, the theosophical movement will remain without any deciding influence on Western cultures, which have as their starting point the life of Christ. The revelations of Eastern initiation would have to set themselves up independently *alongside* the living culture in the West. They can only have a hope of success in evolution if they can eradicate the Christ principle from Western culture. But this would be identical with eradicating the *true meaning of Earth*, which consists in the recognition and realization of the intentions of the *living Christ*. To reveal this in all its wisdom, beauty, and effectiveness is, however, the most profound aim of Rosicrucianism. With regard to the value of Eastern wisdom as an object of study, the only opinion that can be held is that it is of immense importance, because the people of the West have lost their comprehension of what esotericism is; the Eastern people, on the other hand, have preserved this knowledge. But as for introducing the right esotericism to the West, the only conclusion to be drawn is that this must be the Rosicrucian-Christian one, for *this* has sprung out of the Western way of life, and to lose this would be for humankind to deny the sense and destiny of Earth. Only in this kind of esotericism can the harmony between science and religion come to fruition, whereas any other kind of amalgam of Western knowledge with Eastern esotericism produces only such unfruitful bastard products as Sinnett's *Esoteric Buddhism,* for instance. The following diagram illustrates how it should be:

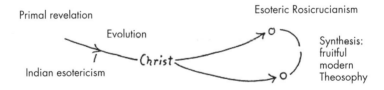

Sinnett's *Esoteric Buddhism* and Blavatsky's *Secret Doctrine* are examples of the following wrong solution:

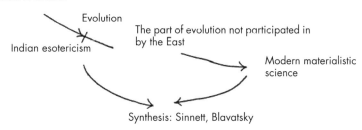

Annie Besant, having declared at the Munich Congress in May 1907 that she was not competent to deal with the subject of Christianity and that she therefore relinquished to Rudolf Steiner any part in the movement insofar as Christianity was concerned, came up with a Christ doctrine very soon afterward that contradicted completely the teachings of Rudolf Steiner. Whereas he always taught that, since the event of Golgotha, Christ had become the leading spirit of the Earth and had only once appeared in a physical body, Annie Besant taught that Christ was a teacher of humankind in the same sense as Buddha and other great spirits, and that his reappearance in the flesh was imminent. That was lurking in the background during the next Theosophical Congress in Budapest in 1909. The foregoing is given greatly added weight by Rudolf Steiner's statements, made about that same time, about a law of occult investigation that makes clear the necessity of fostering our spiritual heritage within the community:

Why should we really bother ourselves about theosophical ideas and theories before we can have experiences in the spiritual worlds ourselves? Some people will say: "We are made aware of the results of spiritual investigation; however, I still cannot see into these worlds. Wouldn't it be better for us simply to be given instructions on how to become clairvoyant ourselves, rather than to be told about the results of clairvoyant investigation? In this way, everyone could accomplish further development themselves." Anyone not involved in occult investigation may believe it would be good if one were not told in advance about such things. But in the spiritual world a very definite law exists, and its significance can be made clear by an example. Let us suppose that in a certain year a genuine trained occultist, chosen at random, had made one or another observation in the spiritual world. Now imagine that ten or twenty years later another occultist, equally experienced, had made the same observation, without having heard of the results arrived at by the first. If you were to believe that this could happen, you would be greatly mistaken, because in actuality, once a fact of the spiritual world has been discovered by an investigator or occult group, one can never investigate it a second time without being aware that it has already been researched. If, therefore, an occultist has investigated a fact in 1900, and another occultist has progressed far enough by 1950 to ascertain the same fact, this investigator can only to do so after becoming aware that it was already researched by someone else. Thus it is that spiritual facts already known can be observed only if one first understands that such communications have already been investigated. That rule establishes universal brotherhood in the spiritual world for all time. It is impossible to enter any realm whatsoever without first uniting oneself with what has already been probed and looked into by the elders of humankind. Provision has been made in the spirit realms to prevent those from becoming a law unto themselves who would say, "I'm not bothering with what is there already; I am going to make discoveries on my own." All the facts that Theosophy disseminates today would never have been observed by anyone, however learned and advanced, unless these facts had been known previously. Because of that— because one is obliged to link up with what has already been investigated—the theosophical movement was established in the way it was.

In a relatively short time many people will have clairvoyant faculties; such people could only see unreality and would not behold the truth in the spiritual world if they had not heard what was already investigated. First of all, one has to learn the truths that Theosophy provides; only then can one observe them. Thus, even occultists must first become acquainted with what has already been investigated, and then, after conscientious study, they can observe the facts themselves. One can say: "Divine beings only fructify a human soul once for its first faculty of insight; if this unique virginal fertilization has taken place, then it becomes necessary for others to direct their attention to what this first soul has achieved, in order to acquire the right to a similar achievement, and to see what the first soul has seen. This rule establishes a universal brotherhood in the innermost depths, a truly human brotherliness. From one epoch to the next, the store of wisdom has been handed on through the Mystery schools, and it has been faithfully guarded by the Masters. And we must also help to maintain this treasure and remain united in brotherhood with those who have already achieved something, if we want to make our way into the higher realms of the spiritual world. What has to be worked for as a moral law on the physical plane constitutes a law of nature in the spiritual world. (Budapest, June 4, 1909)[216]

This exposition makes it comprehensible why the link with the Theosophical Society was necessary. In the first place, the fact that it finally separated was not the result of opinion that differed with Annie Besant about an acknowledgment of the Christ, but of the untruthfulness about actual occurrences connected to running the society. Rudolf Steiner's stance toward the whole problem, in accord with the Masters' intentions, is discerned from the two addresses on December 14–15, 1911.

---

216. *Das Prinzip der spirituellen Ökonomie* (GA 109).

NOTES ON SEVEN LECTURES AND ADDRESSES

AND FROM A LETTER TO ANNIE BESANT

The Masters: Inspirers of the Theosophical Movement

Dresden, September 27, 1904

Address to the newly-formed group [217]

To awaken humankind to an understanding of what is coming in the future, the theosophical movement was called into being by personalities whose powers are far beyond the reach of even the most educated human being. All who are not so completely lacking in modesty that they imagine *their* knowledge to be the sum of *all* knowledge, and *their* power of judgement the highest power of judgement, will soon be able to discern that there are others who possess greater knowledge and greater powers of judgement than they, and they will pay attention to such personalities, and will allow themselves to be instructed by them. After having attained a little insight such people will reach the point where they will say: I still have to walk the path that others have already walked.

As one acquires more insight, one becomes more modest in this respect. One will see more clearly how much remains to be learned, and will be in a better position to find those who can convey something of their elevated qualities to which one has not yet attained. If people are under the impression that there is nothing they can learn from others, then this is a sure sign that they are not very advanced. The more advanced people are, the greater will be their conviction that human beings have attained to various levels of development, and that there have always been those who were spiritual leaders of humankind—those who had advanced beyond everyone else, those

---

217. Note-taker unknown.

most highly-developed ones, the ones who have advanced furthest beyond their fellow human beings. The less-developed people find it most difficult to understand them, and even to recognize them. It was such barely recognized, obscure, but highly developed beings who issued the great spiritual impulse in 1875 that, with the help of the theosophical movement, spread itself far and wide to the humanity that was hungry for it.

It is often asked why these highly-developed beings do not show themselves—why they are not more in evidence. You will find the answer in one of the most profound works produced by the theosophical movement, in the little booklet that, at the same time, contains a world of knowledge: *Light on the Path* [by Mabel Collins]. What it says about these highly-developed individualities who tower above their fellow human beings, who can be present, even in a crowd, without being recognized—how they can be present in Saint Petersburg, London, Berlin or Paris without anyone being aware of it, with the exception of a handful of people—is literally true.

There are reasons, particular reasons, why the advanced leaders of humankind must remain hidden. We cannot concern ourselves with those reasons today. It is, however, necessary that the most exalted leaders build a kind of wall around themselves, and that only those who have been prepared for it by a suitable way of living should have access to them. The movement we call Theosophy has emanated, and will continue to flow, from such beings. Apart from their limitless goodness such beings possess great power, and many things that happen in the world come from these beings without humanity being the least aware of it.

When we talk about new currents in the spiritual life, about a new psychology that appears to deviate from the great theosophical current, this is only seemingly true. The same beings and powers work in both. They speak the language understood by educated people and those in circles devoted to scientific research. For if we look at this "Whitsuntide Revelation," this "speaking in tongues," we see that this is the same as what a theosophist can speak to a member of any race and nation, to any ethnic group in their own language. That is why the theosophist can speak to any people whose hearts are filled with the ancient wisdom, to a people such as the Indians, in Hindi, and to people of other races in other languages.

For those who, in moments of silence, hear the Voice [of the Master] speaking to them, for such men and women the Theosophical Society is merely an outer instrument. It is not a matter of the Theosophical Society being more or less good or more or less bad; it has been built up, as all human institutions have been, on human weakness and human judgement. Even the greatest of the Masters, those who have brought us the theosophical truths and who speak to those who inspire the theosophical movement with life, cannot concern themselves with the outward founding of societies. They leave that to those whose task it is to carry out their instructions, who place themselves at their disposal as their messengers. It does not depend on the outer framework. Nevertheless, we would preserve this, precisely for the reason that we do not overrate it, for we need it and we would be inconvenienced and hindered in our work if we lacked this outer framework to enclose and encompass Europe, America, Asia, Africa, and Australia, and to embrace them all. We wish to draw your attention to the fact that it is not the framework but the spirit needed by people, and it flows through the theosophical movement and to those who desire it. Thus, at the present time a society where theosophists gather together is something quite different, something fundamentally different, from a society where others congregate.

The Nature of the Theosophical Movement and Its Relationship to the Theosophical Society

Berlin, January 2, 1905 [218]

Before starting my journey to southern and western Germany,[219] I should like to speak to you again today about the nature of the theo-

218. From a copy by Franz Seiler; the original was reviewed for the 1984 German edition of this volume and newly checked in 1986.
219. Steiner lectured January 3–13 in Stuttgart, Munich, Nuremberg, and Weimar.

sophical movement and its relationship to the Theosophical Society, for the theosophical movement is of such far-reaching importance that, at the beginning of a new year—which I hope will be propitious for our work—it is right to call to mind the task, aims and functioning of this theosophical movement.

The theosophical movement is not one that can be compared in any way to other present-day movements. People are connected with this movement—which, in its thirty years of existence has in many different ways spread to all parts of the world—and they have always been connected with it in this way from the start.

Since the movement was founded by our most exalted Master's messenger, Mme. Blavatsky, it has gone through many different changes. It has witnessed those in its midst who very soon left again, and others who faithfully and zealously stuck with it. There have been members who came out of curiosity, so that, among the many other interesting things to be learned today, they could also peek into spirit worlds.

The theosophical movement offers human beings a path of development that is not the easiest path to tread. It is reliable rather than being the most comfortable one. It is not a path that can be accomplished in one day, and the highest spirit visions cannot be seen immediately as absolute truth. Rather, intensive work and diligent application are required.

It follows from this that whoever comes into the theosophical movement out of curiosity will leave after a while, because they cannot achieve quickly what they had hoped to take by storm; or they think that the theosophical movement has nothing to offer them. But from the beginning, such inquisitive people cannot be counted on within the theosophical movement, although curiosity is often a roundabout way of arriving at the truth and theosophical knowledge. Curiosity has in many cases changed into a proper theosophical endeavor in the end.

Others come to the theosophical movement to undergo true inner soul development. They earnestly want to become certain of soul and spirit life, and attain mystical depths to become a real part of human development. They are already the better ones. They strive immediately to gain as much knowledge and experience as possible for themselves. In a higher sense this is still an egoistic endeavor. But even the highest seeking after knowledge is an egoistic endeavor and not a selfless one; they are aware that this is not the highest goal. There is a beautiful saying that describes the situation: When a rose adorns itself, it also adorns the garden.

The roundabout path of egoism is, therefore, serious and good, and all who go this way can be worthy and genuine members of the theosophical movement. They are justified in working for their own improvement since only after one has perfected oneself can one become a useful and valuable member of the Society. Of what use is an imperfect person to others; how can one be of use who has only limited insight into life?

Only when one has gained insight into the hearts and souls of others, when one has, to some extent, solved life's riddles for oneself, can one participate in the affairs of the world and of one's fellows in the proper way. For this reason, the way of self-perfection and self-development is a good and proper one. No one can be accused of being egoistic for seeking the way to self-perfection. And all who remain faithful in this will discover that they have not looked in vain within the theosophical movement, that this path leads quietly but surely to what they are seeking.

Some people might say there are other ways. Other ways are not to be attacked or struggled against in any way. I am aware of the service that other spiritual movements render to the world. Not a word of opposition should come from a true theosophist against them. There is no question about this. But whoever seeks the spirit in the highest sense must search for it through self-knowledge. We all carry the spirit within ourselves and basically it is of no use to look for spiritual insight in the world around us if we are not willing, in the true sense of the word, to acknowledge the most accessible spirit of all—that is, the spirit within ourselves.

There are many people who try to perceive the spirit through all kinds of artificial arrangements, and in the process they forget completely that the very same spirit is in the most immediate proximity to themselves—their own soul, their own spirit. We can discover it if we are willing to search for it in the right way. But it lies hidden deep in the human heart, and we have to look deeper and deeper within the recesses of our own soul. What lives in our own soul is the same as what lives outside in the world as soul and spirit. God, who creates in the world, who has created in the world for millions of years, is the same as the God who can be found within the human heart. Just as the scientific researcher studies stones, plants, animals, and human beings in the outer world and tries to understand them according to their physical forces, so no one can understand the soul and spirit who does not truly study them in the outer world. The Spirit who has always created in the world and will continue to create for all eternity, dwells within us as a reflection, as a mirror picture within us. We can struggle upward further and further toward this Spirit, and our own soul will develop that much further.

Thus the endeavor of Theosophy is no less than the endeavor to become conscious of the creative soul-spirit-beings of the universe. What we carry within us today, what we discover when we delve beneath the layers of our soul life, was once created and formed by us. If we could go back—and the theosophist gradually learns to return to primeval times—we would discover the same soul-powers building the universe before there was any physical matter in the external world. We would discover the spirit living as a spark within us, creating in the world before any chemical and physical forces existed. Spiritual and physical forces were working there. Spiritual existence is higher than any physical existence, higher than any bodily existence, and not merely higher, but older.

Thus, from our own hearts and the layers of our soul we can extract the primal enigma and its solution to how the world itself originated. Those who immerse themselves in Theosophy and delve into the sheaths of their own soul-and-spirit-life will find powers that were active before there was an eye to see or an ear to hear. Before there was fire, air, and water on our Earth, there was soul and spirit in the universe that brought everything into being. Something permanent and superior to the physical is found when we delve into the sheaths of our own heart and spirit. And then we bring up from there not what belongs to us, but the upbuilding forces of the universe. All the great teachers have walked the path into the human being. By this means they discovered not just themselves, but their eyes were opened to the stars and to eternity.

How the world came into being, where human beings originated, what the human goals are—both far and near—and what our earthly task is, we can raise all of this from our soul-layers through true self-knowledge. What we know of planet formation, of eras and epochs, of stars and systems, and about the seed of living beings out of solar systems and the heavenly bodies, all of this has been discovered through self knowledge—through self knowledge that has penetrated itself to recognize itself as it exists in spirit today, that has penetrated itself throughout aeons of time. What exists within human beings today leads us to know what has always been within us and, at the same time, in the external world.

If you examine a tree you will see that it possesses annual rings. However, to examine these rings you will first have to cut through the tree. Similarly, the soul has preserved its "rings" for those who can observe them. Every soul acquires such rings. The soul has progressed through cycles, eras, and epochs, and at each point it has accumulated such a ring. These cannot be seen by people today, but when we become clairvoyant we can see what remains as the result of our development. This is the way of self-knowledge, of self-perfection. In this way the world is revealed to us through self-knowledge. Human beings become aware of their own task through such self-knowledge, and comprehend the task of the theosophical movement. They recognize that this movement is essential for humanity, now and for the future.

I can only indicate what I have expressed often. Other epochs preceded our own epoch—other epochs that still possessed spiritual awareness. The Lemurian Epoch still maintained direct contact with the spiritual entities of the world, even though it was not as advanced in its capacity to understand and comprehend, and was later destroyed by fire; it had a direct knowledge of the spiritual world. Humanity has lost its spiritual insight because it was destined to develop its intellectual understanding, to develop an understanding through the senses.

The Lemurian Epoch was followed by the Atlantean Epoch. The Atlanteans also had the capacity to make contact through their soul forces with other, more advanced beings. We know that the Lemurians were led in small colonies to the Atlanteans to form the nucleus of the new race. We also know that toward the end of ancient Atlantis when the floods began to break over and destroy it, that Manu led a small group of people into Central Asia—to the Gobi or Schamo Desert—to form the basis of our own new epoch. There they were protected from the decadent people of the region who had remained behind the Atlanteans and Lemurians. We are the descendants of this handful of people from which the Fifth Epoch sprang.

Our Fifth Epoch will not be destroyed by fire or water, but will experience its twilight differently, so to be led a further step toward a new existence. This new stage is foreseen by theosophists, and they are helping to prepare for the future of humankind and the new epoch. Our epoch will end in a struggle for existence. A small group of people will be saved, and will consist of those who, of themselves, have concluded that they must become leaders, and who once again have sought for soul and spirit.

These days we have to work differently than in previous times. In ancient times human beings were divided up into small cultural districts, and each culture could work only within a small area. Even during the ancient Indian civilization, even during the Persian, Egyptian, Greek, and Roman civilizations, people were restricted to small territories. Now our habitation is the entire Earth. Our technical science, the glory of our epoch, embraces the whole world. There is no more separation. Goods produced in distant lands are distributed over all the world. The Earth has become a common habitation for everyone. Human beings can no longer be differentiated by particular colors, races, and climates. They not only exchange goods but opinions as well. Nothing can remain limited to small groups. Today we have acquired a task by which we can all grow together toward a new future. To apprehend this is the duty of the theosophical movement.

During the first cultural epoch of the Fifth Great Epoch the leaders of humankind were the Rishis of India, about whom almost nothing is known by contemporary historians. Only those who have arrived at a vision of higher worlds through mystery knowledge know of them. The Rishis created a wonderful civilization, which the Vedantic culture only faintly reflects. Everything known to us of the Vedantic culture was created at a much later date. For those who can view the world spiritually, a time is revealed that is undocumented; a time when divinely inspired spirits, such as the Rishis, personally instructed the ancient Indian people; that was a national culture.

Next there was a culture again restricted to a country, the primeval Persian or Zarathustrian culture. Seven Zarathustras existed there. The one usually referred to was the seventh. He was the incarnation of all the previous Zarathustras. The books of the Zarathustrian religion preserve what was written down at a much later date; with these we look back to the second inspired religious belief in Earth evolution.

Evolution then progressed toward the West. There we find the wonderful culture of Egypt, a culture that we are already informed of through books. The *Egyptian Book of the Dead* is a product of the Hermes culture.

Then came Greece and Italy, the original Orphic culture that grew on European soil and nourishes us still. And we then come to the sublime religion of the founder of Christianity, and finally to our own time.

We look up to a series of human religious confessions that have emanated from individual great religious founders. For us these great sublime founders are no less than the members of a spiritual community of beings and individualities who stand high above our human race. They are so exalted that today people can only gaze up in wonder and humility to the great ones who introduced to our development a spiritual impetus. But, when we gaze up at them, we become aware that we are also called on to ascend to such clarity and spirituality. The holy ones have emanated from what we call the Lodge of the Exalted Leaders of Humanity.

Those who brought the Egyptian culture then travelled westward, and when, as ambassadors, they reached the West—Europe—they gave to the European peoples the knowledge compatible with their needs. The White Lodge worked so that every nation could understand it. Every nation had its special requirements during the course of time. Every nation was restricted to narrow limits. What did the ancient Indians know, for example, about what went on in Europe? They lived within quite special social relationships. The great initiates spoke to them in the way that was appropriate. And this is how they spoke to every nation.

Today people are called upon to engage in exchange, not only of goods, but also an exchange of what they believe to be the truth. Human beings are no longer barred from the knowledge that the ancient Rishis taught. So it became necessary for the exalted ones of the Great White Lodge to speak again to humankind. The same beings who were actively engaged in the founding of the Zoroastrian and Egyptian religions; the same being, Jesus of Nazareth, who once offered up his body to Christ the Lord, so that He could be active on the Earth, these beings once more had to speak to humanity, and speak in a new form, a new language, that can be understood by a unified humanity. This is why the exalted ones speak so that their language does not consider the difference between race or language, between sex and social standing. There can no longer be any separate pacts, but humankind must become a community. Our theosophical teaching is such a community, through which we are evolving toward a new epoch. This is the meaning and spirit of the modern theosophical movement.

Those who regard this theosophical movement as the spoken word of those who, from the beginning of humanity, possess the wisdom and the harmony of feeling, know that Theosophy is no less than the pioneer movement that works in advance for the well-being of a new humanity. One who rightly understands the theosophical movement knows that all the great questions that crowd around our doors will have to be solved through the central theosophical movement.

People are searching today for salvation, some through social movements, others along a spiritual path, another a moral path, and yet another through food reform. All such movements are great, important and useful. But these are engaged only in preparation. Their activities will bear fruit only when they become branches of the great theosophical movement. A real advance cannot be made through the external improvement of foodstuffs, industry or manual labor, but only by souls being helped forward. Whoever has thoroughly studied all these movements realizes how they all lead toward the theosophical movement.

Ask people not to act so horribly toward others struggling for existence, but to behave as they would have others behave toward them, then it will become bearable. But write the word "fight" on your ensign and you will achieve nothing. Only through love— uniting with others, and the harmony of all our souls—can salvation be found. Only when we become clear again that we are all beings of soul and spirit, that our soul and spirit are sparks of the primeval fire, and that we are called on to unite in this primeval fire, will we be working toward the welfare of our future. Then we will live on into the time we are destined for, the time we must also create ourselves—and this will depend on the work we do on our own souls.

Many people demand that others should be different, that their class or occupation should be different, and they fight for this. But who can say that this kind of struggle will ever succeed? One thing, however, must succeed: *we can never go wrong if we change ourselves inwardly*, if we all begin to reform our own inner being, to make ourselves better. In this struggle there can be no class distinction, no difference of race, position or sex. And that is the meaning of the theosophical movement that will make it into a great movement and force for the future. That is what we have been taught by the exalted ones who have spoken to us in tones of promise for the future.

Many people have come to the theosophical movement and have said: "You tell us the so-called 'Masters' are at the head of the movement; however, we have never seen them." Now, that is not surprising. Do not think it is the Masters' will that they do not appear among you and speak to you. If it were possible, and if they were allowed, all of them would do so. But I should like to give you a small suggestion as to why the Master must remain separated from those he loves and why he has to choose messengers to convey his word through their physical word.

The laws that direct humankind and the world are immensely superior to anything modern people can conceive. Only those who have learned these sublime laws of the universe, and simply and solely serve them, can guide humankind according to soul and spirit. The Masters have insight, not merely over the years, but over centuries and millennia of time, and they look into the far distant future. The Masters do not give idle teachings to satisfy curiosity, but teachings of great human love that will lead to the future happiness of humanity.

Observe what human beings are like, how they live and how they depend on a thousand daily trivialities—and I shall not even mention these, but only the way people are dependent on space and time, and how difficult it is to get beyond themselves, to attain free judgement, to acknowledge the needs of other human beings. People are constantly bound by many thousands and millions of considerations that make it impossible to achieve a free and independent judgement. But if a person could follow only the innermost voice of the divine depths, then one would be summoned as the leader and guide of other human beings. This is what the Master can do.

Very few people have any idea of the greatness of what the Master speaks of out of free and unrestricted judgement. Only through a feeble glimmer, a faint image, can we voice on the physical plane what the Masters can speak from their elevated dwelling. Land, culture, and education must be considered. What the divine Guide imparts as the great law of the universe can be conveyed to human beings only through a refracted ray. Only those who can listen to the Master so that no flicker of contention arises within their hearts, so that time and space are ignored, and with constant attention to what the Master says with complete devotional surrender—those who do not respond to everything with "yes, but," and know that the Master gives utterance from the Divine—only they are worthy to listen to the word of the Master.

We all fall silent in the face of divine truths. We should end a practice that is most prevalent today—insisting on our own opinions. The Master does not impose his opinion on us, but tries to give us incentive. As long as we indulge in criticism, we remain subject to time and space; as long as this is the case, the voice of the Master cannot reach our ears. When we learn to disregard all that binds us to personal, momentary, and fleeting things—rid ourselves of any consideration of them while creating festive moments, freeing ourselves from our everyday concerns and only intent on the inner voice—then the moment will arrive when the Master can speak to us.

Those who have acquired this great freedom have also attained the possibility of having their own Master; they have advanced far enough that they can be certain of their existence in the light-filled glory of these higher beings. They have given up the principle of "test everything and retain the best," for this principle must be placed to one side by those who wish to draw near to the Master. With this, one is laying down principles with regard to what one actually knows; but if one wishes to learn something new this principle no longer applies. Who can decide what is best—those who have understood it, or those who have not? We must not lose our sense of judgement, we must not be without discernment, but we should be able to enter a mood of detachment if we wish to ascend to such heights. This, first and foremost, must be present in the theosophist as a feeling. And one who lets this feeling penetrate more and more deeply, will be led upward into the heights where conversation with the Master is possible.

Do not ask why the Masters live in seclusion. Truly the Masters reside in Saint Petersburg, Berlin, and London, and are available to those who wish to speak with them, and can do so by acquiring the appropriate frame of mind through self-mastery. If theosophists steep themselves in this attitude of soul then they will become members of the section of humanity that will be elevated to a new and higher form of existence. That is why the theosophical movement is also the most practical one we can have now. Many people raise the objection that it is idealistic, fantastic, and impractical, but a little reflection tells one that it doesn't need to be impractical, for the sole reason that many practical people—that is, people who call themselves practical—consider it to be so. But just look at those who consider themselves practical. It is a strange thing with such people. A few examples will suffice to show what practical people did in the nineteenth century world.

The practical people, for example, possessed a highly impractical postal system until the middle of the nineteenth century. At the time, practical people swore by their practicality as they do today. But then a schoolteacher in England came along and invented the postage stamp. He was an "impractical" idealist by the name of Hill. At the head of the postal system was a "practical" person by the name of Lefield. The latter explained in parliament that nothing would come out of the introduction of the postage stamp and that "practical" people knew it would not work. Traffic might increase, and then there would be insufficient post offices, and therefore the whole thing was a bad idea. This was, in substance, the answer to the "impractical" invention of the postage stamp. Likewise, Gauss invented an electromagnetic telegraph as early as the first third of the nineteenth century. It was never introduced. The idealists were the ones who made the inventions, and the practical people refused to provide the money. It was the same with the railways. What did the practical people do when trains were to be installed? The Berlin postmaster, Nagler, said on that occasion, "Why do we need railways? I arrange for sixteen omnibuses a day to go to Potsdam and nobody uses them. What do we want with a train?" Then the verdict of the Bavarian College of Medicine was given on the construction of railways. The document can be read today.[220]

The doctors thought that railways should not be built, for if people rode in them they would get concussions of the brain; at the very least one ought to line both sides of the track with billboards so that the people as they passed would not suffer concussion or other damage.

---

220. R. Hagen, *Die erste deutsche Eisenbahn*, 1885 (p.45); also Friedrich Harkort, "*Eisenbahnen,*" in the periodical *Herrmann*, No. 26, 1835.

None of the great human achievements have ever come from the heads of those who deem themselves practical people. Practical people have no definite opinion about what constitutes true progress for humanity. Only when people have roused themselves to an appreciation of the great factors that stir civilization, that proceed out of the spirit and soul, and only when they are under spiritual guidance, can they bestow the great impulses on humankind. Unbeknown even to themselves, these inventors were influenced by the Masters. Without knowing it, the chemist in the laboratory or in the factory is influenced by the spiritual hierarchy of the Masters, whom we shall become more closely acquainted with through the theosophical movement.

The theosophical movement will directly affect the activities of the day, and not merely live in the heads and hearts. Yes, in the hearts it will be living, but people will become ensouled right down to the fingertips by it and their whole lives will be altered. It will then be the most practical movement and work directly on everything in our surroundings every hour—even during every minute. That is not said by one who wishes to preach about the movement out of fanaticism, but by one who is called on to speak about it. Many mistakes have been made; one may search in the world for the factors that will bring about social progress, but one will come to realize that progress must be sought within the soul, that progress must spring forth from the soul, even for what must be converted into actions. Where this is our background, let us rightly unite together in the Theosophical Society.

The Theosophical Society is only the outer instrument for those who believe they must participate in the cultural impulse envisaged in the theosophical movement. When the Masters are asked what can be done to contact them, they reply, "People will make contact through the Theosophical Society; by this means they will have the right of possession in their own hands."

In the theosophical movement, the teachings we propagate are the means to enkindle the inner life of others. When a person addresses others, it is not the word that has an effect, but what mysteriously flows through the word. It is not just the sound waves, but the spiritual force that ought to reach us through the word. Through this spiritual force, the Masters' power works on us, the power of the great Leaders works into us so that we can unite in spirit, and our hearts beat in unison. When the current weaves between two hearts, between two souls, then the power of the Masters, who stand behind us, flows through it. That is what it is all about; *it is the inner mood that is important.*

That is why we work in our groups in such a frame of mind; that is why the Masters teach us that we should not acquire knowledge out of curiosity merely to continually accumulate knowledge, but to unite in harmony of feeling. That is why we will never come away from theosophical gatherings the way people come away from other gatherings.

Annie Besant once said that it is not right to make the complaint: "How little I got out of the meeting today!" That is not the point. The theosophist should not say how boring it was, but we should ask: "How boring was I?" We do not come together to learn, but when we create thought-forms that harmonize with one another we exercise the soul, the spirit. Every theosophical gathering, every group meeting, ought to be an accumulator of strength. Every such group meeting works on the environment. The spiritual power does not need anyone to carry it forth. The power of a group meeting such as this spreads in mysterious waves into the whole world. Those who believe in the spirit will know that a powerful activity emanates from such theosophical Lodges. Every theosophical Lodge is an unseen—and, to some, incomprehensible—process. A certain preacher may, for example, be teaching somewhere; likewise a teacher somewhere else. Although they were not in contact with a theosophical Lodge, nevertheless they hit on spiritual words. Chemists and physicists in laboratories receive new ideas—the result of a theosophical gathering.

Only those who have the inner mood just referred to, who cherish and nurture their attributes of love and goodness, and come to the meetings even when there is no interesting speaker present because they know there will be effects not materially visible—only such people are true theosophists. Because some things have come to a standstill in the theosophical movement the Masters have given me the incentive to speak to you in this way. And that is why, on the instructions of the Masters, attention was recently drawn, also in England, America, and India, to the true spiritual mood pertaining to a theosophical Lodge. Leadbeater speaks in this sense in America, Annie Besant in London and India, and that is how we have to speak. It is not a matter of whether we have a preference for a certain person or not, but that we meet together unselfishly. Then we are not just receiving, but also giving. We are giving especially when we give of our soul—and that is the best gift of all. It is also in this sense that we would unite together in our group meetings. The theosophical groups must acquire more and more the quality of bringing every criticism, every attitude of knowing better, to a standstill, so that we work as far as possible in a positive direction and we work upon our souls in the prescribed manner.

When we become convinced that the effects are not outwardly visible, but invisible, this attitude of soul will enable the theosophical movement to become what it is intended to become. All the great spiritual movements have worked in silence and seclusion. No contemporary accounts have been preserved about Christ Jesus. Philo of Alexandria has given us no information about the Master. Only later documents have done this. The Master of Christianity was recognized in His true nature only by the great and faithful ones. Therein lies His strength and the tremendously powerful effect He exerted, which is not in any way exhausted, and will continue to work far into the future.

If you can have faith in the word's spiritual meaning that does not reveal itself through outward success, then you will understand the serious nature of the theosophical movement. Let us truly take this to our hearts at the beginning of a new year, let us gather together in this sense, and from each of our hearts may this New Year message flow, so that we may perform our theosophical tasks in the manner of our exalted Masters who stand above us.

The Original Impulse behind the Theosophical Movement: The Brotherhood Idea

Berlin, January 29, 1906

It is constantly being demonstrated to us how difficult it is for our contemporaries to understand theosophical life. For that reason a few general thoughts on this subject will be expressed. All who feel themselves drawn to Theosophy get the impression that it will fulfill their deepest longings concerning spiritual existence. If, however, we consider the underlying principle of Theosophy that is proper to the present day, if we allow our consciousness to be filled with the idea of the reality of the spirit, then, ultimately, we shall have to learn to acknowledge the dignity of our fellow human beings. We accept the personal side of another's nature because, as human beings endowed with a sentient soul, we do not permit ourselves to harm intentionally the outer being of another. We would also not permit ourselves to attack them in the realm of their personal freedom. But we are still very far from being able to extend our tolerance to the innermost depths of another human soul, because we still have little ability to know—which is mostly theoretical, rather than practical—that feelings and thoughts, indeed everything of a spiritual nature, are quite real. That is clear to all of us. It is also clear to everyone that if I hit someone with my hand it is very actual, very real. But people do not so readily acknowledge that if I send someone a bad thought it is also something real. We have to become aware that the bad thought that I confront a person with, a thought of antipathy or hate, acts on his or her soul in the same way as a hit in the face. The feeling of hate or lack of love that I meet another person with is just like an ordinary external wound that I inflict on a person. Only when we are conscious of this do we become theosophists.

Let us absorb this knowledge into ourselves and be clear about the reality of the spirit within us, so we can comprehend the idea of Theosophy; then something will follow for us that is actually the consequence, the important effect, of such a spiritual concept. To begin with, the members of an educated society will not beat each other up, they will not inflict outer injuries on one another. But what thoughts, what opinions, people of civilized communities have while sitting beside one another! I have no need to speak of that— you know it yourselves. The Theosophical Society has the task of bringing sympathy and respect for each other into people's consciousness. In our time, when it is primarily a question of developing viewpoints and opinions, if seven people are sitting together, then there will be thirteen different viewpoints, and consequently, those people would prefer to split into thirteen factions. That is the consequence of having different opinions, and instead of differing opinions, the theosophical movement has to place the notion of brotherhood into the innermost depths of the soul. We will only fully comprehend Theosophy—the idea of brotherhood—when we can sit together amiably in a group where there is the greatest variety of thoughts. We do not want to merely respect and honor the person of our neighbor, and come together with others in a way that is in full accord with their human dignity, but we also want to afford them recognition in the profoundest depths of their soul. Then we will find it necessary to sit with them and remain faithful to them even when wide differences of opinion occur. Nobody should withdraw from the theosophical community, from the theosophical brotherhood, because of a difference of opinion. That is just the strong point of theosophists—to remain on a basis of fellowship, even when they hold different opinions. We cannot carry through a basic theosophical idea until we can meet together in brotherhood. Only through this will it be possible to uncover the deepest secrets in the soul, to uncover the deepest faculties that lie, as if asleep, at the bottom of the soul; this is only possible when we are clear that we can work together with other people, even though we do not all work in the same way.

I have often said that it is not for nothing that the Theosophical Society was founded in the last third of the nineteenth century. The way that it seeks the spirit is considerably different from other endeavors that also look for proofs of human immortality. There is a great difference in the means used by the Theosophical Society to search for the eternal, and in the means used by other currents directed toward the spirit. Actually, the theosophical movement is nothing other than a popular version of the occult brotherhoods that have secretly encompassed the whole world during the past millennia. I have already mentioned that the greatest and most significant brotherhood in Europe was founded in the fourteenth century as the Rosicrucian Brotherhood.[221] This Rosicrucian Brotherhood is actually the source, the origin, of all other brotherhoods that have been absorbed into European culture. In these brotherhoods, occult wisdom was guarded in strict secrecy. If I were to characterize for you what the people gathered together in these various brotherhoods were hoping for, I would have to say to you: "It was for the high and sublime philosophical teachings and the acts of wisdom that were performed in the occult brotherhoods, of which the Rosicrucian Brotherhood was the most exalted." The teachings and the work that was carried out in these brotherhoods enabled one to become aware of the eternal nucleus of one's being. It raised people to the level where they could find a connection to the higher worlds, to the worlds that lie above us, where we can look toward the leadership of our Elder Brothers, those who live among us and have reached a stage all of you will one day attain. We call these *Elder Brothers* because, anticipating the rest of evolution, they have attained this exalted state at an earlier time; they have attained the assurance of the immortal core of their being, and the activating of the same, so that people can behold the eternal, just as the ordinary person can view the sense world. To achieve this people must follow the example of the Elder Brothers who dwell among us everywhere. These Elder Brothers, or Masters, the great leaders of humankind, have always been the foremost leaders and overseers of the hidden sublime wisdom, through which human beings become aware of the eternal nucleus of their being. Those who, up to the middle of the nineteenth century, wished to be allowed to enter such an occult brotherhood, were subjected to severe tests and trials. Only those could gain admittance to such a brotherhood who showed for certain that their character guaranteed they would never misuse the exalted wisdom

---

221. Lecture in Berlin, November 4, 1904.

for base purposes. Furthermore, their intelligence had to be able to understand and take in that what was imparted to them by the occult brotherhoods. One could only be accepted into such a brotherhood when these conditions were fulfilled, and when a full guarantee was given that one was in a position and right frame of mind to receive the highest teachings.

Though people do not like to believe it, everything of real importance that happened before the French Revolution and into the nineteenth century came from these occult brotherhoods. People did not in the least know how much they were being influenced by the currents that emanated from the occult brotherhoods. Shall I describe a scene to you to illustrate how these brotherhoods work occultly in the world? Let us take the following scene. A very gifted and important man is unexpectedly visited by an apparently unknown person. This unknown person has the knack of bringing about a conversation between himself and the important person— maybe a statesman. Everything happens in a most casual manner and completely "by chance," (and this "by chance" must be enclosed by quotation marks). The conversation is not based on any particular topic, for during the discussion things are spoken of that, quite unnoticed, stick in the mind, in the intellect of the person who receives the visit. Out of this kind of conversation—perhaps only lasting about three hours—a complete change takes place in the person in question. In this way (you may believe it or not) many a great idea of importance to the world has been planted in people's minds. It was in this way that Voltaire's great ideas were kindled in him, without him perhaps having any idea who confronted him as an apparently inconspicuous nonentity, but who, nevertheless, had important things to impart to him. In the same way, some basic ideas were planted in Rousseau and Lessing.

Such effects, emanating from occult brotherhoods, began to fade more and more during the nineteenth century. The nineteenth century was necessarily the century of materialism. The occult brotherhoods had withdrawn. The great Masters of Wisdom and of the Harmony of Sensations and Feelings withdrew, as expressed by a technical expression, "into the East." They ceased their activity in the West. Then something extremely important happened in the West. Let us note this in order to understand the importance of the universal theosophical movement.

In 1841, members of the most secret society realized that important things were due to occur in Europe. To counteract the flood of materialism, it was necessary to introduce a stream of spiritual life into humankind. At the time it was initially as though a kind of difference of opinion would become apparent among the occultists themselves. Some of them said: At this stage, humanity is not yet ripe to receive spiritual facts and experiences; thus we will observe a policy of saying nothing. Those were the conservative occultists. This policy has much to be said for it, for the dissemination of occult truths entails great dangers. The others said: The danger from materialism is so great that something must be done about it, so that at least the elementary things are revealed to people. But, in what form? Humankind had completely forgotten how to apprehend the spirit in its true form, had forgotten how to rise to the spirit world, had completely lost the concept of it, so that a world of that kind no longer existed for them in any form whatsoever. How could one introduce the idea of spirit existence to humankind, who only had a sense of what is material? Why was it so necessary to instill a knowledge of the spiritual world into humanity?

With this we touch on one of the most important secrets, which are presently lying dormant. Now and then I have alluded to the question of why there actually is a theosophical movement and what it is good for. Anyone who can look into the spiritual world knows that whatever exists in outer material form arises out of the spirit—originates in the spirit. There is no material substance that does not owe its origin to the spirit. Therefore, what pertains outwardly to health or illness in the human being derives from a person's disposition, from a person's thoughts. The saying is perfectly true: What you think today you will become tomorrow. You should be quite clear that, if one generation harbors bad and unhealthy thoughts, the next generation and the following age will have to pay for it physically. The old traditional saying is true: The sins of the parents will be visited on their children for so and so many generations.[222] It is not without repercussions that people of the nineteenth century started to think materialistically and turned their thoughts away from anything spiritual. What those of that time have thought will be fulfilled, and we are not so far removed from the time when mysterious illnesses and epidemics will break out in humanity! What we call nervousness will adopt terrible forms no more than half a century from now. Just as there once was pest and cholera, and, in the Middle Ages, leprosy, so there will be epidemics of psychic illness—sicknesses of the nervous system in epidemic form. These will in fact occur because there is something wrong with the spiritual core of human beings. Wherever knowledge of this central core of the human being is present, a person will enjoy good health under the influence of a benign, true, and wise philosophy of life. But materialism denies the existence of the soul, denies the existence of the spirit, undermines people and throws them back upon themselves and upon their surroundings. Health can only be obtained when a person's deep inner being is filled with spirit and truth. The real illness, which follows the undermining of the soul, is the psychic epidemic that confronts us.

We have the Theosophical Society to bring to humankind an understanding of the spiritual core of their being. Its main task is to bring healing to humankind, not to enable one or another person to acquire knowledge of this or that fact. To know that reincarnation and karma are facts—I mean, to merely know this—is not the essential thing; the essential thing is that these thoughts become one with our blood and life, a part of our inner spiritual being, for they are healthful things. Whether we prove them or not, or whether we can establish a scientific principle to demonstrate reincarnation and karma on a strictly mathematical basis, is not the point. There is only one proof of the teachings of Spiritual Science, and that is life itself. Spiritual-scientific doctrines will show themselves to be true if a healthy life grows up under their influence. This will be the real proof of the theosophical doctrines. Whoever wants to prove Theosophy must experience it, and then it will prove

222. Exodus 20:5.

true. Every step and every day must gradually confirm the spiritual-scientific teachings.

That is why the Theosophical Society came into being. How can one convince a materialistic person of the nineteenth century that there is spirit? To begin with the spiritualist movement arose. It evolved simply because no one imagined it would be possible to convince humanity of the existence of the spirit; one had to demonstrate the spirit, to make it visible. Someone in Stuttgart asked why Theosophy was unable to provide Haeckel with palpable proof of the spirit.[223] You see, you have to give a physical proof of the spirit! The first attempt to do this was Spiritualism, which was continued for decades, until the 1860s and 1870s. But then a very unfortunate thing happened. Let us consider this for a moment. You can see in this the difference between the theosophical approach to the spirit and every other approach. We are not for a moment speaking of the truth or untruth of the spiritual phenomena. It is clear that there are phenomena that invoke the physical appearance of spirits from other worlds, so that positive proof can be provided even for those who only accept what is tangible. We have gone beyond the folly of someone saying there is a lot of counterfeit Spiritualism. There are also counterfeit coins, but there is genuine money also.

We shall not discuss further the question of truth, however. But, we do ask what the experience was for one who has attended a spiritualistic seance? Let us assume—all else aside—that we are dealing with genuine revelations. After having introduced this person to the apparition of a dead human being, he will have obtained certain proof of the human soul's immortality. One has had material proof and could convince oneself that the dead continue to exist in a world of some kind, and that they can even be summoned to appear in our world. But this has merely shown that it is not a matter of knowing—that knowing is not the main issue. Let us suppose for a moment that you would all be convinced in this way that a dead person could be brought into our presence through a spiritualistic seance. You would then know that the human soul is immortal. But

---

223. Rudolf Steiner had just returned from a lecture tour.

now one might ask: Does this kind of knowledge have any real significance in a higher sense for a human being's true higher existence? One originally thought so, and believed that people could be raised up another step by being shown that immortality is an actuality. But this is where the spiritual-scientific viewpoint differs considerably from a view of life that wants merely a clear and evident proof of immortality.

Here is a comparison of sorts: I have already spoken many times about all kinds of higher worlds; I have described what it looks like in the astral world and in Devachan; and you know that after death one has to enter first the astral world and then Devachan. Let us suppose that there were many people sitting here who said: We cannot believe what that man is saying—it appears too unlikely! Those who do not believe, who go away and do not return, would, strictly speaking, have to make good their assertion quite on their own. But for those who return, even though they do not believe it, in their case it does not matter. To those who return I would say: You do not have to believe anything I say; it is not a question of belief. You may look at it as deception, or believe that I am telling you something possibly from a world of fantasy—listen, however, and take it in! Much depends on this point. Imagine that I draw the map of Asia Minor for you. Someone might come and say: The drawing he is making of rivers and mountains is a load of rubbish. Then I would reply: I am not concerned that you do not believe me; just get hold of it, have a look at it, and memorize it. When you come to Asia Minor you will find that it is correct, and you will be able to find your way around. That is the point with astronomers also—to venture into higher domains with a map of the district; that is what matters. This also applies to knowledge of higher worlds. We can enter the higher world only if we can absorb some of its nature into ourselves, some of the swaying, vibrating world of the astral; and when Devachan is described you have to absorb some of the nature of this world, which is so very much the opposite of our own. If you would only take in these thoughts and rise to these higher regions, then you would get a feeling for the state of consciousness you have when surrounded by the astral world, for the consciousness you have when surrounded by

Devachan. If you enter into the same condition a seer is in when raised to these worlds, you will encounter something very different from what you meet if you have palpable evidence of "this or that." That is the difference between the spiritual-scientific method and all other ways of gaining certainty about the spirit.

Through Theosophy we endeavor to rise to higher worlds, to gain the capacity to perceive the spirit directly so that we can already feel a breath of the higher worlds here on the physical plane. The spiritualistic view of the world that I described earlier tries to draw the spiritual down into the physical, to place it in front of us as though it were something material. The theosophist tries to raise the human world into spiritual spheres. The spiritualist says: If the spirits are to be made manifest to me, then they must descend to my level. They must "tickle" me, so to speak, and then they will become evident to my sense of touch. The theosophist ascends to them, attempts to draw near to them, and tries to develop the soul so that it can understand the spirit.

You can get an idea of this if you make a simple comparison. It is difficult under present circumstances to raise oneself to the level of higher spiritual beings, even those incarnated in the body. Put yourself in the position you would be in if Christ Jesus were to appear in the present day! How many people would there be, do you think, who would accept Him unreservedly? I would say there might be some who would run to the police if someone appeared making the same claims Christ Jesus once made. But it depends on whether one is ripe enough to see what is living alongside oneself.

Here is a comparison: A lady singer was invited to supper. But she arrived rather late. Her empty chair was between two gentlemen. One of them was Mendelssohn, the other was a gentlemen whom she did not know. She conversed with Mendelssohn, although the other one on her left was very attentive and showed her all sorts of respects. When the meal was over she said to Mendelssohn: Who is that stupid fellow who sat beside me? That is Hegel, the famous philosopher, answered Mendelssohn. Perhaps, if she had been invited to see Hegel, she would most certainly have gone. But, as it was she had no idea who sat beside her; she thought it was a stupid fellow.

So it is with higher individualities. These personalities when incarnated in the body can only be recognized by one who is developed. That is what Theosophy brings about; Theosophy has the task of developing and transforming human beings; it does not demand that spirits should descend to us. If Christ Jesus is to be Christ Jesus, He will have to show Himself as people expect to see Him—as, according to their view, a great person should be; He must not sit like a "stupid fellow" in company.

You see, there is a difficulty concerning our present-day civilized consciousness. But the point is that what lives in higher worlds should not have to descend to us, but we should ascend to it. We should become capable of ascending to the higher worlds. That alone enables us to meet the spiritual worlds in a worthy way when death calls us. Whoever possesses the map, the map drawn up from life, will surely be able to find their way around in Asia Minor. Anyone already familiar here on Earth with what awaits beyond, will enter a known world; they will know what to expect there.

The mere knowledge that such a world exists does not, after all, mean very much. We are confronted here with a very great mystery and another very important fact, and because of this fact the European and American occultists decided to abandon their spiritualistic tactics, and inaugurated the theosophical movement. The great gathering of occultists held in Vienna at that time gave the impulse for the change of tactics.[224]

The introduction of the spiritualist movement was necessary for the undertaking of certain procedures. These procedures, accomplished in civilized countries, were undertaken by American occultists or their Lodges. The spiritualistic path had been decided upon in these Lodges. Its method was to provide certain circles of people with palpable evidence for immortality by a kind of galvanization of certain dead persons. That is to say, above all, the astral corpses of certain dead people were automatically activated on the astral plane

---

224. For further details, see *The Occult Movement in the Nineteenth Century*, Rudolf Steiner Press, 1973, lecture 2, October 11, 1915; also see C. G. Harrison, *The Transcendental Universe: Six Lectures on Occult Science, Theosophy, and the Catholic Faith*, Lindisfarne Press, Hudson, NY, 1993, especially lecture 1.

and directed into the spiritualistic circles on the physical plane. They were supposed to demonstrate immortality. One might ask: Are occultists throughout the world entitled to allow dead people to appear? Certainly; for those who work occultly, there is no boundary between the living and the dead. They can contact the dead in the astral world and Devachan. If so inclined, they can actually provide proof of immortality in spiritualistic circles as I have just related. I would ask you to remember and take note of this. For those who have no experience of these things, it might not be very comprehensible. It is different, however, for occultists. This way of acquiring conviction about immortality proved not only worthless but, in certain ways, extremely dangerous. This way of providing palpable evidence for immortality in the sense world, without improving the human being, was not only worthless, but even very harmful, for the following reasons:

Imagine that the people who have acquired a proof of immortality in this way no longer have a desire to reach the spiritual world; they have become materialists also with respect to the spiritual world. In their knowledge they were spiritualists, in their habits of thought they were no more than materialists. They believed in a spiritual world but imagined it could be apprehended by sensual rather than spiritual means. Thus it happened that those who entered Kamaloka with such materialistic habits of thought were less able than the materialists to recognize what they saw there. Materialists usually imagine that they are in a dream world—that is what usually happens when one goes there. Materialists think they are dreaming, and believe they will wake up at any moment. Human beings find themselves in Kamaloka: they dream, they sleep, they want to wake up.

Those who have gone to a lot of trouble to acquire a conviction of the spiritual world and now perceive that the spiritual world looks quite different after all—they do not merely find themselves in a dream world, but the difference between what they thought the spiritual world would be like and what now appears, works on them like a lead weight. And when human beings enter Kamaloka, where in any case they have enough to cope with, particularly if they cannot have their desires fulfilled—as for instance epicures, whose tastes can only be satisfied when they are in possession of their tongues and their senses, and those are now missing—then it is as though they suffered a burning thirst or as if they were in a burning hot oven. The latter is a somewhat different sensation from the sensation of burning thirst, but it is similar. If you consider all that a human being experiences there, and what must be experienced, one can sum it up in the words: One must learn to live without a body. For those who depend very much on sensual things this is very difficult. For those who have torn themselves free from sensuality it is not at all difficult. Those who have done nothing to raise the level of their soul, have done nothing to develop their soul further, find this difference between what is spiritual and what is sensual as a difference in weight, as a lead weight hung on them. It is really like a difference in weight. What is spiritual requires a very different kind of perception than what is sensual, and in this case the person again expects what is spiritual to be concrete and substantial; and there in the spiritual worlds he finds that what is astral is something totally different. With that the difference seems like a weight dragging one back into the physical world again. And that is the worst part of it.

For these reasons, the genuine Masters of Wisdom abandoned the method intended to give certainty of the existence of higher worlds during the 1850s through the 1870s. The previous method was abandoned and the theosophical path of development was chosen to provide access to the spiritual world. Mainly, it can be traced back to two basic factors. First and foremost, it is necessary to implant a spiritual nucleus in people to protect them from the epidemics of psychic disease. The second is to provide the possibility of entering the spiritual world, of raising oneself up in development and not wishing to draw the spiritual world down to oneself. The spiritual world should not be dragged down to us, but we should be raised to it. By comprehending this correctly, we get an idea, a feeling, for the task of the theosophical movement. In this sense we are entrusted by the theosophical movement with the task of developing ourselves further and further, in order to penetrate the spiritual world. With that, I tend to believe that the idea of brotherhood will mainly come about on its own. We will not then split up into factions. The only reason people split up is because of the wish to remain very materialistically isolated on the physical plane. In reality, we remain separate only as long as we are on the physical plane. As soon as we can rise up to the higher world we become aware of our spiritual brotherhood; spiritual unity enters our consciousness.

I have often tried to present to you—at least in thought-pictures—this idea of brotherhood. It is expressed so beautifully in the words: "That art thou." Let us consider this for a moment. I have said before: If you were to chop off my hand it would very soon cease to be my hand. It can only be my hand as long as it is attached to my organism; otherwise it is no longer a hand, and it withers away. You are also a hand such as this on the Earth organism. Think how it would be if you were to be elevated a couple of miles above the Earth; you cannot live there as a physical human being, and cease to exist as such. You are merely a member of our Earth, just as my hand is a member of my body. The illusion of being independent beings arises only because you walk around on the Earth, whereas your hand is joined to you. But that does not matter. Goethe had something quite specific in mind when he spoke about the Earth Spirit. He meant that the Earth possesses a soul, of which we are the members. He was speaking about something quite specific when he let the Earth Spirit speak the following words:

> In the currents of life, in action's storm
> I float and I wave
> With billowy motion!
> Birth and the grave,
> A limitless ocean,
> A constant waving
> With change still rife,
> A restless heaving,
> A glowing life,
> Thus time's whizzing loom unceasing I ply,
> And weave the life-garment of deity.[225]

---

225. *Faust.* Part 1. Scene 1. Translation by Anna Swanwick. Bohn's Standard Library, 1851.

Thus the physical human being is a member of the Earth organism and a part of an entity. And now look at it from the perspective of soul and spirit, for there it is exactly the same. How often have I stressed that humanity could not live if it had not progressed at the expense of the other kingdoms of Nature. In just the same way, more highly developed human beings cannot exist without the less highly developed ones. There can be nothing spiritual without there being those who have remained behind, just as a human being cannot exist without the animals having remained behind, the animals without the plants, and the plants without the minerals. This is best expressed in Saint John's Gospel in the scene after the washing of the feet: Without you I cannot exist....[226] The disciples are necessary to Jesus, they are the ground on which He exists. That is a profound truth. Take a look at a court of law—a judge sits on the tribunal and feels superior to the prisoner. The judge might reflect, however, and think that perhaps he or she was with the prisoner in an earlier life and, because of neglect, this other person has become a prisoner. Perhaps, if karma had been investigated, it might have shown that the judge was really the one who should have been sitting in the dock. All of humanity is an organism. If you extract a single soul it will not be able to subsist, but will wither and die. A single bond unites us all. That will become clear to us when we attempt to penetrate the higher world, to really rise up and experience what we are in our innermost spiritual core. If a spiritual kernel is living in us it will lead us toward brotherhood. It already exists on higher planes. Earth is only an image of it. The brotherhood that exists on Earth is an image of what is present on higher levels. We deny what we already have within us if we do not cultivate brotherhood among ourselves on Earth.

That is the deeper meaning of the brotherhood concept. For that reason we should continually seek to realize the ideas of Theosophy so that in the most profound depths of our soul we understand each other, and even in the greatest divergence of opinion we can remain together in fellowship. That is the true unity, the true form of brotherhood, that we do not demand from the others that they

---

226. John 13:1–17 (not a literal quotation).

should get along with us by holding the same opinions we do, but because we allow everyone the right to their own opinions. Through such cooperation, the pinnacle of wisdom will be achieved. That is a deeper interpretation of the first of our theosophical maxims. Let us interpret our brotherhood concept in such a way that we say to ourselves: We belong together under all circumstances, however much the opinions of others may differ from ours—differences of opinion can never be a reason for us to separate. We only completely understand one another when we allow each other complete freedom of self-assertion. Certainly we are still a long way from achieving this interpretation of theosophical brotherhood, and it will not come to fruition before theosophical thought has taken root in this way.

Why Is There a Theosophical Movement Today?

Leipzig, April 25, 1906

It is not an accident that there is a theosophical movement. It is a result of the whole development of the nineteenth century and the spread of materialism that became a decisive factor in and around the 1840s. Even during the previous four centuries, materialism was being prepared. To understand this, one must go back to the fifth and sixth centuries. There is a very wrong concept of the spiritual conditions of that time—a very mistaken idea that supposes humanity thought the same as we do today. For example, there was a very different concept of the stars in the thirteenth, fourteenth and fifteenth centuries. Now we only see the material part of them; but during the Middle Ages people saw a spirit in every star. A star was an expression of a spirit for both uneducated and educated people. Thus the whole universe was spiritualized. There is a great difference between supposing there are only physical bodies in the universe and supposing there is also spirit. Human beings of that time felt perfectly safe within a spiritual universe. We do not need, however, to desire a return to this medieval attitude.

Copernicus conquered the universe for the materialistic viewpoint. Research of the physical world reached its climax. Schleiden and others discovered cells. Railways and things of that kind promoted materialism. Then the great leaders of humankind asked: What is to be done? In what way can humanity be shown that there is such a thing as spiritual life? People had an understanding only for what is material. They said: If there is a spirit, it should manifest as spirit. So a trial was actually begun through newly-developing Spiritualism. Since initiates always tried to give instruction in a way people could understand, an attempt was made to produce manifestations, to provide revelations of the other world. To begin with, we must consider what happens to human beings after death. When a person is asleep, the physical and etheric bodies are united and the astral body hovers over the physical. When a person dies, not only does the astral body leave the physical, but the astral and etheric bodies together leave the physical body, which remains behind. The astral and etheric bodies remain together for a short while, and a tableau of the person's life is visible for two or three days. Then these two separate—the ether body dissolves into the general body of life forces and the astral body assumes the state that we call *Kamaloka.* It is disembodied, but it still possesses the habits and tendencies of the physical body. The following example will make it more understandable. The gourmet still has an appetite. That is a quality of the soul, a desire. One no longer possesses gums, but the desire connected with the gums remains as a feeling of burning thirst. In Kamaloka one learns to overcome this desire, for it consumes itself eventually and then the astral body is laid aside insofar as it is the bearer of desires.

Now the possibility arises whereby one can galvanize such discarded astral bodies and invoke their appearance in the sense world. To this end mediums offer their etheric bodies, by means of which the so-called materializations occur. This was the method for showing materialistic humanity what remains behind after death, and the initiates had hoped to convince humankind in this way.

Two embarrassing results occurred, however. First, people were not morally improved by their belief in what Spiritualism showed them; they remained, therefore, without moral advancement. Second, this perspective of things, this conviction, proved to be harmful after death, because the condition of these people was not made easier in Kamaloka, but more difficult. Also, they brought with them the desire that everything of a spiritual nature be satisfied through the senses, because all of these attitudes appeared as a characteristic of Kamaloka. It was an oppressive weight, which lay like lead upon the dead. That was the reason why the initiates said: This cannot continue. The initiates, therefore, had made a mistake, one might say. But even initiates have to gather experience and test things. After this external method had failed, it was generally agreed at the great gathering of initiates that another way must be tried, an inner way, the way of Theosophy. What does this method try to achieve? It seeks to know what lives in human beings themselves as spirit. This spirit is the goal. One can only get to know the spirit when one gives oneself up to it impartially. One must understand what human beings have in common.

Egoism evolved as a parallel phenomenon to materialism. Here is just an example: In general, when one is travelling about, a special stipulation is demanded. All religious questions are excluded as subjects for discussion because of the egoism of opinions. For if there are seven people gathered together, one will find seven viewpoints. Opinions, therefore, are placed higher than universal human love. But brotherhood begins only when human love is placed above personal opinions.

Theosophy exists for this reason—so one truth can be sought through a balancing of opinions. Humanity must become tolerant once more—not merely toward the personality, but also toward the individuality. Tolerance does not mean merely being able to endure things, to let others do as they like, but in this sense it means opening oneself to understanding the other person's individuality. Thus, Theosophy should not be a dogma, but an expression of love. People should help each other—that is, put love before opinions—and that will introduce a common spirit into human evolution. That is the practical side of what must be developed in the theosophical movement.

Initiation Schools of the Past:
The Mysteries of the Spirit, the Son, and the Father

Düsseldorf, March 7, 1907[227]

The theosophical movement did not come into existence through an arbitrary act by one individual, by one or another human being, or by any one society. It is connected with all of human evolution, and as such should be regarded as one of the most important cultural impulses (introduced by those who understand human evolution). If we are to find our way into the mission of the theosophical movement, we must visualize ourselves in the past and future of humanity. Just as individual human beings have developed as individual souls since they first descended from the lap of the gods, so all of humankind has also undergone development.

Just reflect for a moment what variations, what changes, and what developments can be observed on the face of the Earth over the course of the millennia—how thoroughly everything has changed! What we are accustomed to calling "humanity" is only the result of the so-called Fifth Great Epoch, and was preceded by a different kind of humanity—that of the Fourth Great Epoch. They lived on a continent, Atlantis, which we would have to search for somewhere between present-day Europe and America. Our ancestors appeared in a very different form and a very different culture in Atlantis. The Atlantean was not equipped with capacities for thinking and understanding, but instead possessed delicate somnambulistic-clairvoyant forces. Present-day logic, the combinative faculty, science, and art, were not known in Atlantis, for human perception, thinking, and feeling were very different. To combine, do mathematics, calculate, and read as we do today was not possible for a person of that time. But certain spiritual forces of a somnambulistic-clairvoyant nature lived within them. They could understand the language of nature and lived in harmony with all existence. There were no laws or jurisprudence at that time to reconcile one neighbor with another.

---

227. Text according to a partially incomplete version by Alice Kinkel. Additions in parentheses according to different versions.

No, the Atlanteans went out and listened to the sounds of the trees, to the wind, and were told what they had to do.

The memory of ancient Atlantis (*Nibelheim*) has been beautifully preserved for us in the folk legends, which never contain any haphazard or contrived elements. An example of this is the *Nibelungenlied*. The word "*Nibel*" or *Nifel*" suggests that the Rhine and all such rivers are the remains of the floods and watery masses of ancient Atlantis, and the remaining wisdom is depicted as the treasure hidden in them. It is this continent, lying between America and Europe, that we may look to for the seminary of the ancient initiates, where the people resided who were suited to be the pupils of the great individualities we call the "Masters of Wisdom and of the Harmony of Sensations and Feelings."

This initiation school, which flourished during the fourth period of the Atlantean epoch, was located in the middle of the Atlantic Ocean. The pupils were taught quite differently from the way people are taught today. Very differently, but with tremendous power; it was possible for people to work on each other with the force that still resided in words. What is still alive in the peoples of today is a delicate feeling for the inner spiritual occult power of words. The present force residing in words cannot in any way be likened to what it was then. That was something quite prodigious; the word alone stirred up powers in the pupil's soul. A mantram of today does not have nearly the same force as it did when words were not so permeated with thoughts. When these words took effect, the soul forces of the pupil unfolded. One could call it a human initiation brought about by the nature of powerfully effective speech. A distinct language was also spoken there through the fuming and burning of substances such as incense, and so on.

At that time there was a much more direct connection between the soul of the teacher and that of the pupil. And instead of writing in the Mystery Schools of Atlantis there was a delineation of natural processes drawn by the hand in the air, which had a deep effect—even an after-effect—on the spirits of the population of that epoch. (This had a powerful effect on the somnambulant spirit of the population of that time, and it aroused soul powers).

Thus every epoch has its task in human evolution. Our own task of the Fifth Great Epoch or Root-Race is to add what we call the *Manas-principle* to the four members of the human being.[228] That is to say, we have to awaken understanding by means of concepts and ideas. Every epoch is allotted a task: The task of the Atlantean Epoch was the development of the I. Our epoch, the Fifth Great Epoch, has to develop *Manas* or *Spirit-Self.*

The destruction of Atlantis, however, did not mean that its achievements were lost; a small nucleus of people took away with them the most important part of what existed in the training colleges of the adepts. This small band journeyed under the leadership (the great individuality) of Manu (as far as Central Asia), into the region of the modern-day Gobi Desert. And this small troop of people prepared copies of the earlier culture and teachings, but in a form that was more compatible with understanding. It consisted of the former spiritual power translated into thoughts and signs. Out of this center, various cultural streams issued like radii in all directions—first of all the wonderful pre-Vedic culture that for the first time converted in-flowing wisdom into thoughts.

The second culture to emanate from the ancient school of the adepts was the primeval Persian culture. The third was the Chaldean-Babylonian with its wonderful star-wisdom, its magnificent priest-wisdom. Then the fourth, or Greco-Latin, culture flourished, with its personal nuance. And finally the fifth, our own. The sixth and seventh still lie ahead of us. With that I have characterized for you our task in human evolution: to translate into thoughts—to bring down onto the physical plane—what existed until now as cosmic wisdom.

When those of ancient Atlantis listened to the tone that lay between the notes of their music, they heard the name they recognized as that of their God, *Tau.* In the ancient Egyptian Mysteries this tone has been translated into thoughts, into writing, into signs—into the Tau-sign, the Tau-books. Everything to do with knowledge, writing, thought, only came into the world in post-Atlantean times.

---

228. The physical, etheric, astral, and I bodies (or organizations).

Before this no one had written it down. An understanding for this would not have existed. We are presently in the middle of the development toward Manas. Our epoch is nurturing the culture of the intellect, but, at the same time, is bringing egoism to its highest peak. One could say, even though it might sound grotesque, that there was never a time that possessed so much intellect and showed so little understanding, as the present one. Thought is furthest removed from what constitutes the inner essence of things—furthest away from an inner spiritual perception.

When an Atlantean priest traced a sign in the air, the effect was mainly an inner soul experience of the pupil. In the fourth, Greco-Latin, epoch, personal considerations started to take precedence. In Greece personal art arose. In Rome we find the personal element in public administration and so on. In our time we experience egoism, the dry personal element, the dry intellectuality. But our task today is to grasp occult truths in the spirit-self, in the purest element of thought. To grasp what is spiritual in this most refined distillate of the brain, is the true mission of our time. To make this thought so powerful that it contains something of an occult force; that is the task we have so that we can take our place in the future.

Lemuria perished in great outbursts of fire, Atlantis went down under huge floods of water. Indeed, our civilization will also perish through the War of All against All; that is what awaits us. In this way our fifth epoch will perish owing to the most intensified egoism. Simultaneously, however, a small group of people will come together to develop the power of Buddhi, or Life-Spirit, from the power of thought, to carry it over into the new civilization. Everything productive in human striving will grow greater and greater, until the human being's personality will have reached such heights that it will have attained the pinnacle of freedom. In our time every individual person will have to discover a kind of guiding spirit in the inner depths of the soul—Buddhi or the power of the Life-Spirit. If we were to move toward the future so that we could receive into ourselves only the cultural impulses, as in former times, then we should be moving toward a disintegration of the human race.

What do we find today? Everyone wants to be their own master; egoism, selfishness, has reached its peak. A time will come when no other authority whatsoever will be recognized aside from what people place upon themselves, which will be based on the power of voluntary trust. The mysteries that were built on the power of the spirit are called the *Mysteries of the Spirit.* Those that, in future, will be based on trust, are called *Father Mysteries.* Our civilization will end with these. The new impulses relating to the power of trust must appear, otherwise we face the fragmentation of the human race, a culture of universal egoism and selfishness.

During the time of the Mysteries of the Spirit—based on what was, indeed, justified authority, power, and domination of the spirit—there were a few great sages. They possessed wisdom, and only those could be initiated by them who went through severe testing. Now we approach the future Father Mysteries, and we must strive more and more so that every person can become wise. Will this help oppose egoism and disintegration? Yes! Only when human beings have attained the highest wisdom with no variation—in which there is no individual opinion, no personal viewpoint, only a *single* view—will they be able to unite. Were people to remain differentiated as they are, to retain their own point of view and so on, then they would split up again and again. The highest wisdom, however, always engenders the same view among all people. True wisdom is a single entity that unites people again in the greatest possible freedom, without the slightest compulsion. Just as the members of the Great White Brotherhood are always in harmony with one another and with humanity, so will humanity unite one day through this wisdom. Only this wisdom can establish the true brotherhood idea. It is, therefore, unnecessary for Theosophy to take up any other task, it only needs to introduce humankind to this idea through the development of Spirit-Self now and, later, of Life-Spirit. To make human beings free, to enable them to become truly wise—that is the great goal of the theosophical movement; its mission is to allow this truth and wisdom to flow into humanity.

The modern movement of spiritual science began with the most elementary teachings. Many important things were revealed during the (thirty) years since the beginning of this movement, and even more important things will be revealed. The work of the theosophical movement is therefore a gradual dissemination of the wisdom of the Great White Brotherhood, which has its origin in Atlantis. Such work was always prepared over long periods of time. Thus, as preparation for the great unique event of Christ Jesus' appearance, we had all the endeavors of the great founders of religion. Theosophy assumes the role of executrix to the will and testament of Christianity. And that is what it will become. When the Father Mysteries are one day completed—that is to say, when the development of Buddhi is complete in all human beings—then every person will discover the deepest core of his or her being—*Atma* or *Spirit-Body*.[229] The appearance of Christ Jesus was thus prepared by a line of religious founders—Zarathustra, Hermes, Moses, Orpheus, and Pythagoras. All of their teachings followed the same aim: to allow wisdom to flow into humanity in the particular form best suited to the various peoples. Thus, what Christ said is not new. What is new in the appearance and teachings of Christ Jesus, is that the power resided in Him to bring to life what was formerly only teaching.

Through Christianity and the independent recognition of Christ Jesus' authority, humankind has gained the power to unite in the greatest amount of individuation; through a belief in Him, in His appearance, and in His divinity, people can join together in brotherhood. Between the Mysteries of the Spirit and those of the Father

---

229. Rudolf Steiner here uses the term *Geistesmensch*—literally "spirit human being" or, as in previous translations, "Spirit Man." In theosophical language, and in the earliest editions of his book *Theosophy*, it is called *Atman* (as the spirit-self is called *Manas* and the Life-Spirit is called *Buddhi*). It is clear that the *Geistesmensch* or "spirit human being" is the physical body transformed by the I, and that "spirit body" is actually the most unambiguous and least confusing translation. See *The Spiritual Hierarchies and the Physical World*, SteinerBooks, Great Barrington, MA, 2008: "Outwardly, the physical body appears as a physical body, but inwardly it is completely controlled and permeated by the I. At this stage, the physical body is both physical body *and* Atman." Also Steiner's lecture cycle, *The Gospel of St. John*, Anthroposophic Press, 1962, p. 36: "[The human being] will finally reach the point where, by means of the I, the physical body will be transformed also. The part of the physical body that is transformed by the I is called *Atman* or *Spirit-Body*." And p. 116: "... and the physical body will be so greatly metamorphosed that it will, at the same time, be as truly a Spirit-Body, Atman, as it is now a physical body."

there are the *Mysteries of the Son*, for which the School of Saint Paul was the training center, and its leadership was given to Dionysius the Areopagite. Under his care the School enjoyed its time of greatest perfection, for Dionysius taught these Mysteries in a very special way, whereas Saint Paul disseminated the knowledge exoterically.

And now we would like to seek an explanation from a different quarter, to understand what it means that the Mysteries of the Father are approaching. The teachers of the ancient Atlantean School of Adepts, though *not human*, were beings higher than man. They completed their development on other planets—were from ancient planetary development—and they taught the Mysteries of the Spirit to a small, chosen band. Within the Mysteries of the Son, Christ appeared as teacher on certain occasions; thus, there was also a teacher who was not a human being, but a God. Only those who will become teachers in the Mysteries of the Father are human beings. Such human beings have evolved more quickly than the rest of humanity and will be the true Masters of Wisdom and of the Harmony of Sensations and Feelings. They are called the *Fathers*. The leadership of humankind is transferred, therefore, in the Father Mysteries, from beings who have descended from higher worlds into the hands of human beings themselves. That is the important thing.

To prepare people in advance for this, to form a nucleus for this aim, to prepare people for a universal wisdom, for an authority based solely on trust, and primarily to awaken an understanding for this in a small nucleus of human beings: this is the task of Theosophy. The development of material culture reached its zenith in the nineteenth century. That is why the impulse of theosophy entered the world at this time. Together with this, the impulse opposite to materialism was created and was present there—the opposite impulse, which was an impulse toward spirituality. Theosophy is nothing new, nor is the theosophical movement—it is simply the continuation of something that already existed. Materialism and egoism fragment humanity; an individual only regards his or her own interests. Wisdom must reunite a divided humanity. In complete freedom, without any compulsion, humanity will be led together again through wisdom. That is the task of the theosophical movement in our age. We must keep clearly in mind that we have to acquire wisdom in a concrete fashion. We all know the example of the stove—its task it is to make the room warm. No matter how moving the words are that we use to remind the stove of its duty, and no matter how we plead with it to warm the room, it will not comply. Only when we stoke it can it fulfill its task. Thus all chatter about brotherhood and love of one's neighbor is of little avail. Only knowledge gets close to the goal. For every individual, and for humanity in general, the path toward wisdom and brotherhood can only be attained through cognition.

We have now traced this pathway through three varieties of Mysteries. Theosophy must cause a small nucleus of humankind to gain an understanding for what has been said, to awaken comprehension for it in the general populace during the Sixth Great Epoch. That is the task to be fulfilled by Theosophy. A small section of the people of the Fifth Epoch will anticipate this evolution, will spiritualize Manas and develop Spirit-Self. The main portion, however, will attain the heights of selfishness. That core of humanity that will develop Spirit-Self will be the germ of the Sixth Great Epoch, and the most advanced among these—the Masters as we call them—who have evolved from human beings, will then guide humanity. Toward this end the theosophical movement works for spiritual knowledge.

The Mission of the Theosophical Movement

Bielefeld, November 3, 1908

Lecture given at the inauguration ceremony of the group[230]

There is a difference between the founding of an ordinary group and the founding of a theosophical lodge.

By the 1840s human beings had descended furthest into materialism. So that humankind should not perish as a result of this, a

---

230. Source of notes unknown.

spiritual impulse was necessary. The Masters of the White Lodge began an experiment that would have restored to humanity a belief in the spirit and convinced human beings of the existence of spirit underlying material objects. This was accomplished through the impulse of Spiritualism. The Masters also wished to make the spirit visible to people who could believe only in what their senses showed them. But this experiment failed in two ways: first, the people made egoistic use of the spirits who thus appeared to them, by seeking information about all kinds of things for personal reasons. Second, they did not become convinced of the reality of supersensible spirit. They said, "Look! The spirit is visible, just like everything else in the world; therefore, nothing exists that is not evident to our senses."

This attempt was thus a failure. One should not, however, conclude: They must not be great Masters if they can make such errors in experiments. One must remember that people are not automatons, not puppets told how to act, but people are given an opportunity that they can make use of in a variety of ways.

At the end of the 1860s a new spiritual impulse was given. What spiritualism produced after that did not emanate from the Masters. The result of this second impulse was the founding of the Theosophical Society in 1875. It has spread throughout the whole world.

Now a center for spiritual life is also being established here, from which spiritual life must flow into the surroundings. It is not important for theosophical teachings to be made available to the greatest number of people—much more important is the continuous devotion to serious work accomplished in harmony, mutual understanding, and unity within the Lodges. Through this, the Masters of Wisdom and of the Harmony of Sensations and Feelings have the possibility of allowing their strength to flow into such centers as this. And the Masters of Wisdom and of the Harmony of Sensations and Feelings will allow their strength to flow into this center, and will share in the life of the Lodge that works together in harmony and in a regular and devoted way.

All (educated people) seek out societies—whether they be geographical, anthropological, philological, philosophical, or whatever, because such people believe that all cultural efforts have to be propagated socially. But the theosophical movement is different in one way. Theosophists do not wish to be united through common truths, common convictions, and dogmas; they want to be united through what is accessible not only through intelligence, the intellect, but also through the heart—the comprehending, wisdom-filled and, at the same time, loving heart. Theosophists would like to be filled by a life held in common. When they are united, the joined, spiritual life must flow through their hearts. And where there is a theosophical lodge, where any number of present-day theosophical personalities are joined together, they would like to create a center by gathering the strength of soul and spirit, the power from which spiritual life can flow in all directions.

Every gathering, every group, should be a center out of which something invisible flows. It does not matter what is said at these meetings by one or another person, whether a particular person is more or less a scholar, or what one is as a person; it does matter that those gathered together are filled with the proper spiritual life that flows from their midst, so that people of the present day can comprehend it more and more firmly.

It does not depend on what I say here; it does not depend on my words, but on each one of us now gathered here. What passes through our souls during the moments we are united here is what matters. It is irrelevant what a person says, irrelevant how one clothes one's words. In the eyes of those who lead the theosophical movement, what one person says is of no greater importance than what passes through the minds of others. What matters is the spiritual life that must blossom in all the hearts during these moments, emanating into the world and today's civilized humanity. That is the true doctrine of our society.

Why Has What Is Known as the Theosophical Movement Been Included within the Theosophical Society until Now?

Berlin, December 14, 1911

Address given at the General Meeting of the German Section
of the Theosophical Society [231]

You have heard some very beautiful thoughts and ideas expressed by the circle of those gathered here, and have become acquainted with certain of the theosophical movement's difficulties.[232] We have even heard that there are many who regard the state of the Society as a hindrance to their joining it, and further, that they also find the movement is being held in check rather than being advanced by the current state of the Society. Those are weighty matters, especially for those whose hearts are sincerely and properly seeking to be satisfied through Theosophy.

---

231. Text according to notes of unknown source, revised and with additional notes by Bertha Reebstein-Lehmann.
232. This was preceded by Baron A. C. Walleen's statements about his lecture tour in Scandinavia and England. The following notes were made by Rudolf Steiner in connection with this event:

> <u>Walleen</u> = position in TS 1889
> Wedgewood. —Disharmony —
> Headquarters = English people thorough—
> Like to listen to other views—+ Lodge
> founded—Swedes like <u>memories</u>
> of their deeds. After 2nd lecture lady
> not a member. Pity, that it was not for
> a greater auditorium. The whole youth thirsts.
> Theosophy looked at? In England
> no good reputation.—Blavatsky-Institute=
> best beginners <u>outside</u> society.—
> Much chatter about <u>brotherliness</u> = Forgive
> oneself—will practice love=
> attitude toward <u>life</u>—Personal adoration—
> Criticism—not accept everything—
> Danes difficult. Analytical—
> Movement Society—
> Letter to the Corinthians—[sword]=

The question might be raised: Yes, Theosophy, as we understand it, is certainly something real that has flowed, as it were, into the human evolution in our new age; it has created a vessel for itself in the form of the Theosophical Society as we now know it; and it has spread out to various countries; now how is it that, although this vessel has arisen from Theosophy, it does not actually fit very well into this movement at the moment? I think this is a question many of you have the right to ask me, for many of you might ask: Why do you represent what you call the theosophical movement within the Society?

Because I do not wish to take up much time, I cannot explain in detail what, after all, you can easily check for yourselves if you look at the facts—specifically, that the way I propagate Theosophy, and what Baron Walleen meant, has actually very little to do with what we call the Theosophical Society. Anyone could easily conclude this from the facts of recent years. For what connection is there between all that Baron Walleen has spoken about, and, for example, the central points of what we call the Theosophical Society?

Even under the closest scrutiny, one would find very little that has been derived from the Theosophical Society for the movement envisaged here. One can, in a sense, only answer this question historically. I have done this for individuals, and I would like to touch purely objectively on one or two viewpoints. From these facts everyone can draw any conclusions they like about this matter.

First, I had already given those lectures in Berlin, which then appeared as a short abstract in my *Mysticis after Modernism*. I had held other kinds of lectures in one or another circle, and—at the instigation of theosophists and non-theosophists—part of those lectures led to the book *Christianity as Mystical Fact* without ever having my name entered in the register of the Theosophical Society.[233] That is, it did not matter to me, as to how I conducted my theosophical activity, whether my name was entered in the register of the Theosophical Society or not.

Then this fact became known (that I was not a member of the Theosophical Society). I then became acquainted with a person

---

233. CW 7; CW 8, SteinerBooks, Great Barrington, MA, 2000; 2006.

who has since remained attached to that kind of theosophical movement (I represented), but had joined the Theosophical Society long before I did—that is, Fräulein von Sivers. During the time that Fräulein von Sivers was already a member and I was not, we had a conversation in which she asked me why I did not join the Society. And I answered her with a long conversation, the gist of which was this: It will always be impossible for me to belong to a society where one is engaged in the kind of Theosophy permeated everywhere with misunderstood Eastern mysticism, which is the case in the Theosophical Society; for my business would be to recognize that more important occult impulses currently exist, and that it would be impossible to concede that the West has anything to learn from this Eastern mysticism. What I represent would be put in a wrong light if I said: I want to be a member of a society that has Eastern mysticism as its byword. That was the content of the conversation.

Then a further fact emerged—and I only relate facts so that you can judge for yourselves. I held the lectures on mysticism which very soon appeared, much shortened, as the book *Mystics after Modernism.* This book appeared in turn, extracted in English translation in the periodical *The Theosophical Review,* published by Mrs. Besant and Mr. Mead. The extract, or rather the review of this book, then given by Mr. Keightley, was rather different from the translation he has now prepared (1911). I define the matter, as I did then: this fact revealed that the Theosophical Society has demanded nothing from me— has not demanded that I should associate myself with any sort of rules, principles, or dogmas to which I am bound, but has accepted something that came from outside, that came from me. Therefore, what was given was received in a friendly way.

Then other events occurred. The establishment of a German Section was proposed. As a result of what had taken place, a kind of union had in fact occurred between the Theosophical Society and me, insofar as the movement is an expression of the Society. The result of this was that—inasmuch as there was a tendency to establish a German Section—it was suggested to me, on behalf of the leader at the time (Count Brockdorff) of the German Theosophical Society (a branch of the General Theosophical Society) that I should be accepted into the Society and simultaneously made chairman of the German Theosophical Society. As a result, I did not join a Society, but entered the Society to impart to it something not previously present within it. I never put forward any kind of motion to become a member of the Society, but I said to myself: If the Society wants me, they can have me. I also took a precaution then—to draw attention to an external fact—to absolve myself from any payments. I did not pay anything. Then a gratuitous diploma was sent to me from England, and I immediately became the chairman of the German Theosophical Society. If I could go into more detail I would show you that it was a necessary consequence, to keep the fact continually in mind, that I never wanted anything from the Society and never needed to accept any of its principles and dogmas, but it had been agreed that something was required of me.

Then the German Section was founded amid "hoping and fearing, in passionate pain,"[234] amid terrible discussions backward and forward—I will spare you that! A person appeared then (who has since left the Society) who was also an agent of destiny—in an occult connection there would be much to say about it. It so happened that Herr Richard Bresch, who was at that time chairman of the Leipzig group, after talking it over with various persons, went to Count Brockdorff one day and said: If Dr. Steiner is already chairman of the Berlin Lodge, he can also become chairman of the German Section. Many different things were necessary before one could accept the offer to become chairman of the German Section, and I will summarize these necessities in a few words so that you may become familiar with them.

First, it was necessary to represent Theosophy the way we do here and make it known in the world.

Second, it was also necessary that we do not make it too difficult for those who want to work, for we started with very small groups.

Now, in keeping with so many things that happen all the time in occult matters, I had to say to myself: This Society, along with everything that has happened in it, is actually only a hindrance to the

---

234. Goethe's *Egmont*, 3, 2. Translation Anna Swanwick.

theosophical movement. And I believe that Fräulein von Sivers will still remember how I maintained this view in a conversation about Schuré and his relationship to H. P. Blavatsky. In this conversation I described in detail to that person who is closest to me, what a very great obstacle this Society is to the movement. The other thing I had to say to myself, as so often happens in occult matters when one is faced with opposition—one swallows it, imbibes these hindrances, and takes them into one's own constitution, whereby they are, in a sense, eliminated from the world. Those who then belonged to the movement in Germany can confirm that we would have had the most unbelievable obstacles during those years if we had not become the Society ourselves. We would never have found time to do everything necessary at the time to eliminate the obstacles that crowded in from all sides, so that we could fill the movement with a positive content. We could not have avoided going along with the Society; you should not forget that the concentration of misunderstandings, as they now appear in *one* point—others will come, but that does not matter—were embodied in two people.[235] These misunderstandings and, on top of that, all the chatter about brotherliness, was spread abroad throughout the widest circles—this arose on all sides. And, essentially, you see the same story that has happened now to *one* human being [Hugo Vollrath], has happened to a whole Society; it was presented and spread, in the form of a brochure, as the exact opposite of what I told you at the time.[236] That was just the principle of the various societies that had, above all, developed from the idea of sociability.

The same year that I became a member of the Theosophical Society and was elected chairman without a vote— because there was no such thing as a vote then—the Congress of the European Sections took place in London, where the German Section was to be represented for the first time. I had a conversation there with Mr. Mead in the presence of Mr. Keightley, which chiefly concerned my book

235. Wilhelm Hübbe-Schleiden and Ludwig Deinhard; compare with Rudolf Steiner's letter to Marie von Sivers of April 18, 1903 in *Correspondence and Documents: 1901-1925*, Anthroposophic Press, 1988 (GA 262).
236. See footnote on page 252.

Mystics after Modernism, with which he had become acquainted through Keightley's review. On that occasion Mr. Mead let fall the following words—I have to state them as fact, because they are explanatory: "The whole of Theosophy is to be found in your book." Of course the whole of Theosophy cannot be found in such a thin book; a thing like that must be interpreted as: "One can find in that book what leads to the whole of Theosophy." In principle, what has since been "unhidden" lies hidden in this book. I would like to attach this to the question: Is there not inherent in this statement the supposition that one would welcome this particular current of theosophical spiritual life with eagerness? For, if one says: The whole of Theosophy can be found in it, then surprisingly much has thus been affirmed.

As a result of this statement, it was justified to assume that the Theosophical Society might eventually adopt a form that would create a framework for what "can be found in the whole of Theosophy." For there is not in this book, in the remotest way, anything to which someone in the Theosophical Society says "no" at present.

You can see, therefore, that it was then necessary to act as we did. This can be justified from the most occult aspect; for the theosophical movement we have in mind was completely successful in preparing what we could of the theosophical groundwork for it. If this had not occurred then, right at the start, all that followed could not have happened.

Indeed, it is nonsense for me to say this, because I could also say the opposite: It was necessary to act as we did at the time, to make possible everything that has now taken place.

Over the years I have been very careful to engender an understanding for whatever presents itself as a kind of consequence in feelings and sensations. No one can say that I have treated the Society other than in terms of the consequences of the way things were at that time. And something else happened. This was evoked very clearly and decisively in the very beautiful words of our friend Baron Walleen, who said that since that time nothing has changed within our movement, yet, certainly the circumstances outside have changed. Nothing at all within our own movement has changed, but everything has been fulfilled step by step. I will also quote facts here.

Take the situation of the Theosophical Society as it was when I was the General Secretary of the German Section. At that meeting in London I became acquainted with Annie Besant, and at the second Congress a year later, I became acquainted with Colonel Olcott. I mention this because it is necessary to emphasize that nothing happened then that could do anything other than strengthen the belief in our way of representing Theosophy. Olcott said at the time that he was quite surprised to see me—that gave me something to think about for a moment; he said that, after having known about me for a year and a half, he had expected me to be a gentleman of at least his age.

The obstacles that had arisen to these things that had happened until that time had the most diverse causes, but often took the form where someone said: We cannot join the Society because everything that happens there is dictated by Adyar, and run on a completely autocratic principle. I always said to such people (and that is one of the consequences arising from the preconditions): "I find it unfounded to speak like this within the German Section, because I deal with the edicts from Adyar in such a way that I put them aside and do nothing about them; apart from that I just do as I think right." During my first conversation with Colonel Olcott, I told him I would act thus—despite the possibility he might have preferred to hear it from someone his own age—so that he would not remain unclear about it. I have always spoken very warmly about Olcott, for he was really the ideal person to be the founder of such a society. He immediately understood every stirring of freedom and has never opposed such things; it never occurred to him to do so. He did not talk much about such things, but when someone wrote to him to say that the general secretary of the German Section laid aside the edicts from Adyar one after another and ignored them—he put aside such a letter of complaint and paid no attention to it. You see we could work together very well at that time. Then gradually other times approached. And you can see, I am not actually speaking about anything to do with doctrine; neither am I saying that it should have appeared somehow important to give more attention to the program concerned with my mysticism; I am speaking of what happened.

Then, by and by, other things happened. Now it would take a very long time to describe the many other things. One would have to begin with the fact that Olcott died, and that something then occurred that could certainly be interpreted as apparently in harmony with the spirit of the Theosophical Society, but that it is extremely difficult to interpret it this way. I can briefly state that the message then went out from Adyar that the Masters had appeared at Olcott's deathbed and decided who his successor should be.

There are two ways of interpreting such things: I do not now refer to the interpretation of the content. One could possibly say: Under the circumstances, it is absolutely necessary, apart from how the contents are interpreted, to keep this thing within the most restricted circles, and not mention it in the Society. The other possibility would be to talk about it. Such information would then naturally go from mouth to mouth, no longer under control. And that also happened.

Even though no one has done anything contrary to the spirit of the Society, even though no one deserves any kind of blame—for Mrs. Besant had the right to think and act as she pleased, to make use of this revelation and to guide the Society in that way—nevertheless, it is a fact that, since then, we are no longer on a sound footing in the Society. That is definitely a fact.

What our friend Walleen said refers to the judgement of those outside, who are free to ask themselves whether they want to join or not. What I am now saying refers to the internal aspect, to the ground upon which we ourselves stand. There was no longer a sound footing, and from that time on, the question could not be settled about whether one could remain within the Society at all, or whether one should resign. You know that many people from all over the world resigned; one of the most prominent, for instance, was Mr. Mead. Since then, we no longer stand on a sound basis—for many reasons—and most certainly, the opinion of the outer world regarding the Society has become as bad as it is since then. For the most remarkable things have occurred since then, which certainly do not belong to a proper regulation of the Society, but bear the stamp of the Society on them. Different things happened; first came the Leadbeater case—but not the case as such. Those who are familiar with my attitude will know that I took the following view: as a person, Leadbeater has to be supported as broadly as possible. The only bad thing in connection with Leadbeater's case is that it was also held against the Society. That was the second time I stressed that one cannot really work any longer with this Society. It also became known, through indiscretion, that Mrs. Besant at first personally condemned Leadbeater and then, after a short while, sided with him. This fact has also been laid at the door of the Society by the outside world. Next came something that, strictly speaking, also does not belong to a proper regulation of the Theosophical Society; but, it could be considered a kind of dishonesty if I were to remain silent about it or not mention it.

Among many other things, which would take too long to explain, the fact is added that in Munich in 1907 Annie Besant admitted before a witness (Marie von Sivers), who would be ready to so testify at any time, that she was not competent with regard to Christianity. And because of that she, as it were, transferred the movement to me inasmuch as Christianity should flow into it. After having told me this, several matters were attended to, which, from this point of view, could have brought order into the Society. Nevertheless, one could hear from several sides that Dr. Steiner had now separated from Annie Besant: now there will be two separate currents and that this is going to cause disagreement in the Society. That took people unawares. And now a peculiar method of being practical was adopted, which, in fact, consisted of turning everything into its opposite. And "turning of everything into its opposite" has prevailed ever since in a strange way. It is hard to explain what this turnaround signified. At the time one could have said: Yes, many people are leaving the Society because of disagreement! But the truth was this: Many people would have left the Society even if this disagreement had not come about. They only stayed because this current separated in complete social legality after Annie Besant agreed.[237]

---

237. The statements in this section refer to the separation of the Esoteric School.

Something else suddenly appeared two years later in 1909. Please let there be no misunderstanding about it; but without adding any criticism, accept it as fact—which, of course, will be presented in such a way that it is completely justified—that in 1909 Annie Besant announced in many different places a lecture about the nature of Christ. At the time it gradually became known that a rumor was circulating about the idea of a Christ appearing in the flesh, and this idea grew stronger and stronger, eventually culminating with what you know. If, during recent times, the judgement of outside people has become even more unfavorable, then, without doubt, the story of the appearance of Christ in the flesh has largely contributed to it.

From now on a fact has been established that—in the wake of the former fact (of Olcott's death)—appears to make it impossible to separate the purely administrative side from the teaching side. It is a fact, established as a result of the impossibility of such a separation, and that is the unfortunate position the whole Society is placed in today. To begin with this is only a symptom. Surely you have found a hint in my words to the effect that I do not challenge Mrs. Besant's right to name whom she pleases to represent her in the affairs of the "Star of the East." Not only do I not challenge this right of hers, but, up to the present moment, I do not for an instant think it wrong that she has appointed Vollrath. That is also her perfect right, because she has the right to hold a different opinion than I do about Vollrath. But this is not what we are discussing, although I know for a fact that in the near future it will be said that this was being discussed. But the question is something different. Of course, I do not see why someone who says that I have stolen silver spoons cannot also be the representative for something different; but the fact is, after all, that through this it has been made impossible to support the president, to side with her, if she chooses this particular moment for a pamphlet such as this to appear.[238] For one would

---

238. Hugo Vollrath of Leipzig was excluded from the German Section in 1908, but not from the Society. Annie Besant was informed of this by Rudolf Steiner. In 1911 Vollrath demanded his reinstatement and published a libel against Rudolf Steiner. Simultaneously he was elected, alongside Hübbe-Schleiden, to represent the Order of the "Star of the East" in Germany.

have the right—if the president were given further support, even if it were only said, which is a fact, that one loves her—one would have the right to say to me: So, you side with Mrs. Besant, do you? Then you agree with her; you are a fine one!

That is how it stands. Otherwise one would have to say that Mrs. Besant does not know about it. But that is untrue, because she knows the case exactly. I had to inform Mrs. Besant of these things in a detailed reply to a letter she received from the other side (from Vollrath).[239] Apart from that, everyone would say: What powers of judgement has this president you uphold if she does not see that she cannot do things like that? In other words, one is placed in an impossible situation, and we are continually put in such impossible situations. That only bears the stamp of the Society.

I shall not say anything at all about the Genoese Congress, which is also indicative of an impossible situation.[240] But, you see, when two people defend opposing views from the platform, as they did in Budapest in 1909, this is all right in a Society built on the principle of equal rights of opinion. But no other course is open in a society of people. I shall first ask you: Imagine you have had an invitation, and when you go to see the person who has invited you, you bring someone you value very much, and attach great importance to the fact that this particular person is with you. When you come before the person who has invited you, that person says to you: I do not wish to know anything about this other person, who is no concern of mine. Well, how would you react to such a thing? You would take it as a kind of personal insult. It cannot be otherwise. If you introduce someone you value to someone, and the other person refuses to acknowledge this person, it is not good enough, and no communication is possible. Let us now suppose that the Genoese Congress had taken place; then we would have been placed in just such a situation. Apart from what others stood for, we would have had to

---

239. See the letter from Rudolf Steiner at the end of this lecture (p. 372).
240. In September 1911, a Congress of the Federation of the European Sections of the Theosophical Society was scheduled, where the different views of Annie Besant and Rudolf Steiner about the teaching about Christ were to be discussed publicly. Besant cancelled the Congress at the last minute.

refuse to acknowledge, that is, ignore, not a doctrine, but the human being Mrs. Besant brought with her because she saw something quite special about him, and had made ample provision that others should recognize this quality.[241] Every other possibility was ruled out. In this way we would have been forced to insult the president. If one mixes up the affairs of the Society with private concern, then something personal results from this. You may teach the opposite, but when people are put forward who are personally involved, then we get a situation where the Society is radically drawn into what is personal. How does that compare with what Olcott once said? "It does not concern H. P. Blavatsky, it does not concern me, it concerns the thing itself. No personalities should have a part in that." Does that hold true when one just serves up personalities to the Society as if they were part of our teachings? Is that not a departure from the most apparent principle of fellowship? Yes! Even though unconsciously. It is the same when brotherliness is advocated in the way it was criticized today. Where is there any mention in those three points set up by H. P. Blavatsky and Colonel Olcott that brotherliness should be fostered in the way Vollrath states it in the first sentence? What stands in the first sentence is that a "nucleus"—not at all a universal "hash"—a nucleus of individual people, bound together in brotherliness should be built, which has the task of spreading Theosophy throughout the world. Brotherliness is something that can arise on its own, something one keeps a modest silence about. But it goes along with everything else that this universal "hash" is by and by adopted as a statutory matter.

With this, you see, I have presented you with a few facts. But perhaps it was necessary to speak about these things to validate the assertion, to evoke the justified opinion that, without our involvement, we are confronted by an extremely important situation in the Society. And the only decisive factor until now for me personally —not insofar as *you* find it justified for me to speak like this, but for this reason I say it is decisive for *me*—is that I know the

---

241. This refers to Krishnamurti.

opinion of those who are the leaders of our theosophical movement is that we should preserve the Society as long as possible! And that is what makes it so difficult for me to recommend any direct action against any kind of disruption in the Society. One could say: The things of that time are certainly no longer with us—that would not be very correct; but on the other hand, it is true that we have in this Society something that has been provided—not by us, for we did not enter the Society, but were pushed into it—by the founding of our modern theosophical movement. So the destruction of the Theosophical Society as such is definitely not the right thing; the right thing is the positive. And, as far as that goes, that is much more difficult to perform than the negative. The negative is soon done, only one decision is required for that. But the positive requires action that not only comes at the beginning, but has to be prolonged throughout. That is the important point we have to be clear about; and there it will be a matter of having to arrive at truly positive solutions—that is, solutions that, in a certain way, gradually realize Baron von Walleen's beautiful words: that the content always creates the framework when the content is present. But it is always necessary to take the first step. It seems to me, however, that this is something of exceptional significance and importance, and perhaps should not be interpreted quite so simply as some do. For that reason I take the liberty today of making one remark: I shall be obliged to speak to you here at eleven o'clock tomorrow about something that exists in itself already, and has already been instituted on especially festive occasions, but in a way that it will make it a kind of common possession in a very specific way. What can be made known of this matter will be done tomorrow. We shall see then what is intended.[242]

---

242. See "An Esoteric-Social Impulse for the Future: An Attempt to Found a Society for Theosophical Style and Art" on page 373.

Supplementary Material from a Letter to Annie Besant
Concerning the Vollrath case

In the handwritten text for translation into English by Marie von Sivers Rudolf Steiner wrote in February 1909 about the Vollrath case (see preceding pages):

... concerning the affair of Dr. Vollrath in Leipzig I have no intention of interfering in any way with what you, dear Mrs. Besant, as president, deem correct in this case. I would have preferred that the exclusion of Dr. Vollrath from the German Section had not been necessary. It was the Leipzig Lodge and not I who proposed this exclusion. And for me there was only the question: Shall I oppose the exclusion? I was unable to take responsibility for retaining Vollrath. This was not possible, because Dr. Vollrath was *not* to be treated as a mentally-sound person, since he cannot really be held responsible for his actions. These actions are such that they damage the TS very badly if Dr. Vollrath is a member. Above all, our Leipzig Lodge could not function if it were faced with Dr. Vollrath's enterprises. One should certainly feel great sympathy for Dr. Vollrath: But within the TS he is impossible. The letter he wrote to you is again a proof of what this man is capable of. He enumerated six points about me, *despite the fact* that he must have known everything contained in these six points was objectively completely untrue. Thus he told you that I had succeeded in securing for myself a salary of 1,200 and 2000 marks, respectively, from the German Section, despite the fact that it contains not a single word of truth. This sum has been allotted to the furnishing of the Berlin headquarters of the German Section. I have not only declined to accept anything for myself from the Section's account, but also consider it important that not even my traveling expenses are paid from the Section's funds, but by other means.

To speak about the other false statements of Dr. Vollrath appears to me to be an unworthy act and a waste of time. But as to whether or not it is good to let Dr. Vollrath remain a member of the TS, I would not, as I said, like to interfere in your decision. I should only like to draw your attention to the following: Should Dr. Vollrath remain a member of the TS, he will make use of the opportunity in such a way that he will publish his printed accounts that go against all healthy human reasoning—that the President has disavowed the German Section, and me as well, and specifically, that a wrong has been done him. As things are here in Germany the Theosophical Society would be quite unnecessarily damaged by that. It is sufficiently characteristic of Dr. Vollrath that it is only against me that he directs his complaints, for he knows that it was I who kept him from the Society for as long as possible. I naturally do not care about the false accusations by Dr. Vollrath against me, which he will certainly spread in the near future; but it damages the Society if, at the same time, he can say that the President of the TS has disavowed me.

How much I am *opposed*—just as you are, dear Mrs. Besant—to exclusion in general, you may see from the fact that for months the Leipzig Lodge has demanded the exclusion of a Mr. Zawazki, and I have advised against it for the present.... In any case you may rest assured, dear Mrs. Besant, that I would not have permitted the exclusion of Dr. Vollrath if there had been the least chance that we could have hoped for his recovery. One can cope with the destructive activities of healthy people; nevertheless, even though one can personally look upon the unpredictable actions of unsound people with the greatest sympathy, the Society should not be compromised by them. I would rather not speak about how much trouble I have personally undertaken to help Dr. Vollrath.

In ever-remaining warm respect
Dr. Rudolf Steiner

An Esoteric-Social Impulse for the Future: An Attempt to Found a Society for Theosophical Style and Art

Marie Steiner's foreword to the 1947 edition of her privately printed An Impulse for the Future, and What Initially Became of It:

In view of the difficulties of our time and the short time left to us, it appears as a pressing need to rescue what we can of Dr. Steiner's impulses and words still available to us. This includes many things that he only spoke of in serious conversation within intimate circles at certain turning points connected with the further tasks and aims of the movement he inaugurated. Not everything is available as transcripts, and not everything is complete. Even though they are incomplete and perhaps lacking in some finer nuances, one can nevertheless easily sense how diverse and well-adapted the expressions he uses are to the theme—plastically outlined and firm, or lightly dissolving—allowing us to become dimly aware of a light that remains partially hidden due to a lack of words to describe it. This light settles on them like a faint bloom, through which, however, the impulses can work, leading into the future. Rudolf Steiner continually planted forces of resurrection for future activity in our hearts, germs for the future that will spring to life when the soul-sleep comes to an end. Because of the rush of daily life, they are too often buried or caught up, and swept away by the whirl of events. Those who were able to receive into themselves these seeds for the future included some in whom this seed would one day rise to new life and renewed struggle; others—like the stony ground in the Gospel picture—would not immediately offer it any nourishment. Not only nature, but souls themselves are subject to organic laws. Some of what descends spiritually into these souls becomes hardened or perishes, and some proves fertile and transforms into new forms of life. The passage through death, and the downward plunge into chaos with its whirling, seething powers, provides the surety of a later revival of the spiritual element through metamorphosis to higher forms of existence. The law of metamorphosis to new forms of existence is valid in the microcosm as in the macrocosm, in the earthly as well as the planetary existence. Religions have accompanied this along the way, and practiced and explained it in the form of pictures according to race and nationality, and they have attained higher and higher stages of knowledge that are universal in character and illuminate the hidden depths according to the times.

When a certain climax had been reached in this development, and the danger of philosophical abstraction had entered so that the old pictures and signs were no longer sufficient to capture fresh, vibrant life, the Christian impulse came into being, which brought about the great turning point. Still, even when this emerged into the external world from the dark catacombs, the danger of hardened dogmas arose, and the surging, living powers looked for new directions. These new directions were discovered in the Secret Societies, which refused to bend to the authority of Church dignitaries and Council decrees, and they were subsequently persecuted for heresy. Their content, concealing itself from the outer world, lived on again in signs and symbols, which brought a new impulse to art, initially expressing itself in the works of Gothic architecture—the organic growth of plants was worked into stone. New life even flowed into the names; contained in them was what the soul needed to strengthen and raise it up, to help it develop properly before it had acquired an independence of its own. But the educating of human beings to acquire this independence, into which the newly awakened I-forces were to be poured, demanded first of all that they had to pass through abstract intellectualism. For a time, this separated souls from their spiritual origins, so that, in passing through the coldness of isolation, they could find themselves again in the spirit through stirring their higher I. Knowledge of nature, divorced from the spirit, does not supply the soul with forces that will raise it up. Worlds had to be broken by the spirits for this to be experienced and recognized. We stand amid the broken ruins of worlds; a new search has begun for the solution to the riddles of destiny. The life work of Rudolf Steiner can provide the answer to these questions. He commanded a knowledge of all the exact sciences. He can also reveal to us the spirit that was once secreted into the ancient names, and works unseen behind phenomena. We can guess at the motivating powers that lie concealed in the names through his work. Life lines, which we were not ready to grasp, were thrown to us for use in the inevitable shipwreck. Souls were not awake enough, but were trapped in old concepts. Attempts made for social reasons encountered unyielding opposition from the outer world. An intense sorrow can grip us when we realize how little we were able to bring to fruition what we were offered, to become suitable tools in the fiery hands of the helper sent to us in our need. Standing on the wreckage of broken worlds, we must attempt now to recall, out of the remaining fragments of documents, the word that we received and did not take up with sufficient fire of spirit, raising it to the I of humankind through our individual labor. Rudolf Steiner tried to lead us to freedom—not only along the paths of philosophy and science, but also through esoteric training in life; this was intended to transform gradually our old dependence on the teacher into an impulse for freedom and responsibility toward the spirit. Souls that feel anchored in the spirit have to undergo trials. Self-willed trials of this kind always accelerate karma; even those things that prefer to remain hidden from themselves have to be brought to light. Through such tests the efforts of spiritual powers—motivated by deep cosmic purpose intended to elevate human development to a higher stage—have often miscarried. This was true of the French Revolution and likewise before the universal wars of our century.

Rudolf Steiner first spoke to a small circle of his pupils of such missions for the future, and tried to guide those souls to an understanding of the importance of such future missions, which would grow out of human will free from egoism. He repeated these words to a larger gathering he called together at the General Assembly on December 15, 1911. This did not happen during the negotiations of the General Assembly itself; he explained that this would occur outside the program. He began this address in a particularly festive and impressive manner. This is perhaps why the first part of the address was only written down in brief notes, and is not reproduced in his words. He emphasized that the content of this lecture was independent of anything previously given. It concerned a direct communication, so to speak, from the spiritual world. It was like a summons directed toward humanity. Then comes a time of waiting to see what echo there would be. A call such as this usually occurs three times. If the call goes unheeded a third time, it will be taken back into the spiritual worlds for a long time to come. This call was already sent out to humanity on one occasion; unfortunately there was no echo.[243] This was the second occasion. It concerns purely spiritual matters. With every ineffective attempt, conditions and circumstances become more difficult. The following was reported in notes of the transcript:

Address in Berlin December 15, 1911 (Morning)[244]

My dear Friends! I am now obliged to convey to your larger circle an impulse coming from a smaller group of those who are already informed about the matter.[245] First, allow me to say a few introductory words. It should, however, be specially stressed that what is about to be said is not connected with what has occurred until now in this general assembly or with previous actions, thus, it may be given further consideration later if there is a wish for it.

If we look around us in the world today we would have to say to ourselves: The world of today is actually full of ideals. And we could ask ourselves: Is the advocacy of these ideals honest and honorable on the part of those who believe in them and would serve them? In many cases we would have to reply: Yes, it is—insofar as the belief and devotion of single individuals are concerned. If we now ask: How much is usually expected of people—be it an individual or a group—when they are asked by someone to support an ideal that is about to be put forward? Then, by observing life, we would have to respond: In most cases everything, as it were, is demanded of one; first and foremost, however, an absolute and unconditional acceptance of the proposed ideal is demanded. The proposal of such an ideal is usually based on the demand of absolute acceptance, and

---

243. In the December 24, 1923 lecture at the opening of the Christmas meeting, it was stated that the impulse for the anthroposophical movement has flowed "not through earthly choice, but in obedience to the call from the spiritual world."

244. Only incomplete notes exist of this address, written by various members of the audience. Marie Steiner had only Berta Reebstein-Lehmann's shorthand report when she produced copies in 1947. Notes by Mieta Pyle-Waller and Elizabeth Vreede have been discovered since then and included in a 1984 edition. Mieta Pyle-Waller's notes were read by Rudolf Steiner and he made a few corrections. More detailed shorthand notes by Franz Seiler were also used in the first edition from which this present translation is derived.

245. The smaller group was the Esoteric School.

the failure to achieve such accord is usually expressed by some form of negative criticism of those who were not in agreement.

These words are intended to characterize how the principle of an association of people has come about in a very natural way during the course of human evolution; and at this moment, justification of such a principle will not in any way be put in doubt. But now a possibility is offered whereby you can add to all that is worked for in the world through associations, societies, unions, and so on; this cannot be expressed properly in words, because what one wants to express can never be the standard of correctness for such a thing. According to what people can think, they can conflict with reality as soon as they express thoughts in words. Right now something has to be said that would not be considered very credible in the world. So it must be stated: It is possible that the avowal of something may invalidate it as soon as it is put into words. I would like to cite a simple example so you can see the possible danger that something may become untruthful as soon as it is expressed in words. And I would like this simple, elementary example to be taken in conformity with the Rosicrucian principle that has existed since the thirteenth century.

Let us suppose someone expresses the immediate state of his being by saying: "I am silent"; this, by its very nature, cannot hold true, and does not express the truth. Then I would ask you, my dear friends, to notice that it is possible, by verbally asserting something, to negate that same thing in the process. Through what this simple, elementary example —"I am silent"—expresses, you may conclude that it might be applied in countless other cases, and can occur time and time again.

What does such a fact imply? It implies that people who wish to form any kind of association in support of one or another cause are in an extremely difficult situation. The people, with what they hold most precious, could not unite in any way whatsoever, unless their reasons for doing so are such that they are not of this world, but are of the supersensible world. And if we understand what we have been able to gradually take in, of all that derives from modern occultism, so shall we realize that it is an absolute necessity for the near future to stand up for certain things pertaining to this occultism, and to proclaim them to the world. Therefore, in the face of all principles pertaining to societies, in the face of all organizations that have until now been possible, a trial should be made of something that is completely and wholly born from the spirit of that occultism, about which we have so often spoken in our circle. This, however, cannot be done in any way other than by directing our attention completely and wholly to something positive, completely and wholly to something that exists as a reality in the world, and can be cultivated as such. However, realities are, in our language, only those things that belong first and foremost to the supersensible. For the whole world of the senses reveals itself to us as an image of the supersensible world. Therefore the trial will be made, the trial that the supersensible world has to make: the trial not to *found* a community, but to *confer* one.[246]

I have already emphasized on another occasion the difference between *founding* and *conferring*; this was some time ago.[247] It was not understood then, and hardly anyone has given it a thought since. For that reason those spiritual powers known to you under the sign of the Rose-Cross ceased to disseminate the knowledge of this difference to the world.

But the attempt must be made again—and this time energetically—to see if any success can be obtained with a community that is not founded, but conferred. If this result is not achieved—well, it has failed for a time (and it will have to be postponed for a while).

For this reason it is now announced that those who come forward in an appropriate manner will be entrusted with a way of working together that, in the way it is presented, can be directly attributed to

---

246. Translator's note: It becomes clear during the course of this address that the distinction Rudolf Steiner makes between *Gründung* (foundation) and *Stiftung* (something conferred; endowment) is that the former is something instituted by human beings, and the latter a gift from above. One might even try to translate *Stiftung* as "initiative." Rudolf Steiner assigned himself the role of interpreter of the Masters' will. It is obviously not an endowment of money, but of spiritual content. It is similar to the distinction he makes elsewhere between the Theosophical Society and the theosophical movement.

247. Presumably the lecture given at the General Meeting in Berlin, October 22, 1905 (GA. 93).

the individuality we have known since earliest times in the West as Christian Rosenkreutz. What can be said today about what we are entrusted with, is preliminary. For until now, only a part of this endowment could be imparted, but when the possibility arises, it will appear before the world in a comprehensive way. What could be imparted until now concerns one section, one branch of this endowment—specifically, the artistic representation of Rosicrucian occultism.

The first point I must mention to you is that under the direct protection of that individuality—known to the outer world for two incarnations as Christian Rosenkreutz—a style of working together will be conferred that, to begin with, will be distinguished for a while by the provisional name, "Society for Theosophical Style and Art." This name is not the final one, and will be replaced by a definitive one when, in the appropriate manner, the first preparations have been made to proclaim it to the world. What comes under the heading "theosophical style" is still completely in a germinal condition; for it will depend, first of all, on the preparations made to promote an understanding of what it means. "Theosophical art," however, has made its debut in a variety of ways—including the performances in Munich and, primarily, the important start made in connection with our room in Stuttgart. A further important step toward the understanding of such an idea has been made specifically through founding the union for the Johannes-building. These are all things that have been started. Something exists in connection with this that, having been proved already, has in a way been sanctioned.

The matter is this; within the working committees a purely spiritual task must be awakened—a task that will be taken up entirely with a spiritual style of activity and the results of such work. And the thing is, nobody will become a member of this working group (this working style) who is not determined to devote all the strength needed to support the positive side of it. Perhaps you may say I am using lots of words that are not quite understandable. That is bound to be so with regard to a matter of this kind, for it has to be comprehended in its immediate essence.

What could already be accomplished within this institution actually consists of the creation—according to purely occult principles—of a primarily small, minute circle of people, who consider it their task to cooperate with the envisaged aims. This tiny circle of people has primarily been formed so that a start can be made in creating this establishment, so that, in a certain sense, the contents of our spiritual current can be released from my own person and be given its own stability (substance), its independent existence.

Therefore, to begin with, this small circle presents itself to you with *that* sanction; it has received its task by virtue of its own acknowledgment of our spiritual current, and, in a certain sense, it can envisage the principle of sovereignty and independence of all spiritual endeavor, as the unconditional necessity for the spiritual future; and it is prepared to proclaim this to humanity in the way it finds appropriate. Therefore, I myself will only act as the interpreter, within the movement in question, of the principles that, as such, only exist in the spiritual world; as the interpreter of what in this way must be said about its underlying intentions.

On the other hand, a curator will be appointed for the outer care of the establishment. And because, to begin with, the appointments only entail duties—no honors, no privileges—it will be impossible, if it is properly understood, for any kind of rivalries or other misunderstandings to immediately arise. It will therefore be a question, initially, of Fräulein von Sivers being accepted as curator of the movement. This acceptance simply arises from the movement itself; there are no nominations, only assignations: Fräulein von Sivers will be assigned curator of the movement. And to begin with it will be her responsibility to do what she can, in the sense of this establishment, to canvas a sufficient circle of members—not in an outward sense, but only in the sense that she will allow those who seriously intend to cooperate in this way of working to approach her.

Beyond this, within this one branch of our establishment a number of auxiliary branches will be created. And again, single, tested persons who belong to the movement will be appointed to leading positions within these auxiliary branches—insofar as they already exist—with the corresponding duties. This is also a declaration, to start with, that a such person will be conferred with the office of leading such an auxiliary branch. For each of these auxiliary branches an archdeacon will be appointed. We will have an auxiliary branch for art in general. It has been made known in a small gathering that the archdeacon for the general arts will be Fräulein von Eckhardstein—and, indeed, this has been decided in express acknowledgment of the work that this person has done during recent years for theosophical art in general. Further, the curator, Fräulein von Sivers has been provisionally appointed as archdeacon for literature. Beyond that, for the art of architecture, our friend Dr. Felix Peipers has been appointed; for the art of music, our friend Herr Adolf Arenson; for painting, our friend Herr Hermann Linde.

The work is what should concern us—mainly the inner work—and for the first time, this work, independently carried out, especially by these particular people, will be made public. It will be necessary that those who work in this way cooperate to a certain extent; this cooperation will have to be accomplished in a very different way than formerly employed by any other (ordinary) organization. And we shall need a supervisor of this union. As supervisor to such a union the office of curator will be instituted, and this post will be conferred on Fräulein Sophie Stinde. This union will be affected precisely by the way it is formed (the way the people come together). All of this involves work in the time to come; it will have to be done. But the way this union is brought about—that is, the organizing principle—demands that we have a "keeper of the seals." The office of keeper of the seals is allotted to Fräulein Sprengel, and the secretary will be Dr. Carl Unger.

To begin with, this is the little, the tiny circle with which we are concerned. Do not look at it as something that blatantly announces: "Now, here I am!" Regard it as something that does not have pretensions of being anything but a germ that the thing itself can form around. It will be formed, to begin with, so that by the next Epiphany a number of members will have been introduced to it—that is to say, by that time a number of members will have received an agreement that will ask them, to begin with, if they would like to apply for membership. In order that, right at the start, the assurance of absolute freedom in this connection can be given, the decision to become a member will rest entirely with those who wish it themselves. A person will become a member, first of all, by the recognition of this fact. This concerns only what is to happen in the immediate future, until next Epiphany, January 6, 1912.

Thus we have something that is revealed in this through its own nature, as coming from the spiritual world. It will continue to show that it issues from the spiritual world insofar as the membership is only based on the advocacy and acknowledgment of spiritual interests and excludes everything of a personal nature.

This announcement is in itself a divergence from earlier occult principles. We shall not, therefore, apply to the present (moment) an assertion similar to "I am silent." This is announced, and it will take place in full consciousness that it has been announced. But the moment it becomes clear that somebody does not understand today's announcement, that person will, of course, not be persuaded in any way to join this way of working. I do not say "join in this society," or anything of that sort, but I say: "join in this way of working." You will see, however, that if something like this is to come about—if our age with its peculiar characteristics will allow such a thing to take place—then truly we will be able to work in agreement with the spiritual principle that, not only all of nature and all of history, but the whole of what humanity has produced on Earth is grounded in the supersensible world as well. And you will observe that it would be impossible for any respectable person to belong to such a community if that person did not agree with the community as such. If you think that what has been said to you is very strange, then I ask you to accept it in the way it has been said in full consciousness: that everything will be carried out in complete conformity with the rules, with the eternal laws of existence. And this also belongs to the eternal laws of existence: One should give close attention to the principle of *becoming*.

It would be possible at this point, my dear friends, to sin against the spirit of what is to take place here, if one now went out into the world and announced that one or another thing has here been founded. Not only has nothing whatever been founded, but it is a fact that it will never be possible to define what should occur, because everything must remain in a continual state of becoming. And what should actually happen as the result of what has been said today cannot be described at present—no definition, no description of it can be given—and everything one could say would, at the same time, become untrue. For what is to come about is not based on words but on human beings, and not even on human beings but on what the human beings are going to *do*. It will remain in a living flow, in a living state of becoming. Therefore, the only principle that will be laid down today is this: *acceptance of the spiritual world as the basic reality.*

Any further principles will be created only in the course of development. As a tree in the next moment is no longer what it was before, but has added to itself, so should this thing be like a living tree. What this thing is to become must never be prejudiced in any way by what it is now. Therefore, whoever wants to define—as this or that foundation as something or other existing out there in the world—what has been described here as a beginning would immediately succumb to the same error as saying "I am silent" when describing one's present state of being. One who, therefore, uses one or another word in any sense to characterize the matter, is saying something that is untrue anyway. So, to begin with, it entirely depends—for everything will be in a state of becoming—on the fact that people who want this should come together. It merely depends on people coming together who want such a thing. Then the matter will go forward! From all that has been said, you may conclude that the matter will proceed further. In its fundamental principles it will differ from what is inherent in the Theosophical Society. For not one single feature of what has been expressed today can be applied to the Theosophical Society.

I found it necessary to speak about this matter for the simple reason that such things as are connected with this initiative in an organic (organizational) way have already come before the public of our Theosophical Society. And because, through this initiative—intentions that certainly do not lie in the physical world and really have nothing to do with Ahriman—an ideal spiritual counterbalance (or counter-picture) can be created to compare with everything connected with what the outside world has founded. Purely in this connection, therefore, a relationship to what is there already can be seen, that this branch of our initiative, the section for theosophical art, can do something to counterbalance what is bound up with Ahriman on the physical plane.

Therewith it can be hoped that the existence of this branch of our initiative will set an excellent example—and the other branch will also perform its duties in this respect; because, what figures as art—if we can use this expression today—actually has to flow into our civilization from the spiritual worlds through our theosophical movement. It must happen that spiritual life is the basis of what we do everywhere. It will be impossible to mix up or mistake this ideal spiritual movement with any other movement that comes from the outside world and parades itself as a "theosophical movement" wishing to participate. The thing is this: wherever we stand, what is spiritual is the ground that supports us. This was attempted through our festive plays in Munich, through the Lodge building in Stuttgart—within the bounds of what is possible under current circumstances—but everywhere it was attempted to make the moment of spirituality the deciding factor. That is the *conditio sine qua non*, the indispensable condition.... [gap in the text].

Those who have already penetrated a little into what is referred to here will understand me on this. These words are spoken less for their content than for the guiding principles that must be imparted.

From Marie Steiner's concluding remarks:

By the end of the year and the next Epiphany Day, when no further nominations had been communicated, Rudolf Steiner was asked by someone in his audience about when this would occur. He replied, "The fact that this has not occurred is also an answer." Some years later he came to speak of this again in a lecture:

It was once announced in autumn that, because certain impossible symptoms had surfaced in our Society, it had become necessary to form a particular smaller Society, whereby I initially tried to assign certain titles to several intimate and long-standing associates of the Society, by assuming that they would work independently in relation to these titles. I said at the time: If anything comes of it, the members will be informed of it by Epiphany Day. Nobody heard anything, and it follows from this that the "Society for Style and Art" does not exist at all. That is indeed self-evident, for nobody received any communication. It is equally self-evident that if anything had been realized it would have been communicated. The manner and fashion in which the thing was interpreted in one particular instance made it impossible. It was an attempt (Dornach, August 21, 1915).

CONCLUDING REMARKS

BY HELLA WIESBERGER

A sense for what is tragic is the key to an understanding of human evolution. [248]

Like a red thread, the theme runs through these documents that one—if not *the*—decisive problem of Rudolf Steiner's spiritual-scientific activity was the *polarity between Movement and Esoteric School*. Until the Christmas Meeting of 1923/24, Steiner had held to the principle of keeping the leadership of the movement and the Esoteric School strictly separate from that of the Society. This was because it was difficult "to combine what is demanded currently by an official position in the outer world—even chairman of the Anthroposophical Society—with the occult duties related to the revelations of the spiritual world" (Torquay, August 12, 1924). [249] Another time he said: "The anthroposophical movement—really a spiritual current guided by spiritual powers and spiritual forces from the supersensible world, only having their reflection here in the physical world—must not be confused with the Anthroposophical Society, which is simply an administrative society that, as much as possible, takes care of the anthroposophical impulse" (Berne, April 16, 1924). [250]

From the beginning he drew people's attention to this with particular urgency concerning the inner constitution of his Esoteric School:

---

248. Rudolf Steiner, Basel, December 21, 1916.
249. *Die Konstitution der Allgemeinen Anthroposophischen Gesellschaft...* (*The Constitution of the General Anthroposophic Society*), untranslated (GA 260a).
250. Ibid.

These aspects must be kept strictly separate; they must never be mixed together. When one talks about the external Theosophical Society, one must never even mention the occult individualities who stood over its inception. The powers that live on the higher planes, that live for the sake of human evolution outside of the physical body, never interfere in these affairs. They never impart anything other than impulses. Whenever we are engaged practically in extending the Theosophical Society, the great individualities whom we call the Masters are standing by our side; we may turn to them and allow them to speak through us. When it concerns the propagation of occult life, it is the Masters who speak. When it only concerns the organization of the Society then they leave it to those living on the physical plane. This distinguishes the occult current from the framework of the theosophical organization. Allow me to express the difference between the inward-flowing spiritual stream and what manifests through individual personalities; it can perhaps best be expressed: When it concerns spiritual life, then the Masters speak; when it only concerns organization, since error is possible, the Masters remain silent.

(Berlin, October 22, 1905)[251]

After the theosophical movement and the Society were united in 1907 (when Annie Besant, the leader of the Esoteric School, became President of the Society), Rudolf Steiner corrected this, as far as it concerned him, by taking his first Esoteric Working Committee out of Annie Besant's Esoteric School.

Rudolf Steiner tried in no uncertain terms to clear up the problem of the polarity (Movement–Society). In 1911–1912, with the impending exclusion of the German Section from the Theosophical Society and the founding of an independent Society, he neither took office nor became a member of it. He worked as a completely independent

---

251. *Die Tempellegende und die Goldene Legende* (*The Temple Legend and the Golden Legend*). The lecture of October 22 is included in the English edition of *The Temple Legend* (CW 93).

spiritual teacher, and officially had nothing more to do with the administration of the Society. But soon the First World War began (1914), which greatly impaired the life of the Society. Through the establishment of daughter foundations in the post-war years, a strong opposition grew up against Anthroposophy, culminating in the burning of the first Goetheanum on New Years's Eve (1922–1923). It became evident that the Society was not equal to the fight, and the polarity of the "Movement–Society" problem became incomparably more difficult. The question as to how this divergent situation could be resolved now became a decisive personal problem for Rudolf Steiner. Marie Steiner reports that, in many difficult moments of failure, faced with the base conduct of opponents, he said, "Who knows if it would not be better to continue the movement without the Society? I am responsible for all the shortcomings of the Society, and the movement suffers as a result."[252]

The re-organization of the Society began in early 1923 through the founding of national societies, and the decision was made to rebuild the Goetheanum and begin an International Anthroposophical Society on Christmas 1923. Rudolf Steiner held eight lectures in Dornach in June 1923 on "The History and Requirements of the Anthroposophical Movement in Relation to the Anthroposophical Society."[253] He intended to arouse people to self-reflection, to make them aware that the consciousness within the Society demanded that one should find one's way out of external things connected with society into the genuine spiritual reality, for "an anthroposophical movement can only exist in an Anthroposophical Society that is a reality" (sixth lecture). Just then, he was still wrestling with a solution to the problem: movement–Society. As late as November 1923, while in Holland for the founding of the Dutch National Society, he still had grave doubts whether "a continuance with the Society as such was still possible at all." He complained that no one seemed to understand what he was driving at, that it might

252. From Marie Steiner's foreword to the first edition (1931) of *The Anthroposophical Movement*, Rudolf Steiner Press, 1993.
253. This and following quotes from *The Anthroposophical Movement*.

be necessary to continue the work with only very few people within a strict circle."[254] After having concluded soon after to cut the Gordian knot by accepting the personal responsibility for the leadership of the Society—in addition to his activities in the field of spiritual investigation and teaching—he appended the announcement of his decision: "It is a fact that things at the moment must be taken very, very seriously—in bitter seriousness—to avert what I have often spoken about, specifically, that I will find it necessary to withdraw from the Anthroposophical Society" (Dornach, December 23, 1923).

In order to preserve both movement and Society, he concluded "after difficult inner conflicts" to break with the previous occult rule of keeping the leadership of the movement and the Esoteric School separate from the Society. Whenever he spoke about the new constitution in 1924, he declared that this decisive change was its underlying thought and emphasized that, because he himself had become the Chairman of the Society, the movement and the Society had become identical. For him that had the practical implication that, apart from the teaching and the spiritual investigation "to give active expression on the earthly plane to what the spiritual worlds wished to reveal,"[255] he had to accept the whole heavy burden of outwardly running a large organization. It was clear to him what this involved after ten years as the General Secretary of the German Section of the Theosophical Society.

Beyond this, the decision at the Christmas meeting signified for him "the undertaking of new responsibilities toward an anthroposophical movement directly from the spirit realms" (Breslau, June 9, 1924),[256] and something completely new would be inaugurated. For the Society, as well as for the Esoteric School, administrative forms had to be created so that Anthroposophy could be portrayed to the world as fulfilling its "world mission" of providing the necessary soul to the material civilization of our planet Earth (Paris, May 25,

---

254. F. W. Zeylmans van Emmichoven: "Entwickelung und Geisteskampf 1923-1935."
255. Dornach, September 5, 1924
256. *Karmic Relationships: Esoteric Studies*, vol. 7, Rudolf Steiner Press, London, 1973, lecture 3.

1924).[257] He regarded that giving full publicity to the Society and the Esoteric School was one of the main prerequisites for this, along with simultaneous safeguards of conditions essential for the life of the esoteric work. In this way the Society was to become the most modern esoteric society in the world, right down to its constitution. (Berne, April 16, 1924).[258] That is why the lecture courses that had previously been only for members (of an intimate circle) were made available. The new Esoteric School was to be similarly arranged in a way that it would not have any of the characteristics of a secret society. Although the School had not had a proper outward organization between 1904 and 1914,[259] it would now be declared in the statutes a "Free High School of Spiritual Science," with three classes and with sections for the different scientific and artistic branches as the center of activity of the Society. Its members were to be given the right to apply for membership, and people were to be informed in detail about what occurred (Dornach, January 30, 1924).[260]

We can clearly assess once more the supreme quality of Rudolf Steiner's attitude toward the guiding spiritual powers by looking at his momentous decision to resolve the earlier discrepancy between the movement and the Esoteric School and Society by personally intervening to bring about a new synthesis. According to his own statement, he had taken a great risk, not knowing how those spiritual powers that guide the anthroposophical movement from the spiritual worlds would react—yes, he even had to consider the danger that, by taking on the external management, the source of his spiritual enlightenment "that we all rely on entirely when it comes to the matter of spreading Anthroposophy" might dry up (Paris, May 23, 1924).[261] It was certainly proved later that he took the correct

---

257. *Die Konstitution der Allgemeinen Anthroposophischen Gesellschaft...* (*The Constitution of the General Anthroposophic Society*), untranslated (GA 260a)
258. Ibid.
259. The school was even independent of the Society to a great extent, so that many members did not even know of its existence, since the participants were there by the exclusive invitation of Rudolf Steiner.
260. *Die Konstitution der Allgemeinen Anthroposophischen Gesellschaft...* (*The Constitution of the General Anthroposophic Society*), untranslated (GA 260a).
261. Ibid.

action, since his decision was kindly accepted by the guiding spiritual powers, and the stream of revelations became even stronger than before. Nevertheless, because of that, strong forces of opposition simultaneously arose; forces of opposition on a spiritual level "that make use of people on Earth for their own ends" (Paris, May 23, 1924).[262] He experienced this in his own body—during the days when the Society and the Esoteric School were still new—through an attempt to poison him.[263] He could, indeed, repulse this attack on his physical forces at the time, but they remained greatly impaired. For nine months he continued to produce an extraordinary amount of teaching activity and created new administrative forms for the upbuilding of the Society; then he became very ill and, on March 30, 1925, he was called away from his physical work on Earth. The esoteric-social work belonging to the future, and begun by him in grand style, had to be left unfinished.

For, as with anyone of exceptional spiritual stature, Rudolf Steiner's life was also full of tragedy; but for him it was tragedy of a different kind than is usually imagined according to the definition given by the great pre-Christian thinker, Aristotle. Aristotle defined the essence of tragedy as the state of tension arising out of the *inevitable* connection that human beings have with the powers that, at war among themselves, decide human fate. The thing that differentiates the tragedy of Rudolf Steiner's life from this is that, in complete *free will*, he placed himself into the tensions, in order to balance, to bridge the differences, until even his strong powers were completely exhausted.

The significance of his superhuman effort to resolve the conflicting relationship of movement-Society, which led to premature death, can perhaps best be approached by means of a comparison with the polarity of *point* and *circle*. The underlying aim of his work can be demonstrably attributed to a cognitive experience, a kind of archetypal intuition, revealed by the polarity of the point and

---

262. Ibid.
263. January 1,1924. See *Die Konstitution der Allgemeinen Anthroposophischen Gesellschaft*, p.589 of the chronicle (GA 260a, untranslated).

circle.[264] This archetypal intuition—"intuition is centered in a point"[265]—is evidently the same as the first, the most far-reaching of the seven great Mysteries of Life, for the commentary to this Mystery reads as follows:

> Consider how the point becomes the sphere and still remains itself. If you have understood how the infinite sphere is, after all, merely a point, then return, for then the infinite will appear as finite within you.[266]

The inner experience of this polarity is described by a technical term appropriate to this great life-mystery: "the plunge into the abyss," for, to progress from the center to the periphery, an abyss—on other occasions referred to by Steiner as "turning inside out"—must be crossed. Only then can the way to a true understanding of humanity's greatest polarity—the *I-being* and *external world*—be made accessible.

When Rudolf Steiner discovered during his early student days, 1879–1880, through his study of synthetic geometry,[267] that it can actually be calculated and demonstrated that a point lying infinitely distant at the right is the same as a point lying infinitely distant at the left—in other words, the circle is qualitatively the same as the point—the spiritual concept of the mutually interacting double current underlying time—*evolution* and *involution*—became mathematically conceivable to him. The idea of the threefold principle underlying world creation in the sense of a balancing of polarities came to him at that time, and was later worked out methodically.

It can be concluded from this that Rudolf Steiner must have acquired his knowledge of the relationship of *I* to *world* through his experience of "turning inside-out" the point-periphery polarity. This

---

264. "Contributions to the collected edition of the work of Rudolf Steiner" No.49–50 Easter 1975.
265. "The importance of Anthroposophy in the spiritual life of the present day" The Hague, 1922; answers to questions, probably between April 7 and 13.
266. Letter to Günther Wagner, December 24, 1903, 51.
267. See Rudolf Steiner: *Autobiography.*

is clearly recognizable in the case of three of his most representative creations: 1) In the realm of scientific knowledge, the two books that form a polarity in this sense: *Intuitive Thinking as a Spiritual Path: A Philosophy of Freedom* and *An Outline of Esoteric Science*. 2) In the artistic-sculptural realm: the double cupola of the first Goetheanum. 3) In the esoteric-social sphere of the formation of the Society: the double cupola concept of the "spiritual" Goetheanum.

Rudolf Steiner stated that *Intuitive Thinking as a Spiritual Path: A Philosophy of Freedom* and *An Outline of Esoteric Science* belong together, as the main representatives of I-wisdom and world-knowledge in the sense of the polarity of point to circumference. When he was once asked if he had been aware of the spiritual world-architects, the hierarchies described in *Occult Science*, when he wrote *Intuitive Thinking as a Spiritual Path*, he replied that he was aware of them, but that the language he spoke at that time gave him no possibility to formulate it; that only came later. Nevertheless, even though the hierarchies are not formulated as such in *Intuitive Thinking as a Spiritual Path*, they are still contained in it. For, if one penetrates the experience of freedom as Steiner described it there, one becomes aware not only of the human being as a spiritual being, but also of the hierarchies, because they are all contained within human beings. And then the decisive sentence follows: "In spirit vision what is within human beings appears as spiritual environment."[268] In this same sense he drew attention to the point-periphery intuition in connection with knowledge of the I and knowledge of the world, at the end of the lecture cycle where he summed up his arguments:

> In these lectures, we have endeavored to fathom the meaning and significance of humanity by considering the significance of our cosmos. Today, to some extent at least, we have raised the spiritual question of the significance of the human being. And we have tried to establish the significance of the human being,

---

268. From a conversation between Rudolf Steiner and W. J. Stein: "Correspondence of the anthroposophical working committee" 1934, No. 5, "A contribution to the story of Rudolf Steiner's life."

the point at the center of the universe, according to the teachings of the mysteries. In so doing, we tried to solve the riddle of
the center, the human being, from the periphery—the riddle of
the point from the perspective of the circumference! In doing
so, we place our knowledge within the sphere of reality.... Our
knowledge is real when it steps in front of our eyes as the structure and process of the entire cosmos.[269]

The fact that the formative laws underlying the human form can
also be detected in the dynamics of the polarity between point and
periphery, follows from his statement that one can only approach
human beings if one can comprehend, in a "completely inward" way,
that a circle is a point and a point a circle, for the truth is fulfilled in
human beings that "the I-point in the head becomes the circle in the
limb-system that forms naturally" (Dornach, July 5, 1924).[270]

In the same way that nature fashions the human form out of the
dynamics of point and periphery, Rudolf Steiner also constructed
the plan of the first Goetheanum in the form of two intersecting circles, and with that he characterized it: "And the building becomes
the human being."[271] We can even see from the history of the building concept how this building plan developed in Rudolf Steiner's
mind. In 1907, when the concept of the building was first envisioned
at the Munich Congress, the Assembly Hall was still arranged as a single room corresponding to the Rosicrucian initiation temple. It
remained this way for the Munich-inspired model building for
Malsch. But, even during the preparatory work for Malsch in 1908,
Rudolf Steiner had the intuition of extending the single-cupola hall
into a double-cupola room. The importance attaching to this extension becomes understandable from the modern esoteric-historical
task of bringing to the public cultural life supersensible knowledge

269. *The Spiritual Hierarchies and the Physical World,* SteinerBooks, 2008 (CW 110).
270. *Curative Education: Twelve Lectures for Doctors and Curative Teachers,* Rudolf
Steiner Press, London, 1993, lecture 10 (CW 317).
271. From Wilhelm Rath, *The Imagery of the Goetheanum Windows: An Interpretation
in Verse Form,* Rudolf Steiner Press, 1976; Three verses for the rose-colored window
in the south entitled, "The world builds," "I behold the building," "And the building becomes man," (pp. 25–27).

and its thus far hidden center for the work of the initiates—that is to say, the temple—to involve the public.

What arose out of this esoteric-historical task—as the problem of the discrepancy of the "movement" with its necessarily aristocratic character, and the "Society" with its public-democratic character—was the solution brought by Rudolf Steiner through the construction of a ground plan of two intersecting circles. He once characterized their differing constructions (large cupola-room, as auditorium, out of ordinary circle construction; small cupola-room, to be used as a stage and for ritual purposes, out of divisional calculation of a circle) in connection with the polarity of point and periphery, as the "new architectural-artistic idea" (Dornach, June 28, 1914).[272] The burning of the building on New Year's Eve 1922–1923, nullified this attempt to reconcile the opposing principles of I and world, of Movement and Society, through artistic forms. In spite of this great misfortune, rebuilding was never questioned. Rudolf Steiner maintained the thought of the reshaping of the building for a year, until the idea of the intersection of two circles occurred to him in quite a new way.

At the same time, during the destiny filled year of 1923, the idea of shaping the long overdue re-constitution of the Society also evolved out of the point-circle-intuition. In the struggle toward that end, which he continued after the burning of the building until the refounding of the Society on Christmas 1923, the resolve was born to overcome the polarity of movement and Society by placing himself in the center. The concept of the ground-plan of the building also became the forming principle of the body social. The Christmas Meeting of 1923–1924 for the re-founding of the Society and the Esoteric School became the "ideal foundation stone" of a new social double-cupola construction. The Esoteric School in the form of "the Free High School of Spiritual Science" under the sole direction of Rudolf Steiner was intended to serve as the "small cupola," as it were, and was to be connected with the "large cupola" of the democratic-public Society. With this hazardous undertaking,

---

272. *Wege zu einem neuen Baustil—Und der Bau wird Mensch* (*The Way to a Renewed Architecture, and Building for Contemporary Humankind*), untranslated (GA 286).

Rudolf Steiner apparently wanted to bridge the abyss that had existed until then between the aristocratic life of the occult movement and the democratic life of the public society. The awareness of this abyss must have lived within him especially strongly in 1923, while he was still wrestling to evolve the new social form. For, according to existing phrases passed on from an Esoteric Lesson of that year, he spoke of this abysmal situation as a "heroic tragedy" in the history of modern humanity.

The decision at Christmas 1923 cost Rudolf Steiner his life. Marie Steiner has often referred to the "infinite tragedy" connected with the Christmas Meeting.[273] From the tremendous importance he attached to the polarity of Movement and Society, it almost goes without saying that Rudolf Steiner could not appoint a successor for the continuation of the impulse inaugurated at that time: "that henceforth the anthroposophical movement will be formed so that it gives no further attention to anything but what the spiritual world requires of it" (Dornach, April 12, 1924).[274] No one else could act as its mediator, because, as he said in this connection, "of course the Anthroposophical Society would be something quite different, depending on whether it were under my leadership, or somebody else were in charge" (Ibid.).

Although this can be experienced as deep tragedy, it is, nevertheless, a tragedy that summons us to active knowledge and further fruitful work. For what is decisive from Rudolf Steiner's perspective might best be expressed in the word of a meditation he once wrote:

> Earthly embodiment is a vanishing of spirit *into the abyss*;
> On the other hand it is a shining forth *from the abyss.*[275]

Hella Wiesberger

---

273. *The Christmas Conference for the Foundation of the General Anthroposophical Society, 1923/1924*, Anthroposophic Press, 1989 (CW 260).

274. *Die Konstitution der Allgemeinen Anthroposophischen Gesellschaft...* (*The Constitution of the General Anthroposophic Society*), untranslated (GA 260a).

275. No. 634 in the Archive notes.

APPENDICES

PRELIMINARY REMARKS BY THE GERMAN EDITORS OF THE SECOND EDITION

When Rudolf Steiner first began his spiritual scientific teaching, the only theosophical meditational material in German were the two small publications: *Light on the Path* by Mabel Collins and *The Voice of the Silence* by H.P. Blavatsky. According to the available sources, Rudolf Steiner only recommended once this work of Blavatsky which contained Indian mysticism (see letters to Doris and Franz Paulus in Stuttgart, April 14, and May 14, 1904) whereas he often recommended *Light on the Path* which was inspired by a Western Master (cf. appendix A, page 425), especially the first four sentences, which are thoroughly explained in what follows, or the three sentences:

Seek out the way / Seek the way by retreating within / Seek the way by advancing boldly without.

See the explanations of the above in the letter of February/March 1905 (GA 266).

Mabel Collins reports as follows concerning the manuscript of *Light on the Path* in *Broad Views*, May, 1904:

... One day, as a result of long and persistent endeavors, I was raised up from the place where I had been and transferred to a quite different place, where I moved about in another body, quite different from the usual one, to which I reacted with the same clumsiness as does a child with its newly acquired limbs. Like a child, I was led by the hand by a mighty being who showed me what I ought to see and what I was to understand. We stepped across the great floor of a gigantic hall and stopped in front of one of the walls. I observed it with great delight, for it was indescribably beautiful. It scintillated with precious stones;

from the floor to the hazy height of the ceiling every inch of the dazzling wall was covered and the sparkling and glittering was bewitchingly beautiful. I was told to look closely and I noticed that the jewels were grouped together in patterns and signs. This required more than my own attention and necessitated the active help of my guide in order for me to notice that the patterns and signs were letters which formed words and sentences. But I was enabled to observe it and I was told to store up carefully in my mind what I was able to read and to write it down as soon as I reentered my body. And that is what I did. I vividly remember the strange way in which I returned to my sparsely lit room, where my sister-in-law (who had watched me while I was absent) patiently awaited the result. This consisted of few words, of few sentences, the first sentences of *Light on the Path*. In order to see and read them myself I was moved to the wall where everyone can read them who enters this place. It is known by those who read this book as "The Hall of Learning." In like manner, I gradually received the whole content of the little book, which has enjoyed such wide and rich renown since it was given to the world and I believe that much more is inscribed on that wall than I was able to read; what remained was just a scintillating glitter of jewels to my eyes.

Appendix A

Exegesis to *Light on The Path* by Mabel Collins

The following explanations by Rudolf Steiner refer to the opening sentences of
Light on the Path*:*

"These rules were written for all disciples; attend thou to them!
Before the eyes can see they must be incapable of tears,
Before the ear can hear it must have lost its sensitiveness.
Before the voice can speak in the presence of the Masters, it must
     have lost the power to wound.
Before the soul can stand in the presence of the Masters, its feet
     must be washed in the blood of the heart."

What is called "truth" by the intellectual soul (*Kama Manas*), directed toward the finite, is only a sub-species of what the esotericist *seeks* as "the Truth"; because the truth of the intellect applies to what *has become,* to what is *manifest.* And the manifested is only a part of Being. Every object in our surroundings is at the same time *product* (that is, become, manifested) and *seed* (unmanifested, becoming). Only when one thinks of an object as both "become" and "becoming" does one realize that it is a member of the *one life,* the life where time is not outside, but within it. Thus finite truth is only something that has *become;* it must be called to life by a truth that is becoming. The former *comprehends,* the latter *heeds.* All merely scientific truth belongs to the former kind. *Light on the Path* was not written for those who seek only such truth, but was written for those who seek the truth that today is *seed,* so that tomorrow it will be *product,* and for those who do not merely comprehend the "become" but heed the "becoming." Anyone who wants to understand the teachings of *Light on the Path* must make them one's own, and yet love them as something completely independent, as a mother makes her child her own and yet loves as one apart.

When the first four Precepts are understood, they open the door leading to esotericism.

What does a person bring to the objects in order to know them? When people examine themselves, they find that pleasure and pain are *their* answer to the impressions of the sense-world and the supersensible world. It is very easy for people to believe that they have laid aside inclination and disinclination. But they must descend into the most hidden corners of the soul and drag up *their own likes and dislikes,* for only when all such likes and dislikes are consumed by the bliss of the higher Self is knowledge possible. People might think this would make them cold and prosaic, but this is not so. A piece of gold remains the same piece of gold—in weight and color—even though it is made into an ornament. So *Kama* (the astral body) remains what it is—in content and intensity—even when spiritually transformed. Kama-force is not to be eradicated, but incorporated into the content of the *divine fire.* So the tender responsiveness of the eye should not unburden itself with tears, but enrich the impressions it receives. Dissolve every tear and lend its sparkling brilliance to the ray that penetrates the eye. *Thy* pleasure and *thy* pain are wasted strength, wasted for knowledge, because the force expended in such pleasure and pain should stream into the object of knowledge.

Before the eye can see, it must be incapable of tears.

Anyone who still abhors the criminal in the ordinary sense, and still idolizes the saint in that sense, has not rendered the eyes "incapable of tears." Consume all your tears in the will to help. Do not weep over someone stricken with poverty; get to know the situation and help that person! Do not grumble about what is bad; understand it and change it into good. Your tears only dim the pure clarity of the light.

Your *sensations* are all the more delicate, the less *sensitive* you are. Sound becomes clear to the ear if its clarity is not disturbed by encountering rapture or sympathetic feeling as it enters the ear.

Before the ear can hear, it must have lost its sensitiveness.

In other words, this means: let the heartbeats of the other resound in you, and do not disturb them with the beating of your own heart. Open your ear and not your nerve-endings. For these will tell you whether the tone is *agreeable* or not, while your open ear will tell you the tone's true nature. When you go to someone who is ill, let every fiber of *the other's* body speak to you, and deaden the impression made on you.

To take the first two precepts together: Reverse your will; let it be as forceful as possible, but do not let it stream into things as *your own*. Instead, inform yourself about things and then impart your will to them; let your will and yourself stream out of things. Let the light-force of your eyes flow from every flower, every stone; but withhold yourself and your tears.

Bestow your words on dumb things so they may speak through you. These dumb things are not a summons to your pleasure, but a summons to your activity. What they have *become* without you is not there for you, but what they are to become through you is there.

As long as you impress your wish on a single thing without this wish having been born from the thing itself, you are wounding it. But as long as you wound anything, no Master can listen to you. For the Master hears only those who need him; and no one who wishes to impress the self upon things needs the Master. Humankind's lower self is like a pointed needle that wants to engrave itself everywhere. As long as it wants to do that, no Master will want to hear its voice.

> *Before the voice can speak in the presence of the Masters it must have lost the power to wound.*

As long as the sharp needles of the "I will" project from a person's words, the words are emissaries of the lower self. If these needles are removed and the voice becomes soft and pliant, so that it lays itself around the mysteries of everything as a veiling garment, then it weaves itself into Spirit-raiment (*Majavirupa*), and the Master's delicate tone takes it as vesture. With every thought that, in the true sense of the word, a person dedicates to the inner truth of things, a thread is woven into the garment that wraps the Master who appears to that person. From one who becomes an envoy of the world—an organ through whom the depth of the world-riddle speaks—the I pours out the life of the soul in the world; the heart's blood bathes the feet so that they may haste in carrying such a person to wherever work needs to be done. And when the soul is where the lower I *is not*, when it is not where a person exists to enjoy pleasant things, but to where active feet have borne one, the Master also appears there.

> *And before the soul can stand in the presence of the Masters,*
> *the feet must be washed in the blood of the heart.*

Those who remain in themselves cannot find the Master; those who would find the master must allow the strength of the soul—the heart's blood—to flow into all that is done, into active feet.

Here is the first meaning of the four fundamental precepts. To someone who lives with this first meaning, the second meaning can be unveiled, and then the succeeding ones. These occult precepts are occult truths and every occult truth has at least a sevenfold meaning.

The second part of the exegesis refers to Chapter II, paragraphs nos. 17 and 18:

"Inquire of the inmost, the One, its final secret which it holds for you through the ages.

"The great and difficult struggle, the conquering of the desires of the individual soul, is a work of ages; therefore do not expect to gain the prize of victory until ages of experience have been accumulated. When the time of actually mastering this seventeenth lesson is reached, man is on the threshold of becoming more than man."

Wisdom of the deepest kind is embodied in these last paragraphs of the second chapter of *Light on the Path*. Number 17 includes the challenge, "Inquire of the inmost, the One, its final secret." One who illumines the depths of one's "inmost," indeed finds the results of "ages." For what humankind is today has occurred over thousands of years. This inmost has passed through worlds, and "in its womb is hidden the fruits brought with it from these worlds. Our inmost being owes what it has become to the countless formative influences on its structure; it has passed through many kingdoms, and from these has formed itself again and again into organs. Through these organs it could interact with the worlds that formed its environment each time. And what it has gained from this interaction has been taken into new worlds, "in order that thus equipped from the past it might pass on to further stages of ever richer experiences." And so today we make use of the essential kernel of our inmost being in its differentiations in order to have a summation of experiences on the "planet" we call "Earth."

All that we passed through on the "Moon-planet" and earlier planets is "in our inmost being." These experiences were already in this inmost part as it evolved through a *Pralaya* to the stage of "Earth."[276] They were in the *Pitri*-nature of this inmost part as the whole lily is latent in the seed, though the seed, of course, is physically visible.[277] The "Pitri-seed" that was dormant from "Moon" to "Earth" was incarnated in substances of the highest order, perceptible only to the "Dangma's Opened Eye."[278] When the lily seed is sown "in the ground," it so orders the substance of earth, water, and air that a new lily is formed. Similarly, the Pitri-seed in its cycles through Earth existence orders substance so that, over the course of those cycles, the perfected human being gradually arises until, after the Sixth Earth Round and by the beginning of the Seventh, the human being may truly be called the "Likeness of God." Until the middle of the Fourth Round—until the end of the Lemurian Age— the human Pitri-nature shared in the work on its own organism with "sculptors" of a more and less exalted kind; but from this point in time onward, humankind's inmost being has to take over this work itself. K. H. says the following about this work: All that "thou" has to

---

276. *Pralaya* means literally "dissolution," and indicates a period of rest. —ED.
277. *Lunar-Pitri* is a term for the beings referred to as "Angels" in *An Outline of Esoteric Science,* the Hierarchy immediately above humankind. They passed through their human stage on Old Moon and are now at the stage human beings will reach by the time Earth's evolution is complete.
278. *Dangma* = seer.

do is to become "complete Man."[279] Know this: only in your physical nature are you almost human; for only at the end of the Fourth Round will you become fully human, even in your physical nature. Still unorganized, still chaotic, however, are your astral body, your mental body, and your I-body (higher Manas). Just as your physical body is perfected after the Fourth Round, so must your astral body be after the Fifth, your mental body after the Sixth, and your arupa body (higher mental body) after the Seventh Round—when at the end of earthly cycles your should have attained your destiny. And only when you have attained *this* destiny, can you. as normal terrestrial Pitri, move on to the next planet.

Those, however, who wish to take the occult path should consciously and continually work from their inmost being on the organisms of these three higher bodies; that is the point of meditating.

The astral body is organized through raising oneself to the higher Self and through self-examination. In very ancient rounds, forces worked outside humankind, building the physical body's organs as they are today. Likewise, the higher Self within human beings works on the astral body so that it may become a "likeness of the godhead" or "complete Man." The astral body then develops the capacity to experience the mysteries of higher worlds through its organs, as the physical body experiences the secrets of the physical-mineral world through its own sense-organs. We examine ourselves at night regarding our day's experiences. We raise ourselves to the "higher Self" through the familiar formula. In both activities we work on our astral body. Only thus do we make it into an astral organism, a body with organs, whereas before it was only a kind of bearer. The formula is this:

> More radiant than the Sun,
> Purer than snow,
> Finer than the ether
> Is the Self,

279. *K. H.* = Kut Hoomi, one of the Eastern Masters spoken of in the Theosophical Society.

The Spirit in my heart of hearts.
I am this Self
This Self am I.

Strahlender als die Sonne,
Reiner als der Schnee,
Feiner als der Äther,
Ist das Selbst,
Der Geist inmitten meines Herzens.
Ich bin dieses Selbst.
Dieses Selbst bin Ich.

A vista is indeed opened through it toward "a work of ages," as further stated in paragraph 17. Just as thousands of years were needed to attain the external physical stage of "likeness," so will a work of millennia be required before this likeness can be attained for the higher bodies.

Only then does humankind stand on the "threshold of becoming more than Man." And human beings must come to this threshold in the Seventh Round, as at the end of the lunar period (Moon) human beings had to be at the threshold that raised them beyond the stage of Lunar-Pitri.

Through mental meditation on a sentence from the inspired scriptures, the person who meditates organizes the mental body. To take such sentences from the *Bhagavad Gita* or other writings found in theosophical literature, is to work on the organisms of this mental body. It must be repeatedly emphasized that it is far less a matter of going through the sentence intellectually—that should be done for its own sake apart from the actual meditation—than of *living* with the sentence in a completely free field of consciousness.

The sentence itself should say to us what it has to say to us. We should be the *receivers*. When it is an inspired sentence, it begins to live in our consciousness; its living element streams forth, becomes a fullness in us, a content undreamed of before. As long as we speculate about it, we can put into it only what is in us already. In that way we go no further.

The organization of the I-body depends on the devotional extent of our meditation. The greater our attainment through this devotion, the deeper and more earnest it is, the more we become like the Being who will be ourself as we move out of our planetary life toward the tasks that lie before us in a later existence.

The explanations now to be given refer to paragraph 18:

"The knowledge which is now yours is yours only because your soul has become one with all pure souls and with the inmost. It is a trust vested in you by the Most High. Betray it, misuse your knowledge, let it drowse when you should be exerting it, and it is possible even now for you to fall from the high estate you have attained. Great ones fall back, even from the threshold, unable to sustain the weight of their responsibility, unable to pass on. Therefore look forward always with awe and trembling to this moment and be prepared for the battle."

We must come to realize that we are one with all that lives. We must be clear that what we call our private individuality has no life when it tries to separate from others. Then it has no more life than our little finger would have if it were cut off from the whole organism. And what the physical-material severing would be for our little finger, that, for our individuality, would be a knowledge that wished to concern itself only with this individuality. We were *one* when, within an all-divine Being, we entered the planet that was the first of three preceding our Earth; we were within the all-divine Being and yet individual, as each tone in a symphony is individual and yet one with the whole symphony. What we are summoned to call our individuality must allow itself to be affected by what it encounters in the 343 worlds it lives through (seven Planets, seven Rounds on each Planet, seven so-called "Globes" to each Round = 7 x 7 x 7 metamorphoses = 343).

"What we are thus enabled to experience is laid in us as *foundation* from the *very first*. And that is the treasure I entrusted to thee by the Most High." And as the treasure is entrusted to us, so are we to place it in the harmony of the planetary symphony. Anyone who fully understands these things will meet again and again with a certain experience. Any deepening in our inner being remains unfruitful, empty, if we desire it only for ourselves. To strive for *our* personal perfection is really only pandering to a higher egotism. Our knowledge must continually flow from us. This does not mean that we must positively teach all the time. That is something for each person to do whenever enabled to do so. But in everyday life the living result of selflessly acquired knowledge can be felt in the lightest handclasp.

When we really perceive that all life is one, that all isolation is based on Maya, then all inward deepening will be permeated with the lively feeling that we must carry it actively into the All-one life. And thus our deepening is always rewarded by fruitfulness. We are then assured that we cannot fall back. Anyone striving for knowledge solely for the sake of one's own perfection, solely that one may advance on the ladder of existence, can still fall, even when already mounted very high. Above all we must be conscious of the "responsibility" that we take upon ourselves through gaining higher knowledge. Only a certain measure of potential development is allotted to humankind as a whole along the path of evolution. If therefore we make ourselves more perfect, if we appropriate to ourselves a measure of perfection earlier than allowed by normal progress, we are *taking for ourselves* something from the common measure of humanity. We make the scales tip to our side—up flies the balance on the other side. Only through giving in one way or another can we redeem what we have *taken*. We must not think, however, that it would be better not to take. That again means egotism, abstaining from taking to avoid the burden of giving.

Not to take and not to give signifies *death*. But we are to *serve life*. We must acquire the faculty of giving and must therefore burden ourselves with the responsibility of taking. We must be aware of this responsibility at every moment; when we have taken we must constantly consider how we can best give.

This produces a "battle," an earnest, solemn battle. Yet this battle must be; we *may not* shun it, and we must arm ourselves for it continually. The exalted significance of this battle has always been and always will be brought especially before the mystics of every School of Initiation. They were exhorted to fill themselves, permeate themselves, with consciousness of this conflict. When the conflict becomes the very breath of our being—a fundamental soul mood—inner sight and inner hearing are freshly animated. And when we can be calm, *very calm,* on this battleground, the lightning of higher mysteries begins to flash in our astral and mental sky. Feelings and thoughts clothe themselves in symbols that are spiritually-apparent realities, and from the nimbus of these spiritually-apparent realities the voice of the Master sounds, his form is fashioned. The higher *interactivity* has begun for as. We begin to be no longer merely co-actors in the world but are messengers for it. (*Angelos*).

This exegesis of No. 18 is sentence for sentence reality, higher reality to be experienced. And those who permeate themselves with the meaning of this paragraph in this way, become citizens of higher worlds.

Appendix B

Rudolf Steiner's Explanations of *The Voice of the Silence* by H. P. Blavatsky

Enclosure with a letter of August 11, 1904 from Rudolf Steiner to Doris and Franz Paulus. The following explanations refer to the beginning of The Voice of the Silence, *the text of which is given in appendix C.*

The first sentence of *The Voice of the Silence* speaks of the lower soul forces (the *Iddhis* or *Siddhis*) and the dangers presented by these soul powers. To begin with I would like to point out that this booklet, *The Voice of the Silence,* is intended to be used as material for meditation. It has been written entirely out of *occult wisdom,* which is living wisdom—wisdom that affects the whole being of those who allow themselves to be permeated by it meditatively. Yet, as I have told you, it is not a matter of understanding and dissecting this wisdom intellectually, but a complete dedication to its substance. Only those will succeed who, for a short while, can completely free their field of observation from all sense impressions and fill themselves with thoughts belonging to the meditation. Only they can reap its fruits.

I now want to point to something that forms the occult background to *The Voice of the Silence.* I must expressly state, however, that it is not a question of using such knowledge to speculate about *The Voice of the Silence* while we meditate, but of acquiring such knowledge when we are not meditating. Then the latter will become part of our soul and will be effective in us, even though we do not analyze it during meditation.

All truly esoteric sentences are based on knowledge of Earth-evolution and are written from knowledge that considers humankind as being in harmony with the One Universal Life, which is expressed in continually new forms. But human beings must recognize themselves as one of these forms and learn to understand that the processes of ancient evolution have flowed into them, that they themselves are an intermediate form that leads to higher states.

As human beings exist today, they are made up of several bodies—physical, astral, lower spiritual, and higher spiritual. Even higher bodies are merely indicated in present day human beings. Human beings can fully understand themselves only if they understand that the bodies just mentioned have not all attained the same degree of perfection. Whereas, for example, the astral body as such exists at a higher level than the physical body, the present human astral body is less perfect than the physical. One has to differentiate between a particular perfection and perfection as a whole. The human physical body has attained only a certain degree of perfection today *according to its kind*, but its perfection will have been fully attained when the present so-called "Round" of our Earth has come to an end. The astral body, however, exists at a lower state of perfection today, and only in the fifth Round will it have attained the perfection that the physical body possesses after its kind today. The higher bodies of humankind are at a still lower stage after their kind. One can say, therefore, that human beings have a lot of work to do on themselves before the higher bodies will become as organized and integrated as the physical body. Human beings today cannot harm the physical body to the extent that they can harm the higher bodies.

Certainly, one can also do harm to the physical body, but the harm that can be done to one's higher bodies is something very different. These higher bodies are in a kind of embryological state and when we affect them, we act on *dispositions*, not on organs, which have acquired a kind of finished form within the realm of nature. Through our thoughts, feelings, and wishes, we organize our higher bodies. We do this in the same way that the forces of nature did in ancient times when they built our physical organs—our lungs, hearts, eyes, ears, and so on—from lower forms of life. We must view ourselves as the successors of nature on higher planes (levels). Thus, we direct our thoughts, wishes, and feelings so that *we* ourselves organize our higher bodies, as nature has organized our physical bodies—that is what the instructions given in *The Voice of the Silence* wish to bring about. And we place ourselves into the proper line of development if we allow such sentences to affect us in meditation. These sentences are actually spiritual nature-forces, through which we are guided and through which we direct ourselves. If we direct ourselves through them, then our higher bodies become organized, and we receive sense organs and organs of activity for the higher planes; we become clairvoyant, clairaudient, and can act according to the impulses of these higher planes in the same way as we are endowed with sight, hearing, and the faculty to act on the physical plane through the forces of nature.

It is understandable that there are "dangers" connected with such development, presented by the so-called "lower soul forces" whenever the spiritual force is not steered in the right direction. *The Voice of the Silence* has been written so that people can proceed in the right way.

There is *also* a danger that humankind will acquire the wrong feeling toward the statement that the "external world" is a mere world of illusion. That is certainly correct from one perspective, but human beings are not called on to withdraw from the "external world" and take refuge in higher worlds. We should acquire insight into higher worlds, but we should be clear that we must search there for the *origins* of *effects* that are presently in our physical world. We should always remember that we are to delve into our own spirit. Through such inner penetration, we learn to comprehend the spirit that speaks to us from without in every leaf, in every animal, and in every human being. It would be wrong, however, to seek the spirit and to look down upon its organs, because the organs of the spirit are the phenomena, the happenings of *this* world. We must draw our impulses and motives for action in this world from higher planes; the actions themselves must occur between birth and death in *this* world. We should not scorn this world but love it—not merely as it appears to the physical senses, but learn daily and hourly to see how it *expresses* the spirit. One must look in every direction to find the "Thought Producer" on the spiritual plane, in the sense of the third sentence of *The Voice of the Silence*.

Certainly the sense-world becomes by that the world of illusion, but only insofar as humankind regards it in an ordinary way. For example, we might see a thief. As most people view thieves, they see only *illusion*. What is true about the thief is seen when we look with a gaze sharpened by knowledge of the spiritual world. When we look deeply into the occurrences of this world, then our whole mood and our feelings change in relation to external reality, and through such knowledge we develop efficiency in the real world where we live. We have to realize more and more that it is not so much our task to set the world straight as to adjust correctly our illusory views of the world. Only then can we work correctively on the world when we have set ourselves straight by changing our wrong concepts into truth. That is why it says in *The Voice of the Silence*: When one has ceased to hear the many, the ONE may be discerned—the inner sound that kills the outer. Only then and not until then can one forsake the region of *Asat*, the false, and enter the realm of *Sat*, the true.

"Creative Spirit" works around us, outside of us, but "Creative Spirit" also works within us. The outer world will always be revealed to us by this Creative Spirit, which binds itself to us when we keep the "Silver Thread." Therefore we must listen to all that strikes our ears, we must gaze at everything that presents itself to our eyes; we should, however, never allow ourselves to be led externally, but should be clear that within us is the "explainer," the director, who puts everything external in the right light. By breaking the "Silver Thread" within us, we ourselves turn the outer world into a world of illusion that deceives us at every step; through maintaining our inner connection with the spiritual source, all the light of what is true pours over the outer world for our benefit.

We must search our own spirit; then the spirit of the universe will be revealed to us. It is not usually accepted that this is how to gain insight into the higher worlds, but that is what it is.

The "Halls" mentioned in *The Voice of the Silence* are real experiences of human self-knowledge.

It is important for us to have a clear view in our soul of the steps that have been delineated here. It is not necessary for us to understand with the intellect what is meant by "Halls." We must *experience* their meaning. Understanding them is least important, and understanding them does not make any higher powers accessible to us. But also, although we may believe we have long since understood them, we must live with them in this sense over and over: that makes them accessible. Experienced occultists know that understanding esoteric theories is not important. That is why every occultist allows whatever has been known for a long time to live within the soul again and again. A true occultist must never neglect to live in meditation *every day* with the most important and simplest truths. That does not give knowledge in a worldly sense, it gives *strength* and *life* in an occult sense. Just as one loves a child who is constantly present and whom one knows intimately, so the occultist loves the truths and has to be in close contact with them every day, *living* with them. Occult knowledge is thus different from any external cultural knowledge of mere civilization. Once one possesses this, one is finished, as it were, with *understanding* it. But this is not so with occult knowledge. That is something we constantly have in our living surroundings, even though it is familiar to us, just as one enfolds a child in a loving embrace, even though one has known the child for a long time.

The "First Hall" makes clear to us that our ordinary perspective is one of *ignorance,* and that ignorance must remain our lot if we are to remain in what has, as it were, been given to us by nature. All external knowledge is also merely a gathering together of that which ignorance provides us. As long as we are unclear that, in spite of much knowledge, we can remain ignorant, true knowledge and any kind of progress is impossible for us. It depends on our becoming penetrated by the conviction that we should be "learners." Every step in life should be schooling for us. Then we can experience life in the "Second Hall." Our whole attitude to life is changed under the influence of such a conviction. We then come to believe we can learn from *everything* we encounter. We become pupils of the universal wholeness of life, which is constantly revealed to us. And thus we first learn to love, to love the whole universe. And so the desire for isolation, confined within the *narrow* self, melts away, and we learn through pain and joy not to remain static, but to allow ourselves to be taught in this way. And so we come to recognize that our own organism is an organ for comprehending the whole world. We understand that our real self is in no way identical with this organism; we learn to see ourselves as a tool through which the world works on the higher self, and through which our higher self works on the world. Then we soon begin to see, however, that this higher self is a member of the whole spiritual organism, lent to us on trust so that we may consider ourselves messengers of the divine universal will. We feel ourselves more and more as missionaries of the Great Spirit of the Universe. And when we feel like *this* then we get a breath from the atmosphere of the "Hall of Learning."

Then, however, we can raise ourselves to a feeling of what the Third Hall—the "Hall of Wisdom"—is. We experience its connection with Universal Spirit and become aware that the highest knowledge flows into our inner being; we begin to surrender to this current. The Gates of Inspiration open for us. We shall be led truly by our own selves and not by the proddings of the external world. In this way we are *re-born*, because, just as we were previously a "Child of the World," now we become a "Child of the Spirit." The spirit within us shows us the way. An infinite feeling of security and peace descends on us; whatever success we achieve has no influence on our actions—only the vision of what is right. And this feeling of inner security opens our eyes to the "Hall of Bliss" where the *Seven Voices* sound forth.

Each of these Seven Voices has a sevenfold explanation—as do all occult truths—and we thus draw nearer to the ultimate explanation, which is actually not an explanation at all, but spiritual truth itself. We must, however, actively take up the following explanations into ourselves in meditation so that higher meanings and, eventually, realities unfold before us.

We begin with the first (symbolical-allegorical) explanation:

1. During active contemplation of a living experience, call to mind again and again the feeling that the world, as we *first* view it, is external display and illusion. We must steep ourselves in the living belief that this world will reveal truth to us more and more when we immerse ourselves in inner contemplation. It may not be easy to immerse ourselves completely in this mood, because we must remember that this is, after all, *our* world, the world we are called on to love. If it were easy for us to abandon the way we live in this world, it would not be a sacrifice to leave it behind; in that case we would look for a new way of life, just as we hurry from one change to the next in ordinary life. Therefore the Voice that speaks to us in the

moment of saying "goodbye" must be the sweet sound of the nightingale's song; it must be a real leaving from *illusory feelings of life.* When we immerse ourselves again and again for awhile in such a mood, we climb the ladder of mystical perfection.

Then we can discern the *Second Voice* amid the things of this world. The world within us sounds inharmonious as long as we live in illusory feelings. We make judgements and criticize because we discern the disharmony on the *surface* of things. But when we deaden perception of the discord, and when we stifle judgement and criticism, we immerse ourselves in the harmony at the base of everything. We even learn to understand evil. We learn to recognize that evil is power that manifests in the wrong place. If it were in its right place it would be a good force. Thus, what formerly appeared as discord at the basis of all things is transformed into a harmony. To hear and understand without judgement or criticism means that the Second Voice sounds to us from the silence. All occultists are aware that they have been helped tremendously through attempting everywhere to understand things sympathetically, without criticism; then the silver cymbal sounded for them, the cymbal that is only drowned by an outer sense of hearing attuned to the surface of things.

The occultist asks us to "listen into the *heart* of things." Whenever you compare one thing with another, you may find that one thing is more perfected than another. But one cannot discern what a thing is like through such comparison, but only through the *Third Sound,* which is hidden within every object, like the sound hidden in the seashell. Whatever is ugly in nature, whatever is wrong in life, whatever is corrupt within humankind cannot be understood by comparing one thing with another, but through your own listening to the hidden inner depth of every object and being. Go into the silence where nothing forces itself on you, where nothing urges you to make a comparison. Remain spiritually *alone* with every being; the "silence" will reveal to you the muffled sound in every thing and in every being.

After such an exercise, solemnity extends over the whole of our being and what we stand for. We learn to understand the world in its solemnity and dignity. Something has to be aroused in us that fills us with respect for *all* things. This is the moment when everything is revealed to us as the expression of the powerful Whole. We become accustomed to gazing from the smallest up to the Infinite, because in looking at what is smallest the thought will not leave us that, through it, we are listening to the language of the Universe, which speaks to us in most quiet dignity. The comprehension of this in living feeling in our meditation produces the *Fourth Sound.*

Then, however, after having prepared ourselves in this way, the spirit-beings of the world begin to resound for us; they reverberate then like the sounds of trumpets, because not only does the secret of a single object resound, but the sounds of the universe itself. If we would only allow the spirit of the world to speak to us it would sound forth from everything, no longer as the single sound of these objects, but as the harmony of the spheres. That is the *Fifth Sound.*

And this sound can be intensified. We hear it permeating one being with the next. It reveals to us the secrets of the world. When we understand that all things are revealed as one spirit, then we can surrender completely to this revelation. We imagine the world as a Spiritual Sound penetrating everywhere, and everywhere finding an echo. That is the *Sixth Voice.*

We should reach the spiritual meditative experience of the ideas indicated here. We should remain alone in the silence, very quiet, and keep vividly in our minds the pictures that come from the sounds given us by *The Voice of the Silence,* so that we listen to them in imagination with our spiritual ear. Through this we must fill ourselves with such thoughts as given by me in the exegesis of the sounds. Not speculatively, but with living feeling. Then we meditate correctly and fruitfully.

Finally we allow the revelations of the Six Sounds to flow together in a single note. We should not remain fixed in a *single* relationship with the world, but we should become many sided. Whoever has attained to the Sixth Sound has to return to the First, the Second Sound, and so on. We only draw near perfection when we love the single sound just as much as we love the harmony of the whole.

Appendix C

Excerpt from the German translation of H. P. Blavatsky's
The Voice of the Silence

The manuscript of this translation of the first sentences of The Voice of the Silence *is in an unknown handwriting, preserved in the Archive with the manuscript of Rudolf Steiner's "Exegesis to* The Voice of the Silence*" of 1904.*

The latter translation is very different from that commissioned by Franz Hartmann (Lotus Press, Leipzig, n.d.). Its style leads us to assume it has been produced according to advice from Rudolf Steiner—also the many Indian expressions of the original have been replaced by German terms. Corrections made according to comparison with the English original have been inserted within square brackets.

The following instructions are for those unaware of the dangers that arise from their lower soul forces.

Anyone who would discern the Voice of the Spirit outside oneself must first of all understand the nature of one's own inner spirit.

When the pupil views the outer world of the senses as not being of prime importance, such a pupil must seek out the Creator of the Thoughts that turn the sense world into the world of illusion.

Through immersion in thought, the external appearance of what is true can be recognized in its valuelessness.

Thus should the pupil shed external appearances.

For:

When the pupil has recognized that the outer appearance is a quality of reality, then what is outer appearance will be seen in the self, just as one knows on waking that a dream was a dream and not reality.

When one no longer takes the many faces of outer appearance to be as they appear, then one's gaze will fall only on the ONE truth.

Then and only then will the heart be closed to the realm of what is false and open to the realm of truth.

Before the eyes of the soul can see, inner peace must have been achieved, and the eyes of the flesh must have ceased to impose their opinions on it.

Before the ears of the soul can hear, the person's outer illusory picture must have become deaf to loud and soft noises alike, to the howling of dogs [trumpeting of elephants] as to the buzzing of flies [fire-flies].

Before the soul can envisage the spirit and remember its deeds, it must have united with what speaks to the spirit and what is silent to the senses, just as the potter's clay must abandon the powers with which nature has endowed it and, if it wishes to attain form, must unite with the potter's spirit.

Then the soul will both hear and understand:

The Voice of the Silence

and say:

When thy soul smiles while moving in the sunlight of existence— when thy soul sings within its house of clay and flesh—when thy soul weeps within its outer shell of illusion—when thy soul has rent apart the silver thread that binds it to the Creative Spirit, then, O pupil, it belongs to Earth.

When thy soul gives ear to the clamor of the day—when thy soul is filled with the turmoil of the great world of illusion—when thy soul draws back fearfully into itself at the scream of pain, like a tortoise withdrawing into its shell to escape the outer impression, then is thy soul an unworthy House of the Spirit.

But when, grown stronger, thy soul escapes from its material habitation and departing thence, spins further the silver thread but only binds it to its own image, then it has become entangled in the worst of illusions.

The material world, O pupil, is the world of temptation; it leads you along a path of difficult trials, it entices you to believe that your illusory ego is your true I.

This material world, O pupil, is only a gateway to the Light, to prepare you for the place of the True Light, the Light that no storm can extinguish, and which burns without wick or oil.

The High Voice of the Spirit speaks: "If you would behold the gleaming World-Self you must first behold the small glistening flame of your own Self." In order to obtain this knowledge you must recognize that your illusory self is a non-self, then you will be able to rest in the arms of the All-Being. In these arms a Light awaits you that shines not upon birth and death, but upon what lives eternally.

A U M

Appendix D

Notes from H. P. Blavatsky's "*ES Instructions No. III*"

The following "were written by H. P. B. at the time of a grave crisis, or rather series of crises, for the T S in 1889–90. Treachery within the E S itself and persistent and relentless attacks on the T S from without, especially in America, necessitated the striking of a fresh keynote and giving directions for closing up the ranks of the E S."

"... And if the limbs have to defend the head and heart of their body, then why not so, also, the Disciples their Teachers as representing the SCIENCE of Theosophy which contains and includes the "head" of their privilege, the "heart" of their spiritual growth? Saith the Scripture:

"He who wipeth not away the filth with which the parent's body may have been defiled by an enemy, neither loves the parent nor honors himself. He who defendeth not the persecuted and the helpless, who giveth not of his food to the starving, nor draweth water from his well for the thirsty, hath been born too soon in human shape.

"Behold the truth before you: a clean life, an open mind, a pure heart, an eager intellect, an unveiled spiritual perception, a brotherliness for one's co-disciple, a readiness to give and receive advice and instruction, a loyal sense of duty to the Teacher, a willing obedience to the behests of TRUTH, once we have placed our confidence in, and believe that Teacher to be in possession of it; a courageous endurance of personal injustice, a brave declaration of principles, a valiant defence of those who are unjustly attacked, and a constant eye to the ideal of human progression and perfection which the secret science (*Gupta-Vidya*) depicts—these are the golden stairs up the steps of which the learner may climb to the Temple of Divine Wisdom. Say this to those who have volunteered to be taught by you."

These are the words of great Teachers, and I but do the bidding of one of these in repeating them to you.

BIOGRAPHICAL NOTES[280]

ARENSON, ADOLF

(b. Hamburg-Altona 1855–1936 d. Stuttgart-Bad Cannstatt)
Originally a tradesman, he later devoted himself entirely to music study. He was interested in Theosophy, even before the founding of the German Section, and became a member on December 15, 1902. He met Rudolf Steiner at the First General Meeting of the German Section in Berlin in October 1903, and after that, devoted himself entirely to the work connected with anthroposophy. An esoteric pupil of Rudolf Steiner from 1904, and from 1906 the leader of the Stuttgart Esoteric Group. From 1904 to 1913 a member of the Executive Committee of the German Section. An active center of anthroposophical activity soon arose in Stuttgart through his cooperation with his younger friend, and later son-in-law, Carl Unger. They founded the new Stuttgart Branch in 1905, exclusively for the study of Rudolf Steiner's writings, which eventually became the main branch there. From 1910 to 1913, at Rudolf Steiner's request, Arenson composed the music to the four Mystery Plays. He did extensive lecturing on the German language as an introduction and deepening of spiritual science. He wrote on his study of Rudolf Steiner's spiritual science; his main written work: *Guide to Fifty Lecture Cycles of Rudolf Steiner*, Stuttgart 1930, 1984.

BAUER, MICHAEL

(Gössersdorf, Bavaria 1871–1929 Breitbrunn, Bavaria)
Worked as a teacher in Nuremberg from 1900. There he gathered a small circle of people around him who were interested in Theosophy, which was not attached to any organization. Was acquainted with Helene Lübke, who asked him to go to Weimar, where Rudolf Steiner was giving a lecture on March 25, 1904. There he met personally with Rudolf Steiner and Marie von Sivers, whereupon he and his Nuremberg group joined the German Section of the Theosophical Society as the "Albrecht Dürer Branch" October 1904. From 1905 until 1913 he belonged to the Executive Committee of the German Section. In 1913 Marie von Sivers, Carl Unger, and he formed the Central Committee of the Anthroposophical Society. In 1921 he withdrew because of ill health. From 1904 on, he was an esoteric pupil of Rudolf Steiner and the leader of the Nuremberg Esoteric Group.
Margaretha Morgenstern, *Michael Bauer: A Citizen of Two Worlds*, Munich 1950.

---

280. Many of Rudolf Steiner's pupils mentioned here are vividly discussed in the memoirs of Andrei Belyi, Assya [Assia] Turgenieff, and Margarita Voloschin, *Reminiscences of Rudolf Steiner*, Adonis Press, Ghent, NY, 1987.

BESANT, ANNIE, née Wood
(London, 1847–1933 Adyar, India)
Of Irish ancestry, religiously brought up, married Anglican Minister Frank
Besant in 1867, and separated in 1873. A period of important activity as a
free-thinker and a Socialist followed. At the time she was acclaimed the best
public speaker in England, and an expert on hypnotism and spiritualism;
when *The Secret Doctrine* by Blavatsky appeared in 1888 she was asked to review
it. Greatly impressed, she managed to meet Blavatsky, became her personal
pupil, joined the Theosophical Society, and deserted her former companions. After that she devoted herself entirely to Theosophy, and through Blavatsky came into contact with the Masters. After Blavatsky's death, she
succeeded Blavatsky as the leader of the Esoteric School, and after the death
of the Founder-President, Olcott, she became the President of the TS. She
also played a part in public affairs in India. Under her presidency the Central Hindu College in Benares was founded in 1889, from which the Hindu
University developed. During the First World War she was interned by the
Anglo-Indian Government because she supported the Indians in their struggle for home rule. For a time she was also the president of the Indian
National Congress, until 1920 when she retired from active politics. Whereas
she acquired great merit up to her election as President in 1907, after that
time she branched off more and more in the direction of an authoritative
personal cult. That led to great difficulties in the Society and many of the
oldest and best members left or withdrew. The questionable manner of her
leadership of the Society and her propagation of the Order of the "Star of
the East," led to a break with Rudolf Steiner.

   Literature: the theosophical period: Arthur H. Nethercot, *The First Five Lives
of Annie Besant*, London 1961. The difficulties in India: Bhagavan Das, former
General Secretary of the Indian Section of the Theosophical Society; *The Central Hindu College and Mrs. Besant*, Berlin 1914. The split in the Society, the
exclusion of the German Section from the TS, Eugen Levy: *Mrs. Besant and the
Crisis in the Theosophical Society*; and Carl Unger: *Wider literarisches Freibeutertum!
Eine Abfertigung des Herrn Dr. Hübbe-Schleiden*, Berlin 1913 (*Against Literary Free-
booting! A Reproof of Dr. Hübbe-Schleiden*).

BLAVATSKY, HELENA PETROVNA (H. P. B.)
(Ekaterinoslav, Russia, 1831–1891 London)
Daughter of Colonel Peter von Hahn, granddaughter of Lieutenant-General Alexis von Rottenstein-Hahn, of the Mecklenburg family in Russia.
Gifted with strong psychic powers during childhood, but also very self-
willed. At 18, in rebellion against her family, she married the Vice-Governor
of Eriwan (Caucasus) Nikofor von Blavatsky (thirty years older than she),
whom she divorced almost immediately. In the following years she began
long journeys across various continents. In August 1851 in London, she met
her spiritual leader, "Mahatma M" of theosophical literature, whom she had

known in visions since childhood. He instructed her to prepare herself through study and occult training for work within an occult society. In 1873 she travelled to New York on his inner directions to oppose and clarify the spiritualism then rampant in America. This led her to connect with Colonel Olcott, and in the autumn of 1875 the Theosophical Society was founded, the headquarters of which was moved to India in 1879. Whereas Olcott organized and administered the Society, H. P. B. was its spiritual center. She wrote her great works *Isis Unveiled* (1877), *The Secret Doctrine* (1888), *The Key to Theosophy* (1889), *The Voice of the Silence* (1889) and many other things. She left India in 1886 and after that lived—with short stays in Würzburg and Ostende—until her death in London.

By Annie Besant: *H. P. Blavatsky and the Masters of Wisdom*. 1908.

BOESÉ, LOUISE
(d. 1960 Alvère, France)
French with knowledge of languages. She was an early member of the German Section, led work-groups in the Berlin Branch, and, for a time, performed secretarial duties. In 1911 she stood in for Marie von Sivers, when she was ill, to translate Rudolf Steiner's lecture into Italian during the Philosophical Congress in Bologna. From around 1909 until 1922 she took notes of countless lectures by Rudolf Steiner. She lived for many years in Dornach before returning to her French homeland in old age.

BRANDIS, ALMA VON
(Dates unknown)
Member of the German Section from 1906 and esoteric pupil of Rudolf Steiner. She lived in Berlin to begin with, later in America, and from time to time in Dornach. In 1919, with some American friends, she gave a large sum of money toward the cost of continuing the work on the Christ sculpture (The Representative of Humanity).

BREDOW, EUGENIE VON, née Countess Schwerin
(d. 1922)
Member of the German Section from late 1904, and esoteric pupil of Rudolf Steiner. A close friend of Mathilde Scholl. Rudolf Steiner stayed for several days with a small circle of friends on the Bredow estate in Landin, Westhavelland in the summer of 1906 and gave a lecture there on Parsifal (July 29, 1906, GA 97). She also had a residence in Berlin, at 17 Motzstrasse, and was a member of the Executive Committee of the German Section of the Theosophical Society from late 1911 until 1913.

BROCKDORFF, CAY LORENZ, COUNT VON
(Neumünster 1844–1921 Meran)
He and his wife, Countess Sophie von Brockdorff, were connected with the

beginnings of Theosophy in Germany. As a leader of the German Theosophical Society (founded 1894) and head of the Theosophical Library, the Brockdorffs invited Rudolf Steiner in 1900 to give lectures and soon begged him to take over their office since they wanted to retire due to their age. Their daughter Hedda wrote to Rudolf Steiner February 1, 1902 from India: "I have just read a very appreciative article by Bertram Keightley in the January 15 *Theosophical Review* about your new book, *Mysticism at the Dawn of the Modern Age....* I am very pleased that this book has been appreciated in this way and given preference by the English people—who otherwise always say, "Germany is not yet ripe for it," or "What good can come out of Germany?" According to my view, you have really demonstrated that you are not only ripe, but that you—or, shall we say, the German mystics and you with your view of them—are far ahead of the English. In the production of your book I have seen for myself that you first spoke to us as teacher-to-pupils, and I have felt far more sympathy and understanding for what you have said than for the erudition of Adyar; the lessons that we had with you in the library have brought me more profit than the ingenious and learned discourses of Mrs. Besant, whose ability and knowledge I have looked at with astonishment, but my heart has only found solace in you... There are far more members of the Theosophical Society here, and well-read members at that, but I believe that the Society has outlived itself; the best derives from people who are not members on paper, but are nearer to the truth without a diploma from Adyar or London."

COLLINS, MABEL
(Pseudonym for Mrs. Kenningdale Cook, 1851–1927)
A very well-known and prolific writer in the early days of Theosophy, and personal acquaintance of Rudolf Steiner and Marie von Sivers. Steiner particularly valued her little booklet *Light on the Path*, which he called an "inspired" piece of work, and wrote an exegesis to it (in *Guidance in Esoteric Training*). Mabel Collins gave the following account of how the manuscript for this booklet came about:

"As a result of long and continual effort I was one day lifted out of my body, and from the place where I found myself I was carried to another, quite different place, where I moved about in another body, quite different from my usual one, whose sense organs I controlled in a very clumsy fashion like the way a small child controls its newly-acquired organs. Like a child I was taken by the hand by a great being who showed me what I had to look at and taught me its meaning. We crossed the extensive floor of a mighty hall and stopped in front of one of the walls. I observed it with great delight, for it was unbelievably beautiful. It glittered with precious stones; from the floor to the hazily-distant ceiling every inch of the magnificent wall was covered with jewels and the sparkling and glittering was fascinatingly beautiful. I was ordered to look carefully and I observed that the jewels were joined together in patterns and signs. It required more than my own perceptiveness, and the active participation of my guide was needed for me to see that the patterns and signs were letters that formed words and sentences. But I was enabled to see it and was told that I must take careful note of what I read and should write it down as soon as I returned into my body. I did this, also. I recall very clearly the unusual manner of my return to myself in the dimly-lit room, where my sister-in-law, who had been watching over me while I was absent, had patiently awaited the result. The first sentences of *Light on the Path* consisted of a few words in a few sentences. In order to read these words I have been carried off to the place where they are written, where all can read them who go there. The readers of this book know this place as the "Hall of Learning." In the same way, I received bit by bit the whole content of the little booklet that, since it was given to the world, has enjoyed such a broad and rich life of its own, and I suppose that much more is written on the wall than I could decipher—the rest was just a sparkling glow of jewels to my eyes (in *Broad Views*, May 1904).

DEINHARD, LUDWIG
(Deidesheim 1847–1917 Munich)
An engineer and industrialist, he and Hübbe-Schleiden were the oldest members of the German Theosophical Society, and he was the leader of one of the earliest theosophical Branches in Munich 1894–1896. He helped to edit the periodical *Sphinx*, published by Hübbe-Schleiden. From 1900 he co-operated with Günther Wagner in the forming of a German Section and was a member of its Executive Committee from 1902 until 1908. After an initial hesitation, he later attached himself more and more closely to Rudolf Steiner.

His book, *The Mystery of Man*, was highly regarded by Rudolf Steiner.

DESSAUER, FRÄULEIN von—
Nothing is known about her.

ECKHARDSTEIN, BARONESS, IMME von
(1871–1930)
Member of the German Section from end of 1905. During the Munich Festival plays, 1909–1913, Rudolf Steiner gave her important tasks, such as serving as Mistress of the Wardrobe. The "1912–1913 Calendar" was her initiative, for which she drew the zodiacal pictures according to Rudolf Steiner's sketches, and he produced the "Soul Calendar" text. She was also one of his esoteric pupils. In 1914–1915 she helped in building the first Goetheanum in Dornach. Due to differences of opinion with other workers, she left Dornach. When Marie Steiner took up the re-staging of the Mystery Plays after Rudolf Steiner's death, Baroness Imme von Eckhardstein returned to Dornach at Marie Steiner's request and created all the costumes anew. She died immediately after completing this task.

FLEISSNER —
Nothing further known.

GRÄSER, GUSTO
(1879–1958)
Apostle of Nature. See Ulrich Linse *"Barfüßige Propheten. Erlöser der zwanziger Jahre"* Berlin 1983.

HARTMANN, Dr. FRANZ
(Donauwörth 1838–1912 Kempten I.A.)
Medical doctor and theosophist. After an adventurous life, during which he also became personally acquainted with H. P. Blavatsky, he founded the Leipzig Theosophical Society in 1897, which was independent of Adyar.

HENNING, HORST VON
Court musician of Grand Ducal Orchestra in Weimar. He was a friend of Rudolf Steiner, who became godfather to his son. A member of Theosophical Society from 1895 and co-founder of the Weimar Branch of the German Section on May 1, 1903. Esoteric pupil of Rudolf Steiner from 1904.

HOOK, DR. WELLER VAN (1862–1933)
Professor of Surgery in Chicago. General Secretary of the Theosophical Society in America 1907–1912. His son, Hubert, was one of the first pupils entrusted to Leadbeater.

HOOK, MRS. VAN, Wife of Dr. Weller VAN Hook
(no further reference)

HÜBBE-SCHLEIDEN, WILHELM
(Hamburg 1946–1916 Göttingen)
He gained a reputation as publisher of works dealing with colonial interests and voyages of discovery. He became acquainted with H. P. Blavatsky in 1884 and occasionally worked in the Theosophical Society headquarters in India. He was the first to organize the Theosophical Society in Germany. He published *The Sphinx* (1886–1895), a monthly magazine for the life of soul and spirit, which was, at the same time, the official organ of the Theosophical Union (founded by him in 1892) and the German Theosophical Society (founded in Berlin in 1894). He was regarded by Rudolf Steiner as the foremost candidate for the General Secretary post of the German Section at its founding, but he declined. From 1902 to 1903 he was a member of the Executive Committee. In 1911 he was nominated by Annie Besant to represent the "Star of the East," founded in Germany in June that year. Through this he came to oppose Rudolf Steiner. After the separation of the German Section from the Theosophical Society he became General Secretary of the new

German Section. He belonged to the Esoteric School of Theosophy in London and also took part in Rudolf Steiner's esoteric classes. It is not known if Rudolf Steiner gave him any personal exercises.

See Rudolf Steiner's letters to Hübbe-Schleiden concerning the founding of the German Section and his writing: "Serve the Eternal! Of What Use Is the Theosophical Society to Its Members?" Berlin 1902, in second volume of *Rudolf Steiner's Letters*, Dornach, 1953. Further biographical details are given in Emil Bock's: *Rudolf Steiner. Studies in His Biography and Life's Work*, Stuttgart 1961 (in German).

JINARAJADASA, CURUPPUMULLAGE
(Ceylon 1875–1953)
From a Buddhist family. He was discovered by Leadbeater and brought to England, where he studied at Cambridge. He became a theosophist and devoted pupil of Leadbeater and Besant. 1946-1953 President of the Theosophical Society.

JUDGE, WILLIAM QUAN
(1851-1896)
Lawyer. 1875: Joint-Founder and Vice-president of the Theosophical Society, General Secretary of the American Section. Collaborator with Blavatsky. Authorized reader for the ES in America. Dismissed from the Theosophical Society on the grounds of allegedly forged letters from the Masters. Most of the American members separated themselves from the Society in consequence; when Mrs. Tingley took over the leadership after his death, the secessionist movements soon ceased to be taken seriously.

KALCKREUTH, PAULINE, COUNTESS VON
(Düsseldorf 1856–1929 Munich)
Actively engaged in a close working partnership with her friend Sophie Stinde in Munich. From 1911 until 1913 on the Executive Committee of the German Section, and from 1911 on, member of the Executive Committee of the building syndicate. Like her friend Sophie Stinde she was also an esoteric pupil of Rudolf Steiner.

KAMENSKY, MISS
Russian theosophist, founder of the Russian Anthroposophical Society (1908), friend of Marie von Sivers. Born in Saint Petersburg, died in Geneva.

KEIGHTLEY, BERTRAM
(1860–1949)
Coworker and travelling companion of H. P. Blavatsky. Around 1900 he became General Secretary of the Indian Section of the Theosophical Society in Benares, and General Secretary of the European Section in London 1901-

1905. Keightley had a command of German and after the appearance of Rudolf Steiner's *Mysticis after Modernism* he reviewed it in the *Theosophical Review* (January 1902) and published sections of it during the summer. In 1911 the whole translation appeared with the title: *Mystics of the Renaissance.* Rudolf Steiner stayed in the Keightley's home in Bayswater during his first visit to London in July 1902. In 1921 he revised the English translation of *Theosophy* and gave the proceeds for the rebuilding of the Goetheanum.

KILI, MARIE (Dates unknown)
Member in Strasbourg from 1908. When Rudolf Steiner visited Strasbourg, where he lectured August 30, 1908, she was given the first exercise and promised acceptance as a pupil on their next encounter. This may have happened, since she also asked to join the First Class of the Free High School in 1924.

KINKEL ALICE
(Stuttgart 1866-1943)
Member of the Society since 1903. Rudolf Steiner enjoyed staying at her house with Marie von Sivers. At Rudolf Steiner's suggestion she occupied and looked after the Stuttgart home at Landhausstrasse 70. Out of her own initiative, she looked after the book table at all functions from 1906 until the Society was closed by the National Socialists in 1935. We are indebted to her for the transcription of many lectures, notes, and so on.

KOLBE, ADOLF
(Dates unknown)
Hamburg. Member of the Theosophical Society from 1897. Together with Bernhard Hubo he founded the Hamburg Branch. (Pythagoras Branch), which was one of the branches that formed the German Section in 1902. He was a member of its Executive Committee 1905-1913, and an esoteric pupil of Rudolf Steiner.

KÜNSTLER, EUGEN (1869-1942) and MAUD (born CAPON, +1916)
Friends and inmates of Mathilde Scholl's home in Cologne. Members from 1903. Developed the work in Cologne along with Mathilde Scholl. Esoteric pupils of Rudolf Steiner. In 1917 Rudolf Steiner modelled a portrait in relief of Maud Künstler, who died in the meantime.

LAGUTT-von OSTHEIM, DR. JAN
(Poland 1873–1944 Basel)
Polish by birth. Studied in Zürich, then worked with a Basel chemical firm. A small theosophical group gathered around him at the beginning of the century, which then became the Basel (Paracelsus) Group in 1906, of which he was the chairman until 1921. An esoteric pupil of Rudolf Steiner.

LANGEN, MARTHA
(Mariahalden, Zürich 1865–1950 Arlesheim)
Descended from the Counts of Strachwitz of Upper Silesia. After various
domiciles, she lived for years in Eisenach. Founded the Eisenach Branch,
which was consecrated in the presence of Rudolf Steiner on June 13, 1908.
Steiner gave several lectures in her home. From 1915 on, she lived in Dornach. Her poems were published even while she was a young girl. Later she
also wrote dramas—including *Schwarz-Weiss* (*Black and White*), a play about
the Templars, 1926; *Julian* 1928; and *Tycho Brahe* 1929. She became a member of the German Section in 1907 and later an esoteric pupil of Rudolf
Steiner.

LEADBEATER, CHARLES WEBSTER
(Northumberland 1847–1934 Perth, Australia)
Because of his father's profession he spent some of his youth in South
America (Brazil). From 1879 on, he was for several years a priest in the
Anglican High Church. During this time—while he was interested in what
spiritualism had to show—he got to know Sinnett and became a member
of the Theosophical Society in late 1883. In 1884, H. P. Blavatsky gave him
a letter from Mahatma K. H. explaining the prerequisites for pupilship. As
a result, he broke off connections in England and accompanied Blavatsky
to India. Leadbeater lived there for five years, and was the General Secretary of the Sinhalese Section of the Theosophical Society in 1888–1889.
When he returned to London in 1889 to privately tutor Sinnett's son, he
brought the Sinhalese boy, C. Jinarajadasa, whom he had discovered, and
provided him with an education. In London he worked more and more
intensively with Annie Besant who, in the meantime, had also become a
theosophist. After the so-called "Leadbeater case," which caused him to
withdraw from the Society in 1906, he was reinstated by Annie Besant in
1909, and he discovered the child Krishnamurti and inspired the Order of
the "Star of the East." He went to Australia in 1913 and participated in the
founding of the Liberal Catholic Church, in which he became Bishop. He
spent his last 20 years in Australia, but until his death he was considered
the Grey Eminence of the TS. He was considered a very controversial figure in the theosophical movement. See Gregory Tillet: *The Elder Brother,*
London 1982.

LINDE, HERMANN
(Lübeck 1863–1923 Arlesheim, Switzerland)
Painter-artist. A member of the German Section from 1906. He belonged to
the Munich circle around Sophie Stinde. He painted much of the stage scen-
ery for the festival performances 1907–1913, and was one of the founders of
the building syndicate. Called to Dornach for the painting of the large
cupola of the first Goetheanum, he lived there after 1914 and became the

Vice-Chairman of the building syndicate in 1920. He was given much stimulation by Rudolf Steiner for his cycle of pictures illustrating Goethe's *Fairy Story*. He was an esoteric pupil of Rudolf Steiner.

LINK, ANTONIA
(1857-1940 Marburg)
Teacher in Ehrenbreitstein, later in Pfaffendorf, near Coblenz. Friend of Mathilde Scholl. She was a member of the English Theosophical Society and joined the Cologne Branch in 1905, and from the summer of that year was an esoteric pupil of Rudolf Steiner. She was a friend of Keightley who asked her for anthroposophical literature in 1913, because he had withdrawn from Annie Besant. During 1920–1924 she frequently supplied Rudolf Steiner with information about Keightley.

LOHF, BERNHARD
(Dates unknown)
Member of the German Section from 1905 and of the Düsseldorf Branch No.1.

LÜBKE, HELENE
(Dates unknown)
Wife of the art critic, Wilhelm Lübke (d. 1893), who came from the Rhine district. She became a member of the London Theosophical Society and its Esoteric School, probably around the turn of the century. She also belonged to the German Section 1902–1903. In 1903–1904 she lived in Weimar, where she organized three public lectures by Rudolf Steiner in April 1903. The Weimar Branch was founded April 18, 1903 at the time of a members' lecture there. She organized lectures by Rudolf Steiner in Elberfeld 1905–1906 as well as in Düsseldorf. Then she returned to England, where she had lived before 1900.

MEAD, GEORGE R. S.
(1863–1933)
Theosophical writer. Secretary to H. P. Blavatsky during her last years, and occasionally General Secretary of the Theosophical Society in London. Co-editor with H.P.B of her periodical *Luzifer*, founded in London in 1886; later, with Annie Besant, its name was changed to *The Theosophical Review*.

MEAD, MRS. L. M.
Secretary of the ES in London. Left the Theosophical Society with her husband George in 1908 after the readmittance of Leadbeater by A. Besant.

MEEBOLD, ALFRED
(Heidenheim, Brenz 1863–1952 Havelock, New Zealand)
World traveller interested in art, philosophy, and natural science, especially

botany. He became a member of the Theosophical Society in London in 1898. In the following years while living in Munich he cooperated with a group of theosophists around Sophie Stinde and Pauline von Kalckreuth to form a branch that was consecrated by Annie Besant in September 1904, while she was lecturing in Munich. At that time Meebold met Rudolf Steiner for the first time, was not particularly impressed by him, and travelled soon after to India. There he had an unsatisfactory talk with Annie Besant over questions of esoteric training. After his return, Sophie Stinde and Pauline von Kalckreuth persuaded him to visit Steiner to ask for an explanation about an occult experience he had in India. Instead of the requested explanation, Steiner shortly and sharply refused to gratify his wishes, and gave him esoteric exercises instead, saying, "If you follow my methods, the former results will disappear and then we shall have to wait until new ones appear." Meebold remained an anthroposophist to the end of his life and enabled many people to gain a connection to Steiner. In 1916 he published his attempt to write a "soul-biography," *My Path to the Spirit.*

MINSLOFF, ANNA
(Dates unknown)
Russian. Daughter of a well-known Saint Petersburg lawyer. Member of the Theosophical Society. Went to Berlin in 1904–1905, where she met Rudolf Steiner and became his esoteric pupil. She played a significant part in theosophical affairs during those years. According to Margarita Voloschin's accounts (*Die Grüne Schlange*, Stuttgart 1954) and Assia Turgenieff (*Memories of Rudolf Steiner and the Work on the First Goetheanum*, Stuttgart 1972, in German) she was a remarkable person, "highly cultured and filled with burning anxiety about the future of Europe and especially about the dangers that threatened Russia. Gifted with strong, but chaotic clairvoyant faculties, not always able to distinguish between what she saw in this way and the outer reality, she reminds one of the tragic figure of H. P. Blavatsky. She regarded it as her mission to found an esoteric center from which the approaching danger could be combated. She possessed great occult knowledge. Writings and meditations reinforced her influence." She is said to have later turned away from Rudolf Steiner and become estranged from her friends.

MOLTKE, ELIZA VON
(born Countess Moltke-Huitfeldt, Bellevue/Sweden,
1859–1932, Ambach, Upper Bavaria).
Wife of Helmuth von Moltke (the younger, 1906–1914 Chief of the General Staff). Became acquainted with Rudolf Steiner in Berlin soon after the turn of the century. Became a member of the German Section, and after 1904 an esoteric pupil of Rudolf Steiner.

OLCOTT, HENRY STEEL
(Orange, New Jersey 1832–1907 Adyar, India)
Specialist in agriculture, free-lance writer and correspondent for several journals. He rose to the rank of a Colonel in the American Civil War (1861–1865). Later he was in charge of a law practice. Through his interest in hypnotism and mesmerism he submitted a report to a New York paper about the sensational spiritualistic phenomena that appeared in America in 1874. Through this he made personal contact with H. P. Blavatsky, and together they founded the Theosophical Society in New York in autumn 1875, and he remained Founder-President until his death in 1907. He wrote *People of the Other World* (1875) and published the magazine *The Theosophist* in 1879; his *Old Diary Leaves* in 1895 was the record of his work with H. P. Blavatsky.

PAULUS, DORIS and FRANZ
(Dates unknown)
They were apparently members of the Theosophical Society before the founding of the German Section. In 1903–1904 they participated in developing the Stuttgart Branch. From 1904 they were esoteric pupils of Rudolf Steiner. In 1906 they moved to Ascona in Switzerland and asked Rudolf Steiner if they could become pupils of the Esoteric School being transferred to the leadership of Annie Besant who often held esoteric classes in nearby Milan. At the end of 1911 they withdrew from the German Section because of the differing opinions of Annie Besant and Rudolf Steiner.

PEIPERS, DR. FELIX
(Bonn 1873–1944 Arlesheim)
He joined the German Section in 1904 through his friendship since youth with Michael Bauer. Dr. Peipers was head of a private sanatorium in Munich from 1907 and was a member of the Munich Group. He took part in the *Mystery Plays* 1910–1913 (as Benedictus) and was one of the founders of the Building Syndicate. He also served on the Executive Committee of the German Section from the end of 1911 until 1913. He was one of the first medical doctors to apply Rudolf Steiner's methods. He was one of the leading doctors at the Clinical-Therapeutic Institute in Stuttgart from 1921–1924. For health reasons he later lived for many years on Tenerife. He was an esoteric pupil of Rudolf Steiner.

SCHOLL, MATHILDE
(1868–1941 Dornach)
Teacher from the Rhine district. She came into contact with leading figures of the Theosophical Society while acting as governess in Italy, and joined the Society. At the meetings for the founding of the German Section in Berlin October 1902, she became acquainted with Rudolf Steiner and Marie von Sivers and after that she actively committed herself to the work. She was a

member of the Executive Committee of the German Section 1903–1913, and issued the Society's official organ 1905–1914—*The News Sheet for Members of the German Section of the Theosophical Society*—and from March 1913 the *Anthroposophical Society.* She lived in Cologne in the same house as her friends Maud and Eugen Künstler (1902–1903), and they founded the Giordano Bruno Branch in 1904, which grew to be a center with a wide sphere of influence. The Anthroposophical Society was founded there at Christmas 1912. From 1914 on, she lived in Dornach where, until she died, an anthroposophical study group formed around her. She belonged to the Esoteric School of Theosophy even before the spiritual-scientific activity of Rudolf Steiner, and she then became an esoteric pupil of Rudolf Steiner. Through the efforts of Mathilde Scholl and her friends the Künstlers, Cologne became a center for esoteric events, especially for pupils of Rudolf Steiner from the neighboring lands to the west, until the First World War in summer 1914.

SCHURÉ, EDOUARD
(Strasbourg 1841–1929 Paris)
French writer. Member of the Theosophical Society in France. From 1899 he maintained an amicable correspondence with Marie von Sivers, who translated several of his works into German. At the Theosophical Congress in Paris in 1906 he made the acquaintance of Marie von Sivers and Rudolf Steiner, whereupon they both stayed on several occasions as his guests in Barr in Alsace. At that time he also became an esoteric pupil of Rudolf Steiner. One year later, at the Theosophical Congress in Munich, Rudolf Steiner arranged for the premiere of Schuré's reconstructed *Sacred Mystery Drama of Eleusis* that Marie Steiner had translated. In 1909 and 1911 his *Children of Lucifer* was performed. In 1913 he resigned from the Theosophical Society and joined the Anthroposophical Society. After having distanced himself from Rudolf and Marie Steiner as a result of the First World War, he later regretted his action and was reconciled to them on the occasion of a visit to Dornach in 1922.

See: Camille Schneider: *Edouard Schuré, his meetings with Rudolf Steiner and Richard Wagner.* Freiburg im Breisgau 1971.

SELLIN, ALBRECHT WILHELM
(Berlin, Ludwigslust 1841–1933 Munich)
Colonizer in Brazil, later wholesale merchant in Hamburg. Played a part in preparing and founding the "Berlin Society for Experimental Psychology." Within the framework of this Society he experimented 1888–1892 with Max Dessoir, Albert Moll, and others, to discover the difference between animal magnetism and hypnotism. At that time he also became acquainted with Blavatsky's Theosophy, which, however, did not satisfy him. After hearing a lecture by Rudolf Steiner (Hamburg, 1904) he immediately joined the German Section and became an esoteric pupil of Rudolf Steiner. Since he

retired soon after, he could devote himself completely to anthroposophical spiritual science and continued to take leading roles in Rudolf Steiner's *Mystery Plays* 1910–1913, until the age of 70. See: A.W. Sellin, *Memories of the Professional Career and Soul-Life of an Old Man.* Constance, 1920.

SELLING, WILHELM
(Steinau on the Oder 1869–1960 Berlin)
After Grammar School in Breslau he studied machine construction at the Technical College in Mittweida. In 1894 he joined the East African expedition of the political economist Theodor Herzka. The expedition failed and he stayed on as an engineer for the state in Africa. Ill health necessitated his return to Germany shortly before 1900. He took an official post in the Colonial Office, but retired early. In 1903 he heard a lecture by Rudolf Steiner, became a member of the German Section, and devoted himself entirely to the work there. For years he was, among other things, in charge of the library and considered to be the initiator of the youth work.

SINNETT, ALFRED PERCY
(England 1840–1921 London)
Journalist, Editor-in-chief of *The Pioneer* from 1872, a prominent English newspaper in India, printed in Allahabad. He became a friend of H. P. B. and Olcott through his interest in spiritual phenomena. Blavatsky arranged for him to correspond with Mahatma K. H., on the strength of which he wrote *The Occult World* (1881) and *Esoteric Buddhism* (1883). In 1882 he returned to England after he was dismissed from his post. According to the owner of *The Pioneer* he had devoted too much space to occult questions and the work of H. P. B. In England he was active in the Theosophical Society and was Vice-President of the International Theosophical Society 1895–1907.

SIVERS, MARIE von (see STEINER, MARIE)

SIVERS, OLGA von (died 1917 in Saint Petersburg)
Sister of Marie von Sivers. Member of the German Section from its inauguration October 20, 1902. Memorial words by Rudolf Steiner (Berlin, August 21, 1917) in *Rudolf Steiner and Our Dead.* After her death Rudolf Steiner modelled her portrait in relief.

SMITS, CLARA
(St. Johann near Saarbrücken 1863–1948 Laufenburg, Baden)
Member of the Theosophical Society from 1903 and esoteric pupil of Rudolf Steiner. She arranged for lectures by Rudolf Steiner in her home, "Haus Meer," near Düsseldorf. As chairman of the first Düsseldorf Branch, she was a member of the Executive Committee of the German Section 1908–1913. She

consulted with Rudolf Steiner in late 1911 about training for her daughter Lory's career, which led to the development of a new movement art, Eurythmy.

SPINK, KATE
(Dates unknown)
English theosophist. From 1905 she succeeded Keightley as General Secretary of the English Section of the Theosophical Society in 1905.

SPRENGEL, ALICE
(Dates unknown)
Member in Munich from about 1904. She worked as an actress during the annual summer events of the German Section in Munich 1907–1913. She played "Theodora" in Rudolf Steiner's four *Mystery Plays*. As an artist and craftsperson, she accepted the task of making symbolic jewelry for theosophists and, based on that, she was nominated by Rudolf Steiner as "Keeper of the Seals" in his attempt in 1911 to form a Society for Theosophical Style and Art. She went to Dornach in 1914 in connection with the building and helped in a variety of capacities. A pronounced psychopathological element showed in her in 1915, and caused a lot of mischief. Due to this she was excluded from the Society by the Central Executive Committee of the Anthroposophical Society in autumn 1915. She then left Dornach and moved to the Tessin-Switzerland.

STEINER, MARIE, née VON SIVERS
(Wlotzlawek–Governorship of Warsaw, at that time claimed by Russia, 1867–1948 Beatenberg, Switzerland)
From a German-Baltic family (Father, Jakob von Sivers, Lieutenant-General of the Russian Army), she grew up in Saint Petersberg. She trained in speaking and the dramatic arts in Saint Petersburg, Paris, and Berlin. Through Edouard Schuré—whom she had turned to about the translation of his play *The Children of Lucifer*—her attention was drawn to Theosophy and to a first meeting with Rudolf Steiner in November 1900 in the theosophical library in Berlin. She experienced at the time how Rudolf Steiner was being pressed to join the Theosophical Society and how he answered: "That is impossible, because I make a great distinction between Western and Eastern mysticism." One year later, at a social gathering on the anniversary of the founding of the Society November 17, she asked him whether it would be necessary to bring into being a spiritual movement in Europe that considered Christianity. Rudolf Steiner later expressed his view of the importance of this question: "That made it possible for me to work in the way I had visualized. The question had been asked and I was able, according to the spiritual rules, to begin to find the answer to such a question." In January 1902 he undertook the leadership of the German Theosophical Society in Berlin, which had been offered him for some time and, in the spring, when he was offered

the General Secretaryship of the German Section—in process of being founded—he accepted with the condition that Marie von Sivers would be willing to work with him as General Secretary. Thus she became his closest collaborator from 1902 until the end of his working life. She organized not only the construction of the whole Society, but devoted her entire capacities toward the development of an anthroposophical stage art, and founded a private press for Rudolf Steiner's literary work. After his death she continued to publish his works and founded the administrative body for Rudolf Steiner's literary remains (Rudolf Steiner Nachlassverwaltung).

See: *From the Life of Marie Steiner-von-Sivers. Biographical contributions and a Bibliography*, Hella Wiesberger, editor, Dornach 1956.

STINDE, SOPHIE
(1853–1915 Munich)
Participated in the refounding of the Münich Branch in 1904 which became *the* Munich Branch and, after Berlin, one of the main centers for Rudolf Steiner's activity. She was a member of the Executive Committee of the German Section 1904–1913, an initiator of the Building Syndicate in 1911 and its Chairman. "Apart from building up the work in Munich, we are indebted to her for the staging of Dr. Steiner's *Mystery Plays* and, following that, the realization of the building project. She was one of those who first had the courage to conceive this bold plan and present it to Dr. Steiner. This wish was not rejected, but given consideration, and the plan matured in detail. And it was Sophie Stinde who furnished the particulars that created a basis for the realization of the project" (Marie Steiner). She was an esoteric pupil of Rudolf Steiner from 1904 and leader of the esoteric center in Munich. After her death Rudolf Steiner modeled her portrait in relief, as he had done for Maud Künstler and Olga von Sivers.

STOCKMEYER family
Artist Karl H. W. (d. 1930 at 72 in Malsch near Karlsruhe). His wife Johanna kept a boarding house for theosophists in Malsch. Both were members of the German Section from 1907 and esoteric pupils of Rudolf Steiner. In 1909, in the presence of Rudolf Steiner and together with their children Hilde and E. A. Karl and several other theosophists, they founded the Francis of Assisi Branch. At the same time, Rudolf Steiner laid the foundation stone of the model building inaugurated by Stockmeyer.

STRYCZEK-HÜBBE-SCHLEIDEN, PAULA
(d. 1945 Celle)
Had a connection with Hübbe-Schleiden, and was later adopted by him. Belonged to the circle of German theosophists even before Rudolf Steiner's teaching activities. She is said to have led a busy and selfless life at the side of Hübbe-Schleiden, and after his death she kept house for Günther Wagner,

who saw her as his chosen daughter, and she cared for him until his death. According to the eulogy by Marie Steiner, she immediately recognized Rudolf Steiner's supreme importance. In contrast to Hübbe-Schleiden, she remained faithful to the end toward Rudolf Steiner.

UNGER, Dr. (ENG.) CARL
(Bad Cannstatt 1878–1929 Nuremberg)
At 14 he became acquainted with Adolf Arenson, more than 20 years his senior, which led to a lifelong friendship founded on mutual spiritual interests. After Arenson became a member of the Theosophical Society in late 1902, Unger also joined in October 1903. He became personally acquainted with Rudolf Steiner in Stuttgart in the spring of 1904 and was so impressed by him, that he thereafter placed his whole strength at the disposal of this concern. In 1905 he founded a Branch in Stuttgart together with Adolf Arenson for the exclusive study of the works of Rudolf Steiner, and it later became the main branch in Stuttgart. Toward the end of 1904 he also became a personal pupil of Rudolf Steiner. He lectured at the Munich Congress at Whitsuntide 1907 where he summarized the results of his activities in the Branch. This was the beginning of widespread lecturing activity in all German and Swiss branches to introduce and work systematically in Spiritual Science. From 1908–1913 he belonged to the Executive Committee of the German Section, and from 1913-1923 to the Central Executive Committee of the Anthroposophical Society. After the re-founding of the latter he became Treasurer of the German National Society of the General Anthroposophical Society. He was also a member of the Building Syndicate founded in 1911 for the Goetheanum, and was in charge of the building operations for a year during the First World War. At the end of the war 1918–1919 he directed his activity toward the social impulses of Rudolf Steiner [the threefold social order], and amalgamated his machining factory with the associative enterprise *Der Kommende Tag* joint stock company. Untiring in the service of Anthroposophy and the Anthroposophical Society, he was shot by a mentally deranged person on January 4, 1929 immediately before he was to deliver a public lecture in Nuremberg entitled "What Is Anthroposophy?" Marie Steiner called Unger the most devoted and able pupil and collaborator of Rudolf Steiner.

VOLLRATH, DR. HUGO
(Dates unknown)
Theosophical book dealer and publisher (Theosophical Publishing House) in Leipzig. Because he belonged to both the German Section and the so-called "Leipzig Society," and wanted to introduce the very differently-directed intentions of the latter into the German Section, cooperation became very difficult. Mainly through pressure from the Leipzig Society he was excluded from the German Section according to a resolution of the latter at its Seventh General Meeting, October 1908.

WAGNER, AMALIE (1837–1910)
Sister of Günther Wagner, living in Hamburg. Member of the German Section from its founding in 1902 and esoteric pupil of Rudolf Steiner.

WAGNER, ANNA
(1847–1905 Lugano)
Wife of Günther Wagner and esoteric pupil of Rudolf Steiner. It was for her that Rudolf Steiner wrote down the text of the esoteric lesson given in Berlin, October 14, 1905 that, for health reasons, she could not attend (see GA 245). She died soon after.

WAGNER, GÜNTHER
(Hamburg 1842–1930 Herrenalb, Black Forest)
Founder of the firm for Pelikan products in Hanover. A member of the German Theosophical Society in Berlin from 1895. Together with a cousin of Hübbe-Schleiden, and Ludwig Deinhard, he made efforts toward founding a German Section. Wagner lived at that time in Lugano and founded a Branch there that later formed part of the German Section. He was also regarded for a time as a candidate for the office of General Secretary. He attached himself entirely to Rudolf Steiner and became his esoteric pupil. After his wife's death (in 1905) he moved to Berlin. After the war years he retired to the country, cared for by Paula Hübbe-Schleiden (Stryczek), who was like a daughter to him. Up to the last he took part in the affairs of the Anthroposophical Society. Steiner liked to refer to him as the "Senior" member of the Society.

WALLEEN-BORNEMANN, BARON ALFONS
(d. 1941 Copenhagen)
"In the years before the war he was a zealous pioneer of our work, as a lecturer and group leader active in various countries; he was one of the outspoken supporters of the Anthroposophical Association during the battle years of separation from the Theosophical Society in 1912" (Marie Steiner in *What is happening in the Anthroposophical Society, News Sheet for Members* No. 51. 18th year, December 1941)

WOHLBOLD, PROF. DR. HANS
(Nuremberg 1877–1949 Tutzing, Upper Bavaria)
Natural science teacher in Nuremberg and Munich until his dismissal by the Nazis. He and his wife became acquainted with Rudolf Steiner in 1904 and he thus became one of the oldest and outwardly most active members, and later, the leader of the Munich Branch. He engaged in copious lecturing and literary activity in order to transmit an understanding of the spiritual science of Rudolf Steiner. In order to pioneer this work, for example, he joined the circle of people around Oswald Spengler to study cultural morphology. In 1926 he

received an invitation from the National Museum of Weimar to set up an exhibit to demonstrate Goethe's color theory in the way Goethe actually intended it. He also produced a book on Goethe's color theory to be published by Diederichs of Jena.

WOLFRAM, ELISA (1868–1942)
A member of the German Section from 1905, and from 1906 the chairperson of the Leipzig Branch and esoteric pupil of Rudolf Steiner. Active as lecturer and writer. A member of the Executive Committee of the German Section from 1908-1913. "A very gifted lady, impulsive and persevering, strong in work, a fighter who courageously resisted the blows of fate" (Marie Steiner).

ZAWADZKI, CASIMIR (Dates unknown)
Originally a colleague of Dr. Vollrath in Leipzig, later an independent magazine publisher. Among other things he founded an "Association for Theosophy and Occult Science" in 1914 and a publishing company of his own. His writings proved to be a plagiarism of Rudolf Steiner and Annie Besant, and he was excluded from the German Section. See Mathilde Scholl, "Literary Plagiarism. Plagiarisms and false quotations," Berlin 1914.

CHRONOLOGICAL LIST
OF LETTERS, DOCUMENTS, AND LECTURES

General Rules

Individually-Given Exercises

From the Teachings about the Masters of Wisdom and
of the Harmony of Sensations and Feelings

Notes of Seven Lectures and Addresses concerning the Relationship between Movement, Esoteric School and Society

(For Edouard Schuré's personal information)

BARR, SEPTEMBER 9, 1907

RUDOLF STEINER'S COLLECTED WORKS

The German Edition of Rudolf Steiner's Collected Works (the Gesamtausgabe [GA] published by Rudolf Steiner Verlag, Dornach, Switzerland) presently runs to over 354 titles, organized either by type of work (written or spoken), chronology, audience (public or other), or subject (education, art, etc.). For ease of comparison, the Collected Works in English (CW) follows the German exactly. A complete listing of the CWs follows, with literal translations of the titles as they are in German. Other than in the case of the books published in his lifetime, these titles were rarely given by Rudolf Steiner himself, and were often provided by the editors of the German edition. The titles in English are not necessarily the same as the German; and indeed over the past seventy-five years have frequently been different, with the same book sometimes appearing under different titles.

For ease of identification and to avoid confusion, we suggest that readers looking for a title should do so by CW number. Because the work of creating the Collected Works of Rudolf Steiner is an ongoing process, with new titles being published every year, we have not indicated in this listing which books are presently available. To find out what titles in the Collected Works are currently in print, please check our website: www.steinerbooks.org or write to SteinerBooks, 610 Main Street, Great Barrington, MA 01230.

Written Work

Lectures to the Members of the Anthroposophical Society

SIGNIFICANT EVENTS
IN THE LIFE OF RUDOLF STEINER

1829:   June 23: birth of Johann Steiner (1829-1910)—Rudolf Steiner's father—in Geras, Lower Austria.

1834:   May 8: birth of Franciska Blie (1834-1918)—Rudolf Steiner's mother—in Horn, Lower Austria. "My father and mother were both children of the glorious Lower Austrian forest district north of the Danube."

1860:   May 16: marriage of Johann Steiner and Franciska Blie.

1861:   February 25: birth of *Rudolf Joseph Lorenz Steiner* in Kraljevec, Croatia, near the border with Hungary, where Johann Steiner works as a telegrapher for the South Austria Railroad. Rudolf Steiner is baptized two days later, February 27, the date usually given as his birthday.

1862:   Summer: the family moves to Mödling, Lower Austria.

1863:   The family moves to Pottschach, Lower Austria, near the Styrian border, where Johann Steiner becomes stationmaster. "The view stretched to the mountains...majestic peaks in the distance and the sweet charm of nature in the immediate surroundings."

1864:   November 15: birth of Rudolf Steiner's sister, Leopoldine (d. November 1, 1927). She will become a seamstress and live with her parents for the rest of her life.

1866:   July 28: birth of Rudolf Steiner's deaf-mute brother, Gustav (d. May 1, 1941).

1867:   Rudolf Steiner enters the village school. Following a disagreement between his father and the schoolmaster, whose wife falsely accused the boy of causing a commotion, Rudolf Steiner is taken out of school and taught at home.

1868:   A critical experience. Unknown to the family, an aunt dies in a distant town. Sitting in the station waiting room, Rudolf Steiner sees her "form," which speaks to him, asking for help. "Beginning with this experience, a new soul life began in the boy, one in which not only the outer trees and mountains spoke to him, but also the worlds that lay behind them. From this moment on, the boy began to live with the spirits of nature...."

1869:   The family moves to the peaceful, rural village of Neudorfl, near Wiener-Neustadt in present-day Hungary. Rudolf Steiner attends the village school. Because of the "unorthodoxy" of his writing and spelling, he has to do "extra lessons."

1870:   Through a book lent to him by his tutor, he discovers geometry: "To grasp something purely in the spirit brought me inner happiness. I know that I first learned happiness through geometry." The same tutor allows him to draw, while other students still struggle with their reading and writing. "An artistic element" thus enters his education.

1871:   Though his parents are not religious, Rudolf Steiner becomes a "church child," a favorite of the priest, who was "an exceptional character." "Up to the age of ten or eleven, among those I came to know, he was far and away the most significant." Among other things, he introduces Steiner to Copernican, heliocentric cosmology. As an altar boy, Rudolf Steiner serves at Masses, funerals, and Corpus Christi processions. At year's end, after an incident in which he escapes a thrashing, his father forbids him to go to church.

1872:   Rudolf Steiner transfers to grammar school in Wiener-Neustadt, a five-mile walk from home, which must be done in all weathers.

1873-75: Through his teachers and on his own, Rudolf Steiner has many wonderful experiences with science and mathematics. Outside school, he teaches himself analytic geometry, trigonometry, differential equations, and calculus.

1876:   Rudolf Steiner begins tutoring other students. He learns bookbinding from his father. He also teaches himself stenography.

1877:   Rudolf Steiner discovers Kant's *Critique of Pure Reason*, which he reads and rereads. He also discovers and reads von Rotteck's *World History*.

1878:   He studies extensively in contemporary psychology and philosophy.

1879:   Rudolf Steiner graduates from high school with honors. His father is transferred to Inzersdorf, near Vienna. He uses his first visit to Vienna "to purchase a great number of philosophy books"— Kant, Fichte, Schelling, and Hegel, as well as numerous histories of philosophy. His aim: to find a path from the "I" to nature.

October 1879-1883: Rudolf Steiner attends the Technical College in Vienna—to study mathematics, chemistry, physics, mineralogy, botany, zoology, biology, geology, and mechanics—with a scholarship. He also attends lectures in history and literature, while avidly reading philosophy on his own. His two favorite professors are Karl Julius Schröer (German language and literature) and Edmund Reitlinger (physics). He also audits lectures by Robert Zimmerman on aesthetics and Franz Brentano on philosophy. During this year he begins his friendship with Moritz Zitter (1861-1921), who will help support him financially when he is in Berlin.

1880:   Rudolf Steiner attends lectures on Schiller and Goethe by Karl Julius Schröer, who becomes his mentor. Also "through a remarkable combination of circumstances," he meets Felix Koguzki, an "herb gatherer" and healer, who could "see deeply into the secrets of nature." Rudolf Steiner will meet and study with this "emissary of the Master" throughout his time in Vienna.

1881: January: "... I didn't sleep a wink. I was busy with philosophical problems until about 12:30 a.m. Then, finally, I threw myself down on my couch. All my striving during the previous year had been to research whether the following statement by Schelling was true or not: *Within everyone dwells a secret, marvelous capacity to draw back from the stream of time—out of the self clothed in all that comes to us from outside—into our innermost being and there, in the immutable form of the Eternal, to look into ourselves.* I believe, and I am still quite certain of it, that I discovered this capacity in myself; I had long had an inkling of it. Now the whole of idealist philosophy stood before me in modified form. What's a sleepless night compared to that!"

Rudolf Steiner begins communicating with leading thinkers of the day, who send him books in return, which he reads eagerly.

July: "I am not one of those who dives into the day like an animal in human form. I pursue a quite specific goal, an idealistic aim—knowledge of the truth! This cannot be done offhandedly. It requires the greatest striving in the world, free of all egotism, and equally of all resignation."

August: Steiner puts down on paper for the first time thoughts for a "Philosophy of Freedom." "The striving for the absolute: this human yearning is freedom." He also seeks to outline a "peasant philosophy," describing what the worldview of a "peasant"—one who lives close to the earth and the old ways—really is.

1881-1882: Felix Koguzki, the herb gatherer, reveals himself to be the envoy of another, higher initiatory personality, who instructs Rudolf Steiner to penetrate Fichte's philosophy and to master modern scientific thinking as a preparation for right entry into the spirit. This "Master" also teaches him the double (evolutionary and involutionary) nature of time.

1882: Through the offices of Karl Julius Schröer, Rudolf Steiner is asked by Joseph Kurschner to edit Goethe's scientific works for the *Deutschen National-Literatur* edition. He writes "A Possible Critique of Atomistic Concepts" and sends it to Friedrich Theodore Vischer.

1883: Rudolf Steiner completes his college studies and begins work on the Goethe project.

1884: First volume of Goethe's *Scientific Writings* (CW 1) appears (March). He lectures on Goethe and Lessing, and Goethe's approach to science. In July, he enters the household of Ladislaus and Pauline Specht as tutor to the four Specht boys. He will live there until 1890. At this time, he meets Josef Breuer ((1842-1925), the coauthor with Sigmund Freud of *Studies in Hysteria*, who is the Specht family doctor.

1885:   While continuing to work on Goethe, Rudolf Steiner reads deeply in contemporary philosophy (Edouard von Hartmann, Johannes Volkelt, and Richard Wahle, among others).

1886:   May: Rudolf Steiner sends Kurschner the manuscript of *Outlines of Goethe's Theory of Knowledge* (CW 2), which appears in October, and which he sends out widely. He also meets the poet Marie Eugenie Delle Grazie and writes "Nature and Our Ideals" for her. He attends her salon, where he meets many priests, theologians, and philosophers, who will become his friends. Meanwhile, the director of the Goethe Archive in Weimar requests his collaboration with the *Sophien* edition of Goethe's works, particularly the writings on color.

1887:   At the beginning of the year, Rudolf Steiner is very sick. As the year progresses and his health improves, he becomes increasingly "a man of letters," lecturing, writing essays, and taking part in Austrian cultural life. In August-September, the second volume of Goethe's *Scientific Writings* appears.

1888:   January-July: Rudolf Steiner assumes editorship of the "German Weekly" (*Deutsche Wochenschrift*). He begins lecturing more intensively, giving, for example, a lecture titled "Goethe as Father of a New Aesthetics." He meets and becomes soul friends with Friedrich Eckstein (1861-1939), a vegetarian, philosopher of symbolism, alchemist, and musician, who will introduce him to various spiritual currents (including Theosophy) and with whom he will meditate and interpret esoteric and alchemical texts.

1889:   Rudolf Steiner first reads Nietzsche (*Beyond Good and Evil*). He encounters Theosophy again and learns of Madame Blavatsky in the Theosophical circle around Marie Lang (1858-1934). Here he also meets well-known figures of Austrian life, as well as esoteric figures like the occultist Franz Hartman and Karl Leinigen-Billigen (translator of C.G. Harrison's *The Transcendental Universe*.) During this period, Steiner first reads A.P. Sinnett's *Esoteric Buddhism* and Mabel Collins's *Light on the Path*. He also begins traveling, visiting Budapest, Weimar, and Berlin (where he meets philosopher Edouard von Hartman).

1890:   Rudolf Steiner finishes volume 3 of Goethe's scientific writings. He begins his doctoral dissertation, which will become *Truth and Science* (CW 3). He also meets the poet and feminist Rosa Mayreder (1858-1938), with whom he can exchange his most intimate thoughts. In September, Rudolf Steiner moves to Weimar to work in the Goethe-Schiller Archive.

1891:   Volume 3 of the Kurschner edition of Goethe appears. Meanwhile, Rudolf Steiner edits Goethe's studies in mineralogy and scientific writings for the *Sophien* edition. He meets Ludwig Laistner of the Cotta publishing company, who asks for a book on the basic question of metaphysics. From this will result, ultimately, *The Philosophy of Freedom* (CW 4), which will be published not by Cotta but by Emil Felber. In October, Rudolf Steiner takes the oral exam for a doctorate in philosophy, mathematics, and mechanics at Rostock University, receiving his doctorate on the twenty-sixth. In November, he gives his first lecture on Goethe's "Fairy Tale" in Vienna.

1892:   Rudolf Steiner continues work at the Goethe-Schiller archive and on his *Philosophy of Freedom*. *Truth and Science*, his doctoral dissertation, is published. Steiner undertakes to write introductions to books on Schopenhauer and Jean Paul for Cotta. At year's end, he finds lodging with Anna Eunike, née Schulz (1853-1911), a widow with four daughters and a son. He also develops a friendship with Otto Erich Hartleben (1864-1905) with whom he shares literary interests.

1893:   Rudolf Steiner begins his habit of producing many reviews and articles. In March, he gives a lecture titled "Hypnotism, with Reference to Spiritism." In September, volume 4 of the Kurschner edition is completed. In November, *The Philosophy of Freedom* appears. This year, too, he meets John Henry Mackay (1864-1933), the anarchist, and Max Stirner, a scholar and biographer.

1894:   Rudolf Steiner meets Elisabeth Förster Nietzsche, the philosopher's sister, and begins to read Nietzsche in earnest, beginning with the as yet unpublished *Antichrist*. He also meets Ernst Haeckel (1834-1919). In the fall, he begins to write *Nietzsche, A Fighter against His Time* (CW 5).

1895:   May, *Nietzsche, A Fighter against His Time* appears.

1896:   January 22: Rudolf Steiner sees Friedrich Nietzsche for the first and only time. Moves between Nietzsche and the Goethe-Schiller Archives, where he completes his work before year's end. He falls out with Elisabeth Förster Nietzsche, thus ending his association with the Nietzsche archive.

1897:   Rudolf Steiner finishes the manuscript of *Goethe's Worldview* (CW 6). He moves to Berlin with Anna Eunike and begins editorship of the *Magazin fur Literatur*. From now on, Steiner will write countless reviews, literary and philosophical articles, and so on. He begins lecturing at the "Free Literary Society." In September, he attends the Zionist Congress in Basel. He sides with Dreyfus in the Dreyfus affair.

1898:   Rudolf Steiner is very active as an editor in the political, artistic, and theatrical life of Berlin. He becomes friendly with John Henry Mackay and poet Ludwig Jacobowski (1868-1900). He joins Jacobowski's circle of writers, artists, and scientists—"The Coming Ones" (*Die Kommenden*)—and contributes lectures to the group until 1903. He also lectures at the "League for College Pedagogy." He writes an article for Goethe's sesquicentennial, "Goethe's Secret Revelation," on the "Fairy Tale of the Green Snake and the Beautiful Lily."

1888-89: "This was a trying time for my soul as I looked at Christianity. . . .I was able to progress only by contemplating, by means of spiritual perception, the evolution of Christianity . . . .Conscious knowledge of real Christianity began to dawn in me around the turn of the century. This seed continued to develop. My soul trial occurred shortly before the beginning of the twentieth century. It was decisive for my soul's development that I stood spiritually before the mystery of Golgotha in a deep and solemn celebration of knowledge."

1899: Rudolf Steiner begins teaching and giving lectures and lecture cycles at the Workers' College, founded by Wilhelm Liebknecht (1826-1900). He will continue to do so until 1904. Writes: *Literature and Spiritual Life in the Nineteenth Century; Individualism in Philosophy; Haeckel and His Opponents; Poetry in the Present;* and begins what will become (fifteen years later) *Riddles of Philosophy* (CW 18). He also meets many artists and writers, including Käthe Kollwitz, Stefan Zweig, and Rainer Maria Rilke. On October 31, he marries Anna Eunike.

1900: "I thought that the turn of the century must bring humanity a new light. It seemed to me that the separation of human thinking and willing from the spirit had peaked. A turn or reversal of direction in human evolution seemed to me a necessity." Rudolf Steiner finishes *World and Life Views in the Nineteenth Century* (the second part of what will become *Riddles of Philosophy*) and dedicates it to Ernst Haeckel. It is published in March. He continues lecturing at *Die Kommenden,* whose leadership he assumes after the death of Jacobowski. Also, he gives the Gutenberg Jubilee lecture before 7,000 typesetters and printers. In September, Rudolf Steiner is invited by Count and Countess Brockdorff to lecture in the Theosophical Library. His first lecture is on Nietzsche. His second lecture is titled "Goethe's Secret Revelation." October 6, he begins a lecture cycle on the mystics that will become *Mystics after Modernism* (CW 7). November-December: "Marie von Sivers appears in the audience...." Also in November, Steiner gives his first lecture at the *Giordano Bruno Bund* (where he will continue to lecture until May, 1905). He speaks on Bruno and modern Rome, focusing on the importance of the philosophy of Thomas Aquinas as monism.

1901: In continual financial straits, Rudolf Steiner's early friends Moritz Zitter and Rosa Mayreder help support him. In October, he begins the lecture cycle *Christianity as Mystical Fact* (CW 8) at the Theosophical Library. In November, he gives his first "Theosophical lecture" on Goethe's "Fairy Tale" in Hamburg at the invitation of Wilhelm Hubbe-Schleiden. He also attends a tea to celebrate the founding of the Theosophical Society at Count and Countess Brockdorff's. He gives a lecture cycle, "From Buddha to Christ," for the circle of the

Kommenden. November 17, Marie von Sivers asks Rudolf Steiner if Theosophy does not need a Western-Christian spiritual movement (to complement Theosophy's Eastern emphasis). "The question was posed. Now, following spiritual laws, I could begin to give an answer." In December, Rudolf Steiner writes his first article for a Theosophical publication. At year's end, the Brockdorffs and possibly Wilhelm Hubbe-Schleiden ask Rudolf Steiner to join the Theosophical Society and undertake the leadership of the German section. Rudolf Steiner agrees, on the condition that Marie von Sivers (then in Italy) work with him.

1902: Beginning in January, Rudolf Steiner attends the opening of the Workers' School in Spandau with Rosa Luxemberg (1870-1919). January 17, Rudolf Steiner joins the Theosophical Society. In April, he is asked to become general secretary of the German Section of the Theosophical Society, and works on preparations for its founding. In July, he visits London for a Theosophical congress. He meets Bertram Keightly, G.R.S. Mead, A.P. Sinnett, and Annie Besant, among others. In September, *Christianity as Mystical Fact* appears. In October, Rudolf Steiner gives his first public lecture on Theosophy ("Monism and Theosophy") to about three hundred people at the Giordano Bruno Bund. On October 19-21, the German Section of the Theosophical Society has its first meeting; Rudolf Steiner is the general secretary, and Annie Besant attends. Steiner lectures on practical karma studies. On October 23, Annie Besant inducts Rudolf Steiner into the Esoteric School of the Theosophical Society. On October 25, Steiner begins a weekly series of lectures: "The Field of Theosophy." During this year, Rudolf Steiner also first meets Ita Wegman (1876-1943), who will become his close collaborator in his final years.

1903: Rudolf Steiner holds about 300 lectures and seminars. In May, the first number of the periodical *Luzifer* appears. In June, Rudolf Steiner visits London for the first meeting of the Federation of the European Sections of the Theosophical Society, where he meets Colonel Olcott. He begins to write *Theosophy* (CW 9).

1904: Rudolf Steiner continues lecturing at the Workers' College and elsewhere (about 90 lectures), while lecturing intensively all over Germany among Theosophists (about a 140 lectures). In February, he meets Carl Unger (1878-1929), who will become a member of the board of the Anthroposophical Society (1913). In March, he meets Michael Bauer (1871-1929), a Christian mystic, who will also be on the board. In May, *Theosophy* appears, with the dedication: "To the spirit of Giordano Bruno." Rudolf Steiner and Marie von Sivers visit London for meetings with Annie Besant. June: Rudolf Steiner and Marie von Sivers attend the meeting of the Federation of European

Sections of the Theosophical Society in Amsterdam. In July, Steiner begins the articles in *Luzifer-Gnosis* that will become *How to Know Higher Worlds* (CW 10) and *Cosmic Memory* (CW 11). In September, Annie Besant visits Germany. In December, Steiner lectures on Freemasonry. He mentions the High Grade Masonry derived from John Yarker and represented by Theodore Reuss and Karl Kellner as a blank slate "into which a good image could be placed."

1905:   This year, Steiner ends his non-Theosophical lecturing activity. Supported by Marie von Sivers, his Theosophical lecturing—both in public and in the Theosophical Society—increases significantly: "The German Theosophical Movement is of exceptional importance." Steiner recommends reading, among others, Fichte, Jacob Boehme, and Angelus Silesius. He begins to introduce Christian themes into Theosophy. He also begins to work with doctors (Felix Peipers and Ludwig Noll). In July, he is in London for the Federation of European Sections, where he attends a lecture by Annie Besant: "I have seldom seen Mrs. Besant speak in so inward and heartfelt a manner...." "Through Mrs. Besant I have found the way to H.P. Blavatsky." September to October, he gives a course of thirty-one lectures for a small group of esoteric students. In October, the annual meeting of the German Section of the Theosophical Society, which still remains very small, takes place. Rudolf Steiner reports membership has risen from 121 to 377 members. In November, seeking to establish esoteric "continuity," Rudolf Steiner and Marie von Sivers participate in a "Memphis-Misraim" Masonic ceremony. They pay forty-five marks for membership. "Yesterday, you saw how little remains of former esoteric institutions." "We are dealing only with a 'framework'...for the present, nothing lies behind it. The occult powers have completely withdrawn."

1907:   Further expansion of the German Theosophical Movement according to the Rosicrucian directive to "introduce spirit into the world"—in education, in social questions, in art, and in science. In February, Col. Olcott dies in Adyar. Before he dies, Olcott indicates that "the Masters" wish Annie Besant to succeed him: much politicking ensues. Rudolf Steiner supports Besant's candidacy. April-May: preparations for the Congress of the Federation of European Sections of the Theosophical Society—the great, watershed Whitsun "Munich Congress," attended by Annie Besant and others. Steiner decides to separate Eastern and Western (Christian-Rosicrucian) esoteric schools. He takes his esoteric school out of the Theosophical Society (Besant and Rudolf Steiner are "in harmony" on this). Steiner makes his first lecture tours to Austria and Hungary. That summer, he is in Italy. In September, he visits Edouard Schuré, who will write the introduction to the French edition of

Christianity as Mystical Fact in Barr, Alsace. Rudolf Steiner writes the autobiographical statement known as the "Barr Document." In *Luzifer –Gnosis*, "The Education of the Child" appears.1906: Expansion of Theosophical work. Rudolf Steiner gives about 245 lectures, only 44 of which take place in Berlin. Cycles are given in Paris, Leipzig, Stuttgart, and Munich. Esoteric work also intensifies. Rudolf Steiner begins writing *An Outline of Esoteric Science* (CW 13). In January, Rudolf Steiner receives permission (a patent) from the Great Orient of the Scottish A & A Thirty-Three Degree Rite of the Order of the Ancient Freemasons of the Memphis-Misraim Rite to direct a chapter under the name "Mystica Aeterna." This will become the "Cognitive Cultic Section" (also called "Misraim Service") of the Esoteric School. (See: >*From the History and Contents of the Cognitive Cultic Section* (CW 264). During this time, Steiner also meets Albert Schweitzer. In May, he is in Paris, where he visits Edouard Schuré. Many Russians attend his lectures (including Konstantin Balmont, Dimitri Mereszkovski, Zinaida Hippius, and Maximilian Woloshin). He attends the General Meeting of the European Federation of the Theosophical Society, at which Col. Olcott is present for the last time. He spends the year's end in Venice and Rome, where he writes and works on his translation of H.P. Blavatsky's *Key to Theosophy.*

1908: The movement grows (membership: 1150). Lecturing expands. Steiner makes his first extended lecture tour to Holland and Scandinavia, as well as visits to Naples and Sicily. Themes: St John's Gospel, the Apocalypse, Egypt, science, philosophy, and logic. *Luzifer-Gnosis* ceases publication. In Berlin, Marie von Sivers (with Johanna Mücke (1864-1949) forms the *Philosophisch-Theosophisch* (after 1915 *Philosophisch-Anthroposophisch*) *Verlag* to publish Steiner's work. Steiner gives lecture cycles titled *The Gospel of St John* (CW 103) and *The Apocalypse* (104).

1909: *An Outline of Esoteric Science* appears. Lecturing and travel continues. Rudolf Steiner's spiritual research expands to include the polarity of Lucifer and Ahriman; the work of great individualities in history; the Maitreya Buddha and the Bodhisattvas; spiritual economy (CW 109); the work of the spiritual hierarchies in heaven and on Earth (CW 110). He also deepens and intensifies his research into the Gospels, giving lectures on the Gospel of St. Luke (CW 114) with the first mention of two Jesus children. Meets and becomes friends with Christian Morgenstern (1871-1914). In April, he lays the foundation stone for the Malsch model—the building that will lead to the first Goetheanum. In May, the International Congress of the Federation of European Sections of the Theosophical Society takes place in Budapest. Rudolf Steiner receives the Subba Row medal for

How to Know Higher Worlds. During this time, Charles W. Leadbeater discovers Jiddu Krishnamurti (1895-1986) and proclaims him the future "world teacher," the bearer of the Maitreya Buddha and the "reappearing Christ." In October, Steiner delivers seminal lectures on "anthroposophy," which he will try, unsuccessfully, to rework over the next years into the unfinished work, *Anthroposophy (A Fragment)*(CW 45).

1910: New themes: *The Reappearance of Christ in the Etheric* (CW 118); *The Fifth Gospel; The Mission of Folk Souls* (CW 121); *Occult History* (CW 126); the evolving development of etheric cognitive capacities. Rudolf Steiner continues his Gospel research with *The Gospel of St. Matthew* (CW 123). In January, his father dies. In April, he takes a month-long trip to Italy, including Rome, Monte Cassino, and Sicily. He also visits Scandinavia again. July-August, he writes the first mystery drama, *The Portal of Initiation* (CW 14). In November, he gives "psychosophy" lectures. In December, he submits "On the Psychological Foundations and Epistemological Framework of Theosophy" to the International Philosophical Congress in Bologna.

1911: The crisis in the Theosophical Society deepens. In January, "The Order of the Rising Sun," which will soon become "The Order of the Star in the East," is founded for the coming world teacher, Krishnamurti. At the same time, Marie von Sivers, Rudolf Steiner's coworker, falls ill. Fewer lectures are given, but important new ground is broken. In Prague, in March, Steiner meets Franz Kafka (1883-1924) and Hugo Bergmann (1883-1975). In April, he delivers his paper to the Philosophical Congress. He writes the second mystery drama, *The Soul's Probation* (CW 14). Also, while Marie von Sivers is convalescing, Rudolf Steiner begins work on *Kalendar 1912/ 1913*, which will contain the "Calendar of the Soul" meditations. On March 19, Anna (Eunike) Steiner dies. In September, Rudolf Steiner visits Einsiedeln, birthplace of Paracelsus. In December, Friedrich Rittelmeyer, future founder of the Christian Community, meets Rudolf Steiner. The *Johannes-Bauverein*, the "building committee," which would lead to the first Goetheanum (first planned for Munich), is also founded, and a preliminary committee for the founding of an independent association is created that, in the following year, will become the Anthroposophical Society. Important lecture cycles include *Occult Physiology* (CW 128); *Wonders of the World* (CW 129); >*From Jesus to Christ* (CW 131). Other themes: esoteric Christianity; Christian Rosenkreutz; the spiritual guidance of humanity; the sense world and the world of the spirit.

1912: Despite the ongoing, now increasing crisis in the Theosophical Society, much is accomplished: *Calendar 1912/1913* is published; eurythmy is created; both the third mystery drama, *The Guardian of the Threshold* (CW 14) and *The Road to Self Knowledge* (CW 16) are written. New (or renewed) themes included life between death and rebirth and karma and reincarnation. Other lecture cycles: *Spiritual Beings in the Heavenly Bodies and the Kingdoms of Nature* (CW 136); *The Human Being in the Light of Occultism, Theosophy, and Philosophy* (CW 137); *The Gospel of St Mark* (CW 139); and *The Bhagavad-Gita and the Epistles of St. Paul* (CW 142). On May 8, Rudolf Steiner celebrates White Lotus Day, H.P. Blavatsky's death day, which he had faithfully observed for the past decade, for the last time. In August, Rudolf Steiner suggests the "independent association" be called the "Anthroposophical Society." In September, the first eurythmy course takes place. In October, Rudolf Steiner declines recognition of a Theosophical Society lodge dedicated to the Star of the East and decides to expel all Theosophical Society members belonging to the order. Also, with Marie von Sivers, he first visits Dornach, near Basel, Switzerland, and they stand on the hill where the Goetheanum will be. In November, a Theosophical Society lodge is opened by direct mandate from Adyar (Annie Besant). In December, a meeting of the German section occurs at which it is decided that belonging to the Order of the Star of the East is incompatible with membership in the Theosophical Society. December 28: informal founding of the Anthroposophical Society in Berlin.

1913:   Expulsion of the German section from the Theosophical Society. February 2-3: Foundation meeting of the Anthroposophical Society. Board members include: Marie von Sivers, Michael Bauer, and Carl Unger. September 20: Laying of the foundation stone for the *Johannes Bau* (Goetheanum) in Dornach. Building begins immediately. The third mystery drama, *The Soul's Awakening* (CW 14), is completed. Also: *The Threshold of the Spiritual World* (CW147). Lecture cycles include: *The Bhagavad-Gita and the Epistles of St. Paul* and *The Occult Foundations of the Bhagavad-Gita* (CW 146), which the Russian philosopher Nikolai Berdyaev attends; *The Mysteries of the East and of Christianity* (CW 144); *The Effects of Esoteric Development* (CW 145); and *The Fifth Gospel* (CW 148). In May, Rudolf Steiner is in London and Paris, where anthroposophical work continues.

1914:   Building continues on the *Johannes Bau* (Goetheanum) in Dornach, with artists and coworkers from seventeen nations. The general assembly of the Anthroposophical Society takes place. In May, Rudolf Steiner visits Paris, as well as Chartres Cathedral. June 28: assassination in Sarajevo ("Now the catastrophe has happened!"). August 1: War is declared. Rudolf Steiner returns to Germany from Dornach —he will travel back and forth. He writes the last chapter of *Riddles of Philosophy*. Lecture cycles include: *Human and Cosmic Thought* (CW 151); *Inner Being of Humanity between Death and a New*

Birth (CW 153); *Occult Reading and Occult Hearing* (CW 156). December 24: marriage of Rudolf Steiner and Marie von Sivers.

1915:   Building continues. Life after death becomes a major theme, also art. Writes: *Thoughts during a Time of War* (CW 24). Lectures include: *The Secret of Death* (CW 159); *The Uniting of Humanity through the Christ Impulse* (CW 165).

1916:   Rudolf Steiner begins work with Edith Maryon (1872-1924) on the sculpture "The Representative of Humanity" ("The Group"— Christ, Lucifer, and Ahriman). He also works with the alchemist Alexander von Bernus on the quarterly *Das Reich*. He writes *The Riddle of Humanity* (CW 20). Lectures include: *Necessity and Freedom in World History and Human Action* (CW 166); *Past and Present in the Human Spirit* (CW 167); *The Karma of Vocation* (CW 172); *The Karma of Untruthfulness* (CW 173).

1917:   Russian Revolution. The U.S. enters the war. Building continues. Rudolf Steiner delineates the idea of the *threefold nature of the human being* (in a public lecture March 15) and the *threefold nature of the social organism* (hammered out in May-June with the help of Otto von Lerchenfeld and Ludwig Polzer-Hoditz in the form of two documents titled *Memoranda,* which were distributed in high places). August-September: Rudolf Steiner writes *Riddles of the Soul* (CW 20). Also: commentary on "The Chemical Wedding of Christian Rosenkreutz" for Alexander Bernus (*Das Reich*). Lectures include: *The Karma of Materialism* (CW 176); *The Spiritual Background of the Outer World: The Fall of the Spirits of Darkness* (CW 177).

1918:   March 18: peace treaty of Brest-Litovsk— "Now everything will truly enter chaos! What is needed is cultural renewal." June: Rudolf Steiner visits Karlstein (Grail) Castle outside Prague. Lecture cycle: *From Symptom to Reality in Modern History* (CW 185). In mid-November, Emil Molt, of the Waldorf-Astoria Cigarette Company, has the idea of founding a school for his workers' children.

1919:   Focus on the threefold social organism: tireless travel, countless lectures, meetings, and publications. At the same time, a new public stage of anthroposophy emerges as cultural renewal begins. The coming years will see initiatives in pedagogy, medicine, pharmacology, and agriculture. January 27: threefold meeting: "We must first of all, with the money we have, found free schools that can bring people what they need." February: first public eurythmy performance in Zurich. Also: "Appeal to the German People" (CW 24), circulated March 6 as a newspaper insert. In April, *Toward Social Renewal* (CW 23)—"perhaps the most widely read of all books on politics appearing since the war"—appears. Rudolf Steiner is asked to undertake the "direction and leadership" of the school founded by the Waldorf-Astoria Company. Rudolf Steiner begins to talk about the "renewal" of education. May 30: a building is selected and purchased for the future Waldorf School. August-September, Rudolf Steiner gives a lecture course for Waldorf teachers, *Foundations of Human Experience (Study of Man)*(CW 293). September 7: Opening of the first Waldorf School. December (into January): first science course, the *Light Course* (CW 320).

1920:   The Waldorf School flourishes. New threefold initiatives. Founding of limited companies *Der Kommenden Tag* and *Futurum A.G.* to infuse spiritual values into the economic realm. Rudolf Steiner also focuses on the sciences. Lectures: *Introducing Anthroposophical Medicine* (CW 312); *Warmth Course* (CW 321); *Boundaries of Natural Science* (CW 322); *The Redemption of Thinking* (CW 74). February: Johannes Werner Klein—later a cofounder of the Christian Community—asks Rudolf Steiner about the possibility of a "religious renewal," a "Johannine church." In March, Rudolf Steiner gives the first course for doctors and medical students. In April, a divinity student asks Rudolf Steiner a second time about the possibility of religious renewal. September 27-October 16: anthroposophical "university course." December: lectures titled *The Search for the New Isis* (CW 202).

1921:   Rudolf Steiner continues his intensive work on cultural renewal, including the uphill battle for the threefold social order. "university" arts, scientific, theological, and medical courses include: *Astronomy Course* (CW 323); *Observation, Mathematics, and Scientific Experiment* (CW 324); the *Second Medical Course* (CW 313); *Color.* In June and September-October, Rudolf Steiner also gives the first two "priests' courses" (CW 342 and 343). The "youth movement" gains momentum. Magazines are founded: *Die Drei* (January), and—under the editorship of Albert Steffen (1884-1963)— the weekly, *Das Goetheanum* (August). In February-March, Rudolf Steiner takes his first trip outside Germany since the war (Holland). On April 7, Steiner receives a letter regarding "religious renewal," and May 22-23, he agrees to address the question in a practical way. In June, the Klinical-Therapeutic Institute opens in Arlesheim under the direction of Dr. Ita Wegman. In August, the Chemical-Pharmaceutical Laboratory opens in Arlesheim (Oskar Schmiedel and Ita Wegman, directors). The Clinical Therapeutic Institute is inaugurated in Stuttgart (Dr. Ludwig Noll, director); also the Research Laboratory in Dornach (Ehrenfried Pfeiffer and Gunther Wachsmuth, directors). In November-December, Rudolf Steiner visits Norway.

1922:   The first half of the year involves very active public lecturing (thousands attend); in the second half, Rudolf Steiner begins to withdraw and turn toward the society—"The society is asleep." It is "too weak" to do what is asked of it. The businesses—*Die Kommenden Tag* and

Futura A.G.—fail. In January, with the help of an agent, Steiner undertakes a twelve-city German tour, accompanied by eurythmy performances. In two weeks he speaks to more than 2,000 people. In April, he gives a "university course" in The Hague. He also visits England. In June, he is in Vienna for the East-West Congress. In August-September, he is back in England for the Oxford Conference on Education. Returning to Dornach, he gives the lectures *Philosophy, Cosmology, and Religion* (CW 215), and gives the third priest's course (CW 344). On September 16, The Christian Community is founded. In October-November, Steiner is in Holland and England. He also speaks to the youth: *Youth Course* (CW 217). In December, Steiner gives lectures titled *The Origins of Natural Science* (CW 326), and *Humanity and the World of Stars: The Spiritual Communion of Humanity* (CW 219). December 31: Fire at the Goetheanum, which is destroyed.

1923:   Despite the fire, Rudolf Steiner continues his work unabated. A very hard year. Internal dispersion, dissension, and apathy abound. There is conflict—between old and new visions—within the society. A wake-up call is needed, and Rudolf Steiner responds with renewed lecturing vitality. His focus: the spiritual context of human life; initiation science; the course of the year; and community building. As a foundation for an artistic school, he creates a series of pastel sketches. Lecture cycles: *The Anthroposophical Movement; Initiation Science* (CW 227) (in England at the Penmaenmawr Summer School); *The Four Seasons and the Archangels* (CW 229); *The Human Being: Symphony of the Creative Word* (CW 230); *The Supersensible Human* (CW 231), given in Holland for the founding of the Dutch society. On November 10, in response to the failed Hitler-Ludendorf putsch in Munich, Steiner closes his Berlin residence and moves the *Philosophisch-Anthroposophisch Verlag* (Press) to Dornach. On December 9, Steiner begins the serialization of his *Autobiography: The Course of My Life* (CW 28) in *Das Goetheanum*. It will continue to appear weekly, without a break, until his death. Late December-early January: Rudolf Steiner refounds the Anthroposophical Society (about 12,000 members internationally) and takes over its leadership. The new board members are: Marie Steiner, Ita Wegman, Albert Steffen, Elizabeth Vreede, and Guenther Wachsmuth. (See *The Christmas Meeting for the Founding of the General Anthroposophical Society* (CW 260). Accompanying lectures: *Mystery Knowledge and Mystery Centers* (CW 232); *World History in the Light of Anthroposophy* (CW 233). December 25: the Foundation Stone is laid (in the hearts of members) in the form of the "Foundation Stone Meditation."

1924:   January 1: having founded the Anthroposophical Society and taken over its leadership, Rudolf Steiner has the task of "reforming" it.

The process begins with a weekly newssheet ("What's Happening in the Anthroposophical Society") in which Rudolf Steiner's "Letters to Members" and "Anthroposophical Leading Thoughts" appear (CW 26). The next step is the creation of a new esoteric class, the "first class" of the "University of Spiritual Science" (which was to have been followed, had Rudolf Steiner lived longer, by two more advanced classes). Then comes a new language for anthroposophy—practical, phenomenological, and direct; and Rudolf Steiner creates the model for the second Goetheanum. He begins the series of extensive "karma" lectures (CW 235-40); and finally, responding to needs, he creates two new initiatives: biodynamic agriculture and curative education. After the middle of the year, rumors begin to circulate regarding Steiner's health. Lectures: January-February, *Anthroposophy* (CW 234); February: *Tone Eurythmy* (CW 278); June: *Agriculture Course* (CW 327); June-July: *Speech Eurythmy* (CW 279); *Curative Education* (CW 317); August: (England, "Second International Summer School"), *Initiation Consciousness: True and False Paths in Spiritual Investigation* (CW 243); September: *Pastoral Medicine* (CW 318). On September 26, for the first time, Rudolf Steiner cancels a lecture. On September 28, he gives his last lecture. On September 29, he withdraws to his studio in the carpenter's shop; now he is definitively ill. Cared for by Ita Wegman, he continues working, however, and writing the weekly installments of his *Autobiography* and *Letters to the Members/Leading Thoughts* (CW 26).

1925: Rudolf Steiner, while continuing to work, continues to weaken. He finishes *Extending Practical Medicine* (CW 27) with Ita Wegman.

On March 30, around ten in the morning, Rudolf Steiner dies.

INDEX